The Life of
Samuel Johnson

BLACKWELL CRITICAL BIOGRAPHIES

General Editor: Claude Rawson

The Life of
SAMUEL JOHNSON

A Critical Biography

Robert DeMaria, Jr

BLACKWELL
Oxford UK & Cambridge USA

First published 1993

Blackwell Publishers
238 Main Street, Suite 501
Cambridge, Massachusetts 02142
USA

108 Cowley Road
Oxford OX4 1JF
UK

Library of Congress Cataloging-in-Publication Data

DeMaria, Robert.
The life of Samuel Johnson : a critical biography / Robert
DeMaria, Jr.
p.   cm – (Blackwell critical biographies; 2)
Includes bibliographical references and index.
ISBN 1-55786-150-1 (alk. paper)
1. Johnson, Samuel, 1709–1784 – Biography.   2. Great Britain –
Intellectual life – 18th century.   3. Authors, English – 18th
century – Biography.   4. Lexicographers – Great Britain – Biography.
5. Critics – Great Britain – Biography.   I. Title.   II. Series.
PR3533.D39   1993
828′.609 – dc20
[B]   92-23302
                                              CIP

British Library Cataloguing in Publication Data

A CIP catalogue record for this book is available from
the British Library.

Typeset in 10 on 11 pt Baskerville
by Graphicraft Typesetters Ltd., Hong Kong
Printed in Great Britain by T.J. Press Ltd, Padstow, Cornwall.

This book is printed on acid-free paper

To Alex and Davy

Contents

Contents

Illustrations

A Note on the Form of Citation

I have used endnotes with short-title references to works cited in the Bibliography and full references to other works. In addition I have used even shorter titles for a few frequently cited standard works. *Life* stands for G. B. Hill's edition of Boswell's *Life of Samuel Johnson* revised by L. F. Powell, second edition (Oxford: Clarendon Press, 1934–64). *Lives* refers to G. B. Hill's edition of Johnson's *Prefaces Critical and Biographical to the Works of the English Poets* (Oxford: Clarendon Press, 1905); Hill numbers the paragraphs in each of the *Lives,* and I use these more precise numbers, along with the name of a particular life, rather than page and volume references. In reference to those written through 1781 *Letters* means *The Letters of Samuel Johnson,* edited by Bruce Redford, volumes 1–3 (Princeton: Princeton University Press, 1992). For other letters, I use the three-volume edition by R. W. Chapman (Oxford: Clarendon Press, 1952). Because the Johnsonian world is now in between editions of the letters, I will cite them with reference to the old Hill–Chapman numbers as well as the new, authoritative, Redford volume and page numbers. *Yale* is shorthand for the *Yale Edition of the Works of Samuel Johnson* (New Haven, 1958–   ). The other shortened references are easily comprehensible, I believe, and the full reference for any item abbreviated in the notes is easily located in the Bibliography.

In the interest of typographical clarity, I have generally kept the superior reference numbers in each paragraph to a limit of one. Where more than one reference is needed in a single paragraph, I have collected them under an endnote keyed to a superior number added to the last item in the paragraph requiring a note or to the end of the paragraph, whichever seemed more logical in each case.

Preface: Samuel Johnson and Europe

What is the story of Johnson's life? Among the many versions that have
been proposed and elaborated in great detail, perhaps the most famous
is the Cinderella story of the uncouth genius who strides out of obscurity
in the Midlands to become the eponymous lord of a cultural epoch in
London and a symbol of English national pride. This is an exaggeration
even of Boswell's exaggerated story of his Herculean figure, but there is
truth in it, and there is truth in the more temperate version of Johnson's
heroics that stresses his 'achievement', in Walter Jackson Bate's well-
chosen word, the story of how he overcame liabilities and disabilities to
fashion his own greatness, his own sanity, and his own religious peace. But
I would like to propose a somewhat different tale, a story as much about
compromise and alienation as about success.

In my version, Johnson's life begins with a wish to escape the narrow
cultural bounds of his native place, not simply by leaving the fairly sophisticated, cathedral city of Lichfield for the English metropolis, but by
identifying himself with a unified, late Latin European cultural heritage.
Early in life he discovers his natural intellectual superiority to those around
him; his physical debilities – his scars and nervous tics – drive him to
polish this superiority and make it the jewel of his identity. In his father's
bookshop he encounters the great works of European humanism, some of
them in the expensively bound folios of Lord Derby, the foolish purchase
of which drove the business irrecoverably into debt. According to the tale,
Johnson was looking for an apple on the top shelves and found Petrarch
instead, as though experiencing a particularly learned fall from innocence.
He soon aspires to be like Petrarch, and he chooses his heroes from the
succeeding generations of European scholar-poets whose places of origin
were almost irrelevant to their intellectual lives: the likes of Buchanan,
Scaliger, Erasmus, Heinsius, and Burman. In the fairly high social world
of Lichfield circulating around Gilbert Walmesley's residence in the old
Bishop's Palace and in the truly polite world of his cousins in Pedmore

and Stourbridge Johnson identifies himself as an aspiring Latin poet. He writes some courtly verse, and he goes off to college carrying his slender volume of Landesius, a neo-Latin poet of the previous generation, along with works of many other heroes and possible models.

At Oxford, Johnson is somewhat aloof and makes his mark by citing relatively obscure writers, like Macrobius. He contributes the only Latin poem to a miscellany gathered by a classmate. He is undoubtedly put down by the social climate, and he imagines escaping to his world elsewhere, the European intellectual community. He is heard in his room muttering: 'I'll go and visit the Universities abroad. I'll go to France & Italy. I'll go to Padua.'[1] Back in Lichfield, forced to face his penurious economic circumstances after the death of his father, Johnson is torn between making his living as a teacher and making it as a writer. Either is a compromise with his true identity as a scholar-poet. Gradually, writing wins out, although it requires a greater compromise than Johnson can stand at first. In one early enterprise he issues proposals for an edition of Poliziano, a neo-Latin and Italian poet who epitomized the highly cultured state that Johnson hoped to achieve. When this does not work out, Johnson realizes he had better work for an established publisher with capital, but he still tries to maintain his old identity to some degree. He gains entrée into the world of the *Gentleman's Magazine* with his tribute to the editor, 'Ad Urbanum', which alludes to a neo-Latin ode to Pope Urban by a Polish writer, and with Latin and Greek salutes to other members of the staff. Having translated the French of Joachim Le Grand's version of Jerónimo Lobo's Portuguese *Itinerário*, Johnson begins the ill-fated, immense task of translating Paolo Sarpi's *Istoria del concilio Tridentino* (1619), a truly great work of European Reformation scholarship. Johnson makes his greatest contribution to the *Gentleman's Magazine* in imaginative accounts of the English Parliamentary debates, but he keeps a foothold in Europe by starting a column called 'Foreign Books' and soliciting for review important continental publications.

His first important poem and the turning point in his career is *London*, an imitation of Juvenal, printed with the original Latin alongside his version, making his poem a work of scholarly commentary adapted to a wide audience. As one of his many literary jobs, he takes on the task of preparing a sale catalogue for the great Harleian Library. In doing so, he contributes to a money-making project, of course, but he compares the catalogue to the continental European works describing the Barberinian and Thuanian libraries. In precisely the same way he compares his *English Dictionary* to the great productions of the French and Italian academies. The *Dictionary* was naturally a work of great national importance. One early admirer compared its triumphant Anglicity to that of St Paul's Cathedral, but like St Paul's the *Dictionary* has a European design, being based mainly on Latin dictionaries rather than English and finished with an epigram from Horace.

The *Dictionary* of 1755 is Johnson's most thorough and satisfying compromise between his need to write for money in England and his wish to take his place among the great late humanist scholars of Europe. Still, when he revised it in 1773, Johnson addressed a poetic act of humility to his lifelong hero, the poet-scholar and lexicographer Joseph Scaliger. Johnson felt all his life that he had failed and that he had come far short of his expectations for himself. Part of the reason for this is psychological, of course, and part is social, but another part is due to the intellectual compromises he made. The edition of Shakespeare is another brilliant compromise with the scholarly work of Heinsius or Burman on classical writers, and the *Lives of the Poets* rises above 'the penury of English biography' to align itself somewhat with classical and continental forerunners. Still, these are compromises with what Johnson might have done and once imagined himself preparing to do. The long list of prospective scholarly works, which he left in the hands of Bennet Langton shortly before his death, is an outline of the life he failed to achieve.

It was a compromise for Johnson to undertake and conduct a career in English, and he usually resumed his largely private life of classical reading and writing when financial circumstances permitted. Something of Johnson's disappointment with himself comes out in the prefaces to all his scholarly works, and there are always hints therein of his lingering, longing affiliation with the European Latin community. This affiliation appears also in the few fictional works he wrote. They are almost all set outside of Europe and look back upon the continent as a single culture, rather than upon England as a special part of it. If Johnson, like many modern writers, was choosing a point of observation beyond the confines of his identifying place, then that place was Europe as a whole. The early play *Irene* is set at the fall of Constantinople, and the survivors escape the Turks and become émigrés to Europe, bringing Greek civilization with them. *The Vision of Theodore, the Hermit of Teneriffe* takes place on a mountaintop off the west coast of Africa, beyond Europe and outside of the Mediterranean basin. The setting of *Rasselas* in eastern Africa also provides a vantage point outside of Europe. Even the well-travelled Imlac has never been beyond Palestine, and, when he speaks about European culture, he does so without specifying any particular nations. From the grand perspective that Johnson was trying to achieve in his fiction, the divisions among the Europeans were trivial or imperceptible.

In his scholarship Johnson had one foot in Europe, and in his fiction he extends his view over the whole continent. In his life, however, he got no farther away from England than the Hebrides and northern France. He wanted to go farther. He once said that if he had got his pension earlier he would have gone to the Middle East and learned Arabic, like Edward Pococke the orientalist, another of Johnson's intellectual heroes. He dreamed of sailing down the Red Sea, and late in life he actually considered emigrating to India, where he would have joined his friends Robert Chambers and William Jones, pioneering Sanskritists. Johnson was deeply disappointed when his trip to Italy with the Thrales fell through, and late in life he petitioned the ministry for money to allow him to spend the winter in an Italian monastery. On his most famous trip outside of England Johnson was conscientiously unreceptive to the allures of Scotland, except when the journey took him past the haunts of intellectual heroes – Buchanan in St Andrews, for example, and Hector Boethius in Aberdeen. Such places stimulated a kind of spiritual patriotism in Johnson which he displayed in full bloom upon reaching the ancient monastery of Iona. The ruined community of learning and faith represented Johnson's true nationality, and it is telling that his climactic sentence about Iona uses for comparison a description of national feeling, but the 'nation' is not England; it is literally Athens and, by expansion, western Europe: 'That man is little to be envied, whose patriotism would not gain force upon the plain of *Marathon*, or whose piety would not grow warmer among the ruins of *Iona!*'[2]

Seen as beginning with a wish to escape national borders to join himself with an immensely impressive and durable late Latin culture, Johnson's life was a compromise, one with which he was often unhappy. But posterity has made a virtue of necessity and glorified Johnson as a national hero, making him politically nationalistic and xenophobic. Boswell stressed his anti-French and anti-Scots sentiments, and the anti-American remarks in *Taxation No Tyranny* are among his most frequently cited. Despite the brilliant revision undertaken by Donald Greene and others in recent years, Johnson the nationalist survives. In the London *Times* 'Business Diary' on 9 January 1981, for example, Ross Davies gave an account of a conference he attended at Johnson's residence of thirteen months, Pembroke College. Davies punctuates his account with bits of Boswell's Johnson, including a gibe at Scots, and he closes with a deposition from a current resident that he has deceived 'dozens of Americans' about the true location of Johnson's Pembroke rooms. This Davies finds really delightful and finishes ecstatically with the rhetorical question, 'Did not the doctor himself say of them: "Sir, they are a race of convicts and ought to be thankful for anything we allow them, short of hanging"?' Nor is this delight in Johnson's xenophobic nationalism restricted to merely commercial fans. Even a fine, recent scholarly book about Johnson's *Dictionary*, for example, seems to delight in Johnson's Francophobia in his Preface; the author dramatically reports that 'Johnson trains a cold eye on France'.[3] In fact, a close look at Johnson's political writing, especially during the Seven Years War with France, reveals sympathy for the Americans, especially the native Americans, and an equally cold eye trained on England. The attitude Johnson took in politics as in every phase of his life was centrally humanistic, and the excesses of the British colonialists were just as hateful to him as those of the French or Spanish. Johnson's real country was humanist Europe, even when he was making his living writing English political journalism.

My object in the pages that follow is to tell the story of Johnson's life as a compromise with his highest aspirations for a life of European scholarship and European identity. Although there are many fine studies of Johnson, and though my debts throughout this book are enormous, this particular story has not been very much told. Even the possibility of telling it properly has gradually diminished as knowledge of the common Latin culture of Europe has gradually become a matter of specialist interest only. Despite the fine work of Anthony Grafton and a few others, the names of all but the most famous of Johnson's humanist idols are generally unknown. I must apologize, therefore, for presenting the reader with references to so many obscure names. I do not mean to suggest that I move easily and familiarly through this world of scholars; I only want to provide a sense of the intellectual world in which Johnson moved. To bridge the gap a little between Johnson and those who study him I have added some biographical and bibliographical material to the Index.

However, obscurity and the appearance of pretence are not the only risks one runs in discussing Johnson's intellectual background. I thought for some years that I had found an important early model for my approach in the work of Ettore Allodoli. Writing for *La Rinascita* in Florence in 1942, Allodoli surveyed the ways in which 'Nell'Umanesimo settecentesco Samuel Johnson occupa un posto preminente.' Much as I have, Allodoli mentions the many projects that link Johnson to European cultural life. He goes further, comparing him personally and temperamentally to the scholar-poet Poliziano, the bibliophile Magliabechi, and some other Europeans. Allodoli attaches disproportionate weight to some of Johnson's casual references to Italian cultural figures, such as Michelangelo and Pietro Aretino, but I felt I had found a kindred spirit in Allodoli before I realized that the essay is a piece of propaganda.[4]

La Rinascita was the journal of the Centro Nazionale di Studi sul Rinascimento founded by royal decree in Florence in 1937 with the full support of Benito Mussolini. As editor of the journal, Allodoli published contributions from many other distinguished scholars which tended to evince the greatness of Italian Renaissance culture and its persistent influence on Europe throughout the modern period. While building up the importance of Italy in his essay on Johnson, Allodoli was also trying to undermine a source of national pride for the beleaguered English. Much that Allodoli writes is true, but his work turns out to be a monitory example that reveals the political implications that can be hidden in studies that seem to be primarily historical. Allodoli's is perhaps the kind of scholarship that stimulated movement to another extreme in post-war criticism. Years and years of formalism have followed, making various attempts to strip time and place away from authors altogether, as though seeking to replace the Pan-Europeanism of the Fascists with a non-European aestheticism. However, historicism itself should not have been the enemy, and the excesses of formalistic methods have become apparent in recent years, as have their own vulnerability to ethical and political corruption.

One of my principal objects in this book is to resituate Johnson and his works in a European cultural context without introducing, as far as possible, my own national prejudices. As an American, I have had carefully to examine my wish to prove Ross Davies and the London *Times* wrong about

Johnson and Americans. More broadly, I have had to examine my wish to liberate Johnson from England in order to place him in a cultural milieu without national boundaries and equally accessible to all his admirers. I am convinced that Johnson himself inhabited this intellectual world and wished to live in it more thoroughly than he could. However, I realize that residence in his utopia represents only half of the compromise which I have described as characterizing Johnson's life. In treating the other half, I will try to find Johnson where he really was – associating with members of the book trade throughout his life and, mainly in London, working with and among publishers and printers, writing in English for an English audience. (I also provide information in the Index on these less exalted but equally obscure figures.) Like a modern editor in search of the true text, although it no longer exists, I have been in search of the true, historical Johnson, although I know he cannot be entirely separated from the embellishments of earlier accounts nor clearly distinguished during the many parts of his life of which only the evocative traces still survive.

Acknowledgements

In the task of finding the historical Johnson I have benefited enormously from the work and from the advice of many scholars. Like anyone who writes on Johnson, I am indebted to the work of late great Johnsonians like G. B. Hill, L. F. Powell, R. W. Chapman, Aleyn Lyell Reade, and James Clifford. I also wish to acknowledge the formative help I have received from the works or the advice of many scholars still busily at work: David Fleeman, Paul Fussell, Donald Greene, Thomas Kaminski, Alvin Kernan, and Gwin Kolb. My many debts to other scholars are, I hope, adequately registered in the endnotes.

I am grateful to Claude Rawson, who, as general editor of the series in which this book appears, invited me to write it in the first place; his articulation of the object of the series helped me to crystallize my approach, and he saved me many embarrassing errors by reading the book in an earlier draft. I owe a similar debt of gratitude to Andrew McNeillie of Blackwell Publishers. Many others have helped me in various, less pervasive but important ways. OM Brack, Michael Suarez, Bruce Redford, and G. W. Nicholls provided information or comments on my work in draft. Viscountess Eccles, Frank Ellis, and Loren Rothschild are among those who supplied me with photographs of pictures or access to documentary materials in their private possession. I benefited from conversations with colleagues at Vassar College, especially my frequent consultations with Joanne Long and James H. Merrell. Donna Heiland, Bill Gifford, Robert Brown, Rachel Kitzinger, and Ben Kohl also provided casual, intelligent assistance. I am sorry that I cannot now convey my thanks to James H. Day or Irene Grabowski; this would have been a better book if I could have had their guidance and support in the last years of writing it, as I did in the first. The college itself, under the able guidance of President Frances Fergusson and Dean Nancy Dye, provided the necessary 'shelter of Academick bowers' and a sabbatical leave in 1990–91. The National Endowment for the Humanities provided a Summer Stipend. I am also indebted to many librarians, especially Nancy MacKechnie of Vassar College, Vincent Giraud and Stephen Parks of the Beinecke Rare Book and Manuscript Library, and Robert Parks of the Morgan Library. In the final stages of preparing the manuscript for publication I was a Guggenheim fellow, and I enjoyed the luxury of a fellowship at the Center for Advanced Study in the Behavioral Sciences, supported by the Andrew W. Mellon Foundation.

No one can meditate long on Johnson's works and life without acknowledging the importance of personal relationships in all professional achievements. It is a pleasure, therefore, to recognize the support of my family, particularly of my wife, but also of my three living grandparents, my parents, and my two sons.

1

Lichfield

I was bred a Bookseller, and have not forgotten my trade.
Johnson to the bookseller Thomas Cadell, 13 April 1779

Samuel Johnson was born in Lichfield on 7 September, old style, 1709. At this time England had not yet adopted the reformed, Gregorian calendar and its so-called 'new style' of dating. What was 7 September in England was to continental western Europe 18 September, and in England the new year still began on 25 March, according to the Julian method. The need for synchronization or even for precision in dating was not then what it became in the following two hundred years either for nations or for individuals. Johnson found it extraordinary enough to note in his Annals that his father had a watch in 1719, 'which he returned when he was to pay for it', and he did not own one himself until he reached the age of fifty-nine. Johnson's first watch, like his father's, was an extravagance, costing the large sum of seventeen guineas; the small coincidence is a piece of evidence that the son may have inherited from his father a wish to live above his means and to elevate himself above his background. Michael Johnson's father had come to Lichfield, a dignified cathedral city and the second largest town in Staffordshire, from Cubley, a tiny place in Derbyshire. Although his sister married into the upper-class Skrymsher family, thus becoming the sister-in-law of a nurse to James II, Michael Johnson was the son of a day-labourer. Through the excellent system of charities in Lichfield he received an education and at sixteen was apprenticed to a London stationer located in St Paul's Churchyard. Through his father, Johnson's knowledge of English publishing history reached back into the seventeenth century. In his life of Dryden, nearly a hundred years after the fact, Johnson recalled his father's accounts of the extraordinary public demand for Dryden's *Absalom and Achitophel* (1681), which 'he had not known ... equalled but by Sacheverell's trial.'[1]

In 1681 at the age of only twenty-four Michael returned to Lichfield and set up his own business as a bookbinder and bookseller. Like other booksellers of his day, he was also occasionally a publisher and financed works by the Lichfield physician John Floyer, Samuel Shaw, master of a nearby grammar school, and John Bradley, vicar of a nearby parish. The powerful London booksellers employed him as a provincial outlet for subscription sales of Anthony à Wood's *Athenae Oxoniensis* in 1690, and in 1706 he boldly and fatally outbid all comers for the purchase of Lord Derby's library – a collection of some 2900 volumes, reliably described as 'great & noble', consisting 'of most of the Fathers entire, History, especially French, constituted of Folios above the proportion of the other volumes'. This purchase contributed to the debts that dogged Michael throughout his career. Johnson alludes to them in a remark on his parents in his Annals: 'Neither of them ever tried to calculate the profits of trade, or the expenses of living. My mother concluded that we were poor, because we lost by some of our trades; but the truth was, that my father, having in the early part of his life contracted debts, never had trade sufficient to enable him to pay them, and maintain his family; he got something but not enough.' Such accounts as there are of Michael Johnson's sales do not suggest that his clientele would quickly have absorbed Derby's rich and learned stock. His evidently weak catalogue of the library failed to attract new customers, and, all together, Michael Johnson was out of his depth in the venture. Young Samuel found some of Derby's noble folios still on the shelves of his father's shop, and in 1743, when he worked on the sale catalogue of the great Harleian Library, Johnson surely understood the economic value of performing that task well. It is a measure of his ambivalence about his bookselling background, however, that Johnson's preface to the catalogue emphasizes the intellectual value of such works. Throughout his life Johnson took a frank enjoyment in his knowledge of 'the trade', but he also took pains to distance himself from the merely mercantile business of bookselling.[2]

The purchase of Lord Derby's library was overambitious, but Michael Johnson had seriously overreached earlier, in 1695, when he had attempted to expand his business into the production of parchment and vellum, without knowing anything about the craft. Although it was not lucrative, the venture exposed young Samuel to another element of book production, and it took Michael to distant Scotland and Ireland. He returned with tales of far-off lands; he put into his child's hands Martin Martin's *Western Islands of Scotland* (1703) and into his mind a wish to see the Hebrides. When he finally went to Skye in 1773, Johnson employed both his knowledge of Martin and what he had learned from his father when he amazed his host at Ulinish by giving a complete account of the process of tanning.[3]

Michael's excursions, coupled with shorter trips to run extension shops in nearby towns and to conduct auctions all over the county, did not keep him from attaining prominence in Lichfield. Despite his frequent absence and his indictment by the national government for violations of trade laws, Michael held at one time or another most of the important civic posts in the town. In fact, his legal difficulties seem to have helped him in the political world of Lichfield because he was elected to office on a couple of occasions directly after being in trouble with the government. At the time of Samuel's birth, Michael had just become sheriff. In this office he was obliged on the day after Samuel was born to conduct the annual Riding. As James Clifford explains it, 'In those days, before accurate surveys or maps, the boundary line of each parish and township had to be perambulated regularly by as many citizens as possible, so as to perpetuate from generation to generation the remembrance of landmarks and legal boundaries.' On this occasion, Johnson reports in his Annals, his father 'feasted the citizens with uncommon magnificence, and was the last but one that maintained the splendour of the Riding'.[4] Such extravagance of generosity was common in Johnson's father, but it apparently alternated with periods of melancholy, and both sides of his temperament were clearly visible in his son. Johnson struggled with melancholy all his life, and, though he never achieved any civic office, he grandly displayed generosity to those less fortunate than himself.

Johnson's inner life as a child is impossible to recover, but the surroundings in which he grew up are comparatively well documented, and they provide a context for understanding his personal development. Books were an important part of Johnson's surroundings all his life, and from an early age he knew a good deal about them, not only what was in them but how they were produced, what they were made of, how much they cost, and how they were distributed. Johnson added to his knowledge of the book trade throughout his life and was still improving it in his old age. He demonstrated his mastery of the subject in a letter of 1776, for example, and, while travelling in North Wales in 1774, Johnson displayed his ongoing curiosity about his father's trade in a promise 'To note down my Father's stock, expences, and profit.'[5] In a way Johnson was in the family business all his life; he spent a vast amount of his professional life doing booksellers' jobs. Almost everything Johnson produced he wrote on assignment from the publishers and booksellers, everything from advertisements and prefaces to immense projects like the *Dictionary of the English Language*.

Although he was born into the trade and participated in it all of his life, Johnson was determined at an early age to distinguish the business of books from the learning they transmit. In his Annals he makes a comment on his parents' marriage that especially reveals the keenness of his distinction between the trade and learning: 'My father and mother had not much happiness from each other. They seldom conversed; for my father could not bear to talk of his affairs; and my mother, being unacquainted with books, cared not to talk of any thing else. Had my mother been more literate, they had been better companions. She might have sometimes introduced her unwelcome topick with more success, if she could have diversified her conversation. Of business she had no distinct conception;

and therefore her discourse was composed only of complaint, fear, and suspicion.' Johnson's mother Sarah took pride in the social superiority of her family, and she made this her theme in many of the domestic squabbles that young Samuel overheard. She was the daughter of Cornelius Ford, a substantial citizen of Kings Norton, Worcestershire, who was able to pay the considerable sum of £750 for the estate of Haunch Hall in 1649. Ford's older brother Henry was an important lawyer, and a treasured friend was Thomas Hall, a publishing Nonconformist vicar, the uncle of Bishop John Hall. Old Cornelius collected the works of his friend and other Nonconformist writers and left these in his will to members of his family, including his grandson, Cornelius Ford, who notoriously combined the activities of religious divine and townhouse rake. As a teenager Johnson relished his connection with the Fords and undoubtedly appreciated the books as well as the talk of young Cornelius.[6]

Sarah married at the advanced age of thirty-seven; her husband was already forty-nine. Samuel and his younger brother Nathaniel grew up in a household with unusually old parents. What little Johnson reveals about his mother suggests that she was affectionate and proud of her son, though unlearned and ignorantly argumentative with her husband. Johnson's childhood attitude toward her was intolerant and superior, but he took pleasure in making her proud of him. In his Annals he records an incident in which he confides his fears of failing a Latin test to his mother: 'My mother encouraged me and I proceeded better. . . . "We often," said she, dear mother! "come off best, when we are most afraid." She told me, that, once when she asked me about forming verbs, I said, "I did not form them in an ugly shape." "You could not," said she, "speak plain; and I was proud that I had a boy who was forming verbs." These little memorials sooth my mind.' Johnson needed soothing when he thought of his mother later in life because his early treatment of her was evidently harsh. Mrs Thrale reports his remarking, 'I did not respect my own mother, though I loved her: and one day, when in anger she called me a puppy, I asked her if she knew what they called a puppy's mother.' In his Annals Johnson records another instance of his petulance: 'Of the parts of Corderius or Aesop, which we learned to repeat, I have not the least recollection, except of a passage in one of the Morals, where it is said of some man, that, when he hated another, he made him rich; this I repeated emphatically in my mother's hearing, who could never conceive that riches could bring any evil. She remarked it, as I expected.' About thirty years later, in 1749, Johnson emphasized the same moral in *The Vanity of Human Wishes* by picturing the felicity of the carefree, 'needy traveller' and adding:

> Does envy seize thee? crush th' upbraiding joy,
> Increase his riches and his peace destroy.[7]

In later life Johnson recalled his efforts as a literary monitor speaking to an impersonal audience with greater equanimity than those he exerted as a child on behalf of his benighted mother. Yet he was as much himself in one instance as in the other. Until very late in life, when he tried to recapture some of the lost time, Johnson spurned the role of child: as an unwilling dependant, he ventured to lecture his mother, but he took more evasive action with his father. He told Mrs Thrale that 'he absolutely loathed his father's caresses, because they were sure to precede some unpleasing display of his early abilities', and 'an old man's child . . . leads much such a life, I think, as a little boy's dog, teized with awkward fondness, and forced, perhaps, to sit up and beg.'[8] The indignation that Johnson displayed in his attitude to both parents expressed a wish for independence, and the softness he showed towards them or their memories later may be a tribute to their understanding indulgence. Johnson's parents did not crush his spirit, but they were parents, and he was naturally stern in defence of himself; as a result, Johnson felt pain in later life when he remembered his pugnacity, especially with his mother. The depth of this pain and the precise reasons for it would be more comprehensible had Johnson not destroyed shortly before his death the notebooks containing most of his remembrances and confessions about his early life. The fact that he did destroy them suggests that his pain and his remorse were deep.

Whether or not he was naturally vociferous and rebellious, Johnson's childhood struggles for independence were complicated by the fact that he was born with or early contracted several physical ills. His difficult birth may have caused anoxia, a possible source of later problems, but the principal early ailment was scrofula, or tuberculosis of the lymph glands. This probably led to deficient sight in his left eye and a loss of hearing in his left ear. It may have caused some paralysis on the left side of his face, and the boils or blistering tubercles on various parts of his skin, including his neck, left him scarred for life. Although his parents tried to provide proper medical attention, the treatment for Johnson's afflictions was ineffectual or worse. A trip to an oculist in Trysull may have done no harm, but there were at least two operations for the scrofula – one adding to the scars on his face and neck, the other opening a cut in his arm and keeping it open to drain 'bad humours' for six years. At a later date in his childhood Johnson received more scars, this time from a case of smallpox.[9]

By the age of eight Johnson also began showing the signs of an unidentified nervous disorder that modern medicine might have diagnosed as Tourette's syndrome. The tics and gesticulations noted by all of Johnson's biographers, as well as the involuntary vocalizations, repetitions of others' remarks, and the compulsive, ritualized movements when entering a room or walking on pavement with cracks, all suggest the disease named after its nineteenth-century discoverer, Gilles de la Tourette. This syndrome, along with his other disorders, had damaging effects on Johnson's personal and professional lives. His applications to teach in established schools in Solihull and Brentwood and his attempt to run his own school at Edial, for example, were almost certainly ruined by his physical appearance. His failure would have been likely today, and it was almost inevitable in an age that followed Locke's prescription of a tutor who served most importantly as a model of behaviour and deportment for the pupil. Johnson's physical condition may, however, have conferred on him some benefits along with its obvious liabilities. His incapacity to work in more public positions happily pressed Johnson towards the invisible occupation of authorship. In addition, as Oliver Sacks has shown, Tourette's syndrome, with all its debilitations, occasionally lends its victims great verbal and vocal energy; those who can harness this energy sometimes perform with superior strength and speed. The most wonderful suggestion that Johnson enjoyed such extraordinary power occurs in Boswell's account of Hogarth's visit to Samuel Richardson's house where, while offering an apology for George II's harsh treatment of a Jacobite Scot, 'he perceived a person standing at a window in the room, shaking his head, and rolling himself about in a strange ridiculous manner. He concluded that he was an ideot, whom his relations had put under the care of Mr Richardson, as a very good man. To his great surprize, however, this figure stalked forwards to where he and Mr Richardson were sitting, and all at once took up the argument, and burst out into an invective against George the Second. . . . In short, he displayed such a power of eloquence, that Hogarth looked at him with astonishment, and actually imagined that this ideot had been at the moment inspired.' Johnson was capable of astonishing verbal performances, but he often declined conversational engagement altogether until he was provoked or roused to explosive entry into the fray. Diagnosing the diseases of the dead is absurd, of course, and there is an anachronism in superimposing on them our age's medical terminology, but something like Tourette's syndrome would explain both Johnson's reticence and his explosive power as a talker, as well as various symptoms of his movement disorder. Tourette's syndrome is associated with psychological causes, like suppressed rage, that are evident in Johnson's personality, but the illness is neurological and clearly has a biochemical basis: the onset is usually preceded by physical weakness, such as might be caused by scrofula, and the disease is now successfully treated with a drug called haloperidol. Although it is problematic in its own right, diagnosing Johnson's case as Tourette's syndrome has the pleasing effect of short-circuiting efforts to superimpose on him an anachronistic Freudian interpretation of his behaviour. Such features of his behaviour as verbal overkill, heavy remorse, and easy tears are thus seen as the emotional weather he frequently experienced rather than as the mere signs or symbols of something deeper or more essential in his emotional make-up.[10]

The silver lining of Johnson's sufferings with childhood diseases was a trip to London to be 'touched' by Queen Anne for scrofula, which was also known as the King's evil. This was done on the advice of John Floyer, a notable and generally modern physician. Johnson retained all his life a medal he received on the occasion, a dim memory of the Queen herself, and clearer memories of John Nicholson's bookshop, where he and his mother stayed, in the heart of bookselling London. When Johnson finally went down to London as a young man seeking to make his living in the book trade, it was not as a complete outsider or as a newcomer to the profession. He was doing in a way what his father did before him and exploiting, like his mother, the particular world of connections established by Michael Johnson, provincial bookseller.

Much of what Johnson himself tells us about his early life concerns his education. Like other literate men and women of his time, Johnson lived with a Lockean conception of the mind as a *tabula rasa*; consequently, he speaks about his experiences as being literally impressed upon his young and therefore highly receptive mind. In Johnson's account of his childhood, as in Proust's of his (surprisingly), time is a function of impression; speaking of the period that he studied under Humphrey Hawkins, Johnson says, 'The Time [a little over two years], till I had computed it, appeared much longer by the multitude of novelties which it supplied, and of incidents, then in my thoughts important, it produced. Perhaps it is not possible that any other period can make the same impression on the memory.' Later, in connection with work he was doing for a less congenial teacher, Johnson again comments on the growth of a Lockean and surprisingly modern mind: 'In making, I think, the first exercise under Holbrook, I perceived the power of continuity of attention, of application not suffered to wander or to pause. I was writing at the kitchen windows, as I thought, alone, and turning my head saw Sally [Ford] dancing. I went on without notice, and had finished almost without perceiving that any time had elapsed. This close attention I have seldom in my whole life obtained.'[11]

Such self-deprecating reference to his mental lassitude is a salient feature of Johnson's journals throughout his life, as is his focus on reading and writing. What filled Johnson's mind and early became the medium in which he marked time were numbered pages of books and lines of verse. He remembers with great specificity his childhood grammar books and on what parts of them he was examined from the time he started at age seven in Lichfield Grammar School with Humphrey Hawkins. (His remembrances of study at home with his mother, in Dame Oliver's 'kindergarten', and in Thomas Browne's school are unfortunately part of the journal he destroyed in 1784.) His education, or at least his memories of it, centred on Latin grammar, employing the long standard Lily's *Grammar* supplemented by Garretson's and Walker's *Exercises*. Quotations in the *Dictionary* show that Johnson still had these books on his shelves, or in his head, in the late 1740s and early 1750s. For 'literature' the learner read schoolboy editions of moral fabulists like Aesop, and modernized editions of colloquies by Erasmus and Vives. The children's textbook was still the important literary genre that the great early European humanists had made it, and Johnson imbibed humanism as a part of his elementary education. Like almost everyone else of his time, Johnson recognized Locke's pre-eminence as an educational philosopher, but his early training prepared him to resist the most practical aspects of Locke's programme – its emphasis on English rather than Latin, for example, and its elevation of breeding in relation to learning. This is most importantly manifest in the *Dictionary*, which Johnson conceived of, in part, as an educational work.

As a teacher, Johnson continued the tradition of pedagogy in which he had been reared, although as a student he had not always found the programme congenial. In his Annals he reports himself very speedily doing an exercise in Garretson's *English Exercises for school-boys to translate in to Latin*, and showing it to his mother. She replied, he writes, 'Though you could make an exercise in so short a time, I thought you would find it difficult to make them all as soon as you should.' All of his life Johnson retained this odd pair of habits: he was very fast at composition but a terrible procrastinator about writing things down. His schoolmate Edmund Hector reported that some of the other boys used to carry Johnson the quarter mile to school to win his favour, and 'Verses or themes he would dictate to his favourites, but he would never be at the trouble of writing them. His dislike to business was so great, that he would procrastinate his exercises to the last hour.'[12] The pattern of procrastination followed by tremendous speed continued throughout Johnson's professional life, as did the pattern of working for or through others. The procrastinating, dictating boy was father to the man who dictated, among much else, sermons and periodical essays for friends, his own translation of Lobo's *Voyage to Abyssinia*, Vinerian law lectures for Robert Chambers, and several legal briefs for Boswell. In a way, Johnson dictated his greatest poem, *The Vanity of Human Wishes*, to himself, composing it in his mind, scores of lines at a time, unable to bear writing them down until later, and then only writing half lines and counting on memory for the rest.

Along with this aversion to the 'business' of paper and pen went an unusually retentive memory. His childhood friend Hector says, 'He was uncommonly inquisitive, and his memory so tenacious, that whatever he read or heard he never forgot. I remember rehearsing to him eighteen verses, which after a little pause he rehearsed verbatim, except one epithet, which improved the line.' Johnson himself remembered astonishing his mother by memorizing one Sunday's collect almost as soon as she gave it him. Both the *Dictionary* and the *Lives of the Poets* present evidence of Johnson remembering in later life vast amounts of much earlier reading. Johnson's great memory may be partly attributed to his living in an age that was just emerging from a predominantly oral stage of culture in which memory was more vital and so more developed than it was to become when written things (not only books, but bills, deeds, maps, advertisements, tickets, schedules, and all kinds of ephemera) became so much more widely available through the medium of print. The transitional nature of his time is perhaps best expressed in the fact that on the day after Johnson's birth his father, a bookseller and promulgator of the printed word, conducted the Riding, the annual perambulation designed to refresh local knowledge of the town's boundaries at a time, before the spread of printing, when documents containing such information were scarce. Even for his time, however, Johnson's memory was something special, as, on the other hand, was his immersion in print and his capacity to read. The tension is striking. If Johnson's neurological disorder was Tourette's syndrome, his troubles were probably heightened by the solitude and anxiety that accompany the private production of writing. Bodily laziness is also a symptom of the disease, and Johnson may have felt a neurological resistance to the physical engagement of writing. Dictating, because it is not solitary and requires less movement, may have suited him for neurological reasons, and he may have developed his great memory to help himself avoid the solitude of study and the pain of manual inscription. In his intellectual make-up, as in other aspects of his existence, Johnson experienced antagonism. His mentality was formed on the silent and largely private study of books; he was quintessentially literate, but the kind of physicality needed in the literate world was an obstacle for him. One sign of this was his rough treatment of books, bending and breaking them sometimes as he read or 'tore out the heart' of them, as one acquaintance described his assault on the world of print. The physical activities that Johnson enjoyed as a child and a man were those that did not require much eyesight or fine motor control. He liked jumping, swimming, and climbing trees, and he may have acquired some skill at boxing and wrestling from his Uncle Andrew. Johnson's approach to the physical task of reading was better suited to these grosser activities. Yet, Johnson not only dictated but spoke a highly literate, as well as literary, language; he was bookish even as he was verbal. Out of such antagonism Johnson's intellectual life grew, and perhaps it had something to do with the formation of his philosophical, Latinate style, through which he exerts very firm control over his topics in a language that is itself highly materiate, uncommon, and untransparent. Johnson's mother may have been recalling the beginnings of this style when she told Johnson, even early in life, 'You could not . . . speak plain.'[13]

For a variety of reasons, involving his superior abilities, his neurological problems, and his fiercely independent temper, Johnson seems to have had some disdain or dislike for all his teachers. He complained about the ineptitude of Holbrook and the severity of Hunter. Johnson's resentment of Hunter's flogging is notable because on some occasions he acknowledged the efficacy of this pedagogical technique; he once even wrote a defence of a teacher accused of undue severity, for whom Boswell had taken a brief. Johnson's temperament could not bear the affront of discipline by teachers or other so-called superiors. His own feelings left him ambivalent about the treatment of children; he acknowledged the need for discipline, but he also recommended indulgence, and he cherished above all his memories of extraordinary parental softness. Mrs Thrale reports his rejection of Cyrus's filial resignation in Xenophon and concludes that 'Of parental authority, indeed, few people thought with a lower degree of estimation.' Johnson once said he loved his mother because she gave him coffee which she could ill afford, and his fondest memory of his father concerns the softness of his voice when encouraging him to swim. He delights in remembering that he was 'indulged and caressed' by Hawkins, his first Lichfield teacher.[14]

Despite Johnson's complaints, Lichfield Grammar School and his last teacher, Reverend John Hunter, the 'very severe, and wrong-headedly severe' headmaster, probably served him well. The school flourished under Hunter's leadership and produced alumni worthy to stand in the company of earlier notables such as Joseph Addison, Elias Ashmole, William Wollaston, and Bishop George Smalridge. Within Johnson's tenure at the Lichfield School were graduated many distinguished lawyers, including William Noel, a Justice of the Common Pleas, and Chief Justice John Eardley Wilmot; distinguished divines, including Thomas Newton, Bishop of Bristol; and a poet of some note, Isaac Hawkins Browne the elder. Johnson's closest school friends, with whom he maintained lifelong contact, were John Taylor of Ashbourne, a minister for whom Johnson composed most of his sermons; Edmund Hector, a Birmingham surgeon; and Robert James, inventor of a famous fever powder and author of a medical dictionary. David Garrick, a more illustrious alumnus, was seven years Johnson's junior, and so they probably struck up their friendship later, when Garrick was one of Johnson's few students at Edial. Johnsonian lore has loved the tale of Johnson and Garrick coming down, penniless and unwashed, from the remote half-civilized provinces to take the town by storm. But this is a half-truth, at best. Lichfield was comparatively remote from London in the eighteenth century; it was more provincial than now, and it then retained a greater locality in speech, customs, and politics. However, with its cathedral, its two bookshops, and its fine grammar school, it was not a rude or rustic place, intellectually or socially. Many of its citizens had preceded Johnson and Garrick to London and made marks almost as great upon life in the capital. As Aleyn Lyell Reade wrote of Johnson's headmaster: 'not only did Hunter educate a remarkable number of distinguished men, but also . . . he attracted to Lichfield a large proportion of the sons of county gentlemen of Staffordshire and neighbouring areas. Indeed Johnson seems to have enjoyed the society of schoolfellows quite the equal in birth and standing to the youths who now [1922] frequent the best public schools.'[15]

In 1725 Johnson broadened his social and intellectual life with a visit to his cousin Cornelius Ford at Pedmore near Stourbridge; it started out as a long weekend and went so well for host and guest that it became a six-month stay. Johnson had visited his mother's relatives and his uncle Andrew Johnson's bookshop in Birmingham in 1719; he had also been to London as an infant, but this was his first extended trip away from home and family. Ford was lively, worldly, and well educated. Johnson described him as 'a man of great wit and stupendous parts'. Ford moved in the highest circles and was even an intimate of Lord Chesterfield, who presented a living to him shortly after Johnson's visit. When Johnson stayed with Parson Ford it is unlikely that he was pursuing the profligate ways that led to his memorialization in Hogarth's *Modern Midnight Conversation*. However, he was thirty-one, had already been a Cambridge don, a man about town in London, and an associate of well-known poets, including Pope. Over fifty years later Johnson paid tribute to Ford in his life of Fenton, lamenting that his 'abilities, instead of furnishing convivial merriment to the volup-tuous and dissolute, might have enabled him to excel among the virtuous and the wise'. Hawkins reports that, despite the disparity in age and ex-perience, Ford, 'discovering that [Johnson] was possessed of uncommon parts, was unwilling to let him return, and to make up for the loss he might sustain by his absence from school, became his instructor in the classics, and farther assisted him in his studies.' Forty-five years later in a letter to Mrs Thrale Johnson spoke of wishing to revisit Pedmore to review his conversations with Ford. Reade comments that 'This holiday spent with his brilliant cousin must be reckoned among the principal formative influences of his early years.'[16]

Johnson's visit to Ford's neighbourhood was soon renewed and extended because the headmaster of the Lichfield school refused to readmit him after his long, unexcused absence. The Johnsons tried to place Samuel in a Shropshire school as a kind of intern, but this scheme was rejected by the headmaster, Samuel Lea, who in later life pleased Johnson immensely by calling it his greatest claim to fame that he almost taught Samuel Johnson. Cornelius Ford stepped in and, using the influence of his half-brother Gregory Hickman of Green Close, Stourbridge, placed Johnson at the Stourbridge School under John Wentworth on similar terms to those rejected by Lea. Thus Johnson's stay in the Stourbridge neighbourhood was extended to at least a full year.[17]

Exactly what kind of influence was this visit on Johnson at the im-pressionable age of sixteen? Society in the neighbourhood was relatively high and included Lord Lyttelton, who lived at nearby Hagley. Conse-quently, the whole year was a sojourn for Johnson in a privileged social circle of upper-class country gentlemen and ladies. Johnson enjoyed this society as a welcome guest, if not as an equal. Reade points out that 'Johnson's natural status when he came to Stourbridge would be much better than that he held at Lichfield, where he was only known as the son of the local bookseller. At Stourbridge he became the nephew of Dr Ford, for years the leading physician of the town; the cousin of Cornelius Ford, fitted by education and talents to adorn the most brilliant society; and the near connexion of the Hickmans, people . . . of considerable local consequence.' This experience undoubtedly prepared Johnson to feel at home among the recently arrived Thrales of Streatham Park and perhaps always gave him a longing or an aptitude to be 'taken up' by people of an elevated, if not a noble class. Although he may always have been on his guard in the presence of nobility, and he is reported to have disliked Lyttelton, Johnson enjoyed playing the part of the brilliant, well-connected young scholar in the attractive social setting of Stourbridge. He must, indeed, have warmed to the role, for Percy reports that 'At Stourbridge Johnson's genius was so distinguished that, although little better than a school-boy, he was admitted into the best company of the place, and had no common attention paid to his conversation; of which remarkable instances were long remembered there.'[18]

Johnson expanded his reading at Pedmore and Stourbridge, becoming better acquainted with classical writers like Anacreon and Martial, as well as with Ford's favourite English poets – Garth, Congreve, Addison, and Prior. These are all writers whom Johnson continued to read for most of his life. During the period of his visits to Pedmore Johnson also produced most of his extant juvenilia. Johnson's childhood compositions consist entirely of poems, most of them translations or imitations of classical verse. The earliest poem dates from just before the trip to Pedmore. It is a highly conventional lament over the transience of life expressed in the form of an address to an early flower. 'On a Daffodill' begins, 'Hail lovely flower, first honour of the year!' The speaker then offers his best wishes to the flower in pastoral terms that the older Johnson found pretty silly: 'May lambent zephyrs gently wave thy head' (9). Young Johnson may have written the poem to express his feelings for an attractive visitor to Pedmore. He calls her Cleora in the poem, and naturally he makes her share in the life and fate of the blossom. Predictably, we are asked to 'See! Sol's bright chariot seeks the western main' (22) and to recall the swift chariots of time that career towards death in so much *carpe diem* poetry:

> With grief this emblem of mankind I see,
>   Like one awaken'd from a pleasing dream,
> Cleora's self, fair flower, shall fade like thee,
>   Alike must fall the poet and his theme.[19]

Like the early compositions of Pope, Johnson's little poem is in the metaphysical tradition of the previous century. Without making too much of it, it is worth pointing out that he chooses the emblematic and moralizing vein of the metaphysicals in preference to their more argumentative or scientific modes. As an older critic, Johnson would prefer the mental exercise of reading Cowley, but as a young, courtly poet he follows Herrick, who probably wrote the most verse about fading blossoms representative of evanescent earthly life, including at least two about daffodils.[20] However, the distance Johnson establishes in the last stanza between the poet and the emblem he views distinguishes his poem from any of Herrick's on a similar theme. Johnson's major verse goes further away from metaphysical poetry in the same direction by being more visual, emblematic, and impersonal. The 'See!' of line 22 is consistent with the voice of *London* and *The Vanity of Human Wishes*, although the setting and hence the imagery are so different that the connection is obscure. Whether or not it continued to influence his poetry, Johnson continued to read metaphysical poetry, quoting extensively from Cleveland, Cowley, Herbert, and Donne in the *Dictionary*. Despite his well-known criticisms of Milton's *Lycidas* and other pastoral verse, and despite his famous reservations about the value of metaphysical poetry, Johnson undoubtedly knew the tradition well and read in it throughout his life.

Edmund Hector, whose copies are the sources for many of Johnson's early verse, said Johnson 'never much lik'd' 'On a Daffodill' because 'it was not characteristick of the Flower.' However, this represents the application of an aesthetic standard that Johnson developed only gradually and did not express fully until the mid-1750s. In any case, it did not affect his view of some of his other childhood pieces, two of which he found durable enough to merit publication, with minor revisions, when he was an adult. One of these is 'An Ode on Friendship', in which Johnson sings the praises of an ideal celebrated by the Hellenistic philosophers, by Cicero (especially in *De Amicitia*), by many European humanists, and by their progeny, including Bacon and Jeremy Collier, both of whose essays on friendship Johnson quotes in the *Dictionary*. With its reliance on a classical and humanistic foundation, the theme of Johnson's ode is characteristic of his later work, but the poem sounds at first anomalous. It is strange to hear a nearly ecstatic Johnson proclaiming:

> When virtues kindred virtues meet,
> And sister minds together join,
> Thy charms, permanent as great,
> Are all transporting, all divine.[21]

Johnson omitted these lines when he published the poem in 1743, but he restored them in 1766, changing 'sister minds' to 'sister-souls' and 'charms' to 'pleasures'. These changes regularize the metre and substitute marching alliteration for chiming consonance, but the transparent attempt at a kind of metaphysical sensuousness is still startling. The words on the page are made to imitate or embody the action they represent: 'virtues' meets 'virtues' in the same line; the sounds of 'sister' and 'minds' (or 'souls') join as do those of 'charms' and 'permanent' (or 'pleasure'). The advantage Johnson takes of alternative pronunciation in 'join' and 'great' is also surprisingly old-fashioned. However, the poem is like Johnson's well-known work in the way it generalizes a familiar theme and employs an abstract but animated allegorical sketch. Still addressing friendship, he says, 'In vain for thee the monarch sighs, / And hugs a flatt'rer for a friend' (15–16). This line indicates that Johnson's mature style emerged early in his poetic career, but it also suggests that his mature style is partly compounded of the metaphysical sensuousness of the early verse.

The other piece of juvenilia that Johnson later published is a translation of the Horatian ode, 'Integer vitae' (1.22). Johnson's very last translation, written a couple of weeks before his death, was also of a Horatian ode, and he told Boswell very credibly that 'Horace's Odes have been the compositions in which he has taken most delight.' There is obvious delight in Johnson's translation of 'Integer vitae' in which a wolf runs away from a virtuous man, and earthly geography, with a host of exquisite place-names, is displayed as richly irrelevant to the infatuated lover. The conventional, Hellenistic theme is common in Johnson's writing, and there is an obvious appeal in the exciting wild beast and all the foreign places rapidly mentioned, set in contrast to the immovable, true man. Johnson's stanza describing the invulnerability of the virtuous man to hostile places is especially energetic: he needs no guard

> Tho' Scythia's icy cliffs he treads,
>   Or torrid Africk's faithless sands;
> Or where the fam'd Hydaspes spreads
>   His liquid wealth o'er barb'rous lands.
> (5–9)

In a more naked form Johnson wrote out the stoic theme in 'Festina Lente', a task reportedly assigned him by Wentworth, the master at Stourbridge, because it was a motto he especially needed to learn:

> Let reason with superiour force controul
> The floods of rage, and calm thy rufled soul.
> (7–8)

Johnson's surviving translations of other Horatian odes also reveal his attraction to their combination of exotic pleasure and familiar wisdom.[22]
    Johnson's translation of part of *Iliad* 6, the famous scene in which Astyanax is frightened by Hector's helmet and its animate plume, is relatively uninteresting, although, like the whole collection of classical translations, it shows astonishing metrical and linguistic competence for a sixteen-year-old. More interesting is his translation of Addison's Latin poem ΠΥΓΜΑΙΟΓΕΡΟΝΟΜΑΧΙΑ, 'Battle of the Pygmies and Cranes'. Addison's mock epic, written as a collegiate spoof, plays on the same incongruities of scale that Swift later exploited in the first two books of *Gulliver's Travels*. Johnson's English version sounds a little like *The Rape of the Lock*, especially the epic card fight and the genesis of the sylphs, but he, Pope, and Addison were all working in the older, Ovidian tradition of metamorphosis:

> Now in the realms below, the Pygmie shades
> Mix'd with old heroes trace the flow'ry meads,
> And wander sportive o'er th' Elysian plain:
> Or if old women's tales may credit gain,
> When pale-fac'd Cynthia sheds her silver light
> Dispelling the black horrors of the night,
> The shepherds oft' see little ghosts glide by
> And shades of Pygmies swim before their eye.
> They call them fairies; these now free from care
> And giv'n to mirth, the Cranes no longer fear,
> But move their num'rous arms to musick's sound,
> And tread in mystick rings the mossie ground.
> (159–70)

Like Addison, Johnson went from Lichfield Grammar School to Pembroke College, Oxford, and his only extant translation of a modern Latin poem may be an identificatory exercise. But it is also a workout in the kind of mockery that Johnson adopted in his Parliamentary reports, *Debates in the Senate of Lilliput.* Moreover, it suggests an interest in portraying ironic heroism that comes to the fore in some sections of *The Vanity of Human Wishes* and in some of the character sketches in the *Rambler* and the *Idler.* Dick Minim, for example, is a pygmy fighting miniscule battles in the ironic world of literary criticism.[23]

Johnson suggested much about the significance of his visit to Pedmore in 1725–6 when, in 1734, he noted it on the first page of his Annals along with only two other events: his birth in 1709 and his entrance to Oxford in 1728. In between Pedmore and Oxford, however, was a two-year period of considerable importance in Johnson's education. In August 1726, shortly after his return to Lichfield, Johnson acquired a copy of Adam Littleton's *Latin Dictionary* and set himself seriously to an extensive course of reading. He described this period of study as one of the heaviest and widest of his life. He told Boswell he then read, 'not voyages and travels, but all literature, Sir, all ancient writers, all manly: though but little Greek, only some Anacreon and Hesiod'. To this period belongs the story that Johnson was searching for an apple on the shelves of his father's shop, but when he came instead across the works of Petrarch he devoured knowledge instead of an apple. With its possibilities for Miltonic interpretation the story is almost too good to be true, but it credibly suggests Johnson's desultory reading habits. As he told Boswell, 'in this irregular manner . . . I had looked into a great many books, which were not commonly known at the Universities, where they seldom read any books but what are put into their hands by their tutors; so that when I came to Oxford, Dr Adams, now master of Pembroke College, told me, I was the best qualified for the University that he had ever known come there.' On another occasion, Johnson spoke to Boswell of his reading 'very hard' as a young man, and he reflected sadly that he knew almost as much at eighteen as he did in his whole life. Precisely what Johnson read in this period is hard to say, but it probably included Petronius, a copy of whose works he definitely acquired in 1727, and Macrobius, with a quotation from whom he astonished his Pembroke College tutor. Johnson was early trying to get above the common round of classical study for reasons both of curiosity and pride. He recalled that as a boy he had found in a school 'trot' or 'pony' the word *'inlicaturus*, which I did not understand, but used it.' Although the majority of his reading was in the works of central authors like Horace, Johnson made excursions into more remote writers, and he enjoyed the superiority this gave him over less adventuresome readers.[24]

One clue to what Johnson read from 1726 to 1728 is the catalogue of the books he took with him to Pembroke. This exists in the form of a list on the back of his letter to Gilbert Repington, a friend whom he asked to retrieve the books he had left behind when he dropped out of Oxford in

December 1729. It is impossible to say exactly when Johnson acquired, much less when, if ever, he actually read most of these eighty-five books, but the list is interesting nevertheless. Johnson understandably brought with him to college a number of grammar books, some geography and chronology books, Roman historians like Tacitus and Silius, Basil Kennett's Roman history, and such student's books as Quillet's *Callipaedia*, Locke on education, and Barecroft's *Advice to a Son in the University*. With coursework in mind, Johnson also brought editions of the standard Greek and Latin authors; perhaps most notable in this part of the list are the multiplicity of Horatian texts and the presence of such lyric poets as are usually not thought of as Johnsonian fare: Anacreon, Theocritus, Ovid, and Catullus. Johnson also came prepared with works that defined the university curriculum of *literae humaniores*: Quintilian, Longinus, Vida, and Le Clerc. Some other items in the collection suggest more personal interests. The most important of these are several volumes of modern Latin poetry, including two volumes by the great humanists, Julius Caesar Scaliger and his son Joseph, one by George Buchanan, and another by André Deslandes. Supplemented by an ample selection of the latest Roman poets, this part of the collection hints at the young Johnson's aspirations to a place as a poet in the late Latin world of letters that still circulated freely across national boundaries in his childhood and took Europe for its province.[25]

It is clear that Johnson was preparing for Latin schooling, but he did not altogether neglect English poetry. He had with him at Oxford several poets whose lives he eventually wrote: Milton, Dryden, Pope, Garth, Prior, Blackmore, Smith, and Ambrose Philips. Garth and Prior were tastes acquired visiting their devotee, Cornelius Ford, but Johnson read Smith in Lichfield at the suggestion of the poet's close friend, Gilbert Walmesley. In his life of Smith Johnson spontaneously pays tribute to Walmesley's 'amplitude of learning' and 'copiousness of communication'. Walmesley occupied the Bishop's Palace in Lichfield as a gentleman and a bachelor. Though separated by political allegiance and by thirty years, Walmesley and Johnson were close intellectual companions. Like Cornelius Ford, Walmesley was a somewhat dissipated, worldly, and conversationally adept country gentleman whom Johnson admired and, in some respects, emulated. James Clifford goes so far as to say, 'It was Gilbert Walmesley, perhaps even more than Parson Ford at Pedmore, who put his stamp on Sam Johnson's mind.' Donald Greene more strenuously analyses Johnson's attachment to Walmesley, Ford, and the equally grand Dr Taylor: 'They seem to have fascinated and stimulated the young man, and he delighted in their admiration of his growing intellectual and artistic powers. Had he been a lesser person, he would have succumbed to their attraction and to the comfortable security of a ready-made intellectual pattern.' Greene's Johnson, always combative, distrustful of cant, and conscious of social realities, rebelled against the society of these 'pleasant people', becoming a rogue Tory in their midst. 'Perhaps Johnson's Toryism', speculates Greene, 'was in large part the product of such a revulsion from the high-flown idealizing of Hagley and Ashbourne to the realities of a life about which he had no romantic illusions. . . . Perhaps it was an instinctive defensive reaction to preserve his intellectual integrity, his identity even from the too insidious attraction of this new-found world.' Like each commentator's Johnson, Greene's bears the marks of his own mind and his own cultural surroundings. Greene's Johnson, like the critical creations of some other extremely able scholars in the post-war period, is in rebellion against a kind of cant that resembles the nationalistic preaching of Joe McCarthy and Richard Nixon, for which the authorized and necessary propaganda of World War II had prepared the nation. Yet this cultural situation is hardly unique, and Greene's Johnson has great validity. However else one sees Johnson, one must also see the 'potential rebel' that Greene has identified as essential to him.[26]

Undoubtedly, Johnson joined in the intellectual life that Walmesley, Ford, and Taylor offered, and he also undoubtedly opposed and criticized it. Much of what is known about Johnson comes from accounts of his conversation, and it is obvious that he thrived on antagonistic debate. Ford advised him early on: 'You will make your way the more easily in the world, I see, as you are contented to dispute no man's claim to conversation excellence; they will, therefore, more willingly allow your pretensions as a writer.' Boswell describes him in conversation as 'actuated by the spirit of contradiction', and as taking pleasure in it. Johnson's good friend Charles Burney reported that he was naturally so contentious that 'If you said two and two make four, he would say, "How will you prove that, sir?" '[27] Action and reaction, friction, and a lively asperity are qualities of Johnson's thinking, writing, and conversation throughout his life.

Walmesley and Johnson must have argued about politics, but they also discussed less controversial intellectual matters, probably reading books in common or at one another's suggestion. Walmesley was a steady customer of Michael Johnson's bookshop, and his surviving book bills from the period of his steadiest conversation with Johnson suggest that the two may have discussed not only the poetry of Edmund Smith, but also *Gulliver's Travels*, Swift's poetry, the *Dunciad*, and Locke's *Essay concerning Human Understanding*.[28] The civil war was also a likely topic of discussion. Law and the relationship between church and state must have come up in 1727 when Walmesley purchased the legal works of John Ayliffe, who had lost his place and his degrees at Oxford because of a controversial earlier work. The civil war was also a likely topic of discussion. Johnson was examining both sides of the issue, reading Salmasius's *Defense of King Charles I* and Milton's answer to it, his *Defense of the English People*. The debate was still lively in Lichfield, where some episodes of the civil war had left their mark on the structure of the cathedral, and the God-given death of the rebel Lord Brooke was celebrated in a memorial place. But by 1727 surely the issues in the war were settling into socially agreeable subjects, and debate on them could be undertaken without rancour as well as with honour. Given our predominant, Boswellian image of his somewhat slovenly

majesty, it is surprising that the young Johnson was an eager courtier in
the Bishop's Palace, visiting Gilbert Walmesely with the other bright young
men of the town, Robert James and David Garrick. He was contentious,
but he was not entirely hostile, withdrawn, or fixed in his opinions. Nor
was he insusceptible to the charms of higher social life.

The 'potential rebel' also fell in love for the first time during this stay
at home, and he produced a couple of occasional poems about young
women. Edmund Hector's sixteen-year-old sister was the object of Johnson's
first romantic passion, and he spoke sentimentally about the future Mrs
Carless, even much later in life. It is possible that Johnson wrote his birthday
poem to his first love. It is a piece of high greeting card verse, with some
echoes of Pope's *Rape of the Lock* and very little of Johnson's characteristic
sharpness. The speaker begins with the entirely conventional request, 'This
tributary verse receive, my fair, / Warm with an ardent lover's fondest
pray'r.' He then rises only to a modest, surprisingly avuncular admonition:
'My fair, be mindful of the mighty trust, / Alas! 'tis hard for beauty to be
just' (11–12). The other poem that dates from this period is 'An Epilogue
to *The Distrest Mother*', a play by Ambrose Philips, which Johnson and his
friends may have produced for their own entertainment. The epilogue
describes the heaven and the hell reserved for kind and cruel beauties. It
might be read as a sketch for the section on the beauty in *The Vanity of
Human Wishes*, but it is less severe, more courtly, and much more like early
Pope than mature Johnson. In coquette heaven, for instance,

> Perennial roses deck each purple vale,
> And scents ambrosial breathe in every gale;
> Far hence are banish'd vapours, spleen, and tears,
> Tea, scandal, ivory teeth, and languid airs.
>
> (16–19)

Such poetry suggests that, if Johnson was partly in rebellion against the
Whiggish aristocracy at the Bishop's Palace, he was also enjoying himself
and was pleased to contribute to local merriment in the courtly idiom of
genteel verse. He adopted such tones again in his poems and letters to
Mrs Thrale and her daughters, but these similar social successes were many
hard years away.[29]

2

Oxford and Birmingham

Poverty is a great enemy to human happiness, it certainly destroys liberty, and it makes some virtues impracticable, and others extremely difficult.
Johnson to Boswell, 7 December 1782

After nearly two years of intense reading and social gaiety, Johnson had proved himself above shopkeeping and bookbinding. On the strength of a bequest to his mother and a promise of further financial support from a friend of the family, Johnson enrolled in Pembroke College, Oxford. He remained there, in continuous residence, for only thirteen months. The promised funds never materialized, and Johnson was forced to withdraw from college, but there is evidence that the onset of a severe depression was part of the reason that he stayed home after the Christmas vacation of 1729.

The length of Johnson's stay at Oxford, once thought much longer, is now settled, but there is still debate about the nature of his experience there. Hawkins and many succeeding biographers have stressed the great effect that Oxford had on Johnson the High Churchman and Tory: 'the order and discipline of a college life, the reading the best authors, the attendance on public exercises, the early calls to prayer, the frequent instructions from the pulpit, with all the other means of religious and moral improvement, had their proper effect; and though they left his natural temper much as they found it, they begat in his mind those sentiments of piety which were the rule of his conduct throughout his future life, and made so conspicuous a part of his character.' Perhaps this is the effect that the intellectual and religious life of Oxford would have had, if it could have been experienced apart from the social reality of a place in which Johnson was evidently uncomfortable. What is reliably reported about Johnson at Oxford suggests that he adopted in his new surroundings an attitude of hostility, pride, and scorn, which softened only later, like his attitude toward his parents, into regretful respect. His attitude toward his tutor, William Jorden, is representative. While he was at Pembroke, Johnson expressed a contempt for Jorden's work. There is the famous story about Johnson sliding on the ice in Christ Church Meadow instead of attending Jorden's lecture and the one about his declaration to Jorden that he had been sconced twopence for missing a lecture not worth a penny. More importantly and more reliably, John Taylor, who followed him from Lichfield to Oxford, reported that Johnson warned him off Pembroke because of Jorden. According to Boswell's transcription of the materials he received from Taylor, 'The moment that young Taylor lighted at the Crown Inn [Oxford] he hastened to his freind [*sic*] who took him directly into his room and upon Dr Taylor's announcing to him that he had obtained his Father's consent to be admitted of the same College with him, Johnson with that conscientiousness which attended him through life immediately objected and said "I cannot in conscience suffer you to enter here. For the Tutor under whom you must be is such a Blockhead that you will not be five minutes at his lectures till you find out what a fool he is and upbraid me with your looks for recommending you to him."' Taylor went across the street to Christ Church and studied with Bateman. Later in life, however, Johnson expressed affection for Jorden. In recounting the sliding incident to Boswell, he added that Jorden had asked him to his rooms after dinner and offered him a glass of wine, proffering his cordiality as a form of rebuke. Jorden's subtlety was not lost on the impatient twenty-year-old Johnson, nor was it fully appreciated until age and achievement had softened his natural indignation.[1]

Other familiar stories about Johnson at Oxford also tend to support Donald Greene's McCarthy-era characterization of him as 'the angry young man of Pembroke'. He rebelliously refused to respond to the servitor's bed-checking methods; he did not do his assignments and more than once gave facetious reasons for his failure; 'he was', in one account, 'generally seen lounging at the College gate, with a circle of young students round him, whom he was entertaining with wit, and keeping from their studies, if not spiriting them up to rebellion against the College discipline, which in his maturer years he so much extolled.' He described himself later as 'rude and violent. . . . I was miserably poor, and I thought to fight my way by my literature and my wit; so I disregarded all power and all authority.' The buttery books of the college indicate that Johnson was a moderately comfortable commoner, and the anger he explained as the result of poverty must have been partly a form of class anger. As a defender of rank and privilege, Hawkins pauses in his biography to rebuke Johnson for thinking that 'the scholar's, like the christian life, levelled all distinctions of rank and worldly pre-eminence.' Hawkins's accusation is probably not exaggerated, but, even if it is, as a student Johnson undoubtedly asserted the importance of learning and intelligence as against the privileges of birth so scrupulously honoured at Oxford.[2]

Johnson's hostility was not, however, limited to social and financial matters. He reported that he could not stand the superior Latinity of his fellow student John Meeke and sat as far away from him as possible so that he did not have to hear him construe. His scorn for Oxford's social ambience was partly an expression of anxiety about success, and the sphere in which he hoped to succeed was the world of letters in which Latin was still the lingua franca. Literature was to be his province, and he needed to asssert his pre-eminenence there, just as he needed to assert the superiority of letters to high society. Johnson's pretension of not studying was an aspect of this anxious, double assertion. The pose of the nonchalant, naturally brilliant wit is one that Johnson had picked up from the likes of Cornelius Ford, but the seventeenth-century ideal of natural learning was evolving into the ideal of the child prodigy or idiot savant. Boswell draws his subject at times in that character: the infant Hercules of Toryism and the inspired idiot discoursing on politics before the amazed Hogarth fit into this mould. Johnson himself clung to the older ideal, glorifying it in college and, to a degree, in his *Life of Savage*. Despite the appearance he wished to make, however, Johnson did read, write, and study at Pembroke. He visited Taylor to get the substance of Bateman's lectures until a new pair of shoes offered by a snickering and affluent student drove him to exile himself from the grandeur of Christ Church, and in private he went on studying.

Although he failed to produce the annual, mandatory exercise on the Gunpowder Plot to blow up Parliament in 1605, he turned in an elaborate excuse for not doing so called 'Somnium', learnedly modelled on Macrobius. As ostentatiously erudite in its way is Johnson's Latin translation of Pope's 'Messiah' for *A Miscellany of Poems by Several Hands*, edited by a Pembroke student named Husbands.[3] Johnson's is the only Latin poem in a collection of some 300 pages. Most of the pieces belong to genres popular among students in 1729: classical and biblical paraphrase, anacreontics, and courtly pastoral poetry. Johnson's Latin attempt at religious sublimity stands out in this collection in a manner that Johnson adopted in order to thrust himself above his classmates and coevals. The poem contains a self-conscious affirmation of Johnson's vocation as a poet. Following Pope, he dismisses the muses of pastoral poetry and invites the unnameable holy muse of the prophet Isaiah. However, the heavenly flame that Pope finds on the prophet's lips, Johnson locates in his breast, and where Pope asks that the muse 'my voice inspire', Johnson calls for a stronger brew: 'dignos accende furores!' (7: 'kindle up a worthy madness!'). Johnson is distinguishing himself not only from his earlier, more pastoral poetic self but also from the finer but less astounding Pope. In the 'Battle of the Pygmies and Cranes', Johnson took on Addison, as here he challenged Pope. Likewise, in 'Aurora est Musis Amica' he emulated the collegiate skill of Milton.[4]

In one final piece of his college verse worth mentioning Johnson most explicitly declares himself, but he does so with irony. 'The Young Author' reads like a draft of the famous section about the student in *The Vanity of*

Human Wishes. Johnson compares his hapless subject to a peasant whose wish to travel is fatally fulfilled by a tempestuous voyage:

> So the young author panting for a name,
> And fir'd with pleasing hope of endless fame,
> Intrusts his happiness to human kind,
> More false, more cruel than the seas and wind.
>
> (11–14)

Like the aeronautic projector in *Rasselas*, the author falls very suddenly; his fame lasts two verse feet – 'The pamphlet spreads, incessant hisses rise' – and the author retreats to obscurity in the remaining five lines. The theme was a commonplace; Husbands, for one, touched on it in the preface to his *Miscellany*. But the suddenness of the collapse is distinctive, and Johnson's decision to versify this, rather than other commonplaces, shows where his thoughts about his future were tending.[5]

Johnson did not merely 'lounge' at Pembroke. His production of poetry indicates this to a degree, but there is evidence of greater activity in his reading. Johnson told Boswell that 'what he read *solidly* at Oxford was Greek; not the Grecian historians, but Homer and Euripides, and now and then a little Epigram' (i.e. the *Greek Anthology*). While reading Greek *solidly*, Johnson did not neglect Latin. In one diary entry from his college year, he poetically bids farewell to sloth and draws up a brief list of books he wishes to own: Lucretius, Velleius Paterculus, Justinus, and Graevius's edition of Cicero's letters. In another entry, Johnson drew up a chart indicating how many lines of Latin or Greek he could read in so many days, weeks, months, and years, if he read so many lines per day. His arithmetic, as it always would, suggests that Johnson was doing less than he expected of himself, but he expected a great deal. In his biography John Hawkins mentions 'having by him' Johnson's *Adversaria*, a set of notes in which he had laid out an extensive plan of study: 'In this course of learning, his favourite objects were classical literature, ethics, and theology. . . . The heads of science, to the extent of six folio volumes, are copiously branched throughout it.' Hawkins also indicates that most of the outline was not filled in, and therefore most of the pages were blank. The mere fact that he arranged such a book, however, is evidence of ambition and certainly of some effort on Johnson's part.[6]

Johnson's most celebrated act of reading at Oxford is his encounter with William Law's *A Serious Call to a Devout and Holy Life*. Following Johnson's own declarations to him, Boswell says that 'From this time forward, religion was the predominant object of his thoughts.'[7] There is no doubt about the importance of religion in Johnson's life, and his religion has important affinities with the Evangelicalism of Law and his admirer Wesley, as Donald Greene has shown. Law's rules for devotion obviously appealed to Johnson, though he was seldom able to observe them for sustained periods. Like other Evangelicals, Law recommends early rising, a regular course of prayer (every three hours at the cardinal points of the day), proper use of time, and a strict, daily accounting of oneself. Another highly recommended activity is reading in the Bible and in good books generally. Like other activities in the confirmed life, reading should be noted, calculated, and reviewed. Hence, Johnson's compulsive notes on his reading potential are intermingled with his religious convictions and religious fears. If reading Law confirmed him in religion, it also confirmed him in his chosen task of reading, but both commitments have roots in Johnson's earlier life.

The significance of this single reading experience has been overestimated, but several important aspects of Johnson's moral life are outlined in Law, especially his rational absolutism. For Law every argument against extreme transgression is an argument against minor transgression, and 'the sin . . . of hating or despising any one man, is like the sin of hating all God's creation.' Such a strict demarcation of the line between virtue and vice characterizes Johnson's attitudes throughout his life. The political implications of Law's absolutism may also have attracted Johnson, especially while he was at Oxford, because they call for a reduction of all classes and stations of life to a homogeneous, egalitarian Christian life: 'All men therefore, as men, have one and the same important business, to act up to the excellency of their *rational* nature, and to make *reason* and *order* the law of all their designs and actions. All Christians, as Christians, have one and the same calling. . . . The one thing needful to one, is the one thing needful to all.' On the other hand, there are aspects of Law's teaching that Johnson resisted: his anti-theatrical campaign, for instance, and his urgent appeal that prayer be begun with a psalm chanted or sung. In college Johnson also read Mandeville, a writer whom Law strenuously attacked for his pessimistic, Hobbesian view of human nature. Mandeville and Hobbes are excluded from Johnson's great course of reading in the *Dictionary*'s illustrative quotations; he did not wish to recommend such dangerous writers to his audience, but he was unafraid of reading them himself. Johnson's declarations about the importance of Law to his religious life were made, like his selections for the *Dictionary*, with an awareness of his audience and a wish to increase or, at least, not to damage the piety of those he influenced. He trusted himself to navigate a wider course of study and of thought than he could safely recommend to others, and he kept that course largely to himself.[8]

Another language in which Johnson read at Oxford is French. James Gray has recently shown that an experimental government programme of instruction in modern languages was under way at Oxford during Johnson's year. In fact, his Lichfield compatriot Robert James studied French and Italian at St John's College shortly before Johnson's arrival. Although there is no evidence that Johnson had formal instruction in French, he picked up the language (and perhaps Italian) at Oxford. He read in French Joachim Le Grand's *Relation historique d'Abissinie*, the work that he eventually translated for his first major publication. All in all, the evidence suggests that Johnson was not idle during his thirteen months at college. He wrote some publishable verse; he read a great deal; and he picked up at least one additional language. He was perhaps thinking of employing new languages in one of the last recorded scenes of his college life. The Master of Pembroke, going past Johnson's room, 'overheard him uttering this soliloquy in his strong emphatick voice: "Well, I have a mind to see what is done in other places of learning. I'll go and visit the Universities abroad. I'll go to France & Italy. I'll go to Padua. – And I'll mind my business. For an *Athenian* Blockhead is the worst of all blockheads.' This rare hint of Johnson's inner voice is suggestive. Walter Jackson Bate finds in it evidence of Johnson's love of travel. True, but it also indicates something about his wish to leave Oxford, to be out of that particular, English, social scene and, in fleeing the mother country, to be part of a larger, European, intellectual community. An Athenian blockhead is one who thinks his home town is the only civilized place in the world. In Herodotus, Thucydides, and Euripides Johnson would have found plenty of reminders of the stupidity of the boastful, autochthonous Athenian, and it is not hard to imagine that he transferred that critique to the Oxonian scene. Johnson's early preparation to write Latin poetry is one sign and these private mutterings are another of his wish to be unprovincial – to escape not only the Midlands but England itself. Like Goldsmith, who really did go to Padua and get a degree, Johnson wished to be a citizen of the world.[9]

Although he had qualms about Oxford, Johnson did not pack up his belongings when he went home for the Christmas vacation of 1729–30, and he probably expected to return. At home, however, he found his father's fortune and health in decline. Michael Johnson died at the end of the following year, leaving behind many debts and many unfulfilled promises of patrimony. Johnson's psychic state in these circumstances went from bad to worse; his pain was so great that he contemplated suicide, although he was keenly aware of the religious consequences. He discussed his condition with Taylor, and he described it vividly in a letter to his godfather. Dr Swynfen found Johnson's statement so compelling as a philosophical description of a disordered mental condition that he showed it to some friends or associates. When Johnson heard that Swynfen had violated his confidence, he broke permanently and irreconcilably with him. What Johnson said in the letter to Swynfen will never be known. Whatever the exact nature of his problems was, however, it is likely that they were exacerbated by the psychological and social circumstances of late adolescence, by his father's illness, and by the necessity of facing his impecunity. In addition, Johnson's emotional problems were linked to his neurological condition. Like other sufferers of Tourette's or related syndromes, Johnson experienced wide swings in mood and energy. From 1730 to 1734 he felt serious depression, melancholy, and even occasional madness. Although Boswell does not mention it in the *Life*, Edmund Hector told him that Johnson feared madness at this period. Boswell once asked Hector point blank if he had seen in Johnson 'a tendency to be disorde[re]d in his mind. Hector said he had.' His involuntary mutterings and ejaculations were frequent; he took 'peevish fits'; and, like Swift, he exercised compulsively in order to calm himself. In doing so, Johnson may have been following the advice of the physician George Cheyne, especially as it appears in his work on melancholy, *The English Malady*. Johnson praised this book and must have found it highly relevant to his own case. Cheyne traces intellectual disorders (like lowness, vapours, despondency, depression, and terrifying fantasies) to nervous conditions brought on by corruptions in 'the Habit' (the overall condition of the bodily mechanism), which may be caused by a 'latent scropulous or scorbutick Taint'. Cheyne avers that the whole syndrome is sometimes the result of old parents. Though there is no clear evidence that he undertook the recommended dietary regimen of milk and vegetables, Johnson practised abstemiousness during this period, and his long walks fit Cheyne's scheme of therapy. Taking another approach, Johnson also tried to regain control over himself in the early 1730s with religious devotions, apparently acquiring a new Book of Common Prayer for the purpose in 1730.[10]

Johnson was working at getting well, and until the end of this black period he produced very little writing. As far we know, he wrote merely three courtly little poems to ladies, one of them for Morgan Graves, the brother of Richard Graves, author of *The Spiritual Quixote*. These poems are elegant but predictable reminders of Dryden's occasional verse. In addition to Morgan Graves, Johnson consorted at this time with his well-to-do Stourbridge and Pedmore relations, and was introduced by Walmesley to Henry, the brother of Lord Hervey. When he was able, Johnson was playing courtier or court poet still, but he was also looking for a job. Rejecting his inherited trade, he looked for opportunities in academic life instead. He applied unsuccessfully to teach at the Stourbridge Grammar School and then successfully to Market Bosworth. He lived there in the house of the school's wealthy patron, Wolstan Dixie, but Johnson could bear his situation and the arrogant behaviour of his employer no more than six months. In July of 1732 he was back in Lichfield applying, again unsuccessfully, for a teaching post at the Ashbourne Grammar School.

About the time he quit Market Bosworth Johnson received a settlement of twenty pounds from his father's estate and made a notation of it in his diary followed by an exhortation to himself: 'Usque adeo mihi mea Fortuna fingenda est. Interea ne paupertate Vires animi languescant, ne in flagitia Egestas adigat, cavendum' ('At this point my fortune is mine to make. While it is so, care must be taken lest in poverty my mental powers should decay or lest destitution drive me to disgrace.')[11] His resolution is admirable, but Johnson had more trouble making his fortune than preserving his intellectual powers and moral integrity. His estimation of his own 'Vires animi' was justifiably large: he considered bookselling beneath him, and he did not hold schoolmastering in much esteem. His concept of the life of writing had not yet admitted a keen sense of financial opportunity.

Thinking of Latin poetry, looking back to Augustan Rome, the late Empire, neo-Latin Europe, or even to the English poets of the previous century, Johnson thought of the social life of writing as gentlemanly. Even Pope, though he made his fortune at writing, was then carrying on a pretence of courtly carelessness about the business of publication, sales, and profits – Michael Johnson's end of the literary world. As an aspiring young writer, Johnson sought to assume the role of the elegant and learned poet, respected and honoured in the homes of his upper-class associates, a man who has won a social place by dint of his intellectual power.

Although it was years before Johnson fully transformed his conception of himself and his life of writing, he made an important step in that direction when he went to Birmingham in 1732. He lived there with his friend Edmund Hector who reported that Johnson 'was Mr Hector's guest at the boarding table of Mr Warren who was also very civil to him on account of the great use Dr Johnson was to him with his advice in his trade.'[12] Thomas Warren's trade, like Johnson's, was bookselling, but in collaboration the two men soon expanded their literary activities. Warren started a provincial newspaper, *The Birmingham Journal*, and for this single-sheet weekly Johnson wrote his first periodical essays. No trace of these works remains, but in producing them Johnson began his life as professional writer. Not content with mere periodical writing Johnson also proposed to Warren a more scholarly project – a translation and abridgement of a book he had read at Pembroke, *Relation historique d'Abissinie* by Joachim Le Grand, a French translation of an unpublished manuscript by the seventeenth-century Portuguese Jesuit missionary Jerónimo Lobo.

Given his background and interests, Johnson's reasons for undertaking this particular project are not immediately apparent, but the prior question is why a provincial bookseller like Warren accepted the proposal to begin with. Le Grand's *Relation* contains three parts: a translation of Lobo's *Itinerário*, the Jesuit's account of his travels in Abyssinia and his attempts to convert the heretical Christians to Roman Catholicism; a sequel, with sixteen dissertations on religious and scientific questions raised by the text; and a section of supporting documents. Johnson abridged and epitomized the first part, translated the second more fully, and left out the third altogether. Warren was trying hard to succeed financially: *The Birmingham Journal*, his advertisements, sales of stationery, hiring out and exchanging books, binding service, and his disastrous investment in a cotton-spinning machine all suggest his entrepreneurial instincts. The Lobo project was probably designed to profit from well-established public interest both in travel books and in religious controversy. Le Grand's Lobo found a niche in the market as one of a very few English works on Abyssinia, and, like Ludolf's *Aethiopean History* and Geddes's *Church-History of Aethiopia*, Johnson's book is partly a polemic against Roman Catholic colonialism. The combination of the travelogue with religious and political polemic is probably what Warren counted on to turn a profit and also what made the work appealing to Johnson. Warren could take advantage of hostility to

Roman Catholicism, an affinity for dissent, and a suspicion of religious fanaticism that was strong in the Midlands throughout his lifetime. The astonishing publishing success of Dr Sacheverell's defence of the High Church of England was as fresh in his mind as it had been in Michael Johnson's.[13]

For Johnson, this was a bookseller's job, but the project also united him in some important ways with the post-Reformation European intellectual community. Like More and Erasmus, he was enlisting himself against the injustices of colonialism. Like Grotius and Le Clerc, he was on the side of a truly catholic, reformed Christian tradition. Like Fontenelle and Joseph Scaliger, he was trying to correct the errors and superstitions passed down from ancient times and perpetuated by the non-rational, non-empirical habits of the uneducated. Closer to home, Jonathan Swift had recently scored a tremendous publishing success with *Gulliver's Travels*, a mock travel book with obvious political and religious overtones, but Johnson's deeper intellectual associations ran directly to the Renaissance humanists. While he was translating Le Grand, Johnson wrote a proposal for an edition of the great humanist Angelo Poliziano's Latin poems, to be introduced with a history of Latin poetry in the fourteenth and fifteenth centuries. This project reflects Johnson's intellectual inclinations at the time, but in Lobo the admirer of Scaliger and Poliziano had to mingle with the young man out to make a living not by the favour of the court or the patronage of the wealthy but by the indulgence of the public.

The only part of Johnson's first book that is well known at all is the preface. Like his idol, Joseph Scaliger, in *De Emendatione Temporum* and like Sir Thomas Browne in *Pseudodoxia Epidemica*, Johnson sets himself up as a modern investigator determined to believe only what is reliably attested or scientifically proved. Johnson recommends Lobo because he seems to have followed empirical rules himself: 'He appears by his modest and unaffected narration to have described things as he saw them, to have copied nature from the life, and to have consulted his senses not his imagination; he meets with no basilisks that destroy with their eyes, his crocodiles devour their prey without tears, and his cataracts fall from the rock without deafening the neighbouring inhabitants.' Not content, however, with the extent to which Lobo and Le Grand live up to this empirical ideal, Johnson often assists them by additions or embellishments of the text. His translation of the section on the Nile is one of the best examples:

> The ignorance, which we have hitherto been in, of the original of the Nile, hath given many authors an opportunity of presenting us very gravely with their various systems, and conjectures about the nature of its waters, and the reason of its overflows.
>
> It is easy to observe how many empty hypotheses and idle reasonings, the phaenomenons of this river have put mankind to the expence of. Yet there are people so biggotted to antiquity, as not to pay any regard to the relation of travellers who have been upon the spot, and by the evidence of their eyes can confute all that the ancients have written. It was difficult, it was even

impossible to arrive at the source of the Nile, by tracing its channel from the mouth; and all who ever attempted it, having been stop'd by the cataracts, and imagining none that follow'd them could pass farther, have taken the liberty of entertaining us with their own fictions. . . . [True explorers] have demolish'd the airy fabricks of renoun'd hypotheses, and detected those fables which the ancients rather chose to invent of the sources of the Nile, than to confess their ignorance. I cannot help suspending my narration to reflect a little on the ridiculous speculations of those swelling philosophers, whose arrogance would prescribe laws to nature, and subject those astonishing effects which we behold daily, to their idle reasonings, and chimerical rules. Presumptuous imagination! that has given being to such numbers of books, and patrons to so many various opinions about the overflows of the Nile.[14]

The source of the Nile was a topic of literature as early as Herodotus and a subtopic of the theme of human ignorance and error almost as long. In rendering this passage Johnson must have felt a tie with that long tradition, and he takes his own place in it by the many changes he introduces in his version. For instance, Johnson added the following important parts of the passage: 'I cannot help suspending my narration to reflect a little'; 'swelling'; and 'Presumptious imagination!' In much of the rest of the passage he embellished or pointed the French original to such an extent that the whole must be regarded as a work of his own creation. Likewise, in his version of Le Grand's appended dissertation 'Upon the Nile' Johnson translates energetically and creatively. This is especially true when he comes to the passage on theories concerning the overflow of the Nile – the heart of the Egyptian mystery: 'The circumstance which [both the ancients and the moderns] were most in pain about, was the encrease and overflow of this river, the causes of which they were in hopes of finding by contriving imaginary systems, which are now of no other use, than to mortify the aspiring pride of man, to show how contracted is his boasted knowledge, and how vainly he reasons upon subjects which his senses have not made him acquainted with.'[15]

Johnson is similarly strong in his translation of Le Grand's treatment of the fictions invented to explain how the Red Sea got its name, but in many smaller instances he steps in to improve his author's credibility. For example, when Le Grand says of a certain bird, 'The *feitan favez* or devil's-horse looks . . . like a man dress'd in feathers', Johnson feels compelled to qualify the verb with the phrase 'at a distance'. In his translation of several other passages concerning marvellous or strange phenomena Johnson renders Le Grand's third-person impersonal 'on' as 'I'. As Joel Gold has shown, this has a drastic effect on the text and looks like an attempt on Johnson's part to limit the claims for truth his text is making, reducing them to instances of individual observation rather than assertions of established fact. Johnson writes, 'In the province of Agaus, has been seen the unicorn, that beast so much talk'd of, and so little known; the prodigious swiftness with which this creature runs from one wood into another, has given me no opportunity of examining it particularly, yet I have had so near a sight of it as to be able to give some description of it.' Unless this is a gross mistranslation, Johnson must have balked at Le Grand's 'on l'a néanmoins assez bien considéré pour pouvoir décrire.' In composing his *Dictionary* on empirical principles, Johnson similarly rejected the persistent 'on dit' of the Académie Française and replaced it with specimens of actual usage, culled from his own experience.[16]

Like many English Christians with a rationalistic bent, Johnson regarded numerous Roman Catholic beliefs and practices as superstitions. He transmits this conviction in the *Dictionary*, among other ways, by quoting heavily from Edward Stillingfleet's *Defense of the Discourse concerning the Idolatry Practiced in the Church of Rome*. In his translation of the Jesuit Lobo Johnson omits flattering references to the Roman Church, descriptions of Roman rituals and rites, and presumptions of divine favour. For instance, when Lobo describes a lightning storm that kills five people, Johnson omits his conclusion, which appears in Le Grand as 'Dieu par sa bonté infinie, me preserva de cet accident qui coûta la vie à cinq personnes.' Likewise, Johnson will not allow Lobo to quote the Gospels and imply the divine sanction of his mission when he 'shakes the dust off his feet' and departs from a village of unrepentant Abyssinians. Johnson's hostility to the Roman Church is evident, but he is also ready to condemn enthusiastic conceits of divine favour on the part of the Abyssinians. Le Grand describes as improbable the natives' claim to have received their rulers in an uninterrupted line from Cham, the son of Noah, but Johnson feels compelled to add, 'there are no real grounds for imagining that Providence has vouchsafed them so distinguishing a protection.' Johnson may have been playing to the audience for the Birmingham publication *The Shortest Way with the French Prophets*, a pamphlet about Richard Warton and other religious fanatics, published in 1708, and on the public's mind since the 1731 'inspirations' of his daughter Hanna. However, his conception of the topic is profound, and he saw Roman Catholic errors as part of the vast body of human ignorance accumulated over the centuries of unscientific speculation and unexamined belief.[17]

The politics of Johnson's Lobo also stem from profound humanistic convictions, although they pertain particularly to Roman Catholic colonialism. Johnson's translations both of Lobo and of Le Grand's dissertations favour the natives and denigrate the missionaries. He rejects Lobo's description of the Abyssinian Christians as 'hérétiques' and 'schismatiques', calling them instead 'those opposed to the Church of Rome'. By this means, Joel Gold shows, 'the Abyssinians are presented not as heretics or schismatics but rather as a people who are separated from or opposed to the Church of Rome, who wish not to be seduced from the true church, and who desire to hold fast to the faith of their ancestors. In their struggle to retain their old religion and customs against the inroads of the Jesuits, the Abyssinians clearly have Johnson's support.' At other points in the narrative, when religious conviction is not at issue, the cruelty of the missionaries is emphasized, and the natives are usually exculpated. As the maintainers of a native Christian tradition, the Abyssinians have something in common with the English, and Johnson's defence of them carries nationalistic overtones like those in *The Shortest Way with the French Prophets.* However, though it is historically inextricable from nationalistic British sentiments, Johnson's attitude is also part of a more general humanistic hatred of oppression, concern for individual rights, and realism about the motives of conquest. In Le Grand's dissertation on the heretical practice of circumcision in Abyssinia, Johnson strengthens the defence of the natives with a politically charged description of the period in which the practice was introduced: 'About the same time Aethiopia groan'd under the complicated miseries of war, pestilence, and famine.' The attitude revealed in this passage appears consistently throughout Johnson's writing: from Lobo to the journalism on the Seven Years War and even into the late political writings, Johnson agreed with humanists like Bacon whom he cites in the *Dictionary* under 'native' to say, 'Make no extirpation of the *natives*, under pretence of planting religion, God surely will no way be pleased with such sacrifices.'[18]

For the critical biographer, the most striking thing about the whole Lobo project is the extent to which Johnson found in it an approach to lucrative literary work that would serve him for the rest of his career. The approach can almost be reduced to a formula: to make a living at literature, take existing books and work them over (by translating, reviewing, introducing, paraphrasing, criticizing, cataloguing, excerpting, or editing), and, in so doing, find ways of expressing and transmitting important, profoundly conventional philosophical themes. The formula is a sort of rhetoric applied to the print world, bringing together the rhetorician's topoi with the new materials (the materia imprimata) of the print world. One reason for Johnson's amazing output as a writer is that in his first enterprise of any scope he hit upon an efficient method of production. In addition to his method, Johnson also had in place at this early date many of the topics that served him as themes for the rest of his career. Even his most famous topic, the vanity of human wishes, makes an appearance here. The Sieur du Roule is the forerunner of Charles IX, Cardinal Wolsey, and Bishop Laud, all of whom fall from glory because of vanity in *The Vanity of Human Wishes*:

> The Envoy thinking he ought on this occasion [a victory feast] to display all his magnificence, had set out some looking-glasses, which brought all the city to his house; the King's women who are rarely permitted to go out, could not forbear gratifying their curiosity with a view of these rarities, and above all were astonish'd at those glasses which multiply objects, and imagining this could not be the effect of natural causes, represented the Envoy and his retinue as magicians, who had ill designs against the King. The whole show added new incitements to the avarice of the officers, and perhaps of the King himself, so that, a few days after, he sent to demand of the Envoy three thousand piasters, and being refused, let the ambassador know

by Macé his interpreter, that his refusal might bring him and his retinue into danger. The demand was repeated several times, and Mr du Roule still continued obstinate. Not to protract the relation, on the 25th of November the King sent three hundred men to seize the Envoy in his house with all his retinue, and carrying them into the market-place, first cut him in pieces, and afterwards his attendants.[19]

Johnson's translation is pretty close here, though there is some heightening and some adaptation of the passage to the broad, moral topic. Even if it were closer and more literal a translation than it is, however, the point would stand. In his Lobo, as in a great many of his other projects, Johnson found a way of using existing printed material to produce new books and at the same time to transmit essential, profoundly conventional wisdom.

For completing this project Johnson received five guineas. The book itself was not a success, and within a year of publication a second bookseller bought up the remaining sheets, issued a new title page and reduced the price of the book from five to four shillings.[20] A second edition was not produced until after Johnson's death. However, the book was sold in London, and it was reviewed there in the *Literary Magazine*, a digest and review run by Ephraim Chambers, author of the *Cyclopedia* that Johnson quotes heavily in the *Dictionary* and which he later sought to re-edit. Johnson said he formed his literary style on Chambers's Preface, and, shortly after completing the *Dictionary* in 1755, he became editor himself of a journal called the *Literary Magazine*. Hence, although Lobo was not a financial success, it brought Johnson's work to the attention of London bookmen and drew him closer to a circle of people, including Chambers, whose professional lives were models for what his would become.

3

Irene

Let the blindness of the Mahometans confirm you in Christianity.
Johnson to John Hussey on his departure for Aleppo, 29 December 1778

Johnson's nerves were so bad in Birmingham that he lay in bed while Edmund Hector took dictation, compelling Johnson to produce his translation of Father Lobo out of pity for the starving compositor in need of copy. Because he was brought up in 'the trade' Johnson always felt a responsibility, once he was engaged for a project, to keep the presses and the pressmen busy. He knew they had to work to eat, and his heart went out to them, even when he was not inclined to write. After getting Lobo all in press, Johnson went back to Lichfield, and contemplated a more scholarly project. On 15 June 1734, with help from a friend, he borrowed the Pembroke College copy of *Angeli Politiani Opera*, and in August he wrote proposals for an edition of Poliziano. Of the great humanist's many and various works Johnson was drawn to the Latin poetry, consisting of odes, elegies, and epigrams, plus *Sylvae*, an epic celebration of poetry and poets, and a translation of four books of the *Iliad*. How much of this Johnson intended to edit and annotate is unknown, but he evidently conceived an ambitious project. Hawkins and Boswell say the book was to be thirty octavo sheets; at sixteen pages per sheet this is 480 pages, which would have left plenty of room for notes. It would have stretched even Johnson's classical and humanistic scholarship to write a commentary on Poliziano's highly allusive verse, and, if he had done it well, Johnson would have moved into the circle of European scholar-poets that he most admired: he would have been among the likes of Scaliger, Heinsius, Erasmus, and Poliziano himself. Predictably, the proposals stirred insufficient interest in the Midlands, and the project was dropped, probably before it was well under way. The mere fact that he did the proposal, however, shows how Johnson was conceiving of himself at the time and the difficulty he had in reconciling his deep identification with neo-Latin humanism with his need to write for a living.

Still thinking of himself as a poet in November 1734 but hoping to hitch his wagon to a better engine of publication, Johnson wrote to Edward Cave, the editor of the newly established *Gentleman's Magazine*. His first approach was haughty and abortive. He wrote to Cave from Birmingham under the assumed name 'S. Smith', 'As You appear no less sensible than Your Readers of the defects of your Poetical Article, You will not be displeased, if, in order to the improvement of it, I communicate to You the sentiments of a person, who will undertake on reasonable terms sometimes to fill a column.'[1] Johnson proposes replacing some of Cave's 'low Jests' and 'awkward Buffoonery' with 'Poems, Inscriptions' and 'short literary Dissertations in Latin or English'. Cave was unreceptive, but he answered the letter, and he eventually made use of Johnson's many talents in his magazine. However, Cave employed Johnson's learned hand, for the most part, on more prosaic tasks than those proposed by the erudite youth, and he shrewdly elevated the tone of his monthly issue without sacrificing popularity.

Meanwhile Johnson travelled often between Lichfield and Birmingham, and after the death of Harry Porter in September 1734 he courted his widow, the former Elizabeth Jervis. They were married in July 1735. Tetty, as Johnson called his wife, was then forty-six and Johnson still twenty-five. Her two sons (aged seventeen and eleven) resented the marriage deeply and refused the connection with their young stepfather. The nineteen-year-old daughter, Lucy, was a loyal friend for life, but she too was cool at first. On the death of her husband, Mrs Porter had inherited £600, and her family may have felt that Johnson was marrying for money. However, Johnson told a good friend that 'it was a love marriage on both sides', and, as James Clifford remarks, Johnson 'desperately needed physical love as well as affection and mothering'. Mrs Porter was attractive and experienced. She also liked Johnson and upon meeting him declared, 'This is the most sensible man that I ever saw in my life.' It is difficult to be sure exactly what she meant, but many of the qualities that Mrs Porter may have been remarking in calling Johnson 'sensible' are related to 'having sensibility' or 'being capable of delicate or tender feeling,' in the words of the *Oxford English Dictionary*. This quality, in the 1990s called 'sensitivity', was part of the contemporary language of romance; indeed, 'sensibility' was what some contemporary writers considered most attractive in the opposite sex. Much of what is recorded about Johnson – his readiness to tears, his sensitivity to the needs of the Birmingham pressmen and others less fortunate than himself, his abrupt breaks and warm reconciliations with close friends – suggest that Mrs Porter recognized him as a man of 'sensibility' and loved him for it. It is also possible that she was referring mainly to Johnson's moral and ethical conscientiousness; that would not have been surprising in a time of Evangelical revivalism in the Midlands, but there were connections, of course, between the romantic and the ethical forms of sensibility, especially as lovers viewed these qualifies in each other.[2]

In any case, the 'love marriage' was not an unqualified success. The couple were often separated, especially when Johnson was making extended trips to London early in his career; they were somewhat estranged later in Elizabeth's life when she became addicted to alcohol or narcotic medicine; their intellectual companionship was probably limited, though Johnson speaks respectfully of his wife's mind. Yet, the death of his wife in 1752 was Johnson's most painful experience, and this is not the only reason to believe that he shared an emotional intimacy with her that goes far beyond Garrick's famous mimicry of their relations. James Clifford provides an account of a performance witnessed by Joseph Cradock: 'Johnson was portrayed as seated by the side of the bed, hard at work composing a tragedy [Irene]. Rather than join his wife as she wished, he regaled her with ponderous verses, the choicest bits from his play, and in absent-minded concentration he seized the bedclothes instead of his own shirttails and tried to tuck them into his breeches. . . . [Garrick] played first Johnson grabbing at the imaginary sheets and stuffing them down, and then poor Tetty, exposed to the cold air, frantically trying to cling to some of the covering.'[3]

Despite his ponderous ways and his indulgence in some misogynistic humour, Johnson was not the male supremacist that Boswell and the nineteenth century depicted. Nor was the whole century sunk in monolithic male chauvinism. Alternative attitudes were available to men in Johnson's time, and his participation in Samuel Richardson's circle of mixed company suggests that he was eager to explore these alternatives. Like Richardson, Johnson may have accorded literary ladies a kind of respect that he did not extend to his wife. Nevertheless, his interest in female intellectuals and his own emotional sensitivity suggest that he had an aptitude for achieving a companionate marriage of the sort that was in his day becoming more possible than ever before. Ill health and hard times attenuated Johnson's marriage in many ways, but in its beginnings the attachment was warm, promising, and perhaps socially progressive.

Shortly after their marriage the Johnsons established themselves just outside Lichfield, in the town of Edial, in a large 'square brick edifice with a cupola and balustrades at the top'. Here Johnson tried to establish a grammar school. He had served as a tutor to the children of Thomas Whitby, a local gentleman, for a couple of months before his marriage. He had also applied for a position at the grammar school in Solihull shortly after his marriage. He lost this post, as he lost another, at Brewood, in 1736 largely because of his appearance and his nervous tics. Encouraged by his old friend Gilbert Walmesley, Johnson tried again at Edial to make a living by teaching and at the same time to achieve a degree of independence. Other schools would not hire him, and, if they did, he might rebel against the servitude of employment, as he had at Market Bosworth. At his own school, if he could make it profitable, Johnson would be his own master.[4]

Johnson drew up some curricular plans divided into three classes, or forms, with classical reading of increasing difficulty for each. The lessons are standard, starting out with Corderius and Erasmus, moving up to Cornelius Nepos, and then to Ovid, Vergil, and Horace. Johnson had written earlier to Richard Congreve at Oxford, asking him for information about the curricula at other grammar schools and suggesting that he intended to come up with a thoughtful, well-researched proposal. He also recovered his library from Oxford at this time, intending to use the books, many of them students' books, in his teaching. When the school was failing in 1736, he placed an advertisement in the *Gentleman's Magazine* for both June and July: 'At Edial, near *Litchfield* [*sic*] in *Staffordshire*, Young Gentlemen are Boarded, and taught the *Latin* and *Greek* Languages, by Samuel Johnson.' In his extant references to Edial Johnson is determined to describe education as learning only and to leave out breeding, the part of education for which he was unqualified. In later, more successful educational projects, like *The Preceptor* and the *Dictionary*, Johnson treats education more broadly, but his emphasis remains squarely on learning.[5]

In some respects Johnson remained an educator for life, but his career as a teacher was short. Later, from the safety of his professional writer's garret, he could look back on teaching with some equanimity but not without irony. Certainly he thought of himself and Edial when he illustrated the word 'pedagogue' in his *Dictionary* with the following quotation from Dryden:

> Few *pedagogues* but curse the barren chair,
> Like him who hang'd himself for mere despair
> And poverty.

Then, as now, there was a stigma attached to schoolmastering, as Johnson shows in his life of Milton when he speaks of the poet 'degraded to a schoolmaster'; being a failed schoolmaster was even worse. Edial failed after only a year, and there was a special sting in the dismissive description that Boswell's father made of his son's admired friend: as rendered by Walter Scott, the old gentleman's slight was, 'a *dominie*, mon – an auld dominie; he keeped a schule, and cau'd it an academy.'[6]

Johnson had only three boarding and just a few day students. One of these students, however, was David Garrick, who became the most famous and successful actor of his century and remained Johnson's friend for life. Johnson closed Edial officially in February 1737, and on 2 March he went on horseback with young Davy Garrick to London where he hoped to use his literature and learning to achieve independence as an author. It was a serious commitment and a gamble, but it was becoming clear that writing was his trade and London was the place to ply it. Johnson still had some money from his marriage settlement to use as a stake, but he also now had a piece of literary property to sell. While at Edial, Johnson had begun writing a tragedy for the stage. Dramatic poetry still provided writers with their best chance to escape poverty and dependency. At the beginning of the eighteenth century most literary work was very poorly paid; poetry was still half in the manuscript age, and disingenuous prefaces in which poets professed their reluctance to print are indications that the genre was still tied to the old economy of soliciting wealthy and discriminating patronage. Playwrights, however, had long confessed their reliance on the public and unabashedly accepted the financial rewards. Lichfield's own Joseph Addison had made his fortune with *Cato*, a Roman tragedy, and this is precisely the genre in which Johnson chose to perform. By writing *Irene* he hoped to make money while maintaining his dignified identity as a poet with a strong classical background. Although the play was not produced and published until 1749, it was drafted at Edial, and it very much belongs to this early period of Johnson's career.

Johnson knew the story of Irene in the version transmitted by Richard Knolles in his *Generall Historie of the Turkes* (1603). He knew this immense book well and praised it as often as he mentioned it. In Knolles's account, the beautiful Greek Irene is captured by Mahomet II at the siege of Constantinople, and she captures his heart. Mahomet is so taken with Irene that he spends all his time with her and neglects his rule to such an extent that his officers become restless and factious. Mahomet then gathers his chiefs and displays Irene in public. They are astonished by her beauty and understand the reason for Mahomet's irresponsible behaviour.

> Whereunto the barbarous prince answered: *Well, but now I will make you to understand how far you have been deceived in me, and that there is no earthly thing that can so much blind my sences, or bereave me of reason as not to see and understand what beseemeth my high place and calling.* . . . And having so said, presently with one of his hands catching the faire Greeke by the haire of the head, and drawing his falchion with the other, at one blow strucke off her head, to the great terror of them all. And having so done, said unto them: *Now by this judge whether your emperour is able to bridle his affections or not.*[7]

The tale had been told before Knolles by the Italian Bandello in 1554, and at least four English dramatizations of the story had been completed before Johnson's. The extent of Johnson's debt to other authors is uncertain, but what he came up with from his reading was a tale of apostasy and fidelity, uncertainty and conviction. He has two Greek ladies, Irene and Aspasia. Mahomet falls in love first with Aspasia, but, failing to seduce her with promises of earthly glory, he turns his attentions to Irene. Aspasia is rewarded for her fidelity by escape with the equally constant Demetrius. Irene gradually and hesitantly succumbs to the temptations of Mahomet. As soon as she yields, she is falsely implicated in an assasination plot and killed by Mahomet's henchmen. The penitent Cali Bassa, who has revolted from Mahomet, is also killed, as is the treacherous and lustful Abdalla. The constant Mustapha remains to issue the moral:

So sure the fall of greatness rais'd on crimes,
So fix'd the justice of all-conscious Heav'n.
When haughty Guilt exults with impious Joy.
Mistake shall blast, or accident destroy;
Weak man with erring rage may throw the dart,
But Heav'n shall guide it to the guilty heart.[8]

The moral confirms Providence, the divine government of the world. The theme is high and philosophical, and the rough draft shows that Johnson was using his humanistic studies to work it up in a fashion worthy of a man who had proposed an edition of Poliziano. *Macbeth, Paradise Lost, The Essay on Man*, and Dryden's *Aureng-Zebe* may have occurred to him as he composed his play, but his draft notes glide over these to rest on deeper, classical sources. Sketching out Aspasia's response to Demetrius's request that she live a virtuous though indigent life, Johnson writes, 'She knows that the demands of Nature are few – Nor is Providence obliged to provide for desires it has not created – Ingratitude charges Providence as penurious though it satisfies their needs, because not their desires. – Petronius – candidus esse Deus – Claudian – Verona – Martial Vitam quae faciunt – she can exchange the Pomp and Luxury she was born to, for the Magnificence of Nature and chearful Poverty, and having drank of the River sleep with Innocence upon its banks. This Philosophy[,] which she was blamd for by fops and Girls, as unfit for her Sex[,] has taught her.' He refers to three classical poems that together summarized the theme for him. Heinsius's note on 'De Sene Veronensi' in the edition that Johnson owned might have led him to the epigram from Martial, but he seems to have added on his own the Petronius, which begins, in translation, 'Honest Heaven ordained that all things which can end our wretched complaints should be ready to hand.' Other such notes in the draft also suggest that Johnson's preparation for writing *Irene* was partly an act of humanistic scholarship. Like some of the figures within the play, Johnson was himself a Renaissance scholar living in the wake of the fall of Constantinople and one of the Western beneficiaries of the calamity.[9]

Johnson set *Irene* in the historical moment that he and other scholars of his time believed was the crucial moment for the development of humanism and the Reformation. According to the accepted historical view, the fall of Constantinople was a happy fall because the ensuing exodus of Greek scholars from the Eastern empire brought Greek teachers into Italy, at the court of the Medicis, for example, and in Venice where Poliziano lived, thus reviving learning in the West. Believing that the fall of Constantinople enabled the humanistic tradition, with its blend of modern Christianity and ancient philosophy, Johnson could think of it as the genesis of his own mentality. Moreover, he goes a long way toward assembling and presenting that mentality in *Irene*. It is significant that he does so by setting his scene outside of Europe, not merely outside of England, because it suggests that he considered Europe as a whole his intellectual homeland. In his original character sketches for the play Johnson describes Demetrius

as 'A Greek nobleman versed in philosophy and literature' and Aspasia
as 'bred up in all the learning of Greece'. In her successful resistance to
worldly temptation Aspasia displays her conversation with the Greek philosophers and her successful synthesis of them with Christian virtues, such
as humility and faith in Providence. Her philosophical achievement is
so great that she exceeds the limitations of her frail sex: 'All Aspasia but
her Beauty's Man.' Demetrius and Aspasia go off at the end of the play to
Florence, where 'The mighty Tuscan courts the banish'd arts':

> There shall despotick Eloquence resume
> Her ancient empire o'er the yielding heart;
> There Poetry shall tune her sacred voice,
> And wake from ignorance the Western World.[10]

Although he writes about it in terms of Western civilization, Johnson
was struggling with his own intellectual self-creation in the composition of
Irene, and this may explain why, as he always maintained, it cost him more
effort than any of his other works. The rest of Johnson's career of composition is a story of almost fantastic facility and celerity. A few years later
he stayed up all night to produce forty-eight octavo pages of the *Life of
Savage*, duplicating a feat he had achieved earlier while doing a translation
from French. He was painfully slow in producing *Irene* because he was
assembling the dense kernel of thought that was to serve him inexhaust-
ibly as he expressed it more fluently and expounded it more widely
throughout the rest of his career.

In perhaps the most brilliant phrase of his superb article on *Irene*
Bertrand Bronson says the extant draft of *Irene* reveals 'the fragmentary
eruption of Johnson's ideas'. He notes Johnson's 'extraordinary economy
. . . the unwillingness to write more than was necessary'. This economy is
partly the result of Johnson's usual unwillingness to write things down, but
the effect is to reveal that his principal concern while composing the work
was with certain central ideas. As Bronson shows, 'there was in the draft
no general working through the sequence of scenes' and 'hardly a single
block of consecutive conversation'; 'A very large part of the draft . . . looks
like a statement of points for debate', and it is 'more a commonplace-
book than a dramatic sketch'. The powerful effect of such intensity is
evident in a passage that Johnson later distributed among three places in
the finished work:

> And though built on feeble Columns – Its lofty
>   turrets blaze amidst the Sky
> With bright effulgence The travell[er] afar
> Surveys the Glories of the splendid Pile
> It spreads the wide Plain an unregarded Ruin.[11]

In the margin of his page Johnson added the connecting or explanatory
note 'But when an Earthquake comes weak and unsupported'. Then immediately follows a passage unconnected except in its general feeling:

> Amidst his gloomy Guards and fiery Vassals
> The horrid pomp of Ostentatious Woe
> En[v]ies the meanest . . . of celestial Beings
> That wafts diseases from the sleeping Infant.

Next Johnson jots down lines that are likewise vaguely and powerfully related:

> And burning Daemons tremble at her torments
> Some soft decoy to lure me to Destruction
> Thou fountain of Existence I pour the Anguish of my Soul before Thee.

They are fragmentary because they are notes, of course, but some of these disjunctive passages appear to take the form of some post-Romantic and modern poetry. They read at times as though they were taken from the pages of a modernist following in the footsteps of Eliot or Mallarmé. Johnson was not a modernist or a romantic, but the imagery of his fragmentary notes on *Irene* resembles that of Stephen Dedalus's recurrent musings on Blake's 'ruin of all space'. Like Joyce's artist as a young man, Johnson draws violent imagery out of traditional literary materials. In such congeries of lines as the following, as in Stephen's musings, one has the sense of a mind working its way through, and out from under, a burden of accumulated literary stock:

> Horrid as a Murd'rers Dreams, Madman's Laughter
> Slumber of the Soul
> Wilderness of waters – The sinking turrets and receding Shores
> My Soul not oft acquainted with Remorse
> Shrinks from this Heap of aggregated Crime.[12]

Seemingly modern acts of intellectual and emotional association are displayed in Johnson's rough draft, but the organic filaments that unite the work are topics of classical and Christian thought. Sometimes Johnson departs from verse and puts the argument (meaning either plot or moral or both) down in prose. For example, directly after the verse just quoted Johnson writes, 'Aspasia answers to Irenes Insult that this World is not the place where happiness is promised to Virtue, or where her Votaries obtain their Reward.' Bronson locates the very centre of the ideas and debates of *Irene* in a speech that expands upon this topic, finally appearing in act 3, scene 7 of the printed text:

> Reflect that life and death, affecting sounds,
> Are only varied modes of endless being;
> Reflect that life, like ev'ry other blessing,
> Derives its value from its use alone;
> Not for itself but for a nobler end
> Th' Eternal gave it, and that end is Virtue.
> When inconsistent with a greater good,
> Reason commands to cast the less away;

> Thus life, with loss of wealth, well preserv'd,
> And virtue cheaply sav'd with loss of life.
> (26–35)

Bronson says plausibly that Johnson chose the subject of *Irene* mainly because it afforded him 'the opportunity to administer [this] instruction'. Additionally, he says that the two main points of Johnson's play are his arguments against apostasy and the causes of the sudden downfall of Constantinople. Donald Greene has corrected Bronson's cursory treatment of the politics in the play, showing that they are broader and more broadly conservative than Bronson says. Bronson's treatment of Johnson's 'ideas' in *Irene* requires similar correction.[13]

The crucial ethical speech in *Irene* is an argument against apostasy, but it is also something much more general. The message is profoundly conventional, mixing Socratic, Christian, and even more ancient wisdom with confidence in the rational capacity to weigh, measure, or compare. It is almost a versification of Locke's simple ethical scheme, which directed that the greater good always be chosen over the lesser, and that the greatest good of all was eternal reward. Passages of equal importance to the message of the play display a similar ethical generality. Apostasy of every kind is surely punished in *Irene*, but apostasy, even very generally conceived, is too narrow to be called the subject of the key passages:

> How Heav'n in scorn of human arrogance,
> Commits to trivial chance the fate of nations!
> While with incessant thought laborious man
> Extends his mighty schemes of wealth and pow'r,
> And tow'rs and triumphs in ideal greatness;
> Some accidental gust of opposition
> Blasts all the beauties of his new creation,
> O'erturns the fabrick of presumptuous reason,
> And whelms the swelling architect beneath it.
> (2.3.1–9)

> To-morrow's action? Can that hoary wisdom
> Born down with years, still doat upon to-morrow?
> That fatal mistress of the young, the lazy,
> The coward, and the fool, condemn'd to lose
> An useless life in waiting for to-morrow,
> To gaze with longing eyes upon to-morrow,
> Till interposing death destroys the prospect!
> Strange! that this gen'ral fraud from day to day
> Should fill the world with wretches undetected.
> The soldier lab'ring through a winter's march,
> Still sees to-morrow drest in robes of triumph;
> Still to the lover's long-expecting arms,
> To-morrow brings the visionary bride.
> But thou, too old to bear another cheat,
> Learn, that the present hour alone is man's.
> (3.2.19–33)

The draft makes it clear that Johnson created these two passages as parts of a whole and then divided them in the final version of the play. His mind played on the central theme of the work, the central theme of all his works, and stayed with it, regardless of the dramatic necessities of plot or character. The topic is 'the vanity of human wishes'. This particular expression of it owes something to the famous 'tomorrow' speech in *Macbeth*, but it is more directly modelled on a speech in Dryden's *Aureng-Zebe*:

> When I consider life, 'tis all a cheat,
> Yet fooled with hope, men favor the deceit,
> Trust on, and think tomorrow will repay.
> Tomorrow's falser than the former day;
> Lies worse, and while it says we shall be blest
> With some new joys, cuts off what we possessed.
> Strange couzenage! None would live past years again,
> Yet all hope pleasure in what yet remain;
> And from the dregs of life think to receive
> What the first sprightly running could not give.
> I'm tir'd with waiting for this chemick gold,
> Which fools us young and beggars us when old.[14]

When he compiled his *Dictionary* fifteen years later Johnson quoted this passage no less than three times in his illustrative quotations. Johnson's extensive lucubrations on the theme in the late 1730s when he was writing *Irene* are part of the reason that by the time he wrote *The Vanity of Human Wishes* in 1748 the thought was so clear to him that he could compose as many as seventy lines in his head before committing them to paper.

In more conventionally Christian terms, the central thought of *Irene* is that Providence, though obscure to man, is immanent throughout God's creation. However, the aspects of the thought that most engage Johnson concern man's ignorance and the resulting ironies of his existence. In order to mitigate the effects of ignorance one must have faith in unseen Providence and discipline one's desires and passions. Moral philosophy, as it appears in the works of many classical writers, and natural science, with its emphasis on empirical findings, may help to prevent the mind from wandering off in pursuit of the phantoms of glory or those of mere reason. Hence, much of Johnson's reading in classical, biblical, and modern writers came together for him as he crystallized the thought of the play. When he packed *Irene* with him to go to London in 1737, Johnson brought with him not so much a marketable literary commodity as the preparation to produce marketable literature. He had done some preliminary work on it in his translation of Lobo, but in drafting *Irene* Johnson definitely settled on a central theme. He was twenty-eight, not an unusual age for an artist to find his identity or the central myth he wishes to expound.

In fashioning his guiding theme Johnson combined his classical learning with his Christian convictions; his sense of himself as a late humanist with his affinity for late Roman satirists; his hostile arrogance with his

growing acknowledgement of the need for submission to the circumstances
in which he found himself in the world. In addition, as Bronson asserts,
the play was 'Johnson's marriage offering' to Tetty. For this and all the
other reasons cited here, Bronson is correct in concluding that 'in its
way, the *Irene* is a sort of diploma of Johnson's intellectual, emotional,
and aesthetic maturity'.[15] Having graduated, the next step, of course, was
London, and Johnson could heartily concur with Robert South, the great
sermonizer of Fleet Street whom he quoted in the *Dictionary* under 'improvement' (sense 4, 'instruction; edification'): 'I look upon your city as
the best place of *improvement*: from the school we go to the university, but
from the universities to London.'

4

London

---

*The reasons for which you are inclined to visit London, are, I think, not of sufficient
strength to answer the objections. That you should delight to come once a year to the
fountain of intelligence and pleasure, is very natural; but both information and
pleasure must be regulated by propriety. Pleasure, which cannot be obtained but by
unseasonable or unsuitable expence, must always end in pain; and pleasure, which
must be enjoyed at the expence of another's pain, can never be such as a worthy mind
can fully delight in.*

Johnson to Boswell, 19 March 1774

On 5 March 1737, three days after Johnson and Garrick left Lichfield
for London, Nathaniel, Johnson's only sibling, was buried at St Michael's
church beside his father. He was only twenty-four; his death was sudden,
but the cause is unknown. The most important surviving document concerning Nathaniel is a letter to his mother, apologizing for trouble of
some kind that he brought on his family and on friends at Stourbridge
where he evidently intended to set up a bookshop. It looks as though
Nathaniel had borrowed money from friends, assumed family support,
and perhaps done something dishonest to float a venture that failed. The
letter exhibits despair as well as contrition: 'I know not nor do I much
care in what Way of life I shall hereafter live, but this I know that it shall
be an honest one and that it cant be more unpleasant than some part
of my Life Past, I believe I shall go to Georgia in about a fortnight.' In
addition to asking forgiveness of his brother, indirectly, Nathaniel also
indicates that the two did not get on: 'As to My Brothers assisting me I had
but little Reason to expect it when He would scarce ever use me with
common civility & to whose Advice was owing that unwillingness you shewed
to my going to Stourbridge.' Some biographers have conjectured that
Nathaniel committed suicide, although his burial in consecrated ground
argues against it. Whatever Nathaniel's end, Johnson continued to think
about his brother throughout his life. In 1748 he was reading Norris's

Miscellany to find material for his *Dictionary* when he ran across a passage that brought his brother to mind, and he made a rare marginal note concerning the connection. In 1780 Johnson still had Nathaniel in mind and sought information about him from a Miss Prowse of Frome in Somersetshire. One of his last deeds in life was to write an epitaph for his parents and his brother to be placed over their graves in St Michael's. In his letters to Miss Prowse, Johnson described his brother as an 'adventurer', 'likely enough to attract notice . . . a lively noisy man, that loved company'.[1] The older, more serious boy apparently scorned his more affable, mercantile brother; he may have found the loud young man embarrassing, but he lived to feel remorse when reconciliation was impossible.

Garrick's departure from Lichfield was also marked by the death of a family member. His father died a few days after he and Johnson set out; this second death upset the financial plans of the duo, as well as leaving them emotionally confused. They borrowed money from a bookseller named Wilcox, who is famous for suggesting that the physically impressive Johnson would do better to buy a porter's knot and make his living as a stevedore rather than as a writer. For his biographers and his other fans, accounts of Johnson's size and strength have always been a source of pleasure. It seems likely that these accounts have been exaggerated: Johnson is a mythic figure, and we love to read his body as a kind of allegory, reflecting and further enlarging his intellectual power. However, according to Mrs Thrale, 'his Heighth was five Foot eleven without Shoes, his Neck short, his Bones large & His Shoulders broad.' This sole recorded measurement of Johnson confirms the tradition that he was very tall for his day; only three in a thousand Englishmen reached his height at the time. Johnson must have looked especially massive to the bookseller Wilcox as he walked in from the street and stood beside the smallish Garrick who may not have been all of five feet.[2]

Johnson resided first with one Richard Norris, a staymaker with Lichfield connections and a flat near the Strand. He enjoyed the upper-class company of the dissolute Henry Hervey, fourth son of the first Earl of Bristol, an officer who married Catherine Aston of Lichfield. Later he moved to Greenwich, where he walked in the park and continued his work on *Irene*. On 12 July 1738 Johnson wrote to Cave, using his own name this time, to propose a translation of Paolo Sarpi's *Istoria del concilio Tridentino* (1619). Johnson planned to take advantage of popular interest in a theological-political controversy, just as he had in his translation of Le Grand's Lobo. At the same time he was pursuing a scholary interest in Renaissance Italy apparent in the earlier proposal to edit Poliziano. He intended to translate the work from Italian with help from the recent French translation of Pierre-François le Courayer. This disaffected French priest had settled permanently in England, where his dissertation on the English apostolic succession had earned him an Oxford degree, and his translation of an anti-papal work had further stirred up English religious nationalism. Cave published Johnson's proposal and his short biography of Sarpi, but he abandoned the project when the appearance on the scene of a competitor (unfortunately named Johnson) disrupted the advance sales needed to finance so large a book. However, a document once in Boswell's possession evidently indicated that Johnson produced four to eight hundred quarto pages of text and commentary before stopping work in April 1739.[3]

The Sarpi translation fits squarely into the Johnsonian canon because it was mainly as an editor, a compiler, a translator, and a literary historian that Johnson made his way in the world of letters. This fact is observable in Johnson's published works, but it is importantly confirmed by a consideration of his many projected works. Although Sarpi was the projected work on which Johnson made the most progress, he noted many others in a list that he passed on to Bennet Langton near the end of his life. It is a long list dominated by works entered under the rubric 'Philosophy, History, and Literature in general'. (There is a separate heading for the very short list of imaginative or what we might call 'creative' writing.) Among the twenty-four projected editions, translations, and collections that Johnson noted, mostly in the winter of 1752-3, perhaps the most ambitious is a 'History of the Revival of Learning in Europe, containing an account of whatever contributed to the Restoration of Literature, such as controversies, Printing, the Destruction of the Greek Empire, the encouragement of Great Men, with the Lives of the most eminent Patrons and most eminent early professors of all kinds of Learning in different Countries'. His proposed 'History of the State of Venice' and translation of 'Machiavel's History of Florence' would have contributed to the larger project, as would the translation of Sarpi and the edition of Poliziano.[4]

In addition to its affinity with his intellectual interests, the proposed translation of Sarpi's *Council of Trent* was an appropriate task for Johnson in another way. One result of the Tridentine Council was the production at its conclusion (1563) of the Roman Catholic Index of forbidden books and the ten rules *de libris prohibitis* in Pius IV's bull *Dominici gregis custodiae* (24 March 1564). This was one of the most odious rulings ever made by the Roman Church, especially for men like Johnson who grew up in the book trade. Yet, in an enactment of Miltonic justice, the bull brought good out of evil for the Protestant book world. Elizabeth Eisenstein sums up its effect in her intellectual history of printing:

> After the Council of Trent, almost the entire Republic of Letters had to go 'underground' in Catholic Europe. Black-market prices brought profits not to local printers and publishers but to rival firms in foreign Protestant lands. As a later discussion of the Reformation book-trade makes clear, an intriguing asymmetry was introduced by the workings of the Index. It provided Protestant firms with a list of profit-making titles and free advertising while alerting potential Catholic purchasers to the existence of forbidden fruit.

An indirect effect of the Tridentine Index, as Eisenstein shows, was the creation among the French especially of a class of professional, often expatriate writers. For these 'new careerists' the art of writing was not separate from the business of the press, and the 'distinctive occupational culture' in which they participated produced a 'new class of men of letters', epitomized by the *philosophes*. By translating le Courayer's Sarpi, Johnson was supporting this 'new class', illuminating its origins, and making a bid for inclusion in it.[5]

In July 1737 Cave was not quite ready to give Johnson support for his scholarly project because his capital was tied up in another major translation, Du Halde's *Description of the Empire of China*. Still, he must have given Johnson encouragement, and Hawkins is probably right that 'Cave's acquiescence, in the [Sarpi] proposal, drew Johnson into a close intimacy with him.' In late summer 1737 Johnson went home to Lichfield for a brief stay and returned to London with his wife. The couple set up housekeeping first in Hanover and then in Cavendish Square, far west of Grub Street in a recently developed, fresh district of London. From this location Johnson commuted east to St John's Gate in Clerkenwell, the home of the *Gentleman's Magazine*. Johnson told Boswell that when he first laid eyes on this place he 'beheld it with reverence'.[6] The antique phrasing is intriguing because it suggests, like some of his early correspondence with Cave, that Johnson had transferred to the commercial publisher feelings traditionally reserved for patrons of the arts. In his approaches to Cave, Johnson was seeking a patron, but what he found was an employer.

Johnson's first publication in the *Gentleman's Magazine* was the work of a writer seeking preferment. Along with some other friends of the editor Johnson defended Cave and his magazine against the attacks of his competitors at the *London Magazine*. Using Cave's press name, Johnson composed his ode 'Ad Urbanum' in Horatian form, complete with allusions to the Roman master, as well as a glance at one of his most admirable modern imitators, Maciej Kazimierz Sarbiewski. Like the first two lines of the Polish poet's ode to Pope Urban, which earned him a papal laureateship, Johnson's first two lines begin with the vocative 'Urbane'. In the body of the poem, Johnson crowns Cave's learned brow ('fronte . . . erudita') with laurels, praises his industry ('Sedulitas animosa'), and makes him the darling of the muses ('habebis / Participes operae Camoenas'). The poet acknowledges that the *Gentleman's Magazine* itself is not the highest sort of literature, but he describes it as a necessary element in the mythic rainbow of letters: 'sic Iris refulget / Aethereis variata fucis' ('so Iris – the rainbow – shines in the heavens with various colours').[7] 'Fucis', traditionally applied both to nature and to rhetoric, links the vehicle and the tenor of Johnson's conventional but nicely executed metaphor. The poem shows that Johnson knows his Horace and that Cave is able to command the talents of a learned writer.

In the next issue of the magazine Johnson paid his compliments to two of Cave's regular contributors: he wrote an epigram in Latin to Richard Savage and one in Greek to Elizabeth Carter. In the same issue he published a clever epigram to Mary Aston. In both of the poems to women Johnson plays in a courtly fashion with the relations between beauty and power. He styles Elizabeth Carter a Venus with the thunderbolts of Zeus in her eyes (ὄμμασι λαμπρὰ Διὸς Κύπρις ὀιστὰ φέρει). In the more interesting poem of the two, 'To a Lady who Spoke in Defense of Liberty', he casts Mary Aston's liberal political arguments in an ironic light by commenting on the power of her beauty to enslave her interlocutor:

> Liber ut esse velim, suasisti, pulchra Maria:
> Ut maneam liber, pulchra Maria, vale.[8]

(Lovely Mary, you have persuaded me that I must wish for liberty. To remain free, I bid thee, lovely Mary, farewell.)

'Liberty' was a buzz word for Whiggish ideals, and in this trifle the courtly Johnson conflates the political and romantic meanings of the word. He may have traded on the laugh such a jest could evoke among Tory male chauvinists, but his political and intellectual conversation with the Aston women was genuine enough to last a lifetime.

Later in the year Johnson published another poem to Mrs Carter, 'To Eliza Plucking Laurel in Mr Pope's Gardens'. In this poem and its Latin version Johnson's compliment is subtler and more playful than it is in his first to the learned young lady. There is a droll effect in the concourse of Pope, Eliza, and Apollo in so few lines, and the compliment has two strings to its bow, being directed both to Mrs Carter and to Pope in his intangible 'Elysios . . . hortos'. The most interesting of Johnson's poems to Mrs Carter, however, did not appear in the *Gentleman's Magazine* or anywhere else in Johnson's lifetime. 'Quid mihi cum cultu?' ('What good is refinement to me?') contrasts 'probitas inculta' and 'ingenium' with refinement, concluding that the uncultivated state is satisfactory if 'pulchra Eliza' approves it.[9] The poem suggests a young Johnson with provincial manners and a naturally rough temperament self-consciously confiding his fears in his new-found, urban intellectual companion. The poem suggests too a greater degree of intimacy than the others by playing on a point of personal concern. Although their relationship never deepened, it was through Carter that Johnson found his way from Cave's offices in St John's Gate to the more diverse company of writers circulating around another London publisher, Samuel Richardson.

At the end of 1738 Johnson published a complimentary Greek epigram to Thomas Birch, thus rounding out his literary approach to Cave's modern salon. At almost thirty years of age Johnson was still winning his way in the literary world with complimentary verse. Even in the decent obscurity of a learned language such addresses do not sort with our image of the fiercely independent professional writer who rejected the patronage of Chesterfield in one of the world's most famous letters. However, in the midst of making his learned addresses to Cave and company, in the same letter with his poem 'Ad Urbanum', Johnson sent Cave his first great poem. *London* changed everything. Still playing the part of a courtly poet too proud to solicit publication, Johnson transparently pretended that *London* was written by a penurious friend for whom he was the agent. Still playing Maecenas to Johnson's Horace, Cave sent Johnson 'a present' in return and printed part of the poem in the May issue of his magazine. Cave also arranged for publication with Robert Dodsley, Pope's printer, and *London* appeared in folio on 12 May 1738, within a day of the appearance of a new poem by Pope, the first part of *One Thousand Seven Hundred and Thirty Eight. A Dialogue Something like Horace.*

A comparison between the unknown, anonymous author of *London* and the most famous poet in England was inevitable and probably intentional. Both poems belong to the then popular genre of the imitation, in which the poet adapts the language and sentiments of a classical poem to his own times. Both are politically tendentious, containing gibes at Robert Walpole and Orator Henley and patriotic recollections of the Spanish depredations, including the notorious incident in which their coastal guards in the West Indies amputated Robert Jenkins's ear, leaving the evidence to be presented by him to Parliament in 1738 as an inducement to war. Both Pope and Johnson also conclude their poems with wishes for a return to less corrupt, sterner, and prouder times. Whether or not the publishing strategy had anything to do with it, Johnson's poem was a great success. It ran to a second folio edition in a week and a third a couple of months later. Although he anonymously offered to 'be so much the Authours Friend' as to act as publisher, Johnson finally sold the copyright to Dodsley for ten guineas.[10] From this moment until 1762, when he was awarded a civil list pension, Johnson earned his living by writing, not as a matter of gifts from a patron but on business terms. Specifically, in addition to some other work, Johnson was employed as a writer and editor for the *Gentleman's Magazine* at the rate of £100 per year. Although the complimentary verse Johnson produced for Cave and his associates may have cleared the way, *London* was the performance that won him his position.

Boswell says that *London* 'first displayed [Johnson's] transcendent powers', and it 'burst forth with a splendour, the rays of which will for ever encircle his name'. Boswell's romantic description of the poem is confused with his appreciation of its importance in Johnson's rise to prominence, and in some ways *London* was a 'career move'. But what sort of professional identity did Johnson seek to create? Since he wrote it in English, Johnson clearly sought a somewhat wider audience for *London* than for the Latin and Greek verses he published earlier in 1738. Yet the best audience for *London* is learned enough to understand Johnson's method of adapting Juvenal, his implicit commentary on the poem, and his poetical stance with respect to earlier translators and imitators of the third satire, including Dryden, Oldham, Holyday, and Boileau. Like Pope and many other writers of imitations, Johnson published the original Latin along with his

English version, although he limited the original to the particular lines he imitated. He displays to all his conversation with Juvenal, but learned readers may also see his critical acquaintance with the vast erudition that the satire had accrued to itself in ever-growing variorum commentaries. As a pair of researchers have shown, Johnson made great use of Schrevelius's variorum edition, as revised by the powerful scholar J. G. Graevius: 'Johnson drank so deep of this erudition that it became inseparable from his appreciation of the poem itself.' The sort of reputation and career that Johnson sought to build by such a demonstration of Latinity is certainly scholarly, perhaps even pedagogical. Johnson shows his readers a way of interpreting Juvenal that displays his awareness of classical scholarship and his acute perception of Latin phraseology. Although he wrote it in English, Johnson was still proving his worth as a Latin poet and scholar in *London*.[11]

As a translator and a scholar Johnson could no more be servile than he could in any other capacity; the critical premium he places on freedom of translation in the *Lives of the Poets* is implicit in *London*. *London* represents a scholarly and critical reading of Juvenal that tempers the original's hostility, elevates its diction, and renders its message calmer and more philosophical, while retaining much of its sharpness and satiric bite. Johnson was applying the revisionist lesson of his own translation when he said forty years later in the life of Dryden, 'The peculiarity of Juvenal is a mixture of gaiety and stateliness, of pointed sentences, and declamatory grandeur.'[12]

Johnson's interpretation of Juvenal is summed up in his substitution of a character named Thales (two syllables) for the original Umbricius. Almost the whole of each poem is spoken by a character saying farewell to the corrupt metropolis and setting out for a safer life in the country. As their respective historical referents suggest, Johnson's speaker is the more philosophical, the wiser, and loftier of the two. Umbricius was a prognosticator who made his divinations by haruspicy, examining the entrails of sacrificed animals. Juvenal makes him an honest man who refuses to bow to the corruptions of Rome, but Johnson's attitude toward all forms of divination was strictly Christian and condemnatory. Umbricius was therefore unacceptably low for him, and he replaced him with someone quite exalted. In Stanley's *History of Philosophy*, a book that Johnson owned, Thales is the first philosopher, the first and foremost of the seven wise men of Greece. His particular excellence was in speculative learning rather than moral rules or practice. Yet, he was a very great natural philosopher and an astronomer, who humbly limited his predictions to such daily events as the weather. Most importantly, Thales is said to be the first philosopher to acknowledge the eternal God and his Providence in governing the world. As a character he is curiously like Demetrius in *Irene*, who goes off with Aspasia to instruct the West in all parts of learning, especially natural philosophy. Pious philosophers, combining fundamental Christian beliefs with ancient wisdom and natural science, Thales and Demetrius

are embodiments of the Johnsonian hero. Furthermore, the historical
Thales is celebrated for moral wisdom, and he is said to have made politics
'his first study'. But he was the only one of the seven wise men not to rule
a city, and 'He was a great Enemy to Tyrants, and accounted all Monarchy
little better.'[13] These aspects of Thales, having been reported by Cicero,
Plutarch, Diogenes Laertius, Stobaeus, and Thomas Stanley, would have
been known to learned readers in Johnson's time. Whether or not all
contemporary readers noticed, however, Thales is the right character for
elevating the philosophy of Juvenal's third satire and for pointing Johnson's
implicit political attack on the Walpole ministry and the Hanoverian
monarchy. Not so very different from Robert Burton's Democritus Junior,
Johnson's speaker, looking much like his engraving in Stanley's *History*,
is 'Indignant Thales' who 'with contemptuous frown, / . . . eyes the
neighb'ring town' (33–4).

The political dimension in Johnson's poem is more pointed and particular than it is in Juvenal's and more closely linked with the expressions
of pastoral longing that appear in both poems. Whereas Juvenal's Umbricius
is going to devote himself to the Sybil and be true to his sacred art,
Johnson's Thales goes to Cambria (ancient Cornwall) to be a 'true Briton',
meaning both an unconquered native of his land and, in contemporary
political parlance, an opponent of the Walpole regime. Thales longs for
'some' conventional 'happier place' and 'secret cell', but one in which
'the harrass'd Briton found repose' (47), and so the most plaintive piece
of pastoral longing in the poem expresses a political message. The six
lines start and end with echoes of *Paradise Lost*, but the middle couplet,
especially in its rhyming words, overtly suggests Walpole's mishandling of
foreign relations with Spain:

> Has heaven reserv'd, in pity to the poor,
> No pathless waste, or undiscover'd shore;
> No secret island in the boundless main?
> No peaceful desart yet unclaim'd by Spain?
> Quick let us rise, the happy seats explore,
> And bear oppression's insolence no more.
>   (170–5)[14]

The longest pastoral description in the poem is a picture of Edenic life
that could pass for an apolitical opposition between urban impoverish-
ment and country ease, except that the chosen locale is 'Some hireling
senator's deserted seat' (213). Moreover, even the purely pastoral parts of
the poem are tinged with irony. For example, there is an implicit hint of
mockery in the predictability and monotony of a couplet describing the
ideal place elsewhere:

> There ev'ry bush with nature's musick rings,
> There ev'ry breeze bears health upon its wings;
>   (220–1)

Likewise the following question is spoken as though it were merely rhetorical, but the harsh word 'rocks' makes it ironic:

> For who would leave, unbrib'd Hibernia's land,
> Or change the rocks of Scotland for the Strand?
>   (9–10)

Johnson most fully transforms the purpose of the satire by putting the pastoral elements of his material into the service of political meaning. But he also throws in discrete, scathing references to such despised government activities as the pension (51, 73, 200), the excise tax (29), the ways and means (245), the Licensing Act (59), the *Gazette* (72), and the King's loyalty to his native Hanover, though he demurely prints 'k—g' (247). It is no accident that much of what Johnson deplores pertains to government intrusions into printing, publishing, and other aspects of the book trade that were affected by Walpole's general economic policies. Although he dignifies his political message by reference to a common inheritance of rugged independence, Johnson has foremost in mind the rights and privileges of his 'patron', Edward Cave, and the class of professional writers to which he himself now belonged. *London* is a pledge of allegiance to Cave and his fellow publishers, whose work was hindered by licensing, the excise, and competition with the subsidized *Gazette*; it is for Johnson another act of professional identification, mixing neo-feudal fealty to a patron with modern class and trade loyalty.

Despite its political modernity, however, *London* achieves 'declamatory grandeur' and an elevation above that of its model. One reason for this is that Johnson supports the superiority of his main speaker with diction that is higher and more philosophical than Juvenal's. An important feature of this elevated language is its high concentration of abstract nouns. The opening lines of Thales' speech, for instance, rise above their Latin counterpart with a strong infusion of abstractions that suggest epic personifications:

> Since worth, he cries, in these degen'rate days
> Wants ev'n the cheap reward of empty praise;
> In those curs'd walls, devote to vice and gain,
> Since unrewarded science toils in vain;
> Since hope but sooths to double my distress,
> And ev'ry moment leaves my little less;
> While yet my steddy steps no staff sustains,
> And life still vig'rous revels in my veins;
> Grant me, kind heaven, to find some happier place,
> Where honesty and sense are no disgrace.
>   (35–44)

'Worth' and 'hope' have no counterparts in Juvenal's poem, and the precedent for 'science' is 'artibus honestis', which is less philosophical in diction, more particular in meaning, and more mundane. The crucial word 'worth' returns without Latin precedent again in line 126 as a title loosely lavished on a potential patron, and again in the most famous line of the poem, 'SLOW RISES WORTH, BY POVERTY DEPRESS'D' (177). 'Virtutibus' is the Latin word behind Johnson's last use of 'worth', but its oblique case and weak syntactical position prevent it from achieving the abstract sense it has in Johnson's highly concentrated, gnomic line.

Latin *virtutes* regularly refers to physical powers or skills rather than to internal or spiritual qualities. 'Virtues', the English reflex, appears four times in Johnson's poem without precedent in the accompanying Latin. Translating *virtus* as 'virtue' would have been significant, albeit conventional, but introducing the word and returning to it frequently makes it very clear that Johnson intends to interpret Juvenal in philosophical, Christian, general, and therefore moral terms. Thales' last words may be read as the poet's promise to return to his audience and an expression of his intended poetical character. Thales says in due time he will help his friend, the 'I' of the poem,

> In virtue's cause once more exert his rage,
> Thy satire point, and animate thy page.
>   (262–3)

The philosophical 'Indignant Thales' at the poem's end becomes at once Johnson's hero and his muse. Passing, as it were, out of life on his 'wherry', Thales becomes a spiritual guide for Johnson who vows to write 'In virtue's cause'. 'Virtue' means partly 'anti-government' here, but the poem as a whole achieves sufficient dignity and elevation to retain the nobler senses of the word. The statement is at once political, moral, and professional, and in *London* Johnson is seeking an identity as a writer that combines all three dimensions.

The interplay of the tendentious and the elevated are not fully resolved in *London* (or in most satire), but they are not wholly antagonistic forces. Johnson continued to use them in satirical combination in a great variety of ways in his succeeding years as a regular writer for the *Gentleman's Magazine*. His greatest contribution to the publication was his series of Parliamentary reports, *Debates in the Senate of Magna Lilliput*, which he began writing late in 1740. In these dramatizations of the proceedings of a Parliament closed to the press, but susceptible to information 'leaks', Johnson most elaborately unites lofty political and moral considerations with pointed criticism of the government. In the Preface to the first index of the *Gentleman's Magazine* Johnson says that the debates conducted in Parliament during Walpole's ministry include 'such a Series of Argumentation as has comprised all Political Science'. Of the various senses in which 'Political Science' may be taken, the most important and obvious is an educational sense. Almost as abstract and lofty as science in *London*, the word here means an elevated and generalized form of information. In the

Index Johnson goes on to say that the debates 'ascertained the Right of the Crown and the Privileges of the People, so as for ever to prevent their being confounded in the cause either of Tyranny or of Faction'.[15] Such an achievement is the highest goal of political philosophy in terms of the tradition that Johnson knew – the line of liberal political philosophers running from Hooker and Grotius through Pufendorf and Locke. Whether or not the actual debates achieved this degree of science, Johnson's versions of them always move in that direction. He represents debates on particular issues as series of speeches on great themes of seventeenth- and eighteenth-century European politics: liberty, the power of the people, war, law, corruption in government, and the evils of a standing army.

Characteristically, Johnson rises above even this level of generality in his *Debates* to express durable truths about life in terms of the topics that had already become habitual with him, including his master topic, the vanity of human wishes. For example, Lord Newcastle speaks in a debate of 4 December 1741, ostensibly defending the ministry's handling of the war with Spain and its proposal to support the Queen of Hungary in order to maintain the balance of power in Europe, but the underlying theme is Johnson's:

> Futurity impairs the Influence of the most important Objects of Considera-
> tion, even when it does not lessen their Certainty; and with regard to Events
> only probable, Events which a thousand Accidents may obviate, they are
> almost annihilated, with regard to the human Mind, by being placed at a
> Distance from us. Wherever Imagination can exert its Power, we easily dwell
> upon the most pleasing Views, and flatter ourselves with those Consequences,
> which, tho' perhaps least to be expected, are most desired; wherever differ-
> ent Events may arise, which is the State of all human Transactions, we naturally
> promote our Hopes, and repress our Fears, and in time so far deceive our-
> selves, as to quiet all our Suspicions, lay all our Terrors asleep, and believe
> what at first we only wished.[16]

As this passage suggests, the *Debates* are Johnson's preparation for the 'pure wine' of the *Rambler* where general and ethical considerations most magnificently supersede the topical or newsworthy interests of journalism. For this reason and because they constitute Johnson's largest body of prose, the *Debates* are too little read.

Despite their generality and magnitude, the *Debates* belong in a particular historical setting, one that is constructed both by the political circumstances of the day and by the place of journalism and other forms of publication in those political circumstances. The Parliamentary privilege of secrecy, asserted and protected from earliest times, was threatened in a new way in the early eighteenth century. Before 1689 and the Glorious Revolution, Parliament asserted its privilege in order to defend itself most importantly from the intrusion of the king. In the early eighteenth century, it was a growing, increasingly literate and enfranchised public that demanded to know about the proceedings of Parliament in much greater detail than was provided by the *Votes and Proceedings* (later called the *Journals of the House of Commons*). The vehicle for satisfying this public demand shifted in the first two decades of the eighteenth century from the newsletter or pamphlet to the newspaper or journal. Abel Boyer began publishing the *Political State* in 1711, and in 1722 Parliament for the first time explicitly named newspapers in one of its frequently repeated assertions of privilege. Before founding the *Gentleman's Magazine*, Edward Cave worked for the *Gloucester Journal*, helping to supply that publication with Parliamentary information. From its inception in 1731, the *Gentleman's Magazine* was involved in Parliamentary reporting, at first generally summarizing the accounts in the *Political State*, though sometimes relying on other sources. (Boyer himself had cultivated MPs who were willing to give him accounts of the proceedings.) Increased vigilance on the part of the Commons hastened the end of reporting in the *Political State* and culminated in the resolution of 13 April 1738 stating, 'That it is an high Indignity to, and a notorious Breach of the Privilege of, this House, for any News Writer, in Letters, or other Papers (as Minutes, or under any other Denomination), or for any Printer or Publisher of any printed News Paper, of any Denomination, to presume to insert in the said Letters or Papers, or to give therein any Account of, the Debates, or other Proceedings, of this House, or any Committee thereof, as well during the Recess as the Sitting of Parliament; and that this House will proceed with the utmost Severity against such Offenders.'[17] The phrase 'as well during the Recess as the Sitting of Parliament' was added in an amendment to the motion and clearly aimed at curtailing the House's customary tolerance of reports published after the session was over.

This order immediately brought about a new phase in the reporting of the debates, and it was in this particular phase that Johnson made his major contribution. In June 1738, soon after the Commons order was issued and about a month after the publication of *London*, Cave employed Johnson to write an advertisement, in full Swiftian regalia, for the new series of Parliamentary reports. He bills the reports as an 'Appendix to Capt. GULLIVER's Account [of Lilliput], which we received last Month, and which the late Resolution of the House of Commons, whereby we are forbidden to insert any Account of the Proceedings of the *British Parliament*, gives us an Opportunity of communicating in their Room.' The advertisement is full of anger about the order and directs satire at the British Parliament by referring to Britain transparently as Lilliput and wishing for a more complete account of its Laws and Customs: 'Happy had it been for Mankind, had so noble and instructive a Subject been cultivated and adorn'd by the Genius of LEMUEL GULLIVER, a Genius equally sublime and extensive, acute and sagacious. . . . Then might the Legislators of *Lilliput* have been produced as Rivals in Fame to *Numa* or *Lycurgus*; and its Heroes have shone with no less Lustre than *Cadmus* and *Theseus: Felix tanto Argumento Ingenium, felix tanto Ingenio Argumentum!*'– 'Happy it is for the writer to have so great a theme and for the theme to have so great a writer!'[18]

Turning nicely on the ambiguity of 'Argumento' in the mock-heroic, invented Latin tag, Johnson assumes a Swiftian posture of defence. 'Argumentum' can mean either argument, theme, fable, or lesson; it is applied variously to the central element in speeches, plays, and narrative or epic poems. Its ambiguity sums up the message, which is that reports of the debates in future will be cast in a form that makes no more claims for truth than for fiction, no more presentations of particular information than discourses on general, allegorical knowledge, and no more elevation than degradation of its subjects. The gesture of aggressive retreat into fiction is evident in the choice of classical figures, like Numa, whose histories are largely mythical, no less than in the assumption of a Swiftian framework. Swift sought, in vain, to teach politicians and the recently created reading public that print is not information; on Cave's behalf, Johnson tries to teach Swift's lesson without alienating a reading public that was created because of and by means of a hunger for information. As a representative of the *Magazine* and print media in general, Johnson actively campaigns for freedom of the press, for the sake of readers, writers, and publishers. Like *London*, the *Debates* are partly concerned to assert the rights and privileges of Johnson's own emerging class of professional writers and their new 'patrons'.

Although he advertised the inaugural *Debates*, from June 1738 to November 1740 Johnson's part in producing them was limited to editing the copy submitted to the magazine by William Guthrie. Because of the differences in chronology between the actual debates and the published reports, it is difficult to ascertain just when Johnson started writing his own copy, but it was probably late November when he took over the job of inventing speeches, based on reports smuggled out by Cave's man in the gallery, leaks from MPs, political pamphlets, and other newspaper reports. Johnson himself never attended Parliament, and his distance from the event increased his tendency to generalize the nature of the proceedings. In the earliest debates on which Johnson reported, the philosophical moralist and the campaigner for freedom of the press both make their appearance. The subject of the Commons debates of 19 and 25 November 1740 was the ministry's Corn Bill, a law to restrict the exportation of food stuffs, lest they supply the roving Spanish navy and their infamous depredations. In Johnson's presentation, the Whig opposition leader, William Pulteney, begins his attack with a statement of the Commons' purpose that seems aimed more steadily at the edification of Johnson's audience than Pulteney's. He explains pedagogically that the Commons members are representatives of the people and will be rated by posterity solely on the score of their attentiveness to encroachments of the ministry: 'Those are always by the general Suffrage of Mankind applauded as the Patrons of their Country, who have struggled with the Influence of the Crown, and those condemned as Traytors, who have either promoted it by unreasonable Grants, or seen it increase by slow Degrees without Resistance.' Pulteney concludes by pointing his moral with an example from history, taken, like the story of Irene, from Knolles's *Generall Historie of the Turkes*: 'To restrain that Commerce by which the Necessaries of Life are distributed is a very bold Experiment, and such as once produced an Insurrection in the Empire of the *Korambecs* [Turks], that terminated in the Deposition of one of their Monarchs.' The defence of personal liberty is carried on by Barnard who sees a loss for all freedom-loving British subjects in the special loss to be suffered by the great rice-exporting colony of Carolina: 'The Sailor, the Merchant, the Shipwright, the Manufacturer, with all the Subordinations of Employment that depend upon them, all that supply them with Materials, or receive Advantage from their Labours, almost all the Subjects of the *Lilliputian* crown, must suffer at least in some Degree, by the Ruin of *Carolana* [Carolina].' The defence of free enterprise becomes a defence of freedom in a broader political and finally in a moral and philosophical sense: 'There is, indeed, Sir, a Possibility that the Liberty for which I contend may be used to wicked Purposes, and that some Men may be incited by Poverty or Avarice to carry the Enemy those Provisions, which they pretend to export to *Lilliputian* provinces. But if we are to refuse every Power that may be employed to bad Purposes, we must lay all Mankind in Dungeons, and divest human Nature of all its Rights; for every Man that has the Power of Action, may sometimes act ill.'[19]

In the context of debates on all sorts of issues speakers deliver similarly general encomia of freedom, and they undertake similarly broad considerations of popular power. Although there are recognizable differences in the styles of the main speakers whom Johnson records, his propensity to discourse on general topics tends to diminish these differences. The Duke of Argyll, for instance, always notable for the grandeur and magisterial good sense of his remarks, must sound much like Pulteney when he issues a statement very much to the same purpose: 'it ought to be our Care to hinder the Increase of the Influence of the Court, and to obstruct all Measures that may extend the Authority of the Ministry, and therefore those Measures are to be pursued by which Independence and Liberty will be most supported.' No matter who the speaker or what the specific issue at hand, liberty is often Johnson's topic. It rises to the forefront, for example, in the debate on the conscription of sailors, when Sir John Barnard says, 'If these Clauses, Sir, should pass into Law, a Sailor and a Slave will become Terms of the same Signification. Every Man who has devoted himself to the most useful Profession, and the most dangerous Service of his Country, will see himself deprived of every Advantage which he has labour'd to obtain, and made the mere passive Property of those who live in Security by his Valour, and owe to his Labour that Affluence which hardens them to Insensibility, and that Pride that swells them to Ingratitude.'[20]

Johnson consistently elevates liberty to a moral and philosophical ideal, but he is not unaware of its dangerous, Whiggish interpretation. Hence, some of his speakers qualify the ideal of liberty with reminders of other ideals. Lord Lovel, for instance, in a speech made on 13 February 1741 in the Lords debate on the removal of Walpole, says, 'Liberty and Justice must always support each other, they can never long flourish apart. . . . By Liberty, my Lords, can never be meant the Privilege of doing Wrong without being accountable, because Liberty is always spoken of as Happiness, or one of the Means to Happiness, and Happiness and Virtue cannot be separated. The great use of Liberty must therefore be to preserve Justice from Violation, Justice the great public Virtue, by which a Kind of Equality is diffused over the whole Society, by which Wealth is restrained from Oppression, and Inferiority preserved from Servitude.' Although it appears in a different debate and in a different house, this passage answers such remarks of Pulteney's as 'Liberty is never to be injured whatever is suffered or whatever endangered' and 'If we vote away the Privilege of one Class among us, those of another may quickly be demanded; and Slavery will advance by degrees, till the last Remains of Freedom shall be lost.' Likewise, part of the speech of Chancellor Hardwicke in the Lords debate on supporting the Queen of Hungary speaks primarily to Pulteney's and Argyle's remarks on popular support:

> On this Occasion, my Lords, it is necessary to consider the Nature of Popularity, and to enquire, how far it is to be considered in the Administration of public Affairs. If by Popularity is meant only a sudden Shout of Applause obtained by a Compliance with the present Inclination of the People, however excited, or of whatsoever Tendency, I shall without Scruple declare, that Popularity is to be despised. . . . But if by Popularity be meant that settled Confidence and lasting Esteem, which a good Government may justly claim from the Subject, I am far from denying that it is truly desirable; and that no wise Man ever disregarded it. But this Popularity, my Lords, is very consistent with Contempt of riotous Clamours, and of mistaken Complaints; and is often only to be obtained by an Opposition to the reigning Opinions, and a Neglect of temporary Discontents.[21]

As Hardwicke does here, speakers on both sides of the aisle make contributions to the central topics of the *Debates*. Although Johnson was hostile to Walpole's ministry, he does not make Walpole or his defenders speak poorly or to no general, educational purpose. Unlike his competition, Thomas Gordon in the *London Magazine*, Johnson did not obviously and regularly display his political persuasion in the way he reported the debates; he usually preferred to teach deep, non-partisan political commitments. One exception, however, is Johnson's and his publisher's conduct with respect to the issue of freedom of the press or, more properly, the freedom of writers and publishers to live by their trade free from government restriction. Every one of the frequent uses of Swiftian terminology is a blow struck for this issue: Lords are Urgs, London Mildendo, pounds sterling Sprugs, MPs Clinabs, the King the Emperor, France Blefusco, and England Lilliput because the government restricts the press. The particular message is clear every time a proper name appears, though the use of silly, anagrammatic names is also blatantly irreverent, and at times Johnson plays it up for the sake of ridiculing the ministry.[22]

Cave and Johnson also show their concern for freedom of the press very specifically by reporting a debate relating to a seditious paper in which a writer, a publisher, and a printer are hauled before the bar of the Commons and sent to prison for breach of the Commons' privilege and for distributing a 'seditious' pamphlet. Like eight others that Johnson composed, this debate was not reported by the *London Magazine*; it is a significant deviation because it parallels an earlier decision of Cave's to report the Playhouse debates, although his regular source of material, the *Political State*, did not choose to cover them.[23] As Johnson recognized in his later life of Cave, the editor of the *Gentleman's Magazine* was influential in raising the social and economic status of authors, publishers, and the whole business of literature. Cave and Johnson were probably conscious of campaigning for such elevation while working on the *Debates*, and their attention to the so-called 'seditious paper debate' is evidence of their proper interest in a fellow member of the guild.

It was only the previous year (1739) that Johnson himself had written his satirical pamphlet *A Compleat Vindication of the Licensers of the Stage*, in which he assumes a Swiftian persona in order to defend fellow writer Henry Brooke against government censorship of his politically tendentious play *Gustavus Vasa*. The Licensing Act of 1737, which codified the Lord Chamberlain's powers of censoring the London stage, is Johnson's main target in the pamphlet, but he also defends the press. His totalitarian speaker sneers at the natural temper of the 'true Britons' because 'This temper makes them very readily encourage any writer or printer, who, at the hazard of his life or fortune, will give them any information.' He calls 'liberty of the press . . . the darling of the common people'; he argues for the establishment of an *Index Expurgatorius*; and he 'earnestly implore[s] the friends of the government to leave no art untry'd by which we may hope to succeed in our design of extending the power of the licenser to the press, and of making it criminal to publish any thing without an *imprimatur*.' The Tridentine cast of the speaker's remarks derives in part from Johnson's work on his translation of Paolo Sarpi, but the dramatization is fundamentally Swiftian, ending with the modest proposal that 'it may be made a felony to teach to read, without a license from the Lord Chamberlain' and a hope that 'the nation will rest at length in ignorance and peace.'[24] Johnson directly continues his campaign for freedom of the press in his version of the second Parliamentary debate that he reported.

In the House of Commons on 2 December 1740 Lord Thompson read out the 'seditious' paper, *Considerations upon the Embargo on Provision of Victual*, an attack on the proposed Corn Bill. The *Gentleman's Magazine* for December 1741 carried the story (including a reprint of the paper) as 'An Account of a memorable Transaction in the last *British* Parliament, to which nothing is found Parallel in the whole History of *Lilliput*.' Johnson's account of the debate itself did not appear until January 1742 as part of the

1741 *Supplement.* By being a year or more behind the breaking story, Cave and Johnson avoided the fate of their subjects, but they still ran some risk of prosecution for breach of privilege because their report was so critical of the government's action. The scene that Johnson describes is one of the most dramatic in the *Debates*: it is one of the very few that involves a description of physical as well as verbal action, and it is the only scene that involves anyone other than MPs, Lords, and other Parliamentary officials. The writer, William Cooley, who handed out the seditious paper to MPs, is brought before the bar of the Commons. Cooley, whom Johnson does not name, is asked to identify the printer. He deflects the question at first, answering 'that he printed it himself. Which he explained afterwards, by saying, that as he had carried it to the Printer's, he might be said, in the general Acceptation of the Term, as applied to an Author, to be the Printer; he then discovered the Printer [John Hughes of Holborn], and was asked, where was the original Manuscript, which he said he had destroy'd, as he did any other useless Paper.' Even though names are omitted, the amount of detail is surprising and interesting; Cooley evidently gets the best of his examiners by knowing more about the publishing world than they, scoffing finally, one feels, at their outdated interest in the manuscript, as if in a world of print such a thing mattered. With their interest in handwritten materials and conducting their business in the even older form of oral exchange, the Members belong to an antique world; the intrusion of Cooley, with his up-to-date knowledge of publication procedures, suggests this, while the Swiftian regalia deepens the overall impression of the Parliament as a neo-feudal, corrupt court, at least in its handling of this case.[25]

Suspicion turns in another direction when some Members observe that the 'seditious' paper was printed in 'one of the daily Papers' (*The Daily Post*). Cooley 'was asked, who carried it thither? and answered, that he carried it himself. It was then demanded, what he gave for having it inserted, and he answered, that he gave nothing.' Cooley is again defiant, but Henry Archer locates the publisher of the *Post*, John Meres, in the gallery of the House and has him immediately brought before the bar. A debate then ensues on the right of the House to demand self-incriminating testimony from the witness, which supplies an opportunity for Johnson to print another encomium of British liberty: 'Such Treatment', says Sandys, 'is rather to be expected by Slaves in the Inquisition of *Iberia* [Spain], than a *Lilliputian* at the Bar of this House; a House instituted to preserve Liberty, and to restrain Injustice and Oppression.' This debate devolves into a discussion of the statute of limitations on the House's standing order to protect its privilege, a point of much concern to Johnson and his publisher. But the whole matter gets even closer to home when Pulteney responds to Walpole's suggestion that an MP is the true author of Cooley's piece: 'There are, indeed, some Passages which would not disgrace the greatest Abilities, and some Maxims true in themselves, though perhaps fallaciously applied, and at least such an Appearance of Reasoning and Knowledge, as sets the Writer far above the Level of the contemptible Scribblers of the Ministerial Vindications: a Herd of Wretches whom neither Information can enlighten nor Affluence elevate; low Drudges of Scurrility, whose Scandal is harmless for want of Wit, and whose Opposition is only troublesome from the Pertinaciousness of Stupidity.' In *London* Johnson expresses the same hostility to the writers of the official *Gazette,* and he only tempered it slightly in the *Dictionary* in his second definition of 'gazetteer': 'It was lately a term of the utmost infamy, being usually applied to wretches who were hired to vindicate the court.' He clearly enjoys expressing the sentiment in the person of Pulteney whom he makes go on at some length, declaring at one point: 'Why such immense Sums are distributed amongst these Reptiles, it is scarce possible not to enquire; for it cannot be imagined that those who pay them expect any Support from their Abilities.' Johnson had used the imagery of serpents and reptiles to describe the evils of a standing army in *Marmor Norfolciense* (1739), his most virulent attack on the government, and he almost reaches that level of violence here.[26]

When Walpole is finally allowed to answer this attack on his ministry's hacks, he does so only by issuing a grand statement about the nature of political writing, which is reminiscent of the impossible standards of excellence that Johnson sets for the epic poet in his life of Milton and for any poet in chapter 10 of *Rasselas*: 'He that will write well in Politicks, must at the same Time have a complete Knowledge of the Question, and Time to digest his Thoughts into Method, and polish his Stile into Elegance; which is little less than to say, He must be at once a Man of Business, and a Man of Leisure; for political Transactions are not easily understood, but by those who are engaged in them, and the Art of Writing is not attainable without long Practice, and sedentary Application.'[27] Although the speaker is Walpole, the sentiments are Johnson's, and the message of this *debate* is the difficulty and danger of political journalism. There are numerous ways to fail, and success can also be dangerous.

Who ran the greatest risk in political writing and publishing? This is revealed in the epilogue to the debate, most fully provided in Stockdale's edition of the *Debates*. There we are informed that the printer, Hughes, spent a night in jail, the writer, Cooley, about five days, but the publisher of the journal, Meres, remained in custody until the end of the session, or almost 100 days. For all their technological backwardness, the ministers correctly identified the true source of danger to their ways: the publisher with money and a vehicle for the distribution of classified information.[28]

The scene, which seems to be so much about the writers and producers of it, was literally enacted a few years later, in 1747, when Cave himself was brought before the bar of the House of Lords and made to answer for his breach of their privilege. Some of his testimony is worth remarking. As disingenuous as Cooley in his responses, Cave said that he had never heard of anyone being punished for publishing debates. When asked, '"How he came by the Speeches which he printed in *The Gentleman's Magazine*?"' He said, "He got into the House, and heard them, and made Use of a

Black Lead Pencil, and only took Notes of some Remarkable Passages; and from his Memory, he put them together himself." ' With this piece of perjury Cave protected his 'operative', and with another obvious lie he valiantly shielded his authors, Samuel Johnson among them, from prosecution: 'Being asked, "If he ever had any Person whom he kept in Pay to make Speeches for him?" he said, "He never had." '[29]

Although the Gulliverian trappings of the *Debates* work steadily, consistently, and primarily against government censorship, they also conspire here and there to satirize a particular figure or a particular motion in Parliament. The best example is the famous debate in the Commons on the motion to remove Walpole, especially Walpole's concluding defence of himself. Partly because it was printed so long after the event it records, the debate is full of historical as well as philosophical political science. Lord Sandys introduces the motion to remove Walpole with a lengthy recapitulation of the events of his ministry, stressing the usual anti-government points: the failure of the Convention of Pardo, the Excise Crisis of 1733, and the Treaty of Hanover. Sandys converts these historical episodes into general political arguments concerning 'the Interest and the Voice of the People', liberty, and justice:

> Such, Sir, has been the Conduct of Sir *Retrob Walelop*, with regard to foreign Affairs he has deserted our Allies, aggrandised our Enemies, betrayed our Commerce, and endangered our Colonies; and yet this is the least criminal Part of his Ministry. For what is the Loss of Allies to the Alienation of the People to the Government, or the Diminution of Trade to the Destruction of our Liberties? . . . the People will not always groan under their Burdens, in Submission; . . . they will at length resolve to shake them off, and resume into their own Hands that Authority which they have intrusted to their Governors.[30]

Following a common pattern in Johnson's *Debates*, despite their differing opinions, Walpole's defenders contribute to the lessons in political science begun by his adversaries. Fox's contribution is in the important area of political history: 'To place this Affair in its proper Light, it may be necessary to recapitulate some Occurrences which preceded it, and to consider the State of this Nation from the beginning of the late Emperor [George I].' His defence is persuasive, turning on the reluctance of Walpole to drag Britain into war, and the willingness of the opposition to warmonger for the sake of political profit. Johnson sympathized with this position because of its affinities with humanistic anti-war philosophies, but in expounding it he reviews the sore points of Walpole's regime:

> The War has indeed had already one Effect that they may without want of Candour, be suspected of desiring; it has furnished them with numerous Topics of Accusation which they could not have obtained in Time of Peace; it has given them an Opportunity of diversifying their Invectives and enlivening their Harangues, and enabled them to substitute new calumnies in

the Place of those which, though now no longer credited, they had been hitherto forced to repeat. The Excise which had with unwearied Eloquence been for many Years echoed from one side of this House to the other, the Dangers of a Standing Army which had been exaggerated with all the Zeal of ardent Patriotism, and even the Convention which, tho' a later Subject, had been discussed till it was no longer a Terror but a Vexation to Mankind, gave way to more splendid Themes, Themes on which the Imagination might expatiate without Labour, and Eloquence wanton without the Aid of Invention; they harangued now on the Bravery of our Sailors, the Strength of the Nation, the Triumphs of our Ancestors, and the Weakness of *Iberia* [Spain].[31]

After Fox's defence, most of the speeches focus directly on Walpole's corruption, but general political science is still the subject, even in the fierce rhetoric Johnson invents to represent Pitt's contribution. Johnson begins Pitt's speech with a topic he used again in the Preface to Shakespeare: 'It is an established Maxim, Sir, that as Time is the Test of Opinions, Falsehood grows every Day weaker, and Truth gains upon Mankind.' Truth will out, and 'those whose Purity of Intention, and Simplicity of Morals, exposed them to Credulity and implicite Confidence' will have revenge not merely in the removal but in the execution of Walpole. This is principled but extreme, and General Howe quickly recalls Johnson's readers to a more balanced, more 'scientific', and more practical view of government: 'The Business, Sir, of the Senate is to hold the Ballance between the Court and the People, and to preserve at once the Dignity of the Crown, and the Rights of the Nation; nor are we to suffer the Servants of the Emperor, to be torn from him by popular Fury, any more than the Liberties of the People to be sacrificed to the Ambition of a Minister.' Howe corrects Pitt's view of 'the rule of three', the fundamental paradigm of government to which Johnson perpetually recurred, despite his emphasis early in life on the power of the people and late in life on the power of the king. Nevertheless, Pitt's proof of Walpole's guilt by evidence of general testimony and the stability of truth returns in Heathcote's reprise of the Excise Crisis, which climaxes in a magnificent sentence: 'he who does not know that [Walpole's] Name is never mentioned but by his Vassals without Execrations, that his Counsels are considered by every honest Man as the Causes of all our Misery and all our Disgrace, and that the Time of his Degradation or Destruction would be added to those festal Days on which the Overthrow of arbitrary and republican Schemes are annually commemorated, must live in utter Ignorance of the State of his Country, and must have past his Days without Enquiry, and without Observation, either clouded by the Obscurity of a Village, or dazzled by the Glitter of a Court.' Inhabitants of neither locale are part of Johnson's intended audience. Here, as in almost all of his works, Johnson is speaking to the common reader. As Benjamin Hoover has it, 'the audience on which Johnson kept his eye most steadily was the whole reading public of England.' The fact that this was also becoming the voting public is essential in considering the politics of the *Debates*, and it justifies Robert Giddings's conclusion that in this work 'Johnson contributed generously and characteristically to the further development of [England's] political consciousness.' According to Giddings, this achievement allies Johnson, oddly, 'with John Wilkes, William Cobbett, William Hazlitt, and the other ornaments of [England's] radical tradition'.[32]

Pulteney delivers the final, most powerful condemnation of Walpole, dwelling mainly on his corruption and recapitulating much of what has gone before. This leaves only Walpole himself to speak. There is very little real argumentation in the speech, apart from a tired redaction of the contention that he is not, as some, including the *Gentleman's Magazine*, contemptuously styled him, the 'Prime Minister', but merely one among many members of the ministry. ('Prime Minister' did not become an official title until 1905.) This is an important argument, but it had already frequently appeared in the speeches of his defenders, and the main burden of Walpole's remarks is the pathetic representation of himself as a beaten and tired servant of his country. As others have shown, this part of the speech is entirely Johnson's invention. Other accounts, such as those in the *London Magazine* and Coxe's *Life of Walpole*, provide nothing even remotely parallel. Johnson's Walpole presents himself as an object of pity, but the whole effect is altered by the presence of the Gulliverian trappings, and what might have been moving is finally ludicrous: 'All that has been given me', complains Walelop, 'is a little House at a small Distance from this City, worth about seven Hundred Sprugs, which I obtained that I might enjoy the Quiet of Retirement, without remitting my Attendance on my Office.' Everyone knew, and besides Pulteney had just reminded them, of the grandeur in which Walpole lived and luxuriated both in his small suburban house and in the family estate at Houghton, so the denomination of the house's value in sprugs is particularly funny and particularly disruptive of the pathetic effect. The last bit of the speech also fails because of the admixture of Swiftian elements. Walpole refers to his Order of the Garter and in doing so brings in a decoration that seems Lilliputian even without a specially invented name: 'The little Ornament upon my Shoulder I had indeed forgot, but this surely cannot be mentioned as a Proof of Avarice; nor, though it may be looked on with Envy or Indignation in another Place, can it be supposed to raise any Resentment in this House, where many must be pleased to see those Honours which their Ancestors have worn restored again to the Clinabs.' If the little Lilliputian ornament does not do it, the last word certainly tips the passage over into satire, and what might be read without the Swiftian trappings as a sympathetic portrayal of Walpole becomes mockery. Johnson makes Walpole leave the stage as Walelop, Prime Minister of Lilliput, and chief actor among the illustrious Clinabs.[33]

Such partisan effects are rare, however, and when Johnson told Boswell that in the *Debates* he 'took care that the WHIG DOGS should not have the best of it', did not necessarily mean that he made them get the worst of it.[34] One has the impression reading through all of the *Debates* that things fall out pretty evenly. With few exceptions Johnson makes every speaker useful in the project of presenting 'such a Series of Argumentation as has comprised all Political Science'. When it is subjected to Johnson's method of examination, however, 'Political Science' rises into ethics, the most general and therefore the most important science of human nature. In this way, the debates are a departure from the more strictly partisan pamphlets, *Marmor Norfolciense* and the *Compleat Vindication*. Even more than *London* the *Debates* mix grandeur with wit and suggest Johnson's later, more scientific and philosophical achievements in the *Rambler* and the *Dictionary*. Like a great number of the *Ramblers* and like a striking number of the illustrative quotations in the *Dictionary*, many of the speeches in the *Debates* are exercises on standard ethical topics, like those that appear in the titles of Francis Bacon's *Essays Civill and Morall*. The topic of custom, for example, appears in a number of Johnson's speeches, and the various passages, placed side by side, comprise a Baconian essay:

> Customs, if they are not bad are not to be changed, because it is an Argument in favor of a Practice that the people have experienc'd it and approv'd it.

> Hardships, even when real, are alleviated by long Custom; we bear any present Uneasiness with less Regret, as we less remember the Time in which we were more happy; at least by long Acquaintance with any Grievance we gain this Advantage, that we know it in its whole Extent, that it cannot be aggravated by our Imagination, and that there is no room for suspecting that any Misery is yet behind more heavy than that which we have already born.

> Every Man must be convinced by his own Experience of the Difficulty with which long Habits are surmounted. . . . the Law is ineffectual which is to encounter with the Habits and Appetites of the whole Mass of the common People.[35]

Performance on set topics is supremely appropriate to senatorial speeches because such topics are the substance of classical rhetoric, which of course derives from the study of public oratory. By the eighteenth century, however, rhetoric, like other technologies of communication, was more in the service of the pen than the tongue. Johnson began writing a Gutenberg form of classical rhetoric in *Irene*, but the *Debates* represent his most extended effort at the performance of set topics in written speech. He continued the practice in a variety of ways throughout his professional life. The rhetorical system of organizing knowledge into topics of a durable and general kind, so naturally applied to the representation of oratory, was Johnson's way of putting the world together on the page. Moreover, in the *Debates*, as elsewhere, Johnson was drawn to certain topics more than others. The vanity of human wishes is often the underlying topic of speeches on a variety of specific issues, and many of them support Pulteney's assertion that 'unreasonable Hopes are the parents of Disappointment.' Pitt, for instance, uses the ministers as Johnson uses fallen heroes in *The Vanity of Human Wishes* to 'point a moral' when he says they 'ought to be set as Land-Marks to Posterity, to warn those who shall hereafter launch out on the Ocean of Affluence and Power, not to be too confident of a prosperous Gale.' The *Debates* are not always grim in their satire of human life. Folly is mirthful and almost innocent in Cornewall's paean to his native Herefordshire's cider, which 'shall not . . . now want a Panegyrist', and in the description of drinkers of the proposed low-alcoholic-content liquor as 'now ruthlessly condemned to disconsolate Sobriety'. Restoration comedy always in the back of his mind, Johnson here casts Cornwall as Boniface, the panegyrist of Lichfield ale in Farquhar's *Beaux' Stratagem.* Still, the darker side of human nature is predominant. In the same debate, for example, the Bishop of Oxford wisely exhorts us to remember, 'Whatever be the Reason, it may be every Day observed, that the greatest Pleasure of the Vicious is to vitiate others', and 'the natural Depravity of human Nature has always a Tendency from less to greater Evil.'[36]

As Johnson's favourite topics describe it, human nature is not always vicious, but it is incurably weak and fallible. A consciousness of this fallibility is of the highest political and ethical value. Shippen grants wisdom to the patriots who drew up the Act of Settlement when he says, 'They were far from imagining, that they were calling to the Throne a Race of Beings exalted above the Frailties of Humanity, or exempted by any peculiar Privileges from Error or from Ignorance.' Chesterfield likewise displays wisdom when he says, 'we are to consider Mankind, not as we wish them, but as we find them, frequently corrupt and always fallible', and 'no Degree of human Wisdom is exempt from Error.' The most successful, though perhaps the most predictable, defence of Walpole in the Commons debate on his removal is Lord Cornbury's appeal for leniency and due process, 'if it be remembered, that Humanity is a State of Imperfection, that the strictest Virtue sometimes declines from the Right, and that the most consummate Policy is by false Appearances, or accidental Inattention betrayed into Error'.[37]

Johnson's presentation of Walpole on the heels of such a reminder, even separated as it is by Pulteney's recapitulation of his sins, would have been pathetic and moving, if not for the Gulliverian trappings required by the ministry's suppression of Parliamentary reporting. The *Debates* forgive every political opinion by resolving it into the larger field of 'Political Science' and then seeing that as part of the overall study of human nature, in which, according to the Horatian maxim, nothing human can be foreign or odious to the understanding observer. But the writer and publisher cannot forgive the suppression of their trade; condemnation is inscribed in the format forced on the work. Time alone could repeal their implicit decree, but time moved swiftly in this case. Not long after Johnson's death, first Stockdale, his editor, and then Cobbett, the Parliamentary historian, stripped away the Gulliverian trappings of the *Debates* and reprinted them as factual reports. In doing so they gave Johnson's *Debates* the dignified air of official history, but they obscured the history of the text. The editors reduced the *Debates* to information not only by using historical names but also by applying more uniform and business-like typography (standardized capitalization and italics, for example). No matter that every word of the speeches was composed not by the MP to whom it is attributed but by Samuel Johnson. Decontextualized, typographically flattened, and reprinted in an official series, Johnson's characteristically satirical yet profound 'science' is transformed into the official record. This cultural conversion is not unlike the process undergone by Johnson himself. Literary history has translated him out of his real circumstances as a brilliant but struggling writer adapting his talents to the London publishing scene and memorialized him as the archetypal Englishman of his day and the eponymous lord of a whole cultural period. The modern work of Johnsonian biography is to discover the historical Johnson, just as a modern editor would wish to discover the original text of the *Debates in the Senate of Magna Lilliput.*

5

Early Biographical Writings

He is now launched into the world, and is to subsist henceforward by his own powers. The transition from the protection of others to our own conduct is a very awful point of human existence.

Johnson to John Taylor, 13 April 1775

Over two years intervened between the publication of his advertisement for the *Gentleman's Magazine*'s *Debates in the Senate of Magna Lilliput* and the beginning of Johnson's stint writing them. From the middle of 1738 to spring 1739 Johnson was working steadily for Cave in other capacities. In addition to editing contributions, like William Guthrie's versions of the *Debates*, he excerpted or condensed books for *Magazine* readers; decided which poems to print; judged contests; answered correspondents; and wrote advertisements. One of the works that he advertised and condensed was a translation by other members of Cave's staff of Jean Baptiste Du Halde's *Description de la Chine* (1735). First promised to the English public in 1735, the work finally appeared in two volumes in 1740. Johnson must have read, on and off, in Du Halde for years, thereby increasing a stock of knowledge about Eastern, non-European culture that he had begun to build up while researching *Irene*.

Another work abridged by Johnson was a recently published volume of four sermons by Joseph Trapp, 'On the Nature, Folly, Sin and Danger of being righteous over-much'. In the columns of the *Gentleman's Magazine* Trapp's arguments against religious zealots, particularly early Methodists like William Law, were printed beside letters and statements by the Methodists themselves to make a journalistic forum. However, Trapp and his publisher objected to the unauthorized republications of the abridged sermons and threatened to sue Cave for their lost profit. Before the proceedings went very far, Johnson prepared a sort of legal brief for Cave in the form of thirty-one 'Considerations'. They show Johnson involved once more in developing the social construction of authorship and shaping the nature of publication. Johnson's 'Considerations' reaffirm an author's right to own and transfer literary property. But they also assert the right of readers or purchasers to treat the book in any way they see fit. Johnson includes abridgement and translation among the permissible responses of a reader to his book, along with censure, confutation, and examination. He sees abridgement in particular as contributing to the public welfare:

> 19. The design of an abridgement is, to benefit mankind by facilitating the attainment of knowledge, and by contracting arguments, relations, or descriptions, into a narrow compass; to convey instruction in the easiest method, without fatiguing the attention, burdening the memory, or impairing the health of the student.
> 20. By this method the original author becomes, perhaps, of less value, and the proprietor's profits are diminished; but these inconveniences give way to the advantage received by mankind from the easier propagation of knowledge; for as an incorrect book is lawfully criticised, and false assertions justly confuted, because it is more the interest of mankind that error should be detected and truth discovered, than that the proprietors of a particular book should enjoy their profits undiminished; so a tedious volume may no less lawfully be abridged, because it is better that the proprietors should suffer some damage, than that the acquisition of knowledge should be obstructed with unnecessary difficulties, and the valuable hours of thousands thrown away.[1]

The *Gentleman's Magazine* as a whole and a great many of the projects that Johnson worked on throughout his career depended upon such a *laissez-faire* approach to publication. With modern standards for 'permission to publish' in place, for instance, Johnson's *Dictionary*, with its 116,000 citations, may never have been produced. Johnson genuinely believed his ethical justification in 'Consideration' twenty: the dissemination rather than the discovery of knowledge was his life's work, with full Christian emphasis on the two words 'life' and 'work', but it was also his business, and he had an interest in maintaining the legal conditions that supported it. His position remained about the same throughout his life, and he participated in planning the plea in the House of Lords in 1774 against perpetual copyright, because, as he wrote to William Strahan, 'the authour must recede from so much of his claim, as shall be deemed injurious or inconvenient to Society.'[2]

Also in 1739 Johnson fought against government encroachment on the publishing industry in *A Compleat Vindication of the Licensers of the Stage*. Although Cave was as opposed as Johnson to restrictions on publication, he was not the publisher of this fiercely anti-government piece, nor did he publish the even more virulent *Marmor Norfolciense*.[3] The political sentiments Johnson expresses in both pieces may have been too radical for Cave, who justly feared government censure and, as a publisher, ran greater risks than Johnson did as a mere writer. In addition both pamphlets direct satire against the medium of print itself, and this too may have unsettled Cave. In each pamphlet Johnson assumes the character of a speaker whom he obviously expects his audience to reject along with most of his opinions. Both speakers tend, however, to be representative of the medium of print because, as Swift conclusively showed, the anonymity of print enables the creation of unreliable, invisible speakers. Works that intend these speakers to be rejected also weaken confidence in the medium that fosters them, and such confidence was the backbone of Cave's business.

It is not clear that these works precipitated it, but a rift between Johnson and Cave occurred about the time of their publication. From about August 1739 to February 1740 Johnson was out of London, spending part of the time in Lichfield and another part in Ashbourne. Johnson's wife remained in London during this time, and it appears that the pair were experiencing marital difficulties of some kind. This was just after the period of Johnson's closest association with the poet and polemicist Richard Savage, who left London for good in July 1739 in a state of hostility and humiliation and took up residence in less expensive Wales. Johnson's political hostility, his marital problems, and his break with Cave may have been related to his celebrated friendship with Savage. Johnson was obviously taken with Savage; later in life he spoke to Hawkins, Reynolds, and others of their late-night rambles around St James or Grosvenor Square, 'reforming the world, dethroning princes, establishing new forms of government, and giving laws to the several states of Europe, till fatigued at length with their legislative office, they began to feel the want of refreshment; but could not muster up more than four pence halfpenny.' His relationship with Savage excited Johnson in a way that was not conducive to domestic or occupational tranquillity. From May 1739 to June 1740, Johnson made no formal contributions to the *Gentleman's Magazine*. He may have written a brief letter from Oxford, dated 19 November 1739, complimenting Mr Urban on his poetry section in the October issue. Since a complaint about the magazine's poetry had been part of Johnson's first address to Cave, this letter, if it is by Johnson, was probably meant to be a conciliatory and disarming gesture by a prodigal son.[4]

On 31 January 1740 Johnson definitely wrote to his wife and very obviously sought a reconciliation with her. He wrote from Lichfield where he had just participated in the sale of his birthplace and received good news about the possible production of his unsold literary property, *Irene*. He was about to receive twenty pounds for his share of the house and expected at least fifty pounds for his play. Alarmed by the news that Elizabeth had seriously injured her leg and expansive in his new-found fortune, Johnson urged his wife to hire the best possible surgeon and not to deny herself 'any thing that may make confinement less melancholy'. He went on,

> You have already suffered more than I can bear to reflect upon, and I hope more than either of us shall suffer again. One part at least I have often flatterd myself we shall avoid for the future our troubles will surely never

separate us more.... I still promise myself many happy years from your tenderness and affection, which I sometimes hope our misfortunes have not yet deprived me of.... Of the time which I have spent from thee ... my heart will be at ease on Monday to give Thee a particular account, especially if a Letter should inform me that thy Leg is better, for I hope You do not think so unkindly of me as to imagine that I can be at rest while I believe my dear Tetty in pain.

Be assured, my dear Girl, that I have seen nobody in these rambles upon which I have been forced, that has not contribute[d] to confirm my esteem and affection for thee, though that esteem and affection only contributed to increase my unhappiness when I reflected that the most amiable woman in the world was exposed by my means to miseries which I could not relieve. I am, My charming Love, Yours,

SAM. JOHNSON

Johnson's otherwise unexampled use of 'thee' and other expressions of affection in the letter suggest that he was trying to re-establish an intimacy that had been damaged by separation and by whatever 'troubles' led to it. The last paragraph attempts to extinguish jealousy, which was aroused by reports of Johnson's gallantry with the Lichfield ladies, especially Molly Aston, in a tête-à-tête with whom Johnson told Boswell he experienced 'measureless delight'. Although many of her reports have been discredited, perhaps Anna Seward should be believed in saying that 'Johnson was always fancying himself in love with some princess or other.'[5] The poet-courtier was an early role for Johnson, and his return to Walmesley's palace and the gracious homes of Stourbridge revived that spirit.

However the Johnsons' troubles may have ramified in emotional directions, their immediate source was financial. Johnson left London in August 1739 initially to seek the headmastership of Appleby School. In a way he was following in Savage's footsteps by leaving London for a less expensive life. He was also, of course, returning to an earlier scheme of life, in which he had failed at Edial and the many schools where he taught briefly or had his applications for posts rejected. In his attempt to get the Appleby post Johnson had support from the influential Lord Gower, through the intercession of Alexander Pope. Gower wrote to a friend of Swift's in an effort to secure the Dean's help in allowing Johnson to challenge for a Dublin MA, which might have been translated by Oxford or Cambridge into the degree required for the Appleby post. Gower's description of Johnson shows that all was not well behind the scenes at Cave's St John's Gate offices: 'he is not afraid of the strictest examination, though he is of so long a journey; and will venture it, if the Dean thinks it necessary; choosing rather to die upon the road, *than be starved to death in translating for booksellers*; which has been his only subsistence for some time past.'[6] Gower's letter failed to produce anything for Johnson except lifelong enmity to Swift. The Appleby post went to a relation of the founders, as the governance of the school suggested it should, and Johnson rambled in the Midlands until he sold his birthplace, made up with his injured wife, and returned permanently to London and a life of writing.

There is evidence that Johnson's reluctance to judge Cave's poetry contest 'on the Divine Attributes' precipitated their rift, but the work of translation was what sent him over the brink.[7] In 1738 he was at work on *A Commentary on Mr Pope's Principles of Morality or Essay on Man by Mons. Crousaz*. He wrote as many as forty-eight octavo pages of the work in a sitting, but it was 1739 before he finished translating the volume of about 350 pages containing introductory and concluding letters, Crousaz's commentary, and du Resnel's translation of Pope's *Essay on Man* into French verse, with his preface.[8] Johnson added some notes to the translation, and the work was meant to accompany Elizabeth Carter's version of Crousaz's *Examen de l'Essai du M. Pope sur l'homme*, but, as with the Sarpi project, a competitor appeared on the scene. In this case, Carter's translation was rushed into production, while Johnson's was withheld. Although he finished the job in 1739 and production began, the book was withdrawn and not reissued until 1742.

Like the Sarpi, the Crousaz translation failed to advance Johnson's career, but it too was well suited to his intellectual interests. Crousaz's *Commentaire* takes du Resnel's French translation of Pope's *Essay* and responds to it as an ethical and philosophical statement. Crousaz exposes the Leibnitzian system in Pope's poem and condemns the work as arrogant and impious because it implies that human beings are subject to an overarching fatality and therefore incapable of moral action. In addition, Crousaz finds much of Pope's language either equivocal, cant, or nonsensical. For example, du Resnel's Pope says, 'Homme! pour être heureux tu n'as que un seul moyen; / C'est de vivre content des dons de la nature', and Crousaz comments, in Johnson's translation,

> In this Place Mr *Pope* seems to express a great deal in a few Words, but upon Reflection, we learn nothing from him. He tells us that to be *happy* we must be *content*; this is amusing us with a Repetition of Words that have the same Meaning, for it might be said, with equal Truth, that to be *content* a Man must be *happy*. But Mr *Pope* will shew us the Way to this Happiness and Content. Every Man will attain to them, that shall rest satisfied with the Gifts that *Nature* has bestowed, without desiring any thing beyond them. But who is this *Nature* to whom such Deference is to be paid, and who is to set Limits to our Wishes? Is it the Author of our Existence? The Precept is then indisputable, but very extensive, and ought to be very accurately explained.

There are parallels to Crousaz's remarks in many places in Johnson's writings, including chapter 22 of *Rasselas*, 'The happiness of a life led according to nature'. In his life of Pope, Johnson explicitly acknowledges the justice of Crousaz's attack. Moreover, he reflects Crousaz's opinion when he says that Pope's '*Essay* affords an egregious instance of the predominance of genius, the dazzling splendour of imagery, and the seductive powers of eloquence. Never were penury of knowledge and vulgarity of sentiment so happily disguised. The reader feels his mind full, though he learns nothing.'[9]

Johnson found truths in Crousaz which he expressed much as he would later in his own original essays. For example, he might have been tuning up for one of his *Rambler* pieces when he wrote, 'Men, instead of applying themselves with Ardour and Assiduity to solid Knowledge, to the Attainment of just Notions, to a Life of Virtue, and to the Duties which may procure the Approbation of God, trifle away their Lives in the poor Amusement of forming a perpetual Succession of Schemes, uncertain in their own Nature, and which, tho' they should not be disappointed, would yet be far from bringing the satisfaction that is expected from them.' Johnson's translation of Crousaz's warnings about Leibnitzian impiety foreshadow his later attack on Soame Jenyns's optimistic system: 'Nothing can be more impious than to imagine that God is the Cause of Men's Vices, for the sake of making them subservient to good Ends, which would be more effectually produced by Virtue.' Like Crousaz, Johnson preferred empirical explanations of human behaviour and therefore found the notion of the ruling passion morally dangerous. The translator was in agreement with his author when he wrote, 'it is not proper to dwell too long on the resistless Power, and despotick Authority of this Tyrant of the Soul, lest the Reader should, as it is very natural, take the present Inclination however destructive to Society or himself, for the *Ruling Passion,* and forbear to struggle when he despairs to conquer.'[10]

Furthermore, the intellectual tradition in which Crousaz places himself, in opposition to Pope, is one that Johnson found highly congenial. The whole book begins with an epigraph taken from Lactantius's *De falsa sapientia* concerning self-knowledge and human ignorance. Although this may be the only direct quotation of Lactantius in any Johnsonian work, his writings are full of Lactantian sentiments, and he frequently quotes writers who are themselves paraphrasing or redacting parts of *De falsa sapientia.* His own poem Γνῶθι Σεαυτόν ('Know Thyself') and his projected Hymn to Ignorance, are evidence of his own attempts to versify Lactantius's theme. In addition to Lactantius, Crousaz claims Locke as an intellectual parent. This connection is also highly congenial to Johnson, whose works always display an affinity with Locke's way of thinking and nothing but hostility to Leibnitzian or Spinozan schemes that go beyond empirical findings to assume a god-like perspective on the universe.

Nevertheless, Johnson frequently criticizes Crousaz's reliance on du Resnel's translation. At times, he grows fervent in defence of his countryman. For instance, when Crousaz prefers du Resnel's 'soften'd' version of Pope's 'harsh' opening, Johnson comments, 'The Address of one is the Exclamation of a Freeman, that of the other the Murmur of a Slave. – It is unnecessary here to remind the Reader of *Roscommon*'s Observation upon the *English* Poetry compared with the *French,* – – *One Sterling Line / Drawn to French Wire will thro' whole Pages shine.* This Translator cannot but recall it to his Memory, by giving us 8 lines of 12 or 13 Syllables for 2 lines of 10.' Johnson does not maintain this ferocity throughout; there is even a moment when he praises the French translation for being superior to the English original; but he is generally hostile to du Resnel. Even while objecting to Crousaz's reliance on the inferior and inaccurate French version, however, Johnson rarely argues with his philosophical position. For example, when Crousaz complains about Pope's vague use of the word 'Nature', Johnson writes in his footnote, 'Mr Pope, in the Original, has not made use of the Word *Nature* in the Passage here referr'd to; his Expression being only *Lo! the poor* Indian, *whose untutor'd Mind.* But he has, indeed, us'd the Word a few Lines after, *Yet simple Nature to his Hope has given*, &c. to which, perhaps, all that Mr *Crousaz* has written may be apply'd with Propriety.' Johnson will occasionally chastise Crousaz for a 'Disposition to cavil', and he finds him sometimes 'so watchful against Impiety, that he lets Nonsense pass without Censure.'[11] He is sometimes irritated by Crousaz, but he is usually dismissive of du Resnel.

In his notes Johnson becomes increasingly passive and silent as he proceeds through the translation. He barely rouses himself at all in his version of du Resnel's preface, which ends the volume. Once, however, he comes to life to point out that 'the Abbé, in this Comparison, whether by Design or not, ascribes to the Italians, perhaps the highest Perfection of Writing; such Thoughts as are at once new and easy, which, tho' the Reader confesses that they never occured to him before, he yet imagines must have cost but little labour.' Du Resnel intended to denigrate such thoughts by saying, 'the Ideas of the Italian have indeed the Grace of Novelty, but then they generally appear such as might have been easily struck out.' This remark obviously tripped an alarm in Johnson's mind and required a response. That excellence can be defined as the art of combining the new and the familiar was already a critical principle for Johnson twenty-seven years before he wrote that 'Shakespeare approximates the remote, and familiarizes the wonderful' and longer before he praised the *Rape of Lock* for exhibiting the 'two most engaging powers of an author: new things are made familiar, and familiar things are made new.' But this little outburst is isolated in the later parts of the work, and Johnson's critical intelligence was inactive or repressed as he laboured to finish the job. It was this tedious and unprofitable work that drove Johnson to try for the teaching post at Appleby and led him to tell Gower he preferred 'rather to die upon the road, *than be starved to death in translating for booksellers*'.[12]

When he returned to London in 1740, however, Johnson was confirmed in his choice of life. About this time, he took up residence in the Strand and never again lived far from the central publishing district of the City. He avoided the maddening work of translating, and he gradually assumed a less rebellious, more positive political role in his writing. His Parliamentary *Debates* contribute to the establishment of a mainstream, 'scientific' political outlook, and in his other works Johnson embraces what might be called a more mature position, recurring to fundamentals in his literary constructions and suggesting the establishment of general truths and universal ethical standards. His move in the direction of a more constructive literature is best exemplified in his growing attention at this time to biography.

Beginning in 1738, before his sojourn away from London, Johnson wrote nine biographies for the *Gentleman's Magazine* and contributed something to the biographical articles in Robert James's *Medicinal Dictionary* (1743–5). His biographical writing in this period culminated in the publication of *The Life of Richard Savage* in 1744, his most famous and most appreciated biography. These works fall below modern standards for exhaustive research or historical accuracy in biography. Johnson's life as a writer for hire fostered a willingness to rely on existing printed accounts of his subjects and such oral or manuscript evidence as presented itself to him. Some of the errors in his *Life of Savage*, for example, could have been avoided through consultation with his old friend Elizabeth Carter or the equally accessible Aaron Hill, if Johnson had been more systematic in his research. But Johnson found it easier to get his information from an earlier, flawed biography of Savage and various publications in the *Gentleman's Magazine*. As he once told Boswell when evading the young biographer's attempt to arrange an unsolicited interview with the Earl of Marchmont: 'If it rained knowledge I'd hold out my hand; but I would not give myself the trouble to go in quest of it.'[13] Against the cut-and-paste background, however, Johnson wrote some of the most acute sentences in the history of biography. As a craftsman in the age of print Johnson found his materials and published his works primarily in the dominant medium; his restriction to that medium permitted him to write with the uninterrupted speed and intensity that his profession and his personality demanded. But Johnson had a supreme ability to write up his material. Moreover, he could add from his own stock of observations on life so as to bring the subject, in Bacon's phrase, 'home to men's business and bosoms'.

Although he never changed his methods of writing, the genre of biography was the vehicle Johnson used to make a transition from the political writer and journalist of the late 1730s to the philosopher of the *Dictionary* years. For this reason, as Thomas Kaminski says, 'The short lives that Johnson contributed to the *Gentleman's Magazine* form one of the most obvious links between his early career and his later glorification as "the great Cham of literature".'[14]

Johnson's lives of Paolo Sarpi (1738), Admiral Blake (1740), and Sir Francis Drake (1740) are politically tendentious, partly because of their publishing circumstances. The first is implicitly a polemic against Roman Catholicism and colonialism in general because those are the politics for which Sarpi and his recent translator, le Courayer, stood in England in 1738. Furthermore, anti-Catholic sentiment was very nearly anti-Spanish sentiment, which in turn was anti-ministry sentiment because one of the main complaints against Walpole was his weak management of the war with Spain. The implicit politics of the lives of Drake and Blake are even more obvious. Both biographies celebrate English heroes who handled the Spanish as the British should, and whose presence before the public was a reminder of contemporary Britain's disgrace. Lest anyone miss the point, the editors of the *Gentleman's Magazine* provide prefatory paragraphs drawing the contrast between Britain's present and past postures toward Spain. Within the framework provided, certain episodes in the military lives are particularly pointed. For example, Johnson relates a story about Blake that shows 'the Respect with which he obliged all Foreigners to treat his Countrymen'. Some British sailors insulted the people of Malaga by ridiculing their religious practices and were beaten at the behest of a priest. When Blake found out, he demanded that the local political leader bring the priest before him, declaring that '*if the priest were not sent within 3 Hours, he would burn the Town.*' When the priest explained the incident, '*Blake* bravely and rationally answered, that if he had complained to him, he would have punished [the sailors] severely, for he would not have his Men affront the established Religion of any Place; but that he was angry that the *Spaniards* should assume that Power, for he would have all the World know, *that an* Englishman *was only to be punished by an* Englishman.'[15]

Such patriotism modulates at times into more general positions, such as those Johnson develops in his Parliamentary *Debates.* On his voyages, for example, Sir Francis Drake is kind to the natives, 'it being with him an established Maxim, to endeavour to secure in every Country a kind reception to such *Englishmen* as might come after him, by treating the Inhabitants with Kindness and Generosity; a Conduct at once just and politick.' The Spanish, on the other hand, are cruel: 'under the show of Traffick, [they] by degrees established themselves, claimed a Superiority over the original Inhabitants, and harrassed them with such Cruelty, that they obliged them either to fly to the Woods and Mountains, and perish with Hunger, or to take Arms against their Oppressors, and under the Insuperable Disadvantages with which they contended, to die almost without a Battle in defence of their natural Rights, and antient Possessions.'[16]

The Lockean language of 'natural rights' was gradually at this time coming into the mainstream of English political thought, transforming it into the 'liberal tradition' that dominated English politics in the nineteenth century. The same transitional political philosophy appears in Johnson's many speeches against colonization in the *Debates* and again in the *Life of Savage* where he praises 'On Public Spirit' because '*Savage* has not forgotten . . . to censure those Crimes which have been generally committed by the Discoverers of new Regions, and to expose the enormous Wickedness of making War upon barbarous Nations because they cannot resist, and of invading Countries because they are fruitful; of extending Navigation only to propagate Vice, and of visiting distant Lands only to lay them waste. He has asserted the natural Equality of Mankind, and endeavoured to suppress that Pride which inclines Men to imagine that Right is the Consequence of Power.'[17] Such passages display Johnson as the radical opposition patriot that he was early in life, but they also confirm his association with a line of learned writers, running in England from More to Bacon to Locke, who opposed colonial aggression on humanitarian and philosophical grounds.

Even in his early military lives Johnson could get beyond contemporary politics and reflect on more general themes. In 'Drake', for instance, he usually follows a single printed source, even repeating the praises of *la vie sauvage*, but in one instance he wanders from his track to make a philosophical remark: 'It is, perhaps, a just observation, that, with regard to outward Circumstances, Happiness and Misery are very equally diffused thro' all States of human Life. In civilized Countries where regular Policies have secured the Necessaries of Life, Ambition, Avarice, and Luxury, find the Mind at Leisure for their Reception. . . . Among Savage Nations, imaginary Wants find, indeed, no place, but their Strength is exhausted by necessary Toils. . . . But for such Reflections as these [Drake and his crew] had no Time.' Again finding more time for reflection than his subjects, Johnson waxes philosophical in response to his source's general comment on the fact that Drake's diligence as an underling was rewarded with a grand bequest: 'If it were not improper to dwell longer on an Incident, at the first View so inconsiderable, it might be Added, That it deserves the Reflection of those, who, when they are engaged in Affairs not adequate to their Abilities, pass them over with a contemptuous Neglect, and while they amuse themselves with chimerical Schemes, and plans of future Undertakings, suffer every Opportunity of smaller Advantage to slip away as unworthy their Regard. They may learn from the Example of Drake, that Diligence in Employments of less consequence is the successful Introduction to greater Enterprizes.'[18]

Apart from 'Drake' and 'Blake', most of Johnson's early and nearly all of his later lives are about men whose accomplishments are learned or literary. Many are about men who pursued what the eighteenth century still called 'the professions of the gown': divinity, medicine, and law. The majority are about writers. Johnson's choice of biographical subjects leads naturally, as Paul Fussell has shown, to a good deal of concealed autobiography. Fussell finds, for example, that Johnson was speaking equally about himself and his subject in his 'Life of Dr Herman Boerhaave, late Professor of Physick in the University of Leyden in Holland' (1739), but the self that Johnson identifies in Boerhaave is exalted and perfected. Fussell brings this to light in his treatment of the 'physical description', a regular feature of much Johnsonian biography. Johnson writes, 'He was tall, and remarkable for extraordinary Strength. There was in his Air and Motion something rough and artless, but so majestick and great at the same time, that no Man ever looked upon him without Veneration, and a kind of tacit submission to the Superiority of his Genius.' In a parallel passage, Boswell describes his hero's frame as 'majestic' and 'robust', but not all Johnson's physical peculiarities and deformities can be described as 'rough and artless'. In fact, Boswell's concluding 'physical description' descends to irredeemably ugly deformities before the end of the first sentence: 'His figure was large and well formed, and his countenance of the cast of an ancient statue; yet his appearance was rendered strange and somewhat uncouth, by convulsive cramps, by the scars of that distemper which it was once imagined the royal touch could cure, and by a slovenly mode of dress. . . . So morbid was his temperament that he never knew the natural joy of a free and vigorous use of his limbs: when he walked it was like the struggling gait of one in fetters.' Boswell concludes his obligatory paragraph with the exclamation, 'That with his constitution and habits of life he should have lived seventy-five years, is a proof that an inherent *vivida vis* is a powerful preservative of the human frame.'[19]

If Johnson made a tacit comparison between himself and Boerhaave, it was to his cost. In fact, Johnson's 'Life of Boerhaave' may be overstated and hortatory in ethical terms because Johnson was admonishing himself to live up to an appropriate model. This is plausible; there is a streak of autobiography in much of Johnson's writing, but the exhortations in 'Boerhaave' may also derive simply from Johnson's close adherence to his sole source for the biography, a Latin funeral oration on Boerhaave by Albert Schultens.[20] It is dangerous to assume that any particular sentiments expressed here or in any of his early biographies are Johnson's own. Nevertheless, his choice of biographical subjects is telling, and there are emphases in these early lives that, if not originally Johnson's, seem to be his by adoption. For example, in writing about Boerhaave Johnson has occasion to express a conviction that he always held with respect to himself: 'It is, I believe, a very just Observation, that Men's Ambition is generally proportioned to their Capacity. Providence seldom sends any into the World with an Inclination to attempt great Things, who have not Abilities likewise to perform them.' Likewise, though he was following his source in doing so, Johnson sincerely endorsed the scholarly heroism of Boerhaave, who 'continued his search after Knowledge, and determined that Prosperity, if ever he was to enjoy it, should be the consequence, not of mean Art, or disingenuous Solicitations, but of real Merit, and solid Learning.' Some of Johnson's lifelong feelings about patronage seem to well up behind the phrase 'disingenuous Solicitations'. Johnson again writes in happy agreement with Schultens when he describes Boerhaave's 'Oration upon the Subject of *attaining to Certainty in natural Philosophy*; in which he declares, in the strongest Terms, in favour of Experimental Knowledge, and reflects with just severity upon those arrogant Philosophers, who are too easily disgusted with the slow Methods of obtaining true Notions by frequent Experiments, and who, possess with too high an Opinion of their own Abilities, rather chuse to consult their own Imaginations, than enquire into Nature, and are better pleased with the charming Amusement of forming Hypotheses, than the toilsome Drudgery of making Observations.' Johnson may have recalled this passage when he defined 'lexicographer' in his *Dictionary* as 'a harmless drudge', and there may be a philosophical position as well as humour in the definition. In his *Dictionary* and in his thinking generally Johnson was an empiricist, and it is convenient and correct to think of Johnson's empiricism as Lockean, but Locke himself was participating in and drawing upon a scientific tradition growing up around him, to which Johnson also had direct access. Johnson owned several of Boerhaave's books and consulted him both for practical medical advice and in his own amateur chemical experiments. In a less obvious but fundamental way, Boerhaave also influenced Johnson's *Dictionary* and his other major works.[21]

In *Rambler* 114 Johnson refers to 'the learned, the judicious, the pious Boerhaave', and he was happy to exalt him in his biography although he found the exaltation ready-made. Boerhaave's gloriously argued and careful distinction of body and soul, complete with refutations of Hobbes, Spinoza, and Epicurus, was truly heroic to Johnson who later produced his own anti-materialist tract in the penultimate chapter of *Rasselas*. Schultens's depiction of Boerhaave as a Christian stoic hero also appealed to Johnson: Boerhaave's concentration on his studies as he lay paralysed by disease for months on end 'is perhaps an Instance of Fortitude and steady Composure of Mind, which would have been forever the Boast of the Stoick Schools, and increased the reputation of *Seneca* or *Cato*. The Patience of *Boerhaave*, as it was more rational, was more lasting than theirs; it was that *Patientia Christiana* which *Lipsius*, the great Master of the Stoical Philosophy, begged of God in his last Hours; it was founded on Religion, not Vanity, not on vain Reasonings, but on Confidence in God.' Although derision of classical Stoicism was an eighteenth-century literary commonplace to which Johnson subscribed, he frankly admired devoted Christian stoics and rationalists. Grotius is the best example, but in his learning and in his learned piety Boerhaave too was an important model for Johnson. He therefore did not hesitate to translate with full emphasis the conventional concluding exhortation that he found in Schultens: 'So far was this Man from being made impious by Philosophy, or vain by Knowledge, or by Virtue, that he ascribed all his Abilities to the Bounty, and all his Goodness to the Grace of God. May his Example extend its Influence to his Admirers and Followers! May those who study his Writings imitate his Life, and those who endeavour after his Knowledge aspire likewise to his Piety!'[22]

As in his 'Boerhaave', in his 'Sydenham' and his 'Confucius' Johnson praised Christian stoics. Following Du Halde, Johnson describes Confucius' treatise the *Immutable Medium* as 'correspondent to the Μέτρον ἄριστον of *Cleobulus*, and to the common Maxim, *Virtus consistit in Medio*.' Like an Enlightenment Christian, Confucius 'endeavours to shew, that the sovereign Good consists in a Conformity of all our Actions with right Reason.'[23] Johnson simply accepted such Eurocentric treatment of Asians and was no more capable of representing an Eastern thinker accurately than contemporary potters were of putting genuinely Chinese faces on the newly adopted medium of china dishware. Like his fellow craftsmen, Johnson puts a European face on the Chinese subject, the Christian stoic face of Boerhaave.

In writing the biography of Sydenham Johnson again imposes upon a little-known life the categories he found attractive and ready-made in his work on Boerhaave. Like Boerhaave, Sydenham must be a model for students, so Johnson undertakes to refute the vulgar opinion that he achieved his eminence in medicine by the power of his natural gifts, without study and experimentation. The purpose of the 'Life of Sydenham' is 'that those who shall hereafter assume the important province of super-intending the health of others, may learn from this great master of the art, that the only means of arriving at eminence and success are labour and study.' Although the biography is 'polemical' and 'unreliable', as Thomas Kaminski has pointed out, 'Sydenham' shows Johnson launching out on his own in a characteristic way: he uses topics and categories discovered earlier in other writings (like Schultens's *Oratio*) to discuss fresh material. Over years and years of such work Johnson refined and revamped his favourite topics so that they really became his own, largely through a process of abstraction and generalization. In the polemics concerning Sydenham's education Johnson is only part way to such refinement, but his handling of the death of Sydenham suggests the sophistication of his later work. He begins with a general reflection, which produces narrative suspense and expands the gloom of death: 'It is a melancholy reflection, that they who have obtained the highest reputation, by preserving or restoring the health of others, have often been hurried away before the natural decline of life, or have passed many of their years under the torments of those distempers, which they propose to relieve. In this number was SYDENHAM, whose health began to fail in the fifty second year of his age, by the frequent attacks of the gout.' Sydenham's death illustrates the wise saying with which Johnson prefaces it, much as the death of Pope in Johnson's longest biography illustrates another wise saying: 'The death of great men is not always proportioned to the lustre of their lives. Hannibal, says Juvenal, did not perish by a javelin or a sword; the slaughters of Cannae were revenged by a ring. The death of Pope was imputed by some of his friends to a silver saucepan, in which it was his delight to heat potted lampreys.'[24] The tone of the later work is more confident, and Johnson displays in it a witty awareness that he is entering a literary trope, but the rhetorical pattern is the same in both pieces.

Pulling together two biographical pieces that he did for the *Gentleman's Magazine* in 1741 and 1742 respectively, Johnson published as a pamphlet in 1744 *An Account of the Life of John Philip Barretier, Who was Master of Five Languages at the Age of Nine YEARS*. Because Baratier (Johnson used an alternative spelling) was a prodigy of learning who died at the age of nineteen, the life lends itself directly and completely to elements of biography that Johnson was concentrating on in all his lives at this time. Johnson's sources for the first biography were the letters of the subject's father to acquaintances in England, including Elizabeth Carter's father. In his later revisions he used an ancillary account from the father, but the rigours of primary research did not interfere with Johnson's intention to write an exemplary student's life: 'He was always gay, lively, and facetious, a Temper which contributed much to recommend his Learning, and of which some Students much superior in Age would consult their Ease, their Reputation and their Interest by copying from him.' For the edification of students Johnson again emphasizes the value of consulting existing scholarship and the unlikelihood of achieving much by unassisted genius. The episode from which Johnson draws this lesson in the *biography* is Baratier's attempt to develop a method for ascertaining longitude at sea – a sort of philosopher's stone long sought after by inventors in the eighteenth century and frequently the subject of popular prize competitions. Baratier developed his theory within months of taking up the study of geography. The Royal Society recommended his 'Scheme' to the Queen, 'But it was soon found, that for want of Books, he had imagined himself the Inventor of Methods already in common Use, and that he proposed no Means of discovering the Longitude, but such as had been already tried and found insufficient.'[25] Fifteen years later, Johnson created the same kind of sudden, satirical failure in his description of the aeronautical projector who hopes to fly out of the prison of the Happy Valley in *Rasselas*.

In *Barretier* appear other Johnsonian topics, such as the young teacher's understandable dislike for the 'petulance' of students, the uncertainty and unfairness of patronage, and the dangerous infatuation of early success. Another feature of the biography is its documentary inclusion of Baratier's Latin outline of a treatise on '*Egyptian* Antiquities'. The material shows Johnson's continuing interest in Eastern culture, but the technique suggests a connection between his early short biographies and his triumph at the end of this period, the *Life of Savage* (1744). Bibliographies of the subject's writings were a standard feature of biographies at this time, and a generous padding of citation was also common.[26] Both are rare in Johnson's early biographies, however, except for the one instance in *Barretier* and many, many instances in *Savage*, which ushers in a period of nearly antiquarian scholarly activity in Johnson's intellectual life. The archival activity of collection exhibited in Johnson's *Life of Savage* was his regular work for the years in which he worked on the *Catalogue of the Harleian Library* (from 1743 to 1744).

Antiquarian and anthological activity indexes *Savage* to a specific period of Johnson's career, but a number of other features link the new work with all the earlier lives. The moral of the story is very much like the encouragements to hard work central to the biographies of Sydenham and Baratier: 'nothing will supply the Want of Prudence, and . . . Negligence and Irregularity, long continued, will make Knowledge useless, Wit ridiculous, and Genius contemptible.' Unlike Sydenham, Boerhaave, and Baratier, Richard Savage fails to study hard and make good use of his natural gifts, but like them and so many of Johnson's other heroes, he is a gifted student. He is also, in his way, the kind of rational, Christian stoic that Johnson seemed to find at the heart of all good men, although in this respect too Savage is a failed hero. For instance, from Newgate prison Savage writes to one of his friends in London:

I enjoy myself with much more Tranquility than I have known for upwards of a twelvemonth past; having a Room entirely to myself, and persuing the

Amusement of my poetical Studies, uninterrupted and agreeable to my Mind. I thank the Almighty, I am now all collected in myself; and tho' my Person is in Confinement, my Mind can expatiate on ample and useful Subjects, with all the Freedom imaginable. I am now more conversant with the Nine than ever; and if, instead of a *Newgate* Bird, I may be allowed to be a Bird of the Muses, I assure you, Sir, I sing very freely in my Cage; sometimes indeed in the plaintive Notes of the Nightingale; but, at others, in the chearful Strains of the Lark. –[27]

In his comment on this letter, Johnson begins by praising Savage's 'Fortitude', just the stoic quality he praised in Boerhaave, but his new subject will not support a lengthy panegyric, and his comment soon slips into a humorous vein, despite the fact that death is near:

Surely the Fortitude of this Man deserves, at least, to be mentioned with Applause, and whatever Faults may be imputed to him, the Virtue of *suffering well* cannot be denied him. The two Powers which, in the Opinion of *Epictetus*, constitute a wise Man, are those of *bearing* and *forbearing*, which cannot indeed be affirmed to have been equally possessed by *Savage*, but it was too manifest that the Want of one obliged him very *frequently* to practise the other.[28]

The joke is in the way the last sentence extracts 'forbearance' from its philosophical context and places it in the local tavern or house of ill-repute. Then too, the morphologically related terms of the stoic ideal – 'bearing' and 'forbearing' – are brought into a ludicrously direct relationship with each other. In the solemn acceptation of the terms, the one refers to not acting on inner pressures and the other to enduring pressure exerted from without. But in Johnson's playful use of the terms one mechanically activates the other, and Savage becomes a mechanical stoic who cannnot be moral because he is not free. Johnson carefully keeps Christianity out of the equation and is therefore at liberty to be jocular. Johnson does not joke when he exalts Savage for Christian virtues, like the virtue of charity, which Savage exhibits in an almost superhuman fashion when he divides his only coin with the prostitute who testified against him in his murder trial.

Although Johnson means to ridicule Savage a little, the main purpose of his comedy is mitigation. Even in poverty Savage nobly

preserved a steady Confidence in his own Capacity, and believed nothing above his Reach which he should at any Time earnestly endeavour to attain. He formed Schemes of the same Kind with regard to Knowledge and to Fortune, and flattered himself with Advances to be made in Science, as with Riches to be enjoyed in some distant Period of his Life. For the Acquisition of Knowledge he was indeed far better qualified than for that of Riches; for he was naturally inquisitive and desirous of the Conversation of those from whom any Information was to be obtained, but by no means solicitous to improve those Opportunities that were sometimes offered of raising his

Fortune; and was remarkably retentive of his Ideas, which, when once he was
in Possession of them, rarely forsook him; a Quality which could never be
communicated to his Money.

Johnson makes this last remark as though such a communication could
take place, if one just tried hard enough. It is the kind of joke that
shows up in burlesque works like Fielding's *Jonathan Wild* and Gay's *Beggar's Opera*, and Johnson's Savage resembles the heroes of those satirical
works to some extent. Alvin Kernan describes him engagingly as a mixture
of Pistol and Lovewit. Like his literary forerunners, Johnson's Savage earns
the affection of his audience especially when he does not deserve their
approbation.[29]

In a variety of ways Johnson's *Life of Savage* is a defence of his subject.
There are organizing legal metaphors supporting the whole work, and
Johnson takes special pains in his handling of Savage's trial for murder,
printing a plausible version of Judge Page's decision and giving more
space than any previous accounts to Savage's defence, both of which he
researched. Throughout the biography Johnson stresses the extenuating
circumstances of Savage's birth and, as though he were addressing a jury,
encourages his readers to place the blame for Savage's depravity on his
unnaturally cold mother. He askes us to indict her, rather than her son,
urging on us her adultery and cruelty with a misogynistic persistence. The
more subtle part of Johnson's strategy, however, is to place Savage in a
comic setting, one which puts the jury at ease and makes them willing to
confess that they are liable to be lost in the same mists of error as Savage.
Joking is a standard technique of legal oratory, of course, but doing so
partly at the expense of the client is a little more unusual. Perhaps Johnson
had in mind Cicero's techniques, especially in the *Pro Caelio*, where the
orator humorously ventriloquizes the influence his parents exerted upon
his client. Some of the humour even occurs in the murder scene itself.
Johnson takes much of his account from previously printed versions, but
he adds a comic detail about Savage's character that explains how he fell
into the late-night ramble. On the night of the murder, he 'sat drinking
till it was late, it being in no Time of Mr *Savage*'s Life any Part of his
Character to be the first of the Company that desired to separate'.[30] The
word 'first' expressed negatively is a comic figure of speech for 'last' expressed positively. It is a very common kind of joke, and it is consistent
with the colloquial style of narration in *Savage* that Johnson employs as a
way of recommending his defence of his client to the jury.

When the murder is committed, Johnson says only, 'Swords were drawn
on both Sides, and one Mr *James Sinclair* was killed. Savage having
wounded likewise a Maid that held him, forced his way with *Merchant* out
of the House; but being intimidated and confused, without Resolution
either to fly or stay, they were taken in a back Court by one of the Company
and some Soldiers.' The confusion surrounding the murder of Sinclair
results from Johnson's wish to pare the account down to what was clearly

and legally verifiable, but it is obviously meant to operate in Savage's defence. A bit of prevarication shows up in the word 'likewise', which suggests what the passage refuses to say but which Johnson and many of his readers knew from the published account: that it was Savage who killed Sinclair, 'giving him with a drawn Sword, one mortal Wound in the lower part of the Belly, of the Length of Half an Inch, and the Depth of nine Inches.' Confusion, indeterminacy, and the unreliability of testimony are part of the legal defence of Savage, but Johnson expands these qualities in his biography to provide, in addition, an existential apology for Savage. Johnson's penultimate paragraph, with which he originally ended the work, asks the reader to suspend judgement because he cannot know how it felt to be Savage: 'Those are no proper Judges of his Conduct who have slumber'd away their Time on the Down of Plenty, nor will a wise Man easily presume to say, "Had I been in *Savage*'s Condition, I should have lived, or written, better than *Savage*."'[31]

There is something comic about confusion; in confusion there is little malice, and a character in confusion deflects an inclination to judge him. But the representation of confusion and indeterminacy can also turn tragic or come to rest in that part of irony where tragedy and comedy meet. This is the case in Johnson's description of Savage's last words. Savage seems to take on Shakespearian roles at various times in the *Life*: he is a courtier out of Henry IV in the murder scene, Hamlet in his pursuit of his mother, Richard II writing in prison, and often a Coriolanus too proud to live in the real world. At his death, however, he is Lear experiencing a gaping indeterminacy of life: 'The last Time that the Keeper saw him was on *July* the 31st, 1743; when *Savage* seeing him at his Bed-side said, with an uncommon Earnestness, *I have something to say to you, Sir,* but after a Pause, moved his Hand in a melancholy Manner, and finding himself unable to recollect what he was going to communicate, said, *'Tis gone.* The Keeper soon after left him, and the next Morning he died.'[32] We are left staring at confusion and blankness: 'Is this the promised end? / Or image of that Horror –.' Under such circumstances it is impossible to judge clearly; a wise man will not judge.

As Johnson describes it, Savage's whole life is comic in a cosmic, ironic, and nearly tragic way. The grand perspective with which Johnson begins the *Life* makes a framework in which Savage's existence will seem small and comically pitiable: 'It has been observed in all Ages, that the Advantages of Nature or of Fortune have contributed very little to the Promotion of Happiness; and that those whom the Splendor of their Rank, or the Extent of their Capacity, have placed upon the Summits of human Life, have not often given any just Occasion to Envy in those who look up to them from a lower Station.' The reason for this is that 'the general Lot of Mankind is Misery.' Savage roams this 'clouded maze of Fate', so much like the world Johnson sketches in *The Vanity of Human Wishes*, without direction: 'He proceeded throughout his Life to tread the same Steps on the same Circle; always applauding his past Conduct, or at least forgetting it, to amuse himself with Phantoms of Happiness, which were dancing before him.' Savage is the 'wav'ring man' of Johnson's greatest poem, but in this identity he is also Everyman, and that too makes him difficult to judge. Johnson allows himself to have it both ways, mitigating Savage's faults and encouraging his readers to accept the *Life* as a monitory lesson. But Savage benefits even from the monitory indictment because his sins are expiated in the good they do as lessons for others. Both the reader and the subject are redeemed when Johnson says that it is useful to teach the practices of Savage 'that Folly might be an Antidote to Folly.'[33]

For all its attention to legal language, its complex existential defence of Savage, and its grand monitory framework, Johnson's *Savage* also reads like a novel. Part of the reason for this is the inclusion of so many details of Savage's daily life. Many of these details add to the comic tone of the work: Savage's 'nocturnal intrusions' on his friends, his proud rejection of an offered suit of clothes, his refusal to accept an early appointment made by a potential benefactor, and his carriage from place to place by the chorus of writers who are trying to preserve him toward the end of his life. Johnson knew many of the details firsthand and appears himself in the narrative walking the streets of London, and hearing 'the bells chime at midnight', like one of Pistol's friends. Much of what he did not know firsthand he may have heard from firsthand witnesses. The world of printing, publishing, and writing that Savage inhabited was very much Johnson's world, and there is an intimacy in his description of Savage's movements in that world. Such intimacy, for example, enlivens the episode in which Savage sits at a table with the renowned Steele composing a pamphlet, which in the end only pays for the day's meal, though hopes had run ever so much higher in Savage's mind. At times, the fact that Johnson's own mind is furnished with the details of the printing world gives him a special insight into Savage's mind. The idle wishes that filled Savage's time and made up his inner life were composed of the same stuff as Johnson's, and he displays a bond with Savage in describing them:

> This Project of printing his Works was frequently revived, and as his Proposals grew obsolete, new ones were printed with fresher Dates. To form Schemes for the Publication was one of his favourite Amusements, nor was he ever more at Ease than when with any Friend who readily fell in with his Schemes, he was adjusting the Print, forming the Advertisements, and regulating the Dispersion of his new Edition, which he really intended some time to publish, and which, as long Experience had shewn him the Impossibility of printing the Volume together, he at last determined to divide into weekly or monthly Numbers, that the Profits of the first might supply the Expences of the next.[34]

More public and, broadly speaking, political aspects of Savage's Grub Street life also appear in Johnson's biography. The text becomes at times a vehicle for Johnson's defence of his own socio-economic class – the artists of London. In this context, Savage's pride is often ennobled and we are asked to sympathize with him when patrons and booksellers treat him poorly or when his hopes are dashed by events beyond his control, like the death of the generous Queen Caroline. Savage himself created a scapegoat for Grub Street, Iscariot Hackney, in *An Author to be Lett*. This work operates like the *Dunciad* to gather up and discard all the corruptions of the book world in order to exalt true writers as a respectable class of citizens. Johnson praises the pamphlet extravagantly, and he puts his own Savage to some of the same uses that the real Savage puts Hackney. Johnson both invites commiseration with Savage when he suffers in the hands of the old system of patronage or the new market-based system of literature and praises him when he is a proud spokesman for merit: 'in his lowest State he wanted not Spirit to assert the natural Dignity of Wit, and was always ready to repress that Insolence which Superiority of Fortune incited, and to trample the Reputation which rose upon any other Basis than that of Merit.' Furthermore Johnson shows his own loyalty to the rights of authors by chastising Savage when he fails to live up to the ideal of a print-world writer, allowing himself to sink back into the soft oppression of patronage. Johnson consistently registers disgust over Savage's fawning dedications; he criticizes his haughty attitude toward 'the Voice of the People', the common readers upon whom publishing authors depended in the new regime; and he corrects his outburst against the free press.[35] This is not just a bow in the direction of Cave, who was supporting Johnson's work on the *Life of Savage*; it is a declaration of his own political position and an acknowledgement of the importance of the free press in his rise as an author.

6

Miscellaneous Prose

If Ideas are to us the measure of time, he that thinks most, lives longest.
Johnson to Hester Maria Thrale, 8 April 1780

Among Johnson's friends in the 1740s there were many who, for better or worse, took a more progressive attitude towards the world of publication than did Richard Savage. Perhaps the most interesting of these was George Psalmanazar. Johnson said he sat at Psalmanazar's feet, that he would no more have thought of contradicting a bishop, and that he was the most 'uniform' and virtuous man he ever knew. All of this is remarkable because Psalmanazar was a reformed impostor who had tricked the English reading public and the scholarly world with a fabricated, purportedly firsthand account of the island of Formosa (now Taiwan), complete with descriptions of the people, customs, and geography. Most impressive of all is Psalmanazar's invention of the 'Formosan' language, including an alphabetic writing system in which the letters are called 'am, mem, nen, taph, lamdo, samdo . . . fandem, raw, gomera'.[1] He translates the Lord's Prayer, the Creed, and the Ten Commandments into the imaginary language with striking plausibility. There was so little information about Formosa available in England at that time that the hoax went undetected for decades, and Psalmanazar achieved such acclaim that he was invited to Oxford to teach his made-up language. Before Johnson could have met him, Psalmanazar had admitted his literary deception and apparently begun leading an exemplary life. It is notable that he was working on a history of printing in the 1740s because Johnson planned a similar work himself around the same time. Both men were wrapped up in the print world, and both understood the liabilities to truth in the promulgation of print. Psalmanazar's Formosan hoax is just a shade away from Swift's ventriloquistic hoaxes, and it discredited print in the same way. The Johnson of *Marmor Norfolciense* and the *Compleat Vindication* was like the young Psalmanazar in his attitude toward print, and the later Johnson was, like the later Psalmanazar, respectful of the medium and reconciled to its predominance as a vehicle of information and mainstream public opinion.

Many of Johnson's other friends during this period were building their careers by working for the *Gentleman's Magazine*. John Hawkesworth knew Johnson well and achieved success partly by imitating his prose style. A less successful friend was Samuel Boyse, who, like Johnson, wrote poetry and translated French. Johnson was able to provide information on him for John Nichols's *Anecdotes*, the best history of Grub Street: 'This unfortunate man,' writes Nichols, 'by addicting himself to low vices, among which were gluttony and extravagance, rendered himself so contemptible and wretched, that he frequently was without the least subsistence for days together. After squandering away in a dirty manner any money which he acquired, he has been known to pawn all his apparel . . . and in that state was frequently confined to his bed, sitting up with his arms through holes in a blanket, writing verses in order to procure the means of existence.' When Boyse died in Shoe Lane in 1749, he was buried at the expense of the parish. According to Francis Stewart, one of Johnson's amanuenses, he and three of Johnson's other helpers attended the corpse to the grave.[2] Johnson raised a tiny monument to Boyse some time soon after, when he was working on letter 'P' in his *Dictionary*. He inserted the word 'predal' meaning 'robbing' and illustrated it with two lines from Boyse's ode, 'The Olive', written in Spenserian stanzas and dedicated to Robert Walpole as a peacemaker. But respect for the dead did not prevent Johnson from commenting that Boyse's contribution to the English language was 'not countenanced by analogy'.

Perhaps Johnson found Boyse's case monitory because in the early 1740s Johnson put aside his earlier literary aspirations and produced almost nothing but prose, most of it for the *Gentleman's Magazine*. Although the Parliamentary *Debates* and the early biographies are the most substantial works, some of Johnson's occasional contributions to the *Gentleman's Magazine* in the early 1740s deserve attention. Several of these little-known miscellaneous works confirm aspects of Johnson's political, literary, and linguistic commitments in a very compendious way, and, all together, they show his remarkable versatility as a professional writer.

Since they were written at about the same time, it is not surprising that several of Johnson's miscellaneous works resemble the Parliamentary *Debates* in both method and intention. In 1741, for example, over two issues of the *Gentleman's Magazine*, Johnson wrote an 'extract' or 'epitome' of a 1660 pamphlet that Cave was about to reprint, *Monarchy Asserted, To be the best, most Ancient and legall form of Government*. The pamphlet and Johnson's abridgement take the form of a debate between Cromwell and those of his counsellors who want him to assume the title of king. In its day the pamphlet was meant as an apology for the Restoration. Cromwell stiffly and unreasonably refuses the title of king, though his counsellors show that monarchy is the choice of the people and the best way of preserving

English liberty and the English constitution. As Donald Greene suggests, in 1741 the pamphlet may have been reissued as a comment on the fall of Walpole, whose dismissal was then being debated in Parliament. Johnson and Cave dared not report directly on those debates until they were two years in the past, but comparisons between Walpole and Cromwell had been made in public political discourse, and the politics of the pamphlet, given its place of publication, were clear to Johnson's audience. Like Johnson's Parliamentary *Debates*, however, the extract also serves broader, educational purposes. It too generalizes the issues at hand and turns the discussion in the direction of 'political science'. The topic that receives most elaboration is the undesirability of change: 'Long prescription is a sufficient argument in favour of a practice against which nothing can be alledged; nor is it sufficient to affirm that the change may be made without inconvenience, for change itself is an evil, and ought to be ballanced by some equivalent advantage.' As Greene points out, there is no precedent for this in the original pamphlet, and Johnson echoes the sentiment in 1747, in his *Plan of a Dictionary of the English Language.*[3] In fact, this pamphlet abridgement reveals as much about Johnson's budding philological ideas as it does about his politics.

The importance of the people in government, the consent of the people as represented in custom, and 'standing law' are the salient topics of the extract, and they all converge on the question of names. A theory of language is a political theory, and the differences between the monarchists and Cromwell come out in their differing attitudes toward words. Both agree that words are arbitrary tokens of meaning and nugatory in themselves, but the counsellors respect the power of popular usage in fixing the meaning of the word 'king', for example. Cromwell displays his tyranny by believing that he can alter the course of custom and usage: 'That the title of King is not necessary, how long soever it may have been in use, or what regard soever may have been paid it, is plain from the very nature of language: Words have not their import from the natural power of particular combinations of characters, or from the real efficacy of certain sounds, but from the consent of those that use them and arbitrarily annex certain ideas to them which might have been signified with equal propriety by any other. Whoever originally distinguished the chief magistrate by the appellation of King, might have assigned him any other denomination, and the power of the people can never be lost or impaired. If that might once have been done, it may be done now.'[4] It is decidedly Johnson's view, however, that such reinstitution of words cannot be done 'now'. Johnson was fond of the old anecdote explaining that Caesar himself lacked the power to introduce a new word. His audience may have known it too, and the more learned among them drew a line of association from Caesar to Cromwell to Walpole. A willingness to ignore the role of custom in language is an indication of tyranny because it demonstrates a willingness to ignore the voice of the people. In the *Dictionary* Johnson is primarily concerned to record usage, and he rejects the more imperial role imagined for him by Chesterfield and others interested in reforming or perfecting English. His lexicographical commitment is also a political commitment, and Johnson's abridgement of *Monarchy Asserted* is notable for bringing the two spheres into such direct and illuminating contact with each other. It shows Johnson expanding his thinking from politics to language at an early stage in his career, and it suggests that politics was still an implicit subject during his years of immersion in philology.

In another job he did in the early 1740s Johnson made a more direct and particular political statement, part of which he also repeated in the *Dictionary*. He 'extracted', abridged, and analysed a number of pamphlets devoted to schemes for preventing the sale of raw Irish wool to France, England's chief competitor in the international textile trade. In his remarks on the 'extracts' Johnson expresses his ongoing hatred of excise taxes and the corrupt appointments by which they are enforced. He learned this hatred early, when his father was in trouble with excisemen, and he rarely missed an opportunity to express it. In reaction to one pamphlet's proposal of an excise system, Johnson imagines an astonished 'Foreigner' asking a British 'Clothier', 'Why do you . . . expose your whole Lives to the Inspection of Wretches vested with petty Authority?' This description of excisemen returns in the *Dictionary* where Johnson defines 'excise' as 'A hateful tax levied upon commodities, and adjudged not by the common judges of property, but wretches hired by those to whom excise is paid.' Elsewhere in these dissertations on the wool trade, Johnson inveighs against other forms of institutionalized abuse, as, for instance, when he rejects a scheme that would employ oaths to control smuggling. Johnson was always against enforced oaths because he knew that in the desperate circumstances of their execution they would frequently be broken; enforced oaths, therefore, tended to legislate lying and blasphemy, and 'Trade itself', he declares, 'is not to be preserved at the Expence of Virtue.' Overall, in his handling of the wool debates, Johnson is realistic and practical: he opposes the airy schemes of projectors with reminders of how people can be expected to act when their livelihood is threatened. Johnson blatantly recommends one writer's defence of Irish smuggling: 'For a Nation compelled to keep Sheep, and forbidden to make Cloth, what remains but that they export their Wool?' Johnson comments, *'This Allegation deserves to be attended to, not only for its Certainty and its Importance upon the present Question, but as an Instance that the Consequences of* OPPRESSION *seldom fail to fall upon the Authors.'*[5]

Johnson again perceives the operation of divine justice in his 'Dissertation on the Amazons', yet another of his extracts for Cave. He remarks that the Scythian world that once contained the Amazons was 'an Empire of too great Extent to be of long Duration; for it has been in all Ages the Happiness of Mankind that Ambition has defeated its own Designs, by grasping more than can be easily retained.' The most curious thing about this piece, however, is Johnson's apparent credulity about the Amazons. Yet the credit he gives them is reasoned and examined, and in the act of reasoning about credit Johnson is his usually rational self: 'In every History the Obscurity of some Circumstances, and the Suppression of others, produce Difficulties not easily to be removed; and these Difficulties are always greater as the Facts are more remote: But when the general Relation is confirmed by adequate Evidence, we are not to infer from its Obscurity that it is false, but that some Circumstances are omitted, or some contemporary Events entirely forgotten, which would have reconciled all seeming Inconsistencies, and dissipated all Objections.' Eighteen years later in *Idler* 87 Johnson returned to his puzzlement about the Amazons in an essay supporting George Chapman's remark that incredulity is 'the wit of fools'.[6] In both instances Johnson is determined not to allow himself to take the familiar as a standard for the possible but rather to evaluate evidence free from prejudice. In fact, he seems to bend over backwards in favour of the Amazons because they violate unexamined assumptions – in this case, fixed ideas about what is possible for women. Johnson was always reluctant to credit the unproven and the unlikely, and he became more reluctant to do so as he grew older, but the reason for this is that he believed in empirical inquiry, and he was, therefore, also reluctant to determine against whatever had been discredited without examination.

Johnson took up the question of historical truth and historians' credulity again in his essay on the recently published memoirs of the Duchess of Marlborough. Written from firsthand experience in the court of William and Mary and Queen Anne, the Duchess's memoirs were immensely popular for their exposé of the private world of royalty. The book also served as an apology for the author's notoriously haughty behaviour. Despite its tabloid flamboyance, however, it was valuable because it shed historical light on the shadowy, rapidly changing circumstances of court life in a momentous period of British constitutional history: from the Glorious Revolution in 1688 to the Act of Settlement in 1714. Johnson responded to the genuine information in the book with a short disquisition on historical method that is as philosophical as anything he had written earlier. Johnson briskly weighs the liabilities and advantages of memoirs for seekers of historical truth. He warns readers that 'Accounts of publick Transactions . . . written by those who were engaged in them' are not always as true as they might be because, 'very often, proportionate to the Opportunities of knowing the Truth, are the Temptations to disguise it.' An analysis of the memoirist's motives amplifies the warning to credulous readers: 'the Parent of all Memoirs, is the Ambition of being distinguished from the Herd of Mankind, and the Fear of either Infamy or Oblivion, Passions which cannot but have some Degree of Influence, and which may at least affect the Writers Choice of Facts, though they may not prevail upon him to advance known Falsehoods.' Yet Johnson does not recommend extreme scepticism and concludes that 'Distrust is a necessary Qualification of a Student in History' not because truth is undiscoverable but because it is rare: 'Distrust quickens [the student's] Discernment of different Degrees of Probability, animates his Search after Evidence, and perhaps heightens his Pleasure at the Discovery of Truth; for Truth though not always obvious, is generally discoverable, nor is it anywhere more likely to be found than in private Memoirs.'[7] The remainder of the essay is largely mechanical, treating some of the principal personages in the memoirs and providing excerpts in lengthy footnotes, but the opening workout on the topic of historical truth is a fine example of Johnson's thinking over a basic problem of inquiry.

Almost all of Johnson's work for the *Gentleman's Magazine* exploits pre-existent literary material, translating and extracting it, in fact, more often than commenting upon it. Although Johnson's translations and redactions are always somewhat creative, he usually stays pretty close to his source. When he departs from his source or when he has least to go on, as in the Parliamentary *Debates*, Johnson most reverts to profoundly conventional topics, like truth, freedom, and the vanity of human wishes. His essay on epitaphs in 1740 gave Johnson unusual scope, and he used the opportunity partly to make a profound statement about human freedom. He approaches the epitaph as a literary genre, which he defines in Aristotelian terms with special attention to its final cause, the effect on the reader: 'As Honours are paid to the Dead in order to incite others to the Imitation of their Excellencies, the principal Intention of EPITAPHS is to perpetuate the Examples of Virtue, that the Tomb of a good Man may supply the Want of his Presence, and Veneration for his Memory produce the same Effect as the Observation of his Life. Those EPITAPHS are, therefore, the most perfect, which set Virtue in the strongest Light, and are best adapted to exalt the Reader's Ideas and rouse his Emulation.' Johnson goes on to provide examples of epitaphs that fail and some that succeed according to this standard. 'The best Subject for EPITAPHS', he concludes, 'is private Virtue; Virtue exerted in the same Circumstances in which the Bulk of Mankind are placed, and which, therefore, may admit of many Imitators.'[8]

For his exemplary epitaphs Johnson chooses two devoted to slaves. The first is for a woman named Zosima, who resembles Aspasia, the virtuous heroine of *Irene*. Johnson translates the epitaph from the *Greek Anthology* into Latin verse and English prose: 'Zosima, *who in her Life could only have her Body enslaved, now finds her Body likewise set at Liberty.*' Johnson comments, 'It is impossible to read this Epitaph without being animated to bear the Evils of Life with Constancy, and to support the Dignity of Human Nature under the most pressing Afflictions.' Clearly, Johnson is thinking partly of his own life and of the resolution to avoid disgrace which he had made in his diary in 1732 after receiving his disappointing patrimony. Zosima returns frequently in Johnson's work; she exerted a fascination over him because he found her representative of the human predicament and its solution. The other exemplary epitaph in Johnson's essay teaches much the same lesson, although it concerns a more illustrious person, Epictetus, the Stoic philosopher whose works Elizabeth Carter later translated: 'Epictetus, *who lies here, was a Slave and a Cripple, poor as the Beggar in the Proverb, and the Favourite of Heaven.*' Johnson comments, 'In this Distich is comprised the noblest Panegyric, and the most important Instruction. We may learn from it that Virtue is impracticable in no Condition, since *Epictetus* could recommend himself to the Regard of Heaven, amidst the Temptations of Poverty and Slavery: Slavery, which has always been found so destructive to Virtue, that in many Languages a Slave and a Thief are expressed by the same Word.'[9] Ten years later Johnson made exactly the same remark when he wrote the definition of 'caitiff' in the *Dictionary* and compared it to Italian *cattivo* and Latin *fur*. The moral and ethical importance of freedom is a constant in Johnson's writing that spans his political, religious, and literary works.

All that Johnson wrote and edited in the *Gentleman's Magazine* in the early 1740s may never be precisely known, and hence the canon never settled, despite the efforts of many fine scholars. He seems to have translated bits of the 'Αστεια or *Jests of Hierocles*, which looks forward to the satires on the learned that appear in *The Vanity of Human Wishes*, the *Rambler*, and the *Dictionary*. He probably translated fragments of the Roman *Acta Diurna*, or daily transactions, opening with some laudatory remarks about the contribution of newspapers to 'the Emolument of Society' and ending with some ironic glances at journalistic sensationalism. He may have translated a part of *Cryptographia Denudata*, a work designed to teach a universal system for decoding messages sent in any language. Like other Johnsonian philological works, this little exercise contains a moral. The coded message in the first instalment turns out to be a piece of proverbial wisdom to which Johnson was certainly receptive, whether or not he was responsible for its publication in the *Gentleman's Magazine*. 'MAN MUSS ALSO ARBEITEN, ALS WENN MAN NIEMAHLS STERBEN WURDE UND ALSO IN GOTTESFURCHT LEBEN ALS WENN MAN AUGENBLICT DEN TOD VERWARTETE.'[10] ('One must work as if one should never die, and one must live in the fear of God as if one expected death in the twinkling of an eye.')

A more extensive piece of work, which Johnson very probably composed from August 1741 to March 1742, is the *Gentleman's Magazine's* column on 'Foreign Affairs'. With an urbanity resembling the *New Yorker's* 'Talk of the Town', Johnson surveys current events in Europe, but extends his awareness to happenings in such remote places as India, Persia, Cuba, Boston, New York, Montevideo, and Rio de Janeiro. The urbane manner is epitomized in such opening remarks as these: 'If we turn our Eyes towards Germany, we shall find the Face of Affairs greatly changed' and 'The present Commotions of the World arise, for the most Part, from a Revival of antient Claims, and a Desire of rectifying the unjust Distributions of Dominion, which either Force or Policy has formerly procured.'[11]

As in his reading and translation of travel literature, in 'Foreign Affairs' Johnson was extending his observation of mankind from China to Peru. He did so more seriously and extensively, however, in his column on 'Foreign Books', which he apparently invented and ran steadily from November 1741 through September 1742 and intermittently into 1744. The column appeared after 'Books', which was devoted to British publications, and it was organized by country and city of publication. Both columns list titles that Johnson handled more extensively on other occasions. 'Foreign Books' for December 1741, for example, lists *Cryptographia Denudata*, and in April 1742 Johnson recorded the appearance of *La Vie de M. Jean Phillippe Baratier*. Number 25 in the 'Register of Books' for March 1742 is *An Account of the Conduct of the Dowager Dutchess of Marlborough*, and in July of 1742 appeared '*Hierocles* in Aurea Carmina Comment.', which probably included the *Jests*. By instituting 'Foreign Books' Johnson attempted to extend his literary reach and again to assert a European rather than an insular literary identity. The column for March 1742 includes a direct appeal in Latin to the learned European literary community ('Omnes ubique Gentium Eruditos') to provide Johnson with press releases ('Litteras certiorem') concerning their recent works.[12] Johnson could not go to the continent to visit the universities of France and Italy, as he dreamed of doing while at Oxford, but he would not be 'an Athenian blockhead', imagining the rest of the world to be barbaric; he would reach out in the medium of print to the world of European Latin culture. Johnson's reliance on that medium and the paramount importance he attached to it are evident in his note of February 1742 on the appearance in Hamburg of Christian Wolfius's *Monumenta Typographica*: 'This collection [of remarks and essays on printing] cannot but afford a Reception proportioned to the importance of the Art of which it is intended to discover the Original. If the Curiosity of Mankind were regulated by Reason, what Period of History would so much be studied as the Rise and Progress of the great Art of Printing?' As he wrote this comment, Johnson was beginning a project that took on similar dimensions.

7

The Harleian Library

Of those books which have been often published and diver[si]vied by various modes of impression, a royal Library should have at least the most curious Edition, the most splendid, and the most useful. The most curious Edition is commonly the first and the most useful may be expected among the last. . . . The most splendid the eye will discover.

Johnson to Frederick Barnard, librarian to George III, 28 May 1768

In the October 1742 issue of the *Gentleman's Magazine* Johnson advertised his most ambitious project of the 1740s: 'There is preparing for the Press, a Catalogue of the Celebrated Harleyan Library, collected with extraordinary Charge and Assiduity by the two late Earls of Oxford, the like whereof for the Number of Books, Tracts, Prints, and Drawing, amounting to three hundred thousand Articles, of the choicest Impressions, fairest copies, and richest Bindings, have never been offered to Sale.'[1] More than anything he had done before, the preparation of this sale catalogue plunged Johnson into the international sea of books, the waters of which he had been testing almost all his life.

In 1742 Johnson probably received the information needed for the advertisement from his collaborator on the *Harleian Catalogue*, William Oldys. Oldys served as Harley's secretary from 1738 until his death in 1741, but no later than 1731 he had made the Earl's acquaintance, sold him a collection of manuscripts, and prepared catalogues for him. Although not in a class with Humphrey Wanley, Harley's great librarian, Oldys was a practising bibliographer who had written a dissertation on pamphlets and contributed to a collection of them called *Phoenix Britannicus*. He had also published for a brief time the *British Librarian*, a bibliographical journal in which he made notes on rare books and authors. So intimate with the library for sale was Oldys that in tracing the provenance of some rare volumes he quoted his own marginalia. Oldys's familiarity not only with the Harleian but with all the libraries of London is evident in an interesting manuscript which he left unpublished at his death. The text comprises a scholar's guide to London, describing in brief forty-six public and private libraries in and around the city. With the possible exception of the Cottonian, 'not improperly called the English Vatican', Harley's was evidently the most impressive library in London. Oldys reports, 'For libraries in more expressly particular hands, the first and most universal in England, must be reckoned the Harleian. . . . He has the rarest books of all countries, languages, and sciences, and the greatest number of any collector we ever had, in manuscript as well as in print; thousands of fragments, some a thousand years old; vellum books, some written over; all things especially respecting English History, personal as well as local, particular as well as general. He has a great collection of Bibles, &c., in all versions, and editions of all the first printed books, classics and others of our own country, ecclesiastical as well as civil, by Caxton, Wynkyn de Worde, Pynson, Berthelet, Rastall, Grafton, and . . . all the collections of his librarian Humphrey Wanley, of Stow, . . . and the flower of a hundred other libraries.'[2]

It is possible, given contemporary estimates of other libraries, that Harley's was the largest in England. It is remarkable, if not shocking, then, that the bookseller Thomas Osborne was able to purchase the collection, exclusive of the manuscripts, for £13,000 (less than two million pounds in contemporary value).[3] Nevertheless, it was not easy to dispose of such a great number of books, and, as Johnson knew nearly firsthand because of his father's disastrous purchase of Lord Derby's library, there were great risks for the bookseller. Being aware of the dangers himself, Osborne took the unusual step of engaging Oldys and Johnson to prepare a catalogue of the collection. He meant the catalogue to be a book of value in itself and he offered it for sale, much to the chagrin of his customers.

The book catalogue was an established genre of learned literature by the time Johnson and Oldys set to work. There were booksellers' trade catalogues, library catalogues (though few libraries had complete listings), sale or auction catalogues, and some that served both bibliographical and sale purposes. The *Harleian Catalogue* was designed to be of the mixed kind. Although there were already manuscript catalogues of the Harleian collections (one running to twelve folio volumes), it was to printed sale catalogues of other collections that Johnson and Oldys looked for their models. In 'An Account of the Harleian Library', first published in folio with the 'Proposal' in November 1742, Johnson writes on the intellectual value of book catalogues. Significantly, he compares his work to three seventeenth-century continental productions: catalogues of the libraries of Francesco Barberini (Rome, 1681), of the classical scholar Nicolaas Heinsius (Leyden, 1682), and of the polymath Jacques-Auguste de Thou (Paris, 1679). There were many other catalogues, most of them in the Harleian collection, that Johnson could have named, including those for the large English libraries of Richard Smith (London, 1682) and Thomas Rawlinson (London, 1721–34).[4] The richness or fame of the continental catalogues may be what drew Johnson to make his comparison with them, but the juxtaposition to continental European scholarship is characteristic. As later he drew up his *English Dictionary* in comparison (and opposition) to the works of the French and Italian academies, here too he likens his book catalogue to the most impressive productions of the continent.

Johnson himself owned important library catalogues, like *Bernard's Catalogue of British Manuscripts*, and in his 'Account' he describes their value in an inspiring fashion. Within the few pages of his essay, Johnson addresses three possible audiences and finds separate uses of the proposed catalogue for each. Given the quality and rarity of Harley's books, Johnson unwisely shifts the direction of his remarks quickly away from wealthy book collectors to scholars. He appeals to the wealthy mainly by means of the unpromising vehicle of irony: 'THAT our Catalogue will excite any other Man to emulate the Collectors of this Library, to prefer Books and Manuscripts to Equipage and Luxury, and to forsake Noise and Diversion for the Conversation of the Learned and the Satisfaction of extensive Knowledge, we are very far from presuming to hope.' For scholars and critics the book will be more certainly useful by saving them the embarrassment of errors and repetition that could be avoided by consulting existing work in their fields of inquiry before presuming to publish their own contributions. But Johnson reserves the best use of catalogues for a third audience, not strictly limited by economic status or scholarly training. As in most of his literary works, in the 'Account' Johnson addresses a general but learned public when he traces out the study of intellectual history:

> NOR is the Use of Catalogues of less Importance to those whom Curiosity has engaged in the Study of Literary History, and who think the intellectual Revolutions of the World more worthy of their Attention than the Ravages of Tyrants, the Desolation of Kingdoms, the Rout of Armies, and the Fall of Empires. Those who are pleased with observing the first Birth of new Opinions, their Struggles against Opposition, their silent Progress under Persecution, their general Reception, and their gradual Decline, or sudden Extinction; those that amuse themselves with remarking the different Periods of human Knowledge, and observe how Darkness and Light succeed each other, by what Accident the most gloomy Nights of Ignorance have given Way to the Dawn of Science, and how Learning has languished and decayed, for Want of Patronage and Regard, or been overborne by the Prevalence of fashionable Ignorance, or lost amidst the Tumults of Invasion, and the Storms of Violence.

'Literary history' here means the history of learning or what we generally call 'intellectual history', a phrase that Johnson instituted in 1747 in his *Plan of a Dictionary of the English Language*. The field of study itself was one of Bacon's desiderata in the *Advancement of Learning*, but Johnson also deserves credit as a founder of the modern discipline. Johnson appeals for the study of a couple of favourite areas in particular: 'the Works of

those Heroes . . . of the Northern Nations . . . which may plead, at least
in this Nation, that they ought not to be neglected by those that owe to
the Men whose Memories they preserve, their Constitution, their Proper-
ties, and their Liberties'; and 'THAT memorable Period of *English* History,
which begins with the Reign of King *Charles* the First, and ends with the
Restoration'.[5]

In order to make the *Catalogue* useful for these noble and patriotic
ends, Johnson promised 'that the books shall be distributed into their
distinct Classes, and every Class ranged with some Regard to the Age of
the Writers; that every Book shall be accurately described; that the Peculiarities of Editions shall be remarked, and Observations from the
Authors of Literary History occasionally interspersed.' He then gives
specimens of the intended categories. These are very often too broad to
be useful, and their roughly hierarchical order, beginning with divinely
inspired works and ending with works of mere fancy like poetry, is hard
to follow. In addition, the categories overlap and shift between the first
two volumes and the second two ('the fifth volume is not organized at
all'). Overall, the book does not live up to the standard of organization
suggested by the epigraph from the legendary German literary historian
Daniel George Morhof: 'Catalogorum accuratior Notitia ita necessaria est
Polyhistori, ut Mapporum Geographicorum Cognitio pergrinaturo' ('the
very accurate notes of catalogues are as necessary to the polymath as the
knowledge of geographical maps are to the explorer'). Johnson shows that
he is aware of this failure in an advertisement at the beginning of volume
2 which promises more notes in later volumes and an index, like that
added to the catalogue of de Thou's library. Then there is an Index
Titulorum, a list of the heads in volumes 1 and 2. Despite this attempt to
pull themselves up by the bootstraps, Johnson and Oldys's work generally
becomes less forceful as it proceeds. The second two volumes organize the
offerings by size before subject (all folios first), translate much of the
Latin of the first two volumes into English, and provide special sections
on the expensive vellum books. From a strictly bibliographical point of
view also the *Catalogue* is neither consistent nor impressive. There is
much reliance on a few sources, especially J. A. Fabricius on the classics
and Michael Maittaire on incunabula. Moreover, Thomas Kaminski finds,
Johnson and Oldys failed to use the latest and most correct editions of
these reference works.[6]

The reliance of the *Catalogue* on earlier works causes some confusion
for the student who wants to read everything that is really by Johnson;
further confusion derives from the fact that it is impossible to prove that
Johnson, rather than Oldys, wrote any particular entry in the *Harleian
Catalogue*. Oldys was also working on the project from the beginning and
also had the expertise required to write any of the entries. It seems likely,
however, that each collaborator gravitated to his favourite kinds of work:
Oldys probably did most of the antiquarian notes dealing with curious
provenances and relatively local topography and genealogy, while Johnson

immersed himself in works with a heavier intellectual interest: philology, theology, and history. Moreover, even if the originality or the authorship of particular entries is in doubt, it is clear that Johnson was deeply involved in the project, and his involvement is an important and highly revealing event in his intellectual life.

Despite its various deficiencies both as a catalogue and as evidence of Johnson's thinking, the *Harleian Catalogue* provides a great deal of printing history and much information about the world of books as Johnson knew it. The section on English Bibles, for example, provides a list of the most important editions in chronological order, with enough commentary to make the section a lesson on the growth of the English national church. The sufferings of some of the promulgators are recounted, and there is a hagiography of publishers in this testimony to the power of the press. For instance, 'For printing this Bible [edited by Thomas Matthews, 1537], Grafton, the Printer, was persecuted about five Years afterward', and 'Taverner gave so much Offence by this Performance [Old Testament, 1539], that, after the Death of Lord Cromwel, by whom he was protected, he was imprisoned for it in the Tower.' Next we learn that 'A Proclamation was this Year published, commanding, that every Parish Church should procure one of these Bibles [edited by Edward Whitchurch, with an introduction by Thomas Cranmer, 1540], of the largest Form, and place it upon a Desk in some convenient Part of the Church for the Use of the People, under a Penalty of forty Shillings a Month, for Neglect, after the Time limited.' The Bishops' Bible receives special attention, and the King James Version merits a complete list of the fifty-four translators with descriptions of their tasks and overall procedures.[7]

There are other categories in which the contents themselves are telling. Within the general heading of 'History', which is broken down first into regions, there is one called 'Miscellaneous English History, from the year 1665, to 1739, Inclusive'. Under this subheading there are forty-five consecutive entries devoted to runs of contemporary journals, making the whole a quick introduction to the periodical press of the time. The relative numbers of history books listed under the various regions tells a predictable story of Eurocentrism and national interest: French history is second in volume to English, followed by Italy and Spain. But there are numerous volumes on 'Turcica et Persica' and 'India Orientale et Occidentale'. Perhaps Johnson shows his continuing interest in non-Western culture by providing full notes here. There is praise, for example, for Ludovico Marraccio's Koran (Padua, 1698), Leunclavius's *History of Turkish Moslems* (1591), and Thomas Erpenius's translation of Elmacinus's *Historia Saracenica* (1625). For writing *De Gentibus Indiae & Bragmanibus*, the note says, Palladius should be ranked with William Cave, author of *Antiquitates Apostolicae; or the lives, acts and martyrdoms of the Holy Apostles.*[8]

The mere chronological listing of titles is also interesting or instructive under such diverse categories as 'Histoire de Trouble Arrivée en France, par Rapport de la Bulle Unigenitus', 'Books upon Ludicrous and Diverting

Subjects', 'Speeches of Persons Executed for Divers Offenses', 'Miraculous Monstrous and Supernatural', 'Theologica Ascetica', 'During the Troubles of King Charles the First and King Charles the Second', English 'Controversies with the Papists', the 'Quakers', the 'Deists', and the 'Trinitarian Controversy'. The selection and arrangement of these categories allows their contents to display intellectual history, and the display is often enhanced because the titles of the books are given very completely. The way in which a controversy was conducted through the press is suggested, for instance, by a long list of titles under 'Controversies with the Papists' epitomized by the tortuously titled 'Reply of E.T. to D. Collins's Defence of my Lord of Winchester's Answer to Cardinal Bellarmine's Apology (1621)'.[9] Some of the specific arguments also show up in these titles, usually at the expense of the various heretics. Item 3058 in volume 1, for instance, is 'School of the Eucharist, established upon the Miraculous Respect and Acknowledgments which Beasts, Birds, and Insects have rendered to the Holy Sacrament of the Altar, by Tho. Bridoul, Priest (1687)'. Number 3261 is the more broadly comic 'Featley's Dipper's [*sic*] dipt, or the Anabaptists duck'd and plung'd over Head and Ears (1647)'.

The completeness of the titles is such (especially in the first two volumes) that they sometimes contain little tables of contents, abstracts of the books, biographical sketches of the author, and epigraphs. Item 2893, for example, is 'A Boke made by John Fryth, Prysoner in the Tower of London, answeringe unto M. More's Letter, which he wrote against the fyrste lytle Treatyse that John Fryth made concerning the Sacr. &c. with the Artycles of his Examyneycion before the Byshoppes of London, &c. for whych John Fryth was brente in Smythfield, July 4th, 1533, 12ves, *black Letter*, London by Jugge 1598. The Motto of the Title: *Deade Man* [*sic*] *shall rise agayne.*' Under 'Genealogy and Heraldry in English' there is this charming item:

A true History of several honourable Families of the right honourable name of Scot, by Captain Walter Scot, an old Soldier and no Scholar,

> *And one that can write nane,*
> *But just the Letters of his Name* (1688).

Beneath the epigraph from Morhof in volume 1 of the *Catalogue*, Johnson and Oldys placed another from Maittaire that suggests the compilers' wish to go beyond titles and categorization: in translation, 'Whoever undertakes a task like this is engaged not so much in the labor and tedium of consuming contents of books as in the trivial exercise of gathering information by merely turning pages: those who go no further than the title pick up books in vain.' This epigram adds an element of self-awareness to the book, as does the famous passage in Johnson's *Dictionary* when he defines 'lexicographer' as a 'harmless drudge', but this element does not remain present for very long in the *Catalogue*. The best of it is the remark *in propria persona* that follows a printer's excuse for errors in his 1490 edition of St Ambrose. The publisher-editor jokes rather meanly in Latin verse which may be translated as 'Perceptive reader, should you find an error, attribute it to the boy who copied those books of Ambrosius quickly and ignored my instructions.' Johnson cannot resist adding, also in Latin, 'Likewise, reader, if any errors show up in this catalogue, impute it to the same cause.'[10] Johnson is pointing to the meanness of the publisher-editor in a humorous way and having a joke on himself because he had recently complained in the 'Account' that the compilers of the *Catalogue* had to work without the assistance of amanuenses. This may be the last indulgence of this sort in all five volumes, but there is further evidence throughout that, like Johnson's *Dictionary*, the *Harleian Catalogue* is partly the work of an individual scholar with his own individual interests, predilections, and expressions.

In addition to the essential bibliographical matter, the *Harleian Catalogue* supplies a surprising amount of information on ink, binding, and format. As someone who was bred a bookseller, Johnson had an eye for these material features of books, and OM Brack has very credibly argued that Johnson wrote the introduction to works on vellum in volume 3 of the *Catalogue*. It is more characteristic of Johnson's well-known interests, however, that the *Catalogue* contains so much biographical information. As Kaminski shows, these unoriginal sketches can in many cases be traced to a couple of sources. Nevertheless, the kind and amount of biographical information included, the subjects chosen, and, in some cases, the tone are telling. Even if he was just looking it up in a couple of sources, it is interesting that Johnson read and transferred to the *Catalogue* biographies of most of the major and many of the minor church fathers, editors, commentators, and translators in the Christian era. Abstracted from the *Catalogue* these additions would make a handy, though spotty, volume of reference on the history of scholarship, with special reference to fifteenth-century humanism. Indeed, in drawing up the *Catalogue*, Johnson laid the groundwork for his projected work on the 'History of the Revival of Learning in Europe'. The *Catalogue* is richest in biographies of scholars and others who promoted learning, and the longer entries comprise a pantheon of scholarly heroes to whom Johnson bowed on other occasions. The tone of reverence for the scholars is set by his prayer for the manes of Richard Bentley in the 'Account': 'May the Shade at least of one great *English* Critic rest without Disturbance, and may no Man presume to insult his Memory who wants his Learning, his Reason, or his Wit.'[11] Among other figures whom the *Catalogue* reverences are Alcuin, Lascaris, Peter Lombard, Duns Scotus, Waldensis, Postel, Joseph Scaliger, Sambucus, Meursius, Daniel Heinsius, Grotius, de Thou, Boxhorn, Ramus, Mirandola, Bacon, Lipsius, Reuchlin, Chrysolaris, Melanchthon, Sigonius, Poggius, Morhof, Pococke, and Hemmerlin.

The *Catalogue* is an advertising instrument, and praise for the authors of the books for sale was required. But the relative proportions of the laudatory statements are interesting. Heinsius and Grotius receive very high praise, for instance, and Pico della Mirandola is said to merit his conventional accolade as 'phoenix sui seculi', but more space and grander words are spent on the very greatest scholars. If length of entry is an index of greatness, the two greatest scholars of the Reformation, according to the *Catalogue*, were Francis Bacon and Joseph Scaliger. Bacon's *Instauratio Magna* is catalogued with a description of the author as 'a truly great man, distinguished by unusual intellectual gifts: naturally strong perception, a faithful memory, penetrating judgment, and eloquence'. His method and his physics outdo Aristotle, but 'of all his works his Moralia, or Essays, were most pleasing; indeed they are felt to touch the affairs of real people and to come home to their hearts.' Bacon said this himself about his *Essays*, and Johnson repeated the remark again in the *Rambler*. The *Catalogue*, like Johnson's *Dictionary*, also praises Bacon for refining his native language. The eulogy for Scaliger is attached to his quintessential humanistic work *Opus de Emendatione Temporum*, which is called 'immortalitate dignissimum'. Even though he is mostly citing other scholars, Johnson's praise is remarkable (perhaps the only other place in all his works where he offers such high praise is in his treatment of *Paradise Lost* in his life of Milton): 'Born into the noblest family among the royal Veronesians, Joseph Justus Scaliger was a philosopher, a theologian, a lawyer, and a doctor. He has been distinguished with the highest praise by the most learned men because of his extraordinary scholarship. Some of the learned called him the phoenix, and Daniel Heinsius called him the bottomless pit of erudition, the sea of knowledge, the sun of learning, the divine offspring of a divine father [Julius Caesar Scaliger], a godlike man, indeed Nature's greatest work, and no one ever questioned even the most exalted of these titles.'[12]

Such long notes are unusual because printed space was always at a premium. The short note added to Reuchlin's *Rudimenta Hebraica* is much more representative than the lengthy praise of Scaliger, but, brief as it is, the note carries with it an underlying theme that runs throughout the *Catalogue*. Reuchlin 'was a most illustrious philologer, deeply learned in Greek; he was also most assiduous in his study of the Hebrew language. He defended the writings of the Jews against the Monks, protecting them when they were threatened with ruin.' Many other short biographies celebrate heroes in the war against the Roman Catholic Church, and particular attention is paid to those who appear in the Tridentine Council's book catalogue, the *Index Expurgatorius*. Hemmerlin, for instance, 'is ranked in the first Class of Authors, whose Works are condemned by the Church of Rome. In the Catalogue of those Authors, he is said to be *Dignus Flammis, Malleo, &t Incude* [worthy of flames, and to be smashed with a hammer]; which may possibly induce some curious people to peruse him.' Another victim of Roman oppression was Vecchiettus, who, 'in this distinguished book [*De Sacrorum Temporum Ratione*, 1621] tries to show by reason of the solar and lunar calendars, that before the passion of Christ a solemn feast of Paschal dinner was observed. Not only was the book burned, the author was thrown in jail where he remained for many years in darkness and filth rather than retract the least bit of his argument.'[13]

Writers on the opposite side are also sometimes treated, and sometimes generously. The scholar-hero de Thou, for instance, merits this encomium: 'he was so tireless in his display of love for his nation's works and her freedom that he was called the Cato of his day. His history is distinguished by the highest praise from the most learned. He handles religious matters most judiciously and fairly, even though he subscribed to the religion of the Pope.' Such remarks are usually overtly concessional in this way, however, and the Protestant point of view is preferred throughout. Aeneas Sylvius Piccolomini, later Pope Pius II, has this note attached to his *Opera* (1571), to his cost: 'This author entirely approved and defended the decrees of the Council of Basil, which stated that the Pope was subordinate to the Council. However, when he ascended the papal throne, he issued the bull called the Retraction, in which he nullified the appeal from the Pope to the Council. In another bull, written to the University of Cologne, he declared that he would act as his own overseer. . . . Whence it is said, What Aeneas approved Pius condemned.' Real scorn, however, is reserved for the turncoat. As in British politics Johnson despised the 'renegade' Lord Gower, in the politics of the European Reformation, 'This John Nichols was a very Villain, first a Protestant, afterwards went over to the Church of Rome . . . and died miserably.'[14]

Like the forgotten Lydiat and the executed Laud who serve as monitory examples in *The Vanity of Human Wishes*, many scholars in the *Harleian Catalogue* suffer neglect or worse, despite their awesome achievements. Whether death finds the scholar early or late, illustrious or unknown, however, it finds him in the end, and, like all Johnsonian biography, the *Catalogue* tends to dwell on the deaths of its subjects. The bland 'obiit' is all that history allows on many occasions, but where possible the deaths of writers are recorded in more vivid ways. To item 8304 in volume 1, for instance, is added, 'N.B. The Author of this Epistle is Mr John Corbet, a Scotsman; his Head was cut off by two Swineherds, in the Time of the Irish Rebellion in 1641.' The *Catalogue* reminds its readers of death more elegantly by printing a surprising number of epitaphs. Of Pontanus, for instance, we read, 'This author was most illustrious on account of his unusual qualities of mind, especially the eloquence of his speech. The following epitaph, not unworthy of note, he commanded to be inscribed on his tomb: I am Johann Jovianus Pontanus, beloved of the Muses, admired by good men, honoured by kings and lords. You now know who I am, or rather, who I was. In this dark region I cannot know you, traveller, but I beg thee to know thyself.' Johnson found the epitaph in Julius Caesar Scaliger's *De re poetica*, a book he owned most of his adult life, and he translates part of it in *Rambler* 29. It is characteristic of Johnson to find an opportunity of transmitting this profoundly conventional message amidst the labour of producing a commercial work.[15]

Johnson must have remembered his experience in the Harleian Library when he composed his elegiac Preface to the *Dictionary* because he records with especial richness the sufferings of lexicographers. One source of trouble for them, of which Johnson had already had his share, is competition in marketplace. As in his 'Considerations' on Trapp's sermons, Johnson's notes on dictionary-making take a brief for the redactors, abstractors, and epitomizers. Writing on Scapula's Greek–Latin dictionary, for instance, Johnson makes light of the woe the author caused Stephanus, his source: 'Scapula put together an epitome of Stephanus' *Thesaurus*, which sold for less and was therefore snapped up by students so eagerly that Stephanus lost money on his great work; whence he said, humourously, that he had a pain in the *scapula* [shoulder].' Likewise, Johnson defends Stephen Doletus, whose life as a struggling writer ended in immolation for atheism in Paris, 3 August 1546: 'His work has been reproached because it is extracted from Robert Stephanus' *Thesaurus*, but it deserves praise because it presents plainly, precisely, and appropriately things which in Stephanus no one can read without patching together lots of little bits.' Though he might defend some of his competitors and extractors, Johnson reserves the highest praise among lexicographers for Stephanus, and he allows him a pathetic epigram in the tone of Johnson's lugubrious Preface to his own *Dictionary*: 'No one knows how much work this lexicon cost; nor would it occur to anyone to find fault with it, save that you will object, learned reader, that Stephanus diminishes himself when he complains in such melancholy verse as this: This thesaurus has given me rags for riches and replaced the bloom of youth with the wrinkles of old-age.'[16]

As the fullness of the notes on dictionaries suggests Johnson's hand, so does the fact that the *Catalogue* represents its authors as persons whose lives are subject to divine judgement, whatever the value of their works. For instance, it must be noted of the author of *De Etruriae Regionis* (1551), 'This Postell, a Norman who lived for some time among the Venetians, had illicit affairs with spinsters and determined that it was healthful for the women. Returning to France, he tried to defend his findings ... [he was] very learned but apparently depraved and somewhat mad.' What is recorded of a great scholar of oriental languages is his deviation into the heresy of the church in the region he studied, a heresy Johnson knew well from his work on Lobo: 'Selden suggests that Pococke, the learned Orientalist, was given to expounding the Eutychian heresy' (according to which Christ has a single mixed rather than a dual divine and human nature). On the other hand, no matter how great a writer's work, his most lasting monument is a life well lived. Sambucus, for instance, is praised for being a great antiquarian who is most accurate in his readings, but the motto he leaves the world is more valuable: 'Even in the roughest times, one must keep calm and even.'[17]

There are further Johnsonian touches throughout the *Catalogue*. In the sections on travel literature, for example, authors are praised for avoiding the fabulous and reporting what was seen firsthand. Very much like Johnson's praise of Father Lobo is the encomium of *Le Voyage de Corneille*

Le Brun par la Moscovie (1718): it contains nothing but 'what he himself saw with his own eyes and then carefully mulled over'. Prideaux and Geddes, sources for *Irene*, are described in the *Catalogue*, and Johnson ventures to assert that Zizimi's history of such events as the death of Mahomet I and Bajazet, which are background for *Irene*, are eyewitness accounts. There is also a stirring note on Chrysoloras, who, like Demetrius in *Irene*, flees Byzantium to spread learning in the West: 'When Bajazeth the Turk was at the gates of the city, the Byzantine Emperor sent Chrysoloras out to seek help. He wandered over most of Europe until Tamburlaine captured Bajazeth and liberated Greece from fear. Then Chrysoloras settled in Italy and taught the Greek language with such skill that among the graduates of his school were the likes of [Leonardo] Aretino, Filelfo, and Poggio. It may be owing to his efforts at promoting Greek studies that learned exiles received such a warm welcome in Italy after the fall of Constantinople.'[18] It is very much to this company of scholars that Johnson himself looked throughout his early career, and he pays homage to them in the *Catalogue* in an incomplete but nevertheless more demonstrative way than he does anywhere else in his works.

With as many as 50,000 printed volumes, the Harleian Library contained most of the books Johnson saw in the first half of his life and many of those from which he chose his reading for the rest of his life. He may never before or after have been in a larger library. The printed books came up from Wimpole, Edward Harley's Cambridgeshire house, and were placed in twelve rooms in his mansion in Marylebone, where the Earl had hoped they would form the basis of a great public library. Johnson stood among these books, leafing through them and reading occasionally in them as he catalogued them for sale and dispersion. He saw before him and handled many books he already knew well – Juvenal and Horace in the editions he most admired, romances and travel books from his earliest years (like Martin Martin's *Western Islands*), the Lobo he had translated, books he took to school (like Quillet's *Callipaedia*), the Petrarch he discovered while hunting for an apple on his father's shelves (whatever edition that was), the Petronius he acquired in 1726, the Politian he borrowed from Pembroke, the histories he used to research *Irene*, all the sources of Robert James's *Medicinal Dictionary*, and the biographical works on which he had based all his early biographies. There too Johnson saw, some of them for the first time, almost all the books he would use in compiling his *Dictionary*, not only the other lexicons and reference works but most of the sources of quotations and of the preliminary 'History of the English Language'. He used some of the same reference works in both tasks, and he may have acquired some of his reference books for dictionary-making as part of his payment for work on the *Catalogue*. During his days in Marylebone Johnson must have added to his ambitious plans for his prospective works on the history of printing, the history of criticism, the history of the revival of learning, and others. He planned, for instance, a translation of Herodian, and he owned at his death a 1581 edition by

Stephanus, apparently identical to no. 1081 in volume 3 of the *Harleian Catalogue*. To give just one more example, Thomas Percy once spoke of Johnson planning 'a kind of Monthly Review upon a New Plan . . . something like the Acta Eruditorum Leipsiensia'. Johnson catalogued the edition identical to the one he owned as no. 12541 in volume 2 and added high praise of this 'Doctrinae Thesaur[us]', which included 'not only titles but also extracts, a taste of the authors, the heads of their works, the most important contents, etc'.[19] There must have been for Johnson an extensive mixture of memory and desire about the whole experience and a sense of awe for the achievements of scholarship and printing in the previous three centuries. This experience must be accounted an important place in Johnson's life, and the *Harleian Catalogue*, mixed with Oldys's entries and derivative as it may be, is the most direct record of that experience we have.

Another aspect of the event must not be forgotten. The enterprise was mercantile, and Johnson was in the employ of Thomas Osborne whose dreams, though they also involved books, were undoubtedly of a far different kind than Johnson's. The two men collided while Johnson was working for him, and posterity has shown its usual genius for allegory in embellishing the tale. Johnson's own testimony is merely that Osborne 'was insolent and I beat him'. This was apparently in Johnson's own rooms, but the tale is that Osborne upbraided Johnson for reading too deeply in the books he was supposed to be quickly cataloguing for sale, whereupon the fabled Johnson 'knocked Osborne down in his shop, with a folio, and put his foot upon his neck'. Alvin Kernan has read the allegorical picture as 'the author rampant over the defeated bookseller' in his story of Johnson's life of shaping and being shaped by the print world. This is true enough, but the interpretation might be refined to include the sense that Johnson here is representing an older, post-monastic ideal of scholarship and learning as well as an emerging class of authors who had to assert their free-agency against the controling, paternalistic sellers. An older story of how the great Italian humanist Poggio felled his opponent Tortelli with a codex may lie in the background. The identification of Johnson's 'missile' as a Frankfurt Bible also makes him older and monastic, as does the posture of St George that Johnson is made to assume.[20]

Throughout the latter half of the eighteenth century, especially after the establishment of the British Museum in 1753, great English collections of books and manuscripts were gathered in public places. The forty-six libraries in Oldys's manuscript tour of scholarly London were being gradually consolidated. At the same time, literary activity was becoming more and more subject to the rules of the marketplace; rare books were auctioned up in value as commodities, and the world of scholarly devotion, such as that shown by a Scaliger, a Chrysoloras, or a Bentley, was receding, becoming more specialized, more academic, and less heroic. In addition to being a representative of the newly independent author, Johnson felt an intimate connection with an older world of heroic, learned writers. It was as much in defence of his heroes as of himself that Johnson struck down Osborne. For all its failings the *Harleian Catalogue* is the only record left of the printed books in the great Harleian Library, and it is the fullest record of Johnson's ties with the world it celebrates.

In Sir John Hawkins's version of the story about Johnson's assault on Osborne, the thirty-five-year-old writer was interrupted in the process of selecting material for the *Harleian Miscellany* rather than the *Harleian Catalogue*. The *Miscellany* is eight volumes (in a large quarto with double columns of print) of pamphlets and tracts that Osborne bought along with the regular books in Harley's library. (A very few items are printed for the first time, Osborne evidently having swept up some manuscripts in his purchase of the printed books.) Some of the approximately 1700 pieces selected are accompanied by small introductions and footnotes. As in the case of the *Catalogue*, commentary is more prevalent at the beginning of the work and fades out later under the pressures of publication and fatigue. There is a short burst of assiduousness at the beginning of volume 3, however, and here there are ten prefaces by Johnson.[21] How much more Johnson contributed to the selection and description of pieces remains unknown, but the project fell mostly to Oldys, who had worked on the similar collection, *Phoenix Britannicus*, in the previous decade.

The ten pieces that Johnson introduces and probably selected are representative of the rest of the collection and offer no clues about Johnson's further involvement. The last piece Johnson introduces merits some attention because he praises it as full of 'so many Touches of Elegance and Judgment'. The piece is 'A Letter to the Lord Bishop of Cloyne [George Berkeley]' in which the author makes a strong case for the necessity and importance of received knowledge in opposition to radical empiricism or free-thinking. He says, for instance, 'Without what they call *Prejudices*, that is, early Impressions before they can reason, Mankind could have no Opinions at all; because they could not have any Knowledge without Education.' Johnson was a rational and an empirical thinker but not radically so, and his intellectual ties are stronger with Locke's empiricist predecessors than with successors like Berkeley. By printing this letter and praising it Johnson was refuting Berkeley's theory long before the famous incident in 1763 when he kicked a large stone and declared, 'I refute it *thus*.'[22]

It is pleasant to speculate that Johnson had a hand in selecting other pieces for the *Harleian Miscellany*, especially those concerned with the English language, like 'Vindex Anglicanus' (1644), or those that celebrate the 'trade of writing': the heroic couplets in the broadside 'An Essay on Writing, and the Art and Mystery of Printing' (1696) or 'An Account of the Original of Writing and Paper', apparently translated out of Italian with no date. Johnson may have remembered some of the pieces in the *Miscellany* when writing later works of his own. The highly monitory 'Life of Archbishop Laud' (1641), for instance, may have come to him when he was writing *The Vanity of Human Wishes* or 'The English Hermit' when he was writing *Rasselas*. Such speculation is idle, but the *Harleian Miscellany* does contribute to a knowledge of what books were available to Johnson at this time.

Much of the *Miscellany* comprises political pamphlets, and the preservation and wide dissemination of this material has political implications which are part of the politics of all printing. Like the Parliamentary *Debates*, the *Miscellany* increased the avenues of access to politically important information. By publishing this material in a manageable format, the *Miscellany* enabled independent analyses of political happenings that may have dissented from the official word and supported that dissent with documentation. It was heavily marketed throughout the country and boasted the largest list of subscribers of its day, headed by 'the King's Most Gracious Majesty', and including Johnson's mother Sarah who was still running the shop in Lichfield. In his introduction, later known as the 'Essay on the Origin and Importance of Small Tracts and Fugitive Pieces', Johnson finds English liberty gloriously exhibited in the variety of political views printed in the *Miscellany*: 'There is, perhaps, no Nation, in which it is so necessary, as in our own, to assemble, from Time to Time, the *small* Tracts and *fugitive* Pieces, which are occasionally published: For, besides the general Subjects of Enquiry, which are cultivated by us, in common with every other learned Nation, our Constitution in Church and State naturally gives Birth to a Multitude of Performances, which would either not have been written, or could not have been made publick in any other Place.' In his history of pamphlet publication, Johnson links the freedom of the press with dissent and its control with authority. He deplores the licensing of the press under Queen Mary and celebrates its freedom under Elizabeth, when, he says, 'the *Trade of Writing* began.' Although there are no party politics in the work, Johnson's introduction and the *Miscellany* as a whole celebrate the freedom of the press and the rise of writing as a profession. They have, therefore, like so many of Johnson's efforts, a liberalizing, if not a revolutionary political effect.[23]

The weekly, serial publication of the *Miscellany* began on 24 March 1744, to be completed two years later. By late fall 1744 Johnson was no longer working on any Harleian projects, having turned his attention to Shakespeare. His plan was to produce an edition with commentary in ten volumes. Like the *Harleian Miscellany*, his edition of Shakespeare was to be sold by subscription. In order to launch the project, Johnson wrote *Miscellaneous Observations on the Tragedy of Macbeth*, a sixty-four page specimen of the prospective commentary. To this were attached the proposals for the edition with a pair of sample pages showing equal amounts of text and notes. Also included were observations on the recently published edition of Shakespeare by Sir Thomas Hanmer, an unexpected rival. Johnson and Cave, who was again his publisher, shelved the project when Jacob Tonson, a very powerful London bookseller, threatened them with a suit in Chancery Court on the ground that he held the copyright to Shakespeare's works. Johnson did not return to his edition until after the publication of his

Dictionary in 1755, when the new *Proposals* (1756) was published, with Tonson among the backers. Johnson's Shakespeare, in eight volumes, did not appear until 1765. Although it was largely incorporated into the completed work, which will be discussed later, the *Observations* of 1745 is interesting from the point of view of intellectual biography because it provides some evidence of how Johnson glided from the Harleian work into his editorial work on Shakespeare and from that into the *Dictionary*.

At this time Johnson was cultivating an interest in history that verged on antiquarianism. Shortly after his Harleian researches, he planned a dictionary of antiquities, a biblical commentary, and a history of the debates in Parliament, along with a dictionary of English and an edition of Shakespeare. He was working on all these projects at the same time, according to his good friend Bishop Percy. The sort of notes he wrote in the *Observations* suggests how antiquarian all of the work was. In his first note, on the weird sisters, Johnson offers a learned discussion of the credulity which the ignorance and error of mankind have lent to the phantoms of magic and witchcraft. He cites St John Chrysostom and Photius in Greek as he outlines the history of the idea that magic may be responsible for military success. Johnson is not only continuing the sort of historical work he did in the *Harleian Catalogue*, he is also sounding like the learned Christian classicists whose works he recorded and celebrated. Johnson continues his learned note, citing modern sources that he might also have seen in the Harleian Library: Elizabethan reports on the witches of Warbois, King James I's *Daemonologie*, a law on witches passed in the first year of James's rule, and Joseph Hall's *Sussurium cum Deo*. In other notes Johnson uses more strictly antiquarian sources – Thomas Hearne's *Ectypa Varia*, for example, Camden's works, or Hanvil the Monk's *Architrenius*.[24]

In a note on scene 3, there is an example of a connection from the Harleian work through the *Observations* to the *Dictionary*. Discussing the meaning of 'forbid', Johnson says, '[t]o "bid" is originally "to pray", as in this Saxon fragment, / He is wis that bit and bote, &c. / He is wise that prays and improves.' This proverb reappears in the *Dictionary* under 'to boot' where Johnson says, 'bot, in Saxon, is recompense . . . botan is, to repent, or to compensate; as, "He is wis who bit and bote / And bet bivoren dome."' Johnson printed the line in context in his 'History of the English Language', part of the preliminary material in the *Dictionary*. Johnson's source was George Hickes's *Thesaurus*, a magnificent work in three large folios that Johnson certainly examined (and perhaps acquired) while working in the Harleian Library. 'Harmless industry' (as Johnson called Hanmer's editorial work) could multiply the number of other explicit links among the Harleian projects, the *Observations*, and the *Dictionary*. What the correspondence shows is Johnson's commitment at this time to a historical approach that would make his *Dictionary* a precursor of the *OED* and his Shakespeare a precursor of the *Variorum*. The very first line of his first note in the *Observations* expresses this commitment: 'In order to make a true estimate of the abilities and merit of a writer, it is always necessary to examine the genius of his age, and the opinions of his contemporaries.'[25] Johnson applies history to the task of critical evaluation, and he widened its application as his editorial work went on into the 1760s. What intervenes between the beginning and the conclusion of his work on Shakespeare is the *Dictionary*, a project that is part sibling, part offspring, and part parent of the edition, but both works are children of the Harleian projects.

8

Johnson's *Dictionary*

Dictionaries are like watches, the worst is better than none, and the best cannot be expected to go quite true.

Johnson to Francesco Sastres, 21 August 1784

In every account of Johnson's life, 1746 is a pivotal year. On 18 June Johnson signed his contract with the London booksellers to write *A Dictionary of the English Language* and received a promise of 1500 guineas for the work, some of it in advance. Although he had to pay for all the costs of producing the *Dictionary*, including paper and secretarial help, it was a lavish stake which allowed him to establish himself as an independent author. He capitalized on his situation before completing the *Dictionary* in 1755 by publishing several minor and three other major works: *The Vanity of Human Wishes* (1749), *Irene* (1749), and the *Rambler* (1750–2). Although *Irene* had been finished years earlier, this was the most productive period of Johnson's life of writing; it made him successful and assured him of fame just when his career appeared to be dangerously slowing down.

In 1745 the proposed edition of Shakespeare had been scrapped, like so many earlier projects. Johnson was trying to get out of Cave's steady employ and work on a freelance basis. He was decreasing his contributions to the *Gentleman's Magazine* and doing some professional piece-work: a charity sermon for his friend Henry Hervey Aston to preach in St Paul's, for example, and corrections on a long poem by an Irish clergyman named Samuel Madden. However, the Johnsons' finances were so bad that they were forced to sell the chalice Johnson retained as an heirloom and souvenir of his childhood visit to Queen Anne. When Aston paid Johnson for the sermon, he also relieved him from arrest and possible confinement in debtor's prison. Johnson had exhausted his last reserves and was continually in arrears on his mortgage payments on the house in Lichfield where his mother lived and operated the family bookshop. Johnson again considered abandoning writing for a living and explored the possibility of practising law instead. Using Pembroke College connections, he applied to a man named Smalbroke but found, as in his efforts to become a schoolmaster, that the lack of a degree made it impossible for him to switch professions. Johnson was so inactive professionally at the end of this period and therefore so untraceable that some have imagined him in northern England joining forces with the Pretender in the last serious Jacobite challenge to the Hanoverian monarchy.[1]

In 1746 everything changed. There is solid evidence of Johnson's whereabouts and activities at this time: letters exist from Johnson to the principal booksellers concerning the terms of the contract for the *Dictionary,* and a receipt survives, with the same date as the contract, recording Johnson's employment of a secretary, Francis Stewart. Although work on the *Dictionary* may have begun in Holborn, as Boswell thought, the large advance allowed Johnson to stop wandering from flat to flat and to lease an impressive house at Number 17 Gough Square, where he lived from 1747 to 1759. His name appears on the city rolls as a householder for the first time, and fancy has little room to imagine him elsewhere or doing something other than pursuing his literary career in London. The garret was his studio and the workplace for the secretaries, as many as four at a time, who helped him with the *Dictionary.* The house was attended to by servants, and the Johnsons lived with many of the bourgeois comforts available to mid-century Londoners.[2]

In the attic, amidst an array of impressive but motley books, amidst imperfectly repaired furniture, with the help of the mostly Scottish, mostly impoverished Grub Street hacks who served as amanuenses, the *Dictionary* progressed. Johnson began by reading English books with a black lead pencil in hand. He underlined words, the meanings of which he found properly illustrated in the books; he drew vertical lines at the beginnings and the ends of the passages providing the illustration; and he wrote the first letter of the underlined word in the margin of the book. An amanuensis, or a pair of them, transferred the marked passages to slips of paper and alphabetized them according to the words they illustrated. Johnson then wrote the headwords and etymologies on sheets of paper, enumerated the senses of the words as he found them illustrated, and wrote the various definitions over the illustrative quotations, which could then be pasted on. These sheets went in parcels to the printer, William Strahan, as copytext. It took Johnson about three and a half years to perfect this method. As late as 1750 he was still discussing it with his printer, and he had to bear extra paper and copying costs when Strahan's compositors rejected the double-sided copytext that Johnson first submitted. As a recent study suggests, Johnson may have botched the copy by asking his amanuenses to transcribe illustrative quotations directly to copy-pages, hoping he would be able to put their work in order without using the extra step of preparing slips.[3] Finally, Johnson realized the need for movable quotations, which were either pasted in or recopied, sometimes with

changes that only Johnson could have made. His final way of proceeding
was very much the one employed by James A. H. Murray and the other
editors of the *Oxford English Dictionary*.

Unlike earlier English lexicographers, Johnson worked empirically, for
the most part, gathering words and describing their senses as he found
them employed by writers of English prose and poetry. However, Johnson's
empirical procedure was not pure. Like other lexicographers, for example, Johnson consulted other reference works. He used Nathan Bailey's
Dictionarium Britannicum of 1736, some edition of Edward Phillips's *Worlde
of Words*, Ainsworth's Latin–English, English–Latin *Thesaurus*, Skinner's
Etymologicon Linguae Anglicanae, and Junius's *Etymologicon Anglicanum*. He
used several encyclopedias for the vocabulary of technical subjects: Ephraim
Chambers's *Cyclopedia*, Miller's *Gardeners' Dictionary*, Harris's *Lexicon
Technicum*, Quincy's *Lexicon Physico-Medicum*, and Ayliffe's *Pareregon Canonici
Anglicani* (an encyclopedia of church law), among others. There are also
other books that served Johnson almost as reference works either because
they are alphabetically arranged or because they treat a special subject.
Peacham's *Graphice*, for example, came in handy for finding some of the
terms of painting and Moxon's *Mechanical Exercises* served as a reference
work for the terms related to printing and some other trades. Two hundred
years after the publication of the *Dictionary* one reader of Johnson's book
discovered that he had used an index of the moral sentiments in *Clarissa*,
which Richardson had prepared partly at Johnson's behest. Like other
reference books this 'Index Rerum' allowed Johnson to insert headwords,
quotations, or both without relying on empirical research. Johnson had all
these secondary sources around as he composed his *Dictionary*, and he used
his amazing memory to bring in quotations from the Bible and many
other books that he knew well, but the card-file of selected quotations was
his first resort, and he assembled his book primarily by consulting it. He
chose from this considerably larger file approximately 116,000 quotations
to illustrate the meaning of about 40,000 words. Although the role of his
amanuenses, especially Alexander Macbean, has been underestimated,
Johnson's *Dictionary* is largely the product of a magnificent single-handed
effort of reading and writing that began shortly before 30 April 1746 when
he finished a draft proposal (the 'Scheme') and ended on 15 April 1755
when the two large folio volumes made their appearance on the London
market at the high but not prohibitive price of £4 10s.[4]

Although accurate historical investigation often reduces to human dimensions the Herculean achievements of culture heroes like 'Dictionary
Johnson', his major work retains a nearly mythic status. Despite his
protestations that he was merely a 'harmless drudge', Johnson also thought
of his book in heroic terms. Of all his works the *Dictionary* is the one that
most entitles him to a place among the great humanists celebrated in the
Harleian Catalogue. In the printed proposal for the *Dictionary*, the *Plan
of a Dictionary of the English Language* (1747), it is obvious that Johnson
was trying to emulate his scholarly heroes. Like the Preface to the *Harleian*

Catalogue, this first preface to the *Dictionary* measures the prospective book against seventeenth-century French and Italian achievements in the genre. Johnson advertises the fact that he shares a Latin lexicographical tradition with the likes of Crescimbeni and Furetière. He cites several Roman linguists and compares himself to 'the soldiers of [Claudius] Caesar' looking 'on Britain as a new world, which it is almost madness to invade'. As he concludes the *Plan,* Johnson moves into the mode of complaint that he found in the prefaces of some of the great continental dictionaries he perused in the Harleian Library and explicitly compares his work with that of the European academies: 'We are taught by the Roman orator [Cicero], that every man should propose to himself the highest degree of excellence, but that he may stop with honour at the second or third: though, therefore, my performance should fall below the excellence of other dictionaries, I may obtain, at least, the praise of having endeavoured well; nor shall I think it any reproach to my diligence, that I have retired without a triumph, from a contest with united academies, and long successions of learned compilers.'[5]

Some of the Roman manner was for the benefit of Lord Chesterfield, to whom Johnson addressed the *Plan* in the hope of enlisting a wealthy patron. Chesterfield wanted an authoritative (if not authoritarian) dictionary, and he told the audience of the *World,* 'I will not only obey [Johnson], like an old Roman, as my dictator, but, like a modern Roman, I will implicitly believe in him as my pope and hold him to be infallible.'[6] Later, along with his hope of Chesterfield's support, Johnson dropped the parallel between himself and the invading forces of Caesar, but plenty of references to the tradition of Latin lexicography remain throughout the long course of Johnson's work on the *Dictionary.* Significantly, Johnson took the epigram for the whole book from a passage about Latin diction in Horace's *Epistles.* When he finished his revisions for the fourth edition of the *Dictionary* in 1773 Johnson addressed a poem to the most venerated scholar of all those listed in the *Harleian Catalogue,* Joseph Scaliger. Though the poem, Γνῶθι Σεαυτόν ('Know Thyself'), is an act of supplication and humility, Johnson knew that the *Dictionary* had earned him a hearing from the great scholars he admired. That he made his great achievement in a vulgar language, rather than Latin, is evidence of the lateness of Johnson's humanism, but it is also highly representative of the compromise he made throughout his life between his early scholarly dreams and his need to make a profit by writing for the growing audience of English readers.

What of the *Dictionary* itself? In many ways this enormous book is the centrepiece of Johnson's work, and it is important to understand it critically, both as a useful reference book and as a literary performance. Taking it first as a dictionary in the narrow sense, Johnson's work has several important and highly influential features. Although it is larger than any earlier English dictionary, Johnson's *Dictionary* has a smaller wordlist than some predecessors and competitors. One of the reasons his list is smaller is that Johnson is better than most of his predecessors about excluding the mere 'dictionary words' (anglicized Latin words and obscure technical terms) that earlier lexicographers culled from other reference books or simply invented in order to swell their volumes. Although it contains plenty of Latinate words, Johnson's list almost entirely comprises words actually used by English writers. Johnson's etymologies are also better than his predecessors': they do not reflect an advance in linguistic science, but they usually show good sense, and they rely on judiciously selected sources. Johnson pays more attention to the Saxonic element in English than most early lexicographers, and he rejects the sort of speculative etymology that tended to trace words back through Latin and Greek to an imaginary original language.[7] Johnson's definitions are much better than those of his predecessors: they are generally more detailed and carry distinction further into 'shades of meaning', a phrase that Johnson coined in his Preface. His definitions also sometimes have a kind of expressive literary force which is lacking in all other dictionaries written either before or after his.

In passages that Johnson cites in the *Dictionary* John Locke advised lexicographers to supplement their definitions with illustrations; Johnson may have thought this sound advice, but he included no cuts, pictures, or drawings. A probable reason for this is that so much space, and hence money, was spent in providing the two most important and most innovative features of the book: the numerous illustrative quotations and the careful division into numbered senses of most of the words in the list.

Dictionaries of English before Johnson's printed only occasional quotations or merely assigned usage to authorities without citing passages. They all kept to a minimum the enumeration of various senses of headwords. Johnson adopted his practices from great Latin and Greek dictionaries which he had recently catalogued in Harley's library. Of most importance for him were the dictionaries of Basilius Faber and Robert Estienne (Stephanus), both of which had been printed in numerous revised and augmented editions by learned editors of the seventeenth century. Although there were precedents, great importance must be attached to Johnson's decision to include illustrative quotation, to arrange it chronologically under each sense of each word, and, in large measure, to draw his definitions from the usages he so arranged. The practice suggests the empirical method, a kind of Baconian natural history applied to language, that was later assumed in a purer form by Murray and the 'other men of science' who appear on the first title page of the *Oxford English Dictionary*. In the terms of his own century, however, Johnson's historical arrangement of usage was an intellectual form of antiquarian activity – what Johnson called 'literary history' in the 'Account' preliminary to the *Harleian Catalogue* and seminally in the Preface to the *Dictionary*, 'intellectual history'.

The basis of Johnson's method is his conscious, antiquarian choice of historical linguistic facts in preference to prescribed or theoretically correct forms. 'By this method', Johnson says in the *Plan*, 'every word will have its history, and the reader will be informed of the gradual changes of the language.' The choice is fully consistent with his declaration at the beginnning of the *Observations on Macbeth* that authors should be judged by reference to the language and customs of their own time. The principle applied to the evaluation of Shakespeare in his prospective edition is applied to all authors in his prospective dictionary:

> Our syntax, therefore, is not to be taught by general rules, but by special precedents; and in examining whether Addison has been with justice accused of a solecism in this passage,
>
> > The poor inhabitant –
> > Starves in the midst of nature's bounty curst,
> > And in the loaden vineyard *dies for thirst* –
>
> it is not in our power to have recourse to any established laws of speech; but we must remark how the writers of former ages have used the same word, and consider whether he can be acquitted of impropriety, upon the testimony of [Sir John] Davies, given in his favour by a similar passage:
>
> > She loathes the wat'ry glass wherein she gaz'd,
> > And shuns it still, although *for thirst she dye.*

It may be because he wrote the *Plan* with Chesterfield in mind that Johnson stressed the opportunities for the arbiter of correctness provided by his historical collocations. In the event, however, the illustrative quotations in the *Dictionary* serve the historian much more than the arbiter. Although Johnson does a fair amount of 'branding' and 'censuring' of words because they are 'low', 'mean', 'bad', 'ungrammatical', or 'barbarous', he does not usually let such judgements interfere with his more scientific or antiquarian duties.[8]

Although the standards of the arbiter do not often lure Johnson from his primarily historical method of registering the English language, there are other ideals that he follows, despite their empirical impurity. For one thing, he restricts his view of English almost entirely to printed works. I know of no manuscript evidence employed in the *Dictionary*, and spoken language, when it is mentioned at all, is described with pejorative phrases like 'merely oral'. Not even the *OED* makes much use of oral speech; Boswell's reports of Johnson's talk are an interesting exception. The *OED* improves on Johnson's science, however, by using manuscript evidence of the language and by pushing the chronological boundary of English back to 1150. Johnson is comparatively narrow, drawing his data mainly from books written between the times of Sidney (1554–86) and Pope (1688–1744). There is some earlier English in the *Dictionary*, but much of it is confined to etymological notes and the prefatory 'History of the English Language'. Furthermore, among all the books printed in this period, Johnson looks mainly at great works by acknowledged masters of English. Shakespeare, Milton, Dryden, Bacon, Pope, and Addison, for example, all contribute thousands of illustrative quotations, whereas lesser writers, like Beaumont and Fletcher, contribute little, and many popular writers, like Thomas Nash and Robert Greene, are absent. The *OED* is guilty of the same failure, albeit to a lesser degree, and in preferring to record mainly the English of great writers Johnson was certainly not for his time being particularly conservative or prescriptive.[9]

However, Johnson employs another criterion for inclusion that evinces an attachment to the past and a wish to model his *Dictionary* after its Renaissance Latin predecessors. Like some of the great lexicographers he admired, Johnson selected quotations and sources that would present his reader with an encyclopedia of important knowledge. In 1747 he described his prospective collection of quotations hopefully, but, looking back on what he had done in 1755, Johnson adopts a sadder, nearly elegiac tone:

> When first I collected these authorities, I was desirous that every quotation should be useful to some other end than the illustration of a word; I there-fore extracted from philosophers principles of science; from historians re-markable facts; from chymists complete processes; from divines striking exhortations; and from poets beautiful descriptions. Such is design, while it is yet at a distance from execution. When the time called upon me to range this accumulation of elegance and wisdom into an alphabetical series, I soon discovered that the bulk of my volumes would fright away the student, and was forced to depart from my scheme of including all that was pleasing or useful in *English* literature, and reduce my transcripts to clusters of words, in which scarcely any meaning is retained; thus to the weariness of copying, I was condemned to add the vexation of expunging. Some passages I have yet spared, which may relieve the labour of verbal searches, and intersperse with verdure and flowers the dusty desarts of barren philology.

Despite this lamentation, Johnson knows he has transmitted a great deal of English culture in his book, and he rests his pretensions to success on the extent to which he has fostered an understanding of certain English writers, all of them, significantly, of the seventeenth century: 'I shall not think my employment useless or ignoble, if by my assistance foreign na-tions, and distant ages, gain access to the propagators of knowledge, and understand the teachers of truth; if my labours afford light to the reposi-tories of science, and add celebrity to *Bacon*, to *Hooker*, to *Milton*, and to *Boyle*.'[10] As a work of linguistic history Johnson's *Dictionary* illuminates the language used by these writers, but it also reprints and therefore recom-mends their writing, like a grand thesaurus or commonplace book.

In relying on existing writing for his account of English, Johnson was being empirical and modern, but, in making his *Dictionary* also a kind of encyclopedia, he was at the same time pursuing an older, Renaissance ideal of lexicography. Only gradually in the eighteenth and nineteenth centuries did the genres of dictionary and encyclopedia grow really dis-tinct from each other. In the seventeenth century there still persisted a late humanist dream of containing all knowledge in a book of books –

inevitably a lexicon, dictionary, encyclopedia, or thesaurus. J. A. Comenius's unfinished *Lexicon Reale Pansophicum* was a continental example, and in England there was the prospective second edition of Ephraim Chambers's *Cyclopedia*, which was meant to 'furnish the best Book in the Universe', revealing 'the whole vast Apparatus of unwritten Philosophy'. Johnson's *Dictionary* shares in the dream of publishing a book of books that grew up in Europe along with the rise of print and spawned the academies of learning and science to do cooperatively what one individual could not. Johnson is looking back to the dream of comprehensive knowledge in its purer Renaissance form when he talks in the Preface about the fantasies he entertained at the start of his work: 'When I had thus enquired into the original of words, I resolved to show likewise my attention to things; to pierce deep into every science, to enquire the nature of every substance of which I entered the name, to limit every idea by a definition strictly logical, and exhibit every production of art or nature in an accurate description, that my book might be in place of all other dictionaries, whether appellative or technical. But these were the dreams of a poet doomed at last to wake a lexicographer.'[11] The only kind of poet Johnson can mean here is the Renaissance epic poet, but the elegiac line thinly veils the fact that his expectations for himself have remained high. If he has given up trying to be a learned Latin epic poet – Poliziano, Petrarch, or Buchanan – he is still trying to be another Scaliger.

What kept the dreams of the poet alive in the lexicographer were not only his personal aspirations to Renaissance humanism but also the theory of language that Locke had recently articulated for modern philosophy. Johnson recapitulates this theory in his *Dictionary* explicitly by printing a high proportion of Locke's *Essay concerning Human Understanding* in his illustrative quotations, including much of the crucial Book 3, and by using quotations from Locke to define many key philosophical words, such as the word 'knowledge' itself. Following Renaissance humanists like Comenius and Vives, Locke found a near relation between words and things, and he considered language, in effect, the inventory of knowledge – our only way of retaining, managing, and analysing our thoughts. The importance of language struck Locke so forcefully as he wrote his *Essay* that he found himself inventing or identifying a third part of the universe of knowledge in addition to nature and ethics; this he called σημειωτική (semiotics). Following Locke, Johnson is convinced that the relationship between language and knowledge is a matter of convention, but the compact underlying their meanings, like all human things, is irregular, changeable, irrational, and subject to decay. Johnson wishes that 'signs might be permanent, like the things which they denote', but he knows this is impossible. Unlike classical Latin, to whose lexicographers Johnson is always comparing himself, 'our language is yet living, and variable by the caprice of every one that speaks it . . . and [parts of it] can no more be ascertained in a dictionary, than a grove, in the agitation of a storm, can be accurately delineated from its picture in the water.' Despite his sober awareness that language must remain as imperfect as other human things, Johnson does make some efforts to shape both knowledge and language in his book. He acknowledges that he does 'not form, but register the language . . . not teach men how they should think, but relate how they have hitherto expressed their thoughts'; yet he departs from this zero degree of purity in many interesting ways that link his book, albeit vestigially, with the great systematic summas of an earlier age and with the projects of philosophical linguistic reform of the previous century.[12]

Johnson's division and enumeration of the various senses of words represent his best attempt to 'form the language': in the ordering of senses, especially, Johnson displays a willingness to favour formal etymology over empirical history. The first meaning of 'ardour', for example, is 'heat'; Johnson can adduce no illustration of this meaning from literature, but he puts it at the head of the entry in order to organize the whole semantic field as a ramification of the Latin source *ardor*, meaning heat. In his entries for some complex words Johnson tries to recapitulate at the end and assert an organization of which he and his reader have lost sight in their wandering through a clouded maze of human meanings. At number 27 of 'to break', for instance, Johnson says, 'It is to be observed of this extensive and perplexed *verb*, that, in all its significations, whether *active* or *neutral* [transitive or intransitive], it has some reference to its primitive meaning, by implying either detriment, suddenness, or violence.' The phrase 'primitive meaning' implies a view of linguistic creation and semantic organization that Johnson knows he cannot institute, but he often tries to display the real, historical growth of language on a lattice or framework of ideal, analogical ramification, and he sometimes shows impatience with perverse departure from the ideal. Under the second sense of 'prejudice', for example, Johnson writes: 'mischief; detriment; hurt; injury. This sense is only accidental or consequential; *a bad thing* being called *a prejudice*, only because *prejudice* is commonly *a bad thing*, and it is not derived from the original or etymology of the word: it were therefore better to use it less.' Yet Johnson provides examples of the improper uses he deplores, and the philosopher of language gives way thereby to the historical lexicographer.

Despite his lexicographical fidelity, Johnson imposes some restrictions on language because he is continually recalling his wish to present knowledge, his 'dreams of a poet'. To present knowledge is to shape it, and the field of knowledge in Johnson's *Dictionary* has ascertainable dimensions; it expresses certain themes; and it implies an audience of a certain kind. Johnson partially determined the field of knowledge he would present in his selection of sources. In the Preface he describes his research for the *Dictionary* as 'fortuitous and unguided excursions into books', but study of the text reveals that this is only partly true.[13] Johnson undoubtedly grabbed some quotations from books that he happened to have on hand, but the bulk of the quotations come from selected sources. Moreover, whether they were fortuitous or planned, Johnson's choices shaped the

Dictionary and organized its field of knowledge in particular ways. Even his choice of the great sixteenth- and seventeenth-century writers, which was almost inevitable, carries cultural assumptions, as modern students of the literary canon must agree.

In addition to selecting the greatest English writers, however, Johnson made choices that are more obviously determined by extra-lexical concerns. He found works that treat most branches of knowledge, which the need to cover the vocabulary of English would require, but he also employed ideological standards of admission. In the natural sciences, for example, a large proportion of the writers belong to the school of physico-theology and believe that study of the natural world leads to a deeper conviction of the wisdom, power, and glory of God. Representative of the many books of this sort that Johnson chose are William Derham's *Physico-Theology: or a Demonstration of the Being and Attributes of God from His Works of Creation* and John Ray's *The Wisdom of God Manifested in the Creation.* Because Johnson found his illustrative quotations in such books, much of the vocabulary of natural science in Johnson's *Dictionary* is accompanied by reminders of God's benevolent omnipotence. To give just one example, the scientific word 'mundane', which Johnson defines as 'belonging to the world' is illustrated with a pious reminder by Bentley: 'The atoms which now constitute heaven and earth, being once separate in the *mundane* space, could never without God, by their mechanical affections, have convened into this present state of things.'[14]

The *Dictionary*'s whole wordlist is only slightly less imbued than its scientific vocabulary with the sentiments of physico-theology. Part of the reason for this is that Johnson took illustrations of all sorts of words, not just technical words, out of the physico-theological books, and their teaching shows up all over his book. There is enough of this kind of illustration spread all throughout the *Dictionary* to make it sound as if Johnson is speaking in his own voice when he quotes Cheyne under 'to beget': 'My whole intention was to *beget*, in the minds of men, magnificent sentiments of God and his works.'[15] But Johnson does not find such sentiments only in the physico-theologists. Poets, historians, and writers of sermons also supply him with illustrative quotations that make consulting the *Dictionary* almost a kind of catechism. The poems of Milton and Cowley contribute sentiments much like those of the physico-theologists, as do the sermons of some philosophical divines, like Robert South and Francis Atterbury. Sir Walter Raleigh's *History of the World* is much concerned with seeing history as an exhibition of Providence, as is George Hakewill's *An Apologie or Declaration of the Power and Providence of God in the Government of the World.* Johnson uses both liberally.

There is so much reference to God and Providence in the *Dictionary* that the field of knowledge Johnson gives his readers is theologically oriented. This was not the only point of view open to Johnson as a lexicographer or encylopedist. The French encyclopedists – Diderot and d'Alembert – were working at the same time on eliminating the religious and the spiritual dimensions from the field of knowledge. Both Johnson and the French writers chose the deistic encyclopedist Ephraim Chambers as a guide, but Johnson added theology to Chambers, whereas the French continued to remove it. Johnson took the approach he did for a number of related reasons. Partly because his own religious life was complex and painful, Johnson had a deep conviction of the need for basic religious teaching in education and a fear of contributing in any way to the corruption of young souls. Moreover, Johnson and his publishers conceived of his book as an educational work and thought of their audience as consisting importantly of students. A manuscript note on the back of page 7 of the first draft of the *Plan* suggests this, and it is confirmed in the great number of educational texts that Johnson chose as sources of illustrative quotation. The educational writings of Locke and his disciple Isaac Watts are the most prominent, but there are many others, including Ascham's *Scholemaster,* George Abbot's *A Brief Description of the Whole Worlde,* Andrew Bourde's *Fyrst Boke of the Introduction to Knowledge,* Milton's 'Of Education', Bishop Wilkins's *Mathematical Magic,* Felton's *Dissertation on Reading the Classics,* and *English Exercises for school-boys to translate into Latin* by J. Garretson, to name a few.[16]

Partly because it is a book for students, the *Dictionary* displays the field of knowledge as cleft by religion. The nature of this presentation is clearer in *The Vision of Theodore, the Hermit of Teneriffe,* a tale that Johnson appended to *The Preceptor,* an educational textbook on which he was working when he signed the contract to write the *Dictionary.* In that tale the hermit has an allegorical dream in the manner of John Bunyan; he sees the Mountain of Existence encircled by students, young men and women trying to get to the peak. They are guided first by Innocence, then by Education and Reason. However, in order to penetrate the mists that shroud the top of the mountain in obscurity, they must pledge their loyalty to Religion. Reason can merely surmise that her former charges have made it safely to the top. The highest knowledge is vouchsafed only to Religion.[17]

Johnson builds this divided epistemological field into his *Dictionary* not only by quoting from so many educational texts that imply it but also by choosing several texts that are concerned chiefly with the limitations on human knowledge unassisted by revelation. Physico-theology and the assertion of human limitation are related, as their treatment in the immensely influential writing of Lactantius shows, but human ignorance is the main theme in a couple of other works that Johnson quotes frequently: Joseph Glanvill's *Scepsis Scientifica: or Confest Ignorance the Way to Science* and Thomas Baker's *Reflections upon Learning wherein is Shewn the Insufficiency Thereof, in its several Particulars: in order to Evince the Usefulness and Necessity of Revelation.* Johnson's quotation of Glanvil in illustration of 'amplitude' is representative of the effect of this body of quotations on the overall tenor of his book: 'Whatever I look upon, within the *amplitude* of heaven and earth, is evidence of human ignorance.' Citations from many other books contribute to the theme. One of the best and most important is Sir Thomas Browne's catalogue of human error, *Pseudodoxia Epidemica.* The wisdom books of the Bible – Ecclesiastes and Proverbs, for example – are also rich sources of the theme. But Johnson also imported it from less likely places. Locke turns out to be an excellent source, making such contributions as the following: 'When we consider the reasons we have to think, that what lies within our *ken* is but a small part of the universe, we shall discover an huge abyss of ignorance.'[18]

At times Johnson seems to arrange his quotations so as to display the theme of ignorance more forcefully. In an occasional instance, he truncates his authorities so that they make much starker statements of the theme than they intended. Under 'incurably', for instance, Johnson has Locke say, 'We cannot know it is or is not, being *incurably* ignorant.' The passage of the *Essay concerning Human Understanding* from which Johnson abstracted this sentence is about the human inability to know 'real essences' and the confinement of our understanding to bundles of perceptions that we label with names, which we sometimes mistake for essences: 'how can we be sure', writes Locke, 'that this or that quality is in *Gold*, when we know not what is or is not *Gold*? Since in this way of speaking nothing is *Gold*, but what partakes of an Essence, which we not knowing, cannot know where it is, or is not, and so cannot be sure, that any parcel of Matter in the World is or is not in this sense *Gold*; being incurably ignorant, whether it has or has not that which makes any thing to be called *Gold, i.e.* that real Essence of *Gold* whereof we have no *Idea* at all.' The alteration is significant because Johnson usually managed to preserve the sense of his excerpts even though he trimmed a great many of them.[19] Arrangement and selection can be as pointed as abridgement, however, and Johnson makes his book a reminder of human ignorance more often by these means. Ironically, the whole entry under 'explicable' is devoted to ignorance

Explicable. *adj.* [from *explicate.*] Explainable; possible to be explained.

Many difficulties, scarce *explicable* with any certainty, occur in the fabrick of human nature.

Hale's Origin of Mankind.

Great variety there is in compound bodies, and little many of them seem to be *explicable*.

Boyle.

One of the works that Johnson proposed to himself but never wrote was a 'Hymn to Ignorance'. It was a great seventeenth-century theme on which many writers from Fulke-Greville to Cowley performed, and its roots are in Christian literature, going back to Cornelius Agrippa, Nicholas of Cusa, and Lactantius. From thence it can be traced back to the wisdom literature of the Bible with interesting collateral expressions in Socratic teaching. Socrates often wins honour among Christian writers on account of his reply to the report that he is said to be the wisest of the Athenians. He says his superiority, if he has any, is only in that he knows that he is ignorant, whereas others think they know something. Ignorance is a theme of pious writers because a recognition of it leaves room for faith and religion. A hymn to ignorance would be a religious poem: it would be, like so much of Johnson's other writing, ironic and satirical, yet patient about human wishes and human achievements. It would also be a form of homage to the late Renaissance. Although he never wrote his hymn, Johnson assembled a chorus of writers to sing its strains in the illustrative quotations of his *Dictionary*. Wherever one looks at the field of knowledge in the *Dictionary*, it is bounded by ignorance. Medicine, law, history, politics, and even grammar have their unknowables and incommensurables. One effect of this boundary is to make the *Dictionary* an ironic encyclopedic work that reflects on the vanity of human knowledge at the same time that it displays that knowledge in vast and impressive array.

Because the *Dictionary* presents knowledge for the sake of pious or moral ends, its various departments of knowledge all have an ethical cast. Hence, the field of human knowledge is only partly divisible into recognizable academic categories, such as politics, natural history, or literary criticism. The ethical part of knowledge is so pervasive that the whole book is more easily broken into topics like Death, Judgement, Happiness, Freedom, the Vanity of Human Wishes, Truth, Friendship, Money, Matrimony, Youth and Age, Study and Education. These topics are much like those that compilers of commonplace books throughout the eighteenth century used to organize their collections; they are much like the topics treated in Bacon's *Essays*; and, as a group, they are not much different from the approximately 125 heads that occurred to Johnson when he was contemplating a thematic arrangement of the pamphlets in the Harleian Library.[20] The lists of topics in these places suggest a map of what was knowable for Johnson and a set of directions for organizing his experience, his reading, and his writing. The *Dictionary* is, in effect, Johnson's commonplace book; it both evinces the intellectual categories he had available for organizing his thoughts, and it prepares him to express his thoughts readily, like an orator in splendid control of his topics. Johnson had already cultivated himself in this way, but the *Dictionary* prepared yet more ground for him, and the fruits of his study are visible in all of his subsequent works.

To a significant extent the *Dictionary* represents the organization of knowledge in Johnson's own mind, and hence it provides a map of Johnson's intellectual world. But the map is incomplete. Johnson kept his audience of impressionable learners in mind as he composed the *Dictionary*, and he steered his course through safe, mainstream political, religious, and philosophical waters. For ethical reasons, he feared exposing young minds to anything that would endanger their religious principles. For financial reasons, he wished to secure as large an audience as possible for his book, and he aimed, therefore, at a broad but economically stable, politically conservative stratum of British society. Johnson's attempt to be conservative and non-controversial is evident, for example, in his choice of the divines who deliver a vast number of sermons to students who consult the *Dictionary*. Tillotson, South, Atterbury, Smalridge, Stillingfleet, and Jeremy Taylor are the most frequently cited. Johnson's collection of High Church divines, most of whom became bishops, is not representative of his own range of reading in theological literature. Johnson read very widely in theology, either because he considered himself up to the challenge of dangerous writers, like Mandeville, or because he was actually attracted by some heterodoxical views, like those of John Wesley, Isaac Watts, Edmund Calamy, and Samuel Clarke. Some of Johnson's favourite dissenters appear in the *Dictionary*, but most are cited very occasionally or only from their non-religious works.

Many of the political writers Johnson chose were also High Church affiliates, like Temple, Swift, and Arbuthnot. In fact, there is so much citation from politically and religiously conservative writers that one of Johnson's contemporaries, Thomas Edwards, complained in a letter to a friend that Johnson had used his book as a 'vehicle for Jacobite and High-flying tenets by giving many examples from the party pamphlets of Swift, from South's Sermons and other authours in that way of thinking.'[21] Had he looked further than the authors' names, however, Edwards would have found that the sentiments concerning politics and religion in the *Dictionary* are largely non-partisan. In politics the *Dictionary* stresses the importance of freedom; the rule of three (king, nobles, and commons) as it existed *circa* 1689; the corrupting influence of party politics; and the subordination of politics to ethics. Members of virtually all parties could agree with these points by 1755. Johnson printed a great many political statements that had been resolved into the mainstream, and his book provided a useful format for furthering such resolution. Political writing in the eighteenth century, as now, often aimed at making the author's position seem more moderate than it was by adopting a rhetoric full of terms and statements that were acceptable to most voters. The real political punch was often carried by the context (as the anti-ministerial meaning of Johnson's life of Drake was contained in its appearance in an opposition journal at a time when any mention of a war with Spain was politically charged). The *Dictionary* takes all writing out of context and hence tends to normalize political writing particularly. For example, in the *Dictionary* Swift seems to assert a kind of ethical truism under 'qualification': 'It is in the power of the prince to make piety and virtue become the fashion, if he would make them necessary *qualifications* for preferment.' In its own context, Swift's remark was part of an argument for the controversial Test Act, but Johnson's context strips this away leaving a statement with which all can agree. It is so general that it would be useful today, with minor changes, for senators debating, say, the confirmation of a Supreme Court nominee.

The most interesting case of assimilation and normalization of political language in the *Dictionary* concerns Locke's *Two Treatises of Government*. It is a curious fact that Johnson never refers to these works by name, although he quotes them often and names all of Locke's other works, at

least occasionally, in his italicized references. Locke is the abstract philosopher of the *Dictionary*, cited in key discussions of logic and epistemology
all over the book; partly by withholding the titles of his political works,
Johnson also makes Locke the political philosopher of the *Dictionary*. In
doing so, Johnson both exploits and furthers a confusion between Locke's
philosophical writings and his political positions that was already under
way in English cultural understanding. Because of the generality of his
political writings, Locke is a suitable candidate for his posthumous cultural
role, although in their historical context his works justified his own activism
as a violent opponent of James II who supported the Exclusion Bill and
probably participated in the Rye House assassination plot.[22] Despite their
revolutionary intentions, quotations from Locke's demolition of Filmer's
apology for the divine right monarchy do not throw Johnson off his
centrist course; by 1755 virtually all parties and factions believed in constitutional monarchy and an expanded, but certainly not general, political
enfranchisement of individuals. Particular issues that are more controversial
than divine right do not often surface, and usually Locke falls into league
with Hooker and Bacon to help Johnson display politics as a branch of
ethics. Johnson's citation of Locke reiterating the biblical golden rule in
illustration of 'social' is representative: 'To love our neighbour as ourselves
is such a fundamental truth for regulating human society, that by that
alone one might determine all the cases in *social* morality.' Still, Johnson
was apparently wary enough of the revolutionary suggestions in Locke's
Two Treatises to keep their names out of his book.

Even though the *Dictionary* has the effect of reconciling political opponents and reducing extremist views to a gathering mainstream of belief,
Johnson simply excludes some views and some writers. Harrington's left-
wing *Oceana* is not in the *Dictionary*, for instance, even though it is recommended reading in *The Preceptor*; on the right wing, Filmer is an
unacceptable political theorist. But the most interesting and pointed exclusion is that of Hobbes. Not only is Hobbes excluded, but Johnson
seems to have gone out of his way to make the *Dictionary* refute him by
taking many quotations from a couple of books by John Bramhall:
Castigations of Mr Hobbes (1658) and *A Defence of True Liberty from Ante-Cedent
and Extrinsecall Necessity, being an Answer to a Late Book of Mr Thomas Hobbs
of Malmesbury, intituled, A Treatise of Liberty and Necessity* (1655). The
presence of these books in the *Dictionary* suggests that the most dangerous
aspect of Hobbes's thinking is his determinism. In Johnson's *Dictionary* the
words 'determinative' and 'necessitation' are protected from Hobbesian
contamination by illustrations from Bramhall, but the defence continues
on and off throughout the book. The common word 'but', for instance,
in the the third sense ('the particle which introduces the minor of a
syllogism') is illustrated by Bramhall: 'If there be a liberty and a possibility
for a man to kill himself today, then it is not absolutely necessary that he
shall live till tomorrow; *but* there is such a liberty, therefore no such necessity.' This point obviously has political implications, but it is of primary

importance in religion and ethics. The religious and ethical aspects of political ideas concern Johnson most, and Hobbes's whole political philosophy must be defeated because it rests on ethically unacceptable limitations of freedom. Just as he did in his essay on epitaphs a few years before, Johnson remarks in the *Dictionary* on the important connection between ethics and freedom displayed in the semantic field of the word 'caitiff'.[23] The need for personal freedom is an absolute in Johnson's ethical thinking that overflows into his political views. His exuberance in writing the etymology of 'caitiff' suggests the strength of his feeling about the importance of freedom:

> Ca'itiff. *n.s.* [*cattivo*, Ital. a slave; whence it came to signify a bad man, with some implication of meanness; as *knave* in English, and *fur* in Latin; so certainly does slavery destroy virtue.
>
> Ἥμισυ τῆς ἀρετῆς ἀποαίνυται δούλιον ἦμαρ. Homer.
>
> {The day of slavery destroys the better half of virtue}
>
> A slave and a scoundrel are signified by the same words in many languages.]

This kind of special reminder is extraordinary, but the connection between freedom and virtue is continually present in Johnson's book. Quotations from Locke frequently reinforce the connection; the message is clear in the passage that Johnson chose to illustrate the sixth sense of 'to link': '. . . the ideas of men and self-determination appear to be connected.' This is a point that Johnson often reiterated in his recorded conversations with Boswell, who liked to entertain deterministic notions and the exoneration from guilt that they imply. Johnson, who rarely fled from guilt, probably believed everything he said to Boswell or wrote in the *Dictionary* about freedom and morality. However, its presence in the *Dictionary* or in his conversations with Boswell is not hard evidence that Johnson believed something without qualification; it only tells us how important he felt it was to teach the point to others, especially the young and impressionable. Hester Mulso (later Mrs Chapone), a contributor to the *Rambler* and one of the few living writers quoted in the *Dictionary*, once reported a conversation in which she accused Johnson of harbouring the Hobbesian view that 'the human heart is naturally malevolent.' She said she found her evidence in the *Rambler*, whereupon Johnson answered, 'that if he had betrayed such sentiments in the Ramblers, it was not with design, for that he believed the doctrine of human malevolence, though a true one, is not a useful one, and ought not to be published to the world.'[24] The *Dictionary*, like the *Rambler*, is not a record of individual opinion or personal expression but a representation of the field of knowledge from an ethical point of view adjusted for the edification of students. What Johnson says in the *Dictionary* or in any of his published works should not be equated with what he thought privately. The correspondence between the two is

undoubtedly significant; Johnson was certainly not shamming; but studying him deeply one has the sense that his inner life and his private thinking were more various and more troublous than his public presentations.
The sense that he possessed such innerness – developed from reports of
his conversation, his reading, his diaries, and letters – is an important part
of Johnson's enduring appeal.

The *Dictionary* has been frequently cherished (and occasionally attacked)
for its expressions of personality, its quirkiness, individuality, and oddity.
Although it is, for the most part, rational, empirical, public, and impersonal both philologically and ideologically, there are expressions of personality in the *Dictionary*. Perhaps because it is such a pleasure to note
them, they have received a disproportionate amount of attention. Johnson's
way of commenting on usage is more personal and less institutional than
the system of abbreviations or codes that characterizes twentieth-century
dictionaries. His own voice is audible when, for instance, he passes
judgement on Dryden's attempt to justify his use of 'to falsify' to mean 'to
pierce': '*Dryden*, with all this effort, was not able to naturalise the new
signification, which I have never seen copied, except by some obscure
nameless writer, and which indeed deserves not to be received.' More
personal sounding still and more famous are the self-deprecatory remarks
Johnson makes under 'Grubstreet', 'dull', and 'lexicographer'. In defining himself as 'a harmless drudge' or saying that 'to make dictionaries is
dull work' Johnson is drawing attention to himself, though such playfulness in scholarly works is a convention of humanistic scholarship. Johnson
also very occasionally displays his own point of view on political subjects:
'*Bolingbroke was a holy man*' is Johnson's example of 'irony . . . a mode of
speech in which the meaning is contrary to the words'; his definition of
the fourth sense of 'leader' is 'One at the head of any party or faction: as
the detestable Wharton was the *leader* of the whigs.'[25] Too much has been
made of Johnson's apparently partisan definitions of 'Whig' and 'Tory',
his seemingly anti-Scottish description of the use of oats, and the rest of
the 'gems' that are so infrequent in the *Dictionary*. The sober truth is that
the voice of the author of the *Dictionary* is only very occasionally audible
amidst all the voices of all the authorities he brings together in the illustrative quotations, and usually that voice is commenting on merely lexicographical matters.

There is a deeper, paradoxically more conventional form of self-
expression in the emphasis that Johnson gives to certain topics in the
Dictionary. The *Dictionary* contains, for example, a great many passages that
serve as reminders of death. This is partly a reflection of the contents of
English literature written in the seventeenth century, the period of
Johnson's heaviest reading for his book. But Johnson went out of his way
to make sure his readers would see a death's head on every page. Jeremy
Taylor's *Holy Dying* was perhaps an obvious choice; less obvious choices
were William Wake's *Preparation for Death*, and John Graunt's *Natural and
Political Observations . . . Made upon the Bills of Mortality*. No matter whether

he found them in books devoted to the theme or elsewhere, many of the quotations in Johnson's *Dictionary* tend to comprise a sermon on the theme of Ecclesiastes 7: 2, which illustrates the nineteenth sense of 'to lay': 'It is better to go to the house of mourning than to go to the house of feasting; for that is the end of all men, and the living will *lay* it to his heart.' As he did in his translation of the *Jests of Hierocles*, in the *Dictionary* Johnson also transmits many witticisms about death. The illustration of the word 'joke' provided by Pope is in fact a version of the Hieroclean jest in which a philosopher decides to see if crows really do live 200 years by getting a young one:

> Link towns to towns with avenues of oak,
> Inclose whole downs in walls, 'tis all a *joke*!
> Inexorable death shall level all.

This was a punchline that cast a great deal of human activity into a ludicrous light for Johnson, and his inclination to be aware of such grim elucidation is a part both of his melancholy disposition and of the persistent irony of his literary works. As a literary quality it is visible in the *Harleian Catalogue* and most evident in the *Lives of the Poets*, where so many of the deaths are written as ironic climaxes or gallows humour. This humour is present in the *Dictionary* too, and it is a more important part of what makes the *Dictionary* Johnson's own than the celebrated but rare gems in which he hails Grub Street as his 'Ithaca' or Lichfield as his 'magna parens'.

The overall selection of quotations, which displays knowledge as an array of certain ethical topics, and the particular emphasis on some of those topics unite the *Dictionary* most importantly with the rest of Johnson's writing. Still, there are moments when Johnson's personality breaks through in a pointed way, and there may be some even more poignant though less obvious moments of personal expression. In reading the *Dictionary* all the way through, there are times when it appears to be a kind of personal diary, a registration in literary quotations of Johnson's private life over the nine years or so during which he composed it. The late Eugene Thomas, who studied the making of the *Dictionary* very thoroughly, thought that Johnson purchased and began excerpting the melancholy poetry of Samuel Garth in 1749 to suit his own mood. There do seem to be patches of increased gloom here and there in the *Dictionary*. Johnson's treatment of the word 'bridal', for instance, is so unexpectedly full of memento mori that one is tempted to guess that this part of the *Dictionary*, probably composed in 1749, is, like the infusion of Garth, a registration of grief over Elizabeth Johnson's increasing illness. Somewhat more reliably, parts of Johnson's life of reading can be traced in the sudden appearance of new authors. The sole illustration from Jane Collier under 'to prink' shows that Johnson read the droll *Art of Tormenting* in 1753, when Richardson printed it and perhaps sent it to his friend to help him find examples of very current words. His involvement with the literary career of Charlotte

Lennox starts to appear in the S entries with citations of *The Female Quixote*, which he read in proof, and *Shakespeare Illustrated*, which he introduced. Perhaps these appearances also indicate something about Johnson's social life, which may have been expanding after 1753, when he is known to have contemplated remarriage.[26]

In a broader way, some of the ebb and flow of Johnson's energies are visible in the variable assiduousness that he gave to his task. A reader of the whole *Dictionary* cannot but rejoice that Johnson hurried through the letter Z. Even the vast sea of S is proportionally small – only a little longer than C, whereas the *OED* makes it double the size of C. Such figures do not permit a very precise assessment of Johnson's moods or energies on a given day or in a given season of lexicographical work, but there is an important association between Johnson's life of writing and his life, and this association is most important in the *Dictionary*. As some of his best biographers, Paul Fussell and Walter Jackson Bate, have shown, Johnson identified his life and his work, looking frequently to the parable of the talents in the second book of Samuel for self-admonition. He felt, perhaps obsessively, under the eyes of a divine task-master, and between 1 January 1748 and 3 April 1753 Johnson wrote several prayers beseeching the Almighty for diligence in 'the duties which in thy Providence shall be assigned me'. The last of these is appended to a diary entry stating that Johnson that day began the second volume of the *Dictionary*: 'O God who hast hitherto supported me enable me to proceed in this labour & in the Whole task of my present state that when I shall render up at the last day an account of the talent committed to me I may receive pardon for the sake of Jesus Christ. Amen.'[27] The *Dictionary* was Johnson's work, in religious terms and in existential terms. His prayers in periods when he was not productive are filled with lamentations about the days passing over him unmarked and almost, therefore, unperceived.

Lexicography was partly a way of marking time for Johnson, and he resumed it with some gusto later in life. He not only heavily revised his book for the fourth edition of 1773, he also made thousands of additions and revisions that never found their way into print. The manuscript evidence suggests that Johnson did the work compulsively or, at least, that he had an attraction to what he called 'that *muddling* work' in his account of his attempt to get the job of revising Chambers's *Cyclopedia*. His exclamation upon missing the opportunity is also telling; he exclaimed, 'It is gone, Sir', as if he were announcing a death. It was a grave loss for Johnson because in dictionary work he found a way of marking his existence in continuous literary labour. If there was something neurotically obsessive about his need, there was also great sanity in Johnson's adjustment to it and the use he made of it. In making the *Dictionary* Johnson found a way to live that was both spiritually and economically viable. The work he produced as a result is a permanent contribution to English literature that testifies to the power of Johnson's will as well as to the character of his mind.[28]

9

The Vanity of Human Wishes

The Dr fell to repeating Juvenal's tenth satire, but I let him see that the province was mine.

Johnson to Mrs Thrale, 20 June 1783

The *Dictionary* is unique in many respects, but in its mixture of educational and moral aims and in its sense of audience Johnson's great book is one of a coherent group of projects that he worked on in the late 1740s: *The Preceptor*, the *Dictionary*, *The Vanity of Human Wishes*, and the *Rambler* all exhibit a new focus in Johnson's literary vision. In this group of works Johnson substitutes attention to the moral and ethical ends of education for his earlier examination of more specifically political matters (though he was always philosophical to a degree), and he decisively modifies his presentation of his learning. Beginning with *The Preceptor*, Johnson speaks more about the general lesson of learning than about any of its particulars. It was characteristic of Johnson's mind to leap to the ultimate of any series of deductions, and the ultimate lesson of learning is the Lactantian teaching that learning leaves off where revelation begins. Such teaching subordinates all studies to wisdom and sees religious humility as their most important goal. Johnson allegorized the lesson at the end of *The Preceptor* in *The Vision of Theodore*. Although the fable may be read as a refutation of deism, its lesson is so traditional and so broad that the work does not seem at all polemical.[1] Learning is only one avenue of human desire. The same lesson of humility may be taught by considering other human wishes, and Johnson does touch on the full range of mortal desire. Yet he pays special attention to the temptations of learning in the late 1740s and beyond; the effect of this attention is to preserve a special address to students in his works and to lend them an autobiographical quality. This quality was always somewhat present, but from the late 1740s on there is a stronger sense of Johnson looking back on his eager, scholarly ambitions, as on an earlier and fading self.

Johnson's greatest poem, *The Vanity of Human Wishes*, is a distilled statement of the central theme of his work of the late 1740s. His shift in interest from Juvenal's more obviously political third satire, which he imitated in *London* in 1738, to the grandly philosophical tenth a decade later is representative of the change in Johnson's writing. Johnson's advancing maturity and improved economic circumstances undoubtedly played a part in this change, but it should not be attributed solely to personal causes. Although Johnson is in some ways an expressive writer, he was a professional writer capable of separating his personal and public lives. He continued to carry on a scholarly life that was concerned with particulars rather than the grand ends of learning, and he continued to be interested in particular political issues after he shifted his professional literary focus away from these areas.

The change in Johnson's literary focus stems partly from his wish to broaden his audience and thereby achieve greater professional independence. His chief agent in effecting this change was the publisher Robert Dodsley. Although Johnson was acquainted with him by 1738 when he published *London*, it was in the late 1740s that Dodsley replaced Cave as his most important professional connection. It was Dodsley's *Preceptor* on which Johnson worked; Dodsley recommended Johnson to a group of six other booksellers and together with them issued the contract for the *Dictionary*; Dodsley bought the rights to *The Vanity of Human Wishes* late in 1748; and he published the long-languishing *Irene* in 1749. Johnson called Dodsley his patron, and he frequented Dodsley's shop at Tully's Head. This place was an important enough social and intellectual venue for Johnson that he said, imagining himself again in a Latin cultural scene, 'The true Noctes Atticae are revived at Honest Dodsley's house.'[2]

To some extent, Johnson's works in this enormously productive period of his life are cast in the mould of Dodsley's own productions – both his own compositions and his publishing projects. This is necessarily true of Johnson's work on *The Preceptor* because Dodsley designed the whole collection, but the *Vanity* also seems written with Dodsley in mind, and it eventually became a part of *A Collection of Poems by Several Hands,* an anthology Dodsley brought out earlier in the same year that he purchased the rights to Johnson's great poem.[3] There is a general likeness between Johnson's works of the late 1740s and early 1750s and Dodsley's in that those of each author are concerned with popular education and the inculcation of ethically beneficial habits. Dodsley's poems, such as *Pain and Patience* (1745) and *Public Virtue* (1753), are more homely and less learned attempts to teach the lessons of Johnson's *Vanity*. Although it is mainly a lexicographical work, Johnson's *Dictionary* in a grander and more indirect way accomplishes the educational goals of Dodsley's *Preceptor* or his immensely successful collection of wise sayings, *The Oeconomy of Human Life* (1750). *Rasselas* (1759) resembles Dodsley's *Oeconomy*; both works employ transparent oriental frameworks and imitate biblical wisdom literature. Dodsley's and Johnson's careers are also similar in some ways to

Richardson's because he too taught morality in popular literary forms. Johnson's most obvious distinctions from the two others are his learning, his address to a more learned audience, and the scope of the material he 'moralized'. Dodsley instituted morality in presenting the basic school curriculum of *The Preceptor*; Richardson in presenting a guide to social life in the form of a novel; but Johnson in presenting a dictionary of the English language and the full round of knowledge it conveys. In *The Vanity of Human Wishes* Johnson displays the moral blueprint of his *Dictionary*.

The *Vanity* is a great poem, and it therefore deserves and rewards treatment as a literary phenomenon unfettered by any but aesthetic and intellectual associations. As T. S. Eliot shows in his introduction to the Haslewood Press edition, the *Vanity* belongs in the artistic world defined by the poetry of Juvenal, Dryden, Pope, and Horace. It is also, however, an artefact of Johnson's professional life in the late 1740s. Johnson told a friend that he composed the first seventy lines in Hampstead, where his wife was staying for her health, and he added, 'The whole number was composed before I committed a single couplet to writing.' In part of a telling description of his general method of composing verses, Johnson especially mentions the *Vanity*: 'I have generally had them in my mind, perhaps fifty at a time, walking up and down in my room; and then I have written them down, and often, from laziness, have written only half lines. I have written a hundred lines in a day. I remember I wrote a hundred lines of "The Vanity of Human Wishes" in a day.' The editors of the Yale edition of the poem use evidence from the manuscript to conclude that 'all of the poem was composed before any of it was set down, and it was then written rapidly.'[4] This nearly oral form of composition was possible for Johnson because of his extraordinary memory, but also because of the oratorial organization of his mind around commonplaces and conventional topics. The *Vanity* was particularly well suited to this form of composition because it is so concentrated and distilled a workout on the topics that Johnson had been cultivating and arranging in his mind for the *Dictionary* and *The Preceptor*.

In one of the best of all the critical essays on Johnson's writing, Lawrence Lipking describes *The Vision of Theodore* and *The Vanity of Human Wishes* as the essential works for the student learning to read Johnson correctly.[5] He cites the ease with which both were composed and Johnson's fondness for them in later life as evidence of their affinities with what and how Johnson most characteristically and essentially wished to communicate in imaginative writing. Johnson arrived at this formulation, which Lipking describes brilliantly, in 1748, in his fortieth year, at a certain stage in his professional career – a stage that was shaped by his growing financial independence, his work on the *Dictionary*, and his involvement with Dodsley. Both the *Vanity* and the *Vision* use the ancient fable of the 'Choice of Hercules' to teach readers to prefer virtue to beauty; both add the orthodox Christian insight that revelation and faith alone can lead to the heights of true happiness; both construct allegorical, dreamy visions, obscured by mists; and, partly in the construction of these frameworks, both fictions add an element of irony to their own presentations, turning the student, thus, away from a reliance on poetic formulations and back upon an examination of himself. If the *Vanity* is the spirit of Johnson's mature work, the *Dictionary* is its body, and its family of publishing projects, including *The Preceptor*, are the atmosphere in which they thrived. Each of these elements exerted influence on the others, but, even in examining his most essential work, we are looking at what Johnson wrote and published rather than directly at what he thought.

Unlike *London*, *The Vanity of Human Wishes* was printed without the original lines from Juvenal on the page. The numbers of the Latin verses corresponding to the various sections of the English poem were supplied in footnotes, but, as the typography suggests, Johnson's second imitation of Juvenal is less a scholarly exercise than his first. The grandeur and profound conventionality of Juvenal's theme in his tenth satire enable Johnson to be more independent. Juvenal was himself working within a rich tradition that can be traced to Socratic writings, Pindar, Horace, Seneca, and anonymous verses collected by Valerius Maximus in a work that Roman poets regularly used to help them compose poetry. Johnson knew many of these sources directly, was reminded of them by available commentaries on Juvenal, and may have taken his title from one of them – Seneca's dialogue *De tranquillitate animi* which speaks about 'vanitatem cupiditatium nostrarum'. Johnson also knew the biblical expositions of the theme, especially in the wisdom literature, and he was in the midst of reviewing its modern manifestations in many of the works he excerpted in the *Dictionary*. Johnson printed direct, poetic statements of the theme out of Dryden's version of Juvenal's tenth satire (under 'conduct', for instance), Richard Corbet's *Iter Boreale*, which moralizes the story of Wolsey much as Johnson does in the *Vanity* ('weight') and 'To his Son, Vincent Corbet' ('wealth'), Pope's *Essay on Man* ('joke'), Prior's juvenile exercise 'On Exodus 3. 14' ('unnavigable') and his long poem in three books *Solomon on the Vanity of the World* ('to pursue'), to give just a few examples. Many prose works that Johnson quotes in the *Dictionary* also contribute strands of Juvenal's theme. Under 'to turn', for instance, Johnson cites Addison retelling a Socratic version of the theme: 'Socrates meeting Alcibiades going to his devotions, and observing his eyes fixed with great seriousness, tells him that he had reason to be thoughtful, since a man might bring down evils by his prayers, and the things which the gods send him at his request might *turn* [sense 9] to his destruction.' Similarly, Locke provides a prose version of Juvenal's conclusion under 'for': 'A sound mind in a sound body is a short but full description of a happy state in this world: he that has these two has little more to wish *for*, and he that wants either of them will be but little the better for any thing else.' By the time he finished the *Dictionary*, Johnson added to it many lines from his own *Vanity of Human Wishes* (under 'relax', for instance), thus displaying a double responsiveness to the theme – both anthologizing and rewriting it in his great book. In *Rambler* 66, written after the *Vanity* and shortly after his completion of A, B, and C for the *Dictionary* (3 November 1750), Johnson quotes Juvenal's tenth satire; by this time he has seen so many statements and restatements of the theme that he is almost tired of it: 'The folly of human wishes and persuits has always been a standing subject of mirth and declamation, and has been ridiculed and lamented from age to age; till perhaps the fruitless repetition of complaints and censures may be justly numbered among the subjects of censure and complaint.'[6]

As it appears in Plato, Ecclesiastes, Corbet, Robert Burton, Locke, Prior, and the rest, the theme of Johnson's *Vanity* is traditional and easy to summarize: human beings often wish for the very things that will do them harm rather than good; there are simple inner qualities that really bring happiness and are therefore worthy of prayer, including, as the ancients could not know, Christian faith. However, Johnson's particular expression of the theme is distinctly his own and significantly alters its meaning. Many of the most striking elements of Johnson's work appear in the opening of the poem:

> Let observation with extensive view,
> Survey mankind, from China to Peru;
> Remark each anxious toil, each eager strife,
> And watch the busy scenes of crouded life;
> Then say how hope and fear, desire and hate,
> O'erspread with snares the clouded maze of fate,
> Where wav'ring man, betray'd by vent'rous pride,
> To tread the dreary paths without a guide,
> As treach'rous phantoms in the mist delude,
> Shuns fancied ills, or chases airy good;
> How rarely reason guides the stubborn choice,
> Rules the bold hand, or prompts the suppliant voice;
> How nations sink, by darling schemes oppress'd,
> When vengeance listens to the fool's request.
> Fate wings with ev'ry wish th' afflictive dart,
> Each gift of nature, and each grace of art,
> With fatal heat impetuous courage glows,
> With fatal sweetness elocution flows,
> Impeachment stops the speaker's pow'rful breath,
> And restless fire precipitates on death.
>
> (1–20)

The scene of Johnson's poem is allegorical. The principal figure is a collective man, like Everyman; Johnson's 'wav'ring man' is situated in 'the clouded maze of fate', which is as broadly allegorical as the landscape of *Pilgrim's Progress*. The cloudy, misty atmosphere is reminiscent of *The Vision of Theodore* and of much allegorical dream poetry, especially *The Cloud of Unknowing*, although Johnson may not have known this particular work. In such works human life is depicted as unenlightened by revelation; the representation is so conventional as almost to approach parody: 'now we

see as through a glass darkly', to cite the wisdom literature from which so
many allegorical mists derive. The device is as obvious as the fictitious
'Bramin' Dandamis whom Dodsley set up as the author of his *Oeconomy of
Human Life*. To the familiar backdrop, however, Johnson adds a profusion
of large-scale abstractions. Nearly every line introduces at least one new
abstraction, and almost every one is engaged in a dramatic, visualizable
activity. Within a few lines we find enough characters for several chapters
of Bunyan or many cantos of *The Faerie Queene*: 'hope and fear, desire and
hate', pride, reason, vengeance, and fate all enter between lines 5 and 15.
In addition, almost all the other nouns in these lines are abstract and
heading in the direction of personification: 'airy good', 'the stubborn
choice', and 'the bold hand', for instance, all approach the aesthetic independence of allegorical personification. Johnson's 'wav'ring man' is all
but lost in the rush of human passions, which, because of their personification, are externalized and hence subtracted from him. Their movements are sudden: the figures in this scene 'sink', 'wing', 'shun', 'stop',
and 'precipitate'. All the verbs indicate actions; there are no forms of
the verb 'to be' and no verbs representing states of being. The scene is
agitated, violent, 'crouded', hot and hellish, as befits a representation of
passion or ardour: there is 'fatal heat' and 'restless fire', and Johnson
originally wrote in line 5 about 'hot desire and raging hate'.[7] Not only is
man bereft of revelation in this scene, he is also, like the failed students
in *The Vision of Theodore*, without control over his passions.

As in most great writing, the verse itself here tends to embody what it
represents, and the reader experiences the sense as crowded, dense, and
obscure. The syntax is difficult, approaching the 'Pindarick' mode that
Johnson later criticized in the *Lives of the Poets*. The variety of clauses made
to depend on a single verb and the abrupt changes of verbal mood make
it hard for the reader to take in everything at once. In this respect, as John
Sitter argues, the poem participates in the preference for odes in England
in the 1740s at the expense of easier epistolary verse, like much of Pope's
or of Johnson's *London*. There is an irony in the reader's experience of
crowding and density in view of the invitation in the beginning of the
poem to see all and presumably know all. 'Observation', belonging as it
does to the world of human vision, is plunged into confusion, and readers
receive their only reliable instructions at the end of the poem when God
is invoked, 'whose eyes discern afar'.[8]

The same kind of irony that turns observation into confusion turns each
wish in the poem's catalogue of wishes into something dreaded. As in
other allegorical writing, the reader continues throughout to participate
to a degree in the action of the poem. In lines 37–44, for instance, the
reader is brought into relation with the happy traveller and addressed:

> The needy traveller, secure and gay,
> Walks the wild heath, and sings his toil away.
> Does Envy seize thee? Crush th'upbraiding joy,

Increase his riches and his peace destroy;
Now fears in dire vicissitude invade,
The rustling brake alarms, and quiv'ring shade,
Nor light nor darkness bring his pain relief,
One shews the plunder, and one hides the thief.

The effect of the reader's intrusion is to turn an innocent scene into one that resembles the hellish confusion depicted in the opening of the poem. As this is also the effect of the general passion for wealth, the reader is made the locus of the poem's evils. Many times, readers are commanded to 'see', 'mark', or 'hear' the true state of the world in contrast to their own more fanciful visions, but the poet expects no active or positive response: as viewers of the happy traveller add darkness, hearers of the history of Laud sleep, and those questioned about the liabilities of beauty make no reply at all, like the allegorical representative of Beauty in the poem, who grows deaf to Virtue's call.

Like Juvenal's poem, Johnson's proceeds through a list of common wishes, finding the disaster concealed in each: in succession, we learn the fallibility of the wishes for wealth, status, power, knowledge, fame, long life, and beauty. Each section brings in some historical as well as allegorical figures, and each tends to comprise a somewhat independent poem. There is not much discernible order in the placement of the intermediate sections, though the last two – long life and beauty – approximate the truly desirable things presented in the last sections of the poem. The overall structure of Johnson's poem, like Juvenal's, is based on an old epigrammatic technique in which a series of items are rejected in favour of a last item, which alone is truly eligible. Pindar excelled at employing this form (later called the priamel) within the larger structures of his praise poetry, but Johnson uses it only for overall organization, making his speaker sound as much like an orator utilizing his prepared inventory of places and exempla as a lyric poet singing an ode.

There is no organic unity in the poem and no centre; there is an introduction summarizing the human condition, exempla, and a conclusion with intimations of a better life beyond. But if there is one part in the middle of the poem that calls for greater attention than the others, it is the section devoted to the wish for learning. This wish receives the most elaborate treatment relative to its Latin counterpart. In the corresponding lines Juvenal is concerned only with the wish for eloquence, and he writes mainly about the way that the enviable eloquence of Cicero and Demosthenes led to their respective deaths. Juvenal draws a quick sketch of the votary of eloquence (lines 115–17), a poor schoolboy with a servant guarding his little satchel ('angustae vernula capsae'). Most of Johnson's lines 135–64 take off from this tiny sketch, leaving ten lines on Laud to serve as a counterpart to Juvenal's stories of Demosthenes and Cicero.

Encouraged by Mrs Thrale's report that Johnson wept when perusing his lines about the student in later years, many readers have found an autobiographical reason for his elaboration of this section of the poem. Johnson has modernized Juvenal in a way that makes autobiography a plausible part of the interpretation: he replaces Juvenal's 'eloquium' with his own more literate scholarly goal of 'learning' or 'letters', and he sets the scene in Oxford, his own alma mater. But the exemplum is still more conventional than personal, containing many of the same elements as the obviously general opening of the poem. There is the heat of passion: the student indulges a 'gen'rous heat' and 'Through all his veins the fever of renown / Burns from the strong contagion of the gown' (137–8). As in the opening, there are 'phantoms' (of Melancholy), 'mists' (of doubt), and an inadequate mortal light – 'Reason . . . with her brightest ray' (145). In Johnson's enumeration of the scholar's woes as 'Toil, envy, want, the patron, and the jail', 'patron' is a revision of the earlier 'garret' made in 1755 (for Dodsley's collection) and supposed to be a direct comment on Johnson's anger at Chesterfield for failing to serve as his patron when he wrote the *Dictionary*. It may be, but patronage is as conventional an author's complaint as the inadequacy of his accommodations.

Like other aspects of the *Vanity*, Johnson covered the ills of scholarly life in the *Dictionary* and in *The Vision of Theodore*.[9] Some of the failed students in Theodore's dream are undone by wicked patrons in the service of Avarice, and others end up in the 'Bowers of Intemperance' or the 'Maze of Indolence' (ending in Melancholy). These places are aesthetically and thematically consistent with the scene in the *Vanity* in which, only if all goes well, will 'Sloth effuse her opiate fumes in vain' (150), and 'Beauty blunt on fops [not scholars] her fatal dart' (151). Outlining the dreams of the scholar, the speaker of the *Vanity* says to the reader, 'Are these thy views? proceed, illustrious youth, / And virtue guard thee to the throne of Truth!' (141–2). There is an ironic edge to his tone and an implicit suggestion that such success is unlikely and ultimately inadequate. The allegorical platform on which the irony rests is also present throughout *The Preceptor*. The frontispiece of *The Preceptor*, for instance, depicts wisdom (looking like Athena) guiding a youth to the temple of virtue and the rotunda of honour. A careful reader will see that in the *Vanity* Johnson has reversed the guide and the goal to suit his ironic version of the student's life, but the subject and the allegorical manner of presentation are the same. Ultimately, too, the message of the *Vanity* is much like the message of the frontispiece, contained in Dodsley's hackneyed stanza, which begins:

> The Youth, who, led by WISDOM's guiding Hand,
>   Seeks VIRTUE's Temple and her Law reveres:
> He, he alone, in HONOUR's Dome shall stand.

The *Vanity* expands Juvenal's sketch of the student so greatly because, like *The Preceptor*, the *Dictionary*, and other works that Johnson and Dodsley worked on during the late forties and fifties, Johnson's greatest poem is conscious of an address to students – readers in the process of educating themselves, in or out of school, and using English as the best available road to the learning and wisdom of literature. The audience for the *Vanity* is broader and less select than the audience for *London*; it is an audience of learners who may not even know Latin but desire the advantages of reading, including the wisdom of the classical tradition. As the Parliamentary *Debates* reached out to an expanding audience of voters and furthered their expansion, Johnson's projects of the forties and fifties reached out to a growing reading public. The *Vanity* may not be a popular poem, but it distils the lessons that Johnson found in literature as a whole and offers them in a concentrated form to a wider audience than he addresses in most of his serious poetry. In reaching out to such readers, Johnson is some distance from his earlier aspirations to excellence in Latin poetry, yet he still displays his preparation to follow in the footsteps of Poliziano and other admirers of silver age Latin poetry.

Much attention has focused on the ending of the *Vanity* because of its obvious philosophical departure from Juvenal. In the closing lines, Johnson clearly asserts his belief that wishing, hoping, and fearing are part of the human condition and not to be eliminated without a loss of humanity. He also introduces God and the possibility of eternal reward. In the shorthand of the history of ideas, Johnson rejects Juvenal's Stoicism both for its suggestion of human perfectibility and for its implication that the mind can gain absolute command over the passions. Elizabeth Carter's preface to her translation of Epictetus provides just the sort of critique of Stoicism that Johnson is following in the *Vanity*: she says, for instance, 'Neither [the Epicureans nor the Stoics] seem to have understood Man in his mixed Capacity; but while the first debased him to a mere Animal, the last exalted him to a pure Intelligence; and both considered him as independent, uncorrupted, and sufficient, either by Height of Virtue, or by well-regulated Indulgence, to his own Happiness.'[10] Johnson is always conscious of the 'mixed Capacity' of human beings. Like Locke, Johnson considers pleasure a legitimate end of life, as long as one remembers the superiority of the pleasures of virtue and religion.

After 345 lines of describing failed wishes, Juvenal writes twenty-one lines on proper wishes; he remains ironic, and his tone is condescending. 'If you must wish,' he says, 'wish for sanity, health, and fortitude – strength, that is, of mind, body, and soul.' Having spent seven lines on these Stoic virtues, Juvenal then has a final little laugh at the suppliant: 'monstro quod ipse tibi possis dare' ('I prescribe only what you can give yourself' – 363). In other words, wishing is not necessary. The soul or the mind in Juvenal is capable of being self-sufficient, and it is we human beings who make ourselves either independent or not: 'nos te, / nos facimus, Fortuna, deam caeloque locamus' ('we, we are the ones who make you a goddess, Fortuna, and place you in the heavens' – 365–6).

Johnson adopts Juvenal's condescending tone to some extent; 'fires' (357) and 'fervours' (359) in the final description of praying link this kind of wishing with all the overheated kinds that appear earlier in the poem.

In the last line of his poem Johnson appears to approximate the self-sufficiency prescribed in Juvenal. Having added 'love' (361) and 'faith' (363) to the Stoic description of the happy man, Johnson concludes:

> These goods for man the laws of heav'n ordain,
> These goods he grants, who grants the pow'r to gain;
> With these celestial wisdom calms the mind,
> And makes the happiness she does not find.

There is no self-sufficiency, however, because 'celestial wisdom' does the making, and the mind is merely a seeker. 'Celestial wisdom' is emphatic because 'wisdom' alone meant for Johnson a religious as well as a practical kind of knowledge. The biblical associations are revealed in a quotation from Tillotson that Johnson inserted in the *Dictionary* in illustration of 'strain': 'According to the genius and *strain* of the book of Proverbs, the words wisdom and righteousness are used to signify all religion and virtue.' Wisdom is the kind of knowledge that unites human and divine knowledge. It goes beyond observation and reason to include a sense of the perspective that can only be achieved in the hereafter, beyond the mist that shrouds the top of the Mountain of Existence in *The Vision of Theodore.* By adding 'celestial' to 'wisdom' Johnson makes it clear that he is speaking about religious knowledge, which is only available through divine revelation and prayer.

In rejecting Juvenal's Stoicism Johnson is undoubtedly representing something of his own thinking, but, like his addition of a long section on the student, his ending is also designed for the audience he sought at this period of his career. Stoicism is very much the error of the schools, as it is the error of those students who forget to heed Johnson's admonition in his section on the wish for learning: 'Pause a while from letters, to be wise.' In *The Vision of Theodore* the error of Reason is the Stoic's vain imagination of self-sufficiency. 'I looked then', says Theodore, 'upon the Road of *Reason,* which was indeed, so far as it reached, the same with that of *Religion,* nor had *Reason* discovered it but by her Instruction. Yet when she had once been taught it, she clearly saw that it was right; and *Pride* had sometimes incited her to declare that she discovered it herself, and persuaded her to offer herself as a Guide to *Religion,* whom after many vain Experiments, she found it her highest Privilege to follow.' By invoking 'celestial wisdom' in his conclusion and urging wisdom in his expanded section on the student, Johnson makes his imitation of Juvenal's tenth satire a student's poem. His message is like the message delivered in the prose conclusion to *The Preceptor,* which immediately precedes the *Vision.* The unidentified author of this piece says that many 'Men of Learning . . . miscarried only because they were too soon satisfied with their Acquisitions, and fell into Folly or into Crimes not because they had gained Learning, but because they wanted Wisdom.' Sounding very much like the speaker of Johnson's admonition to students, the valedictory Preceptor tells his graduates: 'Pause therefore for a Time at the Portal of Life; and forbear to step forward, however the Prospect may allure you, till you have added to your other Acquirements that Wisdom, of which the Beginning is the Fear of God, and the Purpose and Effect eternal Felicity.'[11]

The cautious optimism of the endings of *The Preceptor* and the *Vanity* are further evidence of Johnson's continual sense of audience. In Γνῶθι Σεαυτόν, a Latin poem employing a similar allegorical landscape but written for himself and a few friends, the student is not able to escape the misty, delusive atmosphere. Here Johnson is himself the student, and his failure is more fully a failure of intellect and intellectual fortitude than of wisdom or religious understanding. His idol, Joseph Scaliger, is received into a heavenly, lighted upper world of wisdom (Sapientia), but Johnson must go on toiling in a crepuscular, hellish world, much like the unredeemed world described in the opening of the *Vanity*:

> Sed sua regna videns, loca nocte silentia late
> Horret, ubi vanae species, umbraeque fugaces,
> Et rerum volitant rarae per inane figurae.[12]

It sounds like Milton's Limbo described in Vergilian terms, but the passage could be accurately rendered in language reminiscent of the *Vanity*: Observing with extensive view her own dominions, my mind trembles at a world sunk in dreary darkness, where mere phantoms, fugitive mists, and nebulous glimmers of real things flit through the nothingness that is there. It would be going too far to say that the religious ending of the *Vanity* is a pose struck for the benefit of the same impressionable and unsophisticated flock that Johnson addressed in *The Preceptor*. To begin with, there are complications in the tone of the *Vanity*, notes of desolation that are much less muted than they are in *The Vision of Theodore*. But Johnson is always conscious of his audience, and what he says to the fairly large audience he hoped for in the *Vanity* is more optimistic, more religious, and less ironic than what he says to a small sophisticated audience, using the same imagery. Compared with the works he intended to publish, Γνῶθι Σεαυτόν shows that what is loosely called Johnson's thought is often refracted through the medium of a publishing project, with all the awareness of audience that any such project implies, and the *Vanity of Human Wishes*, for all its greatness and genius, is partly a bookseller's job.

10

The *Rambler*

You talk of writing and writing as if you had all the writing to yourself. If our Correspondence were printed I am sure Posterity, for Posterity is always the authours favourite, would say that I am a good writer too. Anch' io sonô Pittore.

Johnson to Mrs Thrale, 27 October 1777

The publication of *The Vanity of Human Wishes* in January 1749 was designed to precede another popular success in Johnson's literary career. The 6th of February was opening night for *Irene*, the play Johnson had nearly completed about twelve years before. His former pupil at Edial, David Garrick, produced his friend's play with a star-studded cast and lots of fanfare at the famous Drury Lane Theatre. Johnson occupied the author's box, wearing a splendid red waistcoat with gold brocade, and perhaps heard, as one spectator reported, 'the whisper . . . strong and prevalent, that the *poet was a prodigy of learning*'.[1] This flattering and appropriate response had its backhand side, however, for the audience was apparently less moved by the play than astonished by its author. Although the overall critical reaction was mixed, there was a strong sense that the play lacked the desirable pathos of tragedy. There was also a hostile response to the on-stage murder of Irene, whom Mahomet II was made to strangle with a Turkish bowstring. The audience hooted this indecorous bit of action off the stage, but with a slight change the play continued on for a very respectable run of nine nights, thus including three author's benefit nights.

Johnson netted nearly £200 from the production and received another £100 for the copyright from his publisher, Robert Dodsley. This income, added to the £1575 that he was promised for the production of the *Dictionary*, might have given Johnson some real financial solidity and a degree of cherished independence. Yet, he had to produce sheets of the *Dictionary* for his publishers in order to receive his money, and he was contracting debts for the supplies and the secretarial assistance he needed to compile his great book. Johnson was probably still in the red as a lexicographer when *Irene* was produced. He began buying material and paying amanuenses in 1746, but it was not until September 1749 that some part of the *Dictionary* was 'almost ready for the Press' and not until 20 October 1750 that the first three letters of the alphabet had been received and printed. The first real evidence of a payment to Johnson from the booksellers appears in William Strahan's printing ledger dated December 1750.[2] Johnson may have been able to borrow money on the strength of his contract, but the *Vanity* and *Irene* helped keep him afloat while he worked on the *Dictionary*, although they also distracted him from the larger work.

On the evidence that exists concerning the progress of the *Dictionary* and Johnson's other projects, it looks as though he finished a good deal of his reading in primary sources by late 1748 and began serious composition of the text in 1749, using reference works and some continued reading to fill out his entries. It was a long pull through the sea of words, and, as John Hawkins tells it, Johnson required 'distractions' from his lexicographical work for personal as well as economic reasons. Hawkins gives this account of the Ivy Lane Club, the first of Johnson's several celebrated social groups:

> One effort however he made to soothe his mind and palliate the fatigue of his labours, which I here relate.
> The great delight of his life was conversation and mental intercourse. That he might be able to indulge himself in this, he had, in the winter of 1749, formed a club that met weekly at the King's head, a famous beef-steak house, in Ivy lane near St Paul's, every Tuesday evening. Thither he constantly resorted, and, with a disposition to please and be pleased, would pass those hours in a free and unrestrained interchange of sentiments, which otherwise had been spent at home in painful reflection. The persons who composed this little society were nine in number [excluding Johnson]: . . . Dr Salter [an aged Cambridge divine] . . . Dr Hawkesworth, – Mr Ryland, a merchant, a relation of his, – Mr John Payne then a bookseller, but now or very lately chief accountant of the bank [of England], – Mr Samuel Dyer, a learned young man intended for the dissenting ministry, – Dr William M'Ghie, a Scots physician, – Dr Edmund Barker, a young physician, – Dr Richard Bathurst, also a young physician, and myself [yet another physician].

This is not the world-famous company that Johnson kept in the club that centred about him from 1764 on, but the Ivy Lane participants were either learned, like Salter and Dyer, upwardly mobile (like Payne and Hawkins), or both. The number of doctors is notable and continues an association with members of that profession which Johnson began in Lichfield with James, Hector, and Swynfen. There is a strong medical presence in the *Dictionary* and in Johnson's reading and conversation throughout his life. Bathurst was evidently his favourite member of the club, and after his death Johnson spoke of him to Mrs Thrale as 'my *dear, dear* Bathurst, whom I loved better than ever I loved any human creature' and called him 'a man to my very heart's content: he hated a fool, and he hated a rogue, and he hated a *whig*; he was a very good *hater*.'[3]

With Bathurst Johnson must have had an agreeably rough good fellowship, but it was with Dyer that he employed his powers of conversational debate. Dyer was well versed in religious controversy and was gradually working his way further out from religious orthodoxy into the embrace of moral philosophies, which, like Socratic thought, were ethical without being religious, except in an abstract way. These philosophies tended, like Shaftesbury's, to assume the goodness of man and the systematic, though obscure, benevolence of the natural order. Beginning with his commentary on Crousaz's critique of Pope's *Essay on Man*, Johnson carried on a lifelong public debate with the optimistic philosophers who tried to discuss morality without recourse to religion – meaning an acknowledgement of sin, repentance, forgiveness, death, and final judgement. His argument with Dyer is an episode in that lengthy debate. Hawkins remarks of the 'altercation between Johnson and Dyer . . . it might be observed, as Johnson once did of two disputants, that the one had ball without powder, and the other powder without ball; for Dyer, though best skilled in the controversy, was inferior to his adversary in the power of reasoning, and Johnson, who was not always master of the question, was seldom at a loss for such sophistical arguments as the other was unable to answer.' Hawkins adds to the general agreement he finds among his acquaintance 'not only that in conversation Johnson made it a rule to talk his best, but that on many subjects he was not uniform in his opinions, contending as often for victory as for truth: at one time *good*, at another *evil* was predominant in the moral constitution of the world. . . . At this versatility of temper, none, however, took offence; as Alexander and Caesar were born for conquest, so was Johnson for the office of a symposiarch, to preside in all conversations.' The 'symposiarch' is a well-known feature of Johnson's social personality. Despite Boswell's acknowledgements that Johnson talked for victory, however, his 'versatility' is less widely known and appreciated. As a part of this, Hawkins stressed Johnson's 'talent of humour': 'by means of this he was enabled to give to any relation that required it, the graces and aids of expression, and to discriminate with the nicest exactness the characters of those whom it concerned.'[4] Boswell's Johnson is such a monumental figure that he lacks the evident talents the real Johnson had for acting and even mimicry. This is a flexibility that is also present in his writing, although it likewise is hidden by the imposing grandeur of his style.

The conversations in Ivy Lane influenced what Johnson wrote in the early 1750s. To give a small instance, Johnson was jabbing Dyer more directly than Bolingbroke when he gratuitously ridiculed his pretensions to piety while defining 'irony' in the *Dictionary*. The arguments with Dyer spilled over on occasion into the numbers of the *Rambler*, but John Payne, a less learned member of the club, exerted more influence on Johnson's periodical essays because he was, with Joseph Bouquet, the publisher of

the *Rambler*. Although Johnson's brilliant series of essays deserves comparison with great predecessors like the essays of Montaigne and Bacon,
Payne and Bouquet's publishing list provides another important context.
Their books included works of religious controversy, such as *Canons of
Controversial Writing extracted from a late controversy between a reverend divine
of the Church of England and a dissenting gentleman* (1751); collections of
non-controversial sermons; devotional writings by Johnson's St John's Gate
acquaintance Moses Browne; some religious exhortations occasioned by
traumatic current events, such as the great London earthquake of 1750;
and philosophical religious writing, such as Thomas Nettleton's *Treatise on
Virtue and Happiness* (1751) and *A Philosophic Ode on the Sun and the Universe*
(1750). They also published fiction with a moral, like Charlotte Lennox's
first novel (which Johnson persuaded the Ivy Lane Club to stay up all
night celebrating), and at least one book of polite instruction, a translation of Toussaint's *Les Moeurs* (1749). A proposal from them to Johnson
(or the other way around) for a series of philosophical, moral essays aimed
at the edification and instruction of an educated audience would have
been consistent with their publishing interests.

Whether the series was initiated by its publishers or its writer is unclear,
but *Rambler* Number 1 appeared on Tuesday, 20 March 1750 and was
followed every Saturday and Tuesday in succession until the last, Number
208, appeared on Saturday, 14 March 1752. By May 1752 Johnson was
submitting copy for the *Dictionary* at a rapid rate and being paid accordingly. Meanwhile, for each number of the *Rambler* he received two guineas.
Johnson wrote all but four of the *Ramblers* and included contributions from
others in only three of the remaining 204. But even this income was
insufficient, and he was forced at this time to borrow money from John
Newberry, a publisher unconnected with the *Dictionary* for whom he did
a short, scathing biography of the fiery and enthusiastic interregnum
President of St John's College, Francis Cheynel.[5]

Hawkins puts Johnson unrealistically above the financial considerations
involved in the genesis of the *Rambler,* but his account reveals much about
its place in Johnson's intellectual growth:

> The same necessity . . . of seeking relief from the fatigue of compiling his
> dictionary . . . induced him to undertake, what most other men should have
> thought an additional fatigue, the publishing a periodical paper. The truth
> is, that not having now for a considerable space committed to writing aught
> but words and their significations, his mind was become tumid, and laboured
> to be delivered of those many and great conceptions, which for years it had
> been forming. The study of human life and manners, had been the chief
> employment of his thoughts, and to a knowledge of these, all his reading,
> all his conversation, and all his meditations tended. By these exercises, and
> the aid of an imagination that was ever teeming with new ideas, he accumu-
> lated a fund of moral science, that was more than sufficient for such an
> undertaking, and became in a very eminent degree qualified for the office
> of an instructor of mankind in their greatest and most important concerns.[6]

In this description as well as in his description of Johnson as symposiarch, Hawkins may have been imbuing the forty-year-old Johnson with some of the sixty-year-old's presence. Yet this is the passage of Johnson's life – from the publication of the *Vanity* in 1749 to the publication of the *Dictionary* in 1755 – when he took on the mature character that Boswell eventually glorified with such pompous titles as the 'Great Cham'. It is difficult to tell how dramatic the personal transformation was. Johnson was no longer sitting at the feet of great men like George Psalmanazar; nor was he pounding the pavement around Grosvenor Square with the likes of the irrepressible Savage. In the Ivy Lane Club, he was the centre of attention; his volubility and the confidence of his address improved accordingly. Yet the Oxford freshman who held back, refusing to impress his new tutor on cue, retained some reticence all his life, and much of the grand transformation occurred in Johnson's literary persona only.

Hawkins is correct in calling the *Rambler* an expression of 'moral science', if 'science' is taken in the same sense that Johnson meant it when he called his Parliamentary *Debates* 'political science'. In both cases Johnson elevates his material to a level of generality that permits conformation with durable, received truth. But his transferal of 'science' from politics to the more general field of moral life germane to the *Rambler* continues the work of synthesis and generalization apparent in the *Vanity*. Yet the *Rambler* also represents a new aesthetic departure because Johnson speaks almost directly in the first person singular. He is not completely free from dramatic presentation of the sort he used in the Parliamentary *Debates* or *Irene*, but he is not assuming the mask of another author, as in *London* or the *Vanity*, and there is no special professional task, such as lexicography, bibliography, or translation, through which his voice is filtered. Johnson is not exactly equivalent to Mr Rambler, but the mask is in many ways a self-portrait.[7] In the *Rambler* Johnson found a distinctive voice and created a literary persona that he enjoyed being.

Nevertheless, the *Rambler* is a literary project with a literary heritage. Although the obvious precedent is Addison's *Spectator*, Johnson's essays, like so much of his writing, look back to the seventeenth century for some elements of their form and theme. As in the *Dictionary*, Johnson is highly responsive in the *Rambler* to the writers who brought their Christian humanism into the age of the new sciences and new scholarship: writers like Boyle, Locke, and Milton, among the English, Scaliger, Le Clerc, Fontenelle, and La Bruyère, among continental writers. Earlier humanists – Erasmus, Montaigne, Thomas More, and Pontanus, for instance – are also in Johnson's background and sometimes appear, but most relevant of all to the voice of the *Rambler* is Bacon. Johnson imitates the approach of Bacon's *Essays*, as Hawkins was among the first to perceive, and he discusses many of the same topics. Johnson praises Bacon's *Essays* both in the *Harleian Catalogue* and in the *Rambler* itself by citing Bacon's dedication. In the *Catalogue* he translates from Bacon's Latin version, but in the *Rambler* he excerpts Bacon's English. After yet another of the many *Ramblers* on the vanity of literary wishes and the ephemerality of almost all kinds of writing, including lexicography, Johnson concludes: 'There are, indeed, few kinds of composition from which an author, however learned or ingenious, can hope a long continuance of fame. He who has carefully studied human nature, and can well describe it, may with most reason flatter his ambition. Bacon, among all his pretensions to the regard of posterity, seems to have pleased himself chiefly with his essays, "which come home to mens business and bosoms," and of which, therefore, he declares his expectation, that they "will live as long as books last."'[8]

Having said this, Johnson then retreats a little from an identification with the greatness of Bacon and sets out for himself a humbler but also more Christian ideal: 'It may, however, satisfy an honest and benevolent mind to have been useful, though less conspicuous; nor will he that extends his hope to higher rewards, be so anxious to obtain praise, as to discharge the duty which Providence assigns him.' The extent to which this statement is personal is revealed by a comparison of it with the prayer Johnson wrote upon beginning the *Rambler*:

> Almighty God, the giver of all good things, without whose help all Labour is ineffectual, and without whose grace all wisdom is folly, grant, I beseech Thee, that in this my undertaking thy Holy Spirit may not be witheld from me, but that I may promote thy glory, and the Salvation both of myself and others, – Grant this O Lord for the sake of Jesus Christ. Amen. Lord bless me. So be it.

Johnson's undertaking is as serious as Bacon's, and his prayer is not unlike one of Bacon's making called 'The Writer's Prayer': 'Thou, O Father, who gavest the visible light as the first-born of thy creatures . . . be pleased to protect and govern this work, which coming from thy goodness, returneth to thy glory. . . . if we labour in thy works with the sweat of our brows, thou wilt make us partakers of thy vision and thy sabbath.'[9]

Not every number of the *Rambler* accords with such high seriousness, but a great many do, and Mr Rambler is more intensely serious than Addison's Mr Spectator and most of his progeny. Although there are some pauses in it, the whole series of *Ramblers* resembles a seventeenth-century sequence of sonnets in its devotion to the exploration of a single but infinitely complex idea. The idea Johnson explores is the vanity of human wishes, but like that of Sir Philip Sidney in *Astrophel and Stella*, his first task is to find a voice. Number 1 speaks directly to the problem by discussing 'The difficulty of the first address on any new occasion'. Johnson even makes a half-joking comparison between the lover and the writer that suggests a parallel between his essays and a sonnet sequence: 'In love, the state which fills the heart with a degree of solicitude next that of an author, it has been held a maxim, that success is most easily obtained by indirect and unperceived approaches; he who too soon professes himself a lover, raises obstacles to his own wishes, and those whom disappointments have taught experience, endeavour to conceal their passion till they believe their mistress wishes for the discovery. The same method, if it were practicable to writers, would save many complaints of the severity of the age, and the caprices of criticism.'[10] Johnson describes the dilemma of the writer more directly as a choice between 'submission' and 'arrogance'. As always in Johnson's rhetorical world, each choice has its dangers, and failing to choose is fatal. Johnson chooses arrogance because the brevity of his performance will prevent disgust, but his resolve is not strong: he talks more about quitting and escaping than proceeding with his task.

In Number 2, one of the greatest *Ramblers,* Johnson presents and enacts in compact and forceful language the operation of the human mind in its restless flight from present life to the anticipation of future joys or woes. This constitutes a psychology that explains why the world neglects speakers of truth, but it does not dispel Mr Rambler's troubling uncertainties about his own enterprise:

> It may not be unfit for him who makes a new entrance into the lettered world, so far to suspect his own powers as to believe that he possibly may deserve neglect; that nature may not have qualified him much to enlarge or embellish knowledge, nor sent him forth entitled by indisputable superiority to regulate the conduct of the rest of mankind; that, though the world must be granted to be in ignorance, he is not destined to dispel the cloud, nor to shine out as one of the luminaries of life. For this suspicion, every catalogue of a library will furnish sufficient reason; as he will find it crouded with names of men, who, though now forgotten, were once no less enterprising or confident than himself, equally pleased with their own productions, equally caressed by their patrons, and flattered by their friends.[11]

This is hardly Johnson's first entrance on the literary scene, but Mr Rambler is a novice, and Johnson is identifying himself more closely with his speaker than he ever has before in a work of imagination.

One cause of the writer's anxiety in Number 2 is the unreliability of his audience: 'He that endeavours after fame by writing, solicits the regard of a multitude fluctuating in pleasures, or immersed in business, without time for intellectual amusements; he appeals to judges prepossessed by passions, or corrupted by prejudices.'[12] Number 3 proposes a solution to this problem by means of an allegory in which the goddess Criticism yields her sceptre to Time, thus freeing authors from the prepossessions and prejudices of contemporary judges. The allegory is consistent with Johnson's other critical writings, including the Preface to Shakespeare, his grandest exploration of the role of time in literary evaluation, but it is also part of his attempt to settle the voice of Mr Rambler.

Having soothed his anxieties about popularity, Mr Rambler discusses popular fiction in Number 4 and fearlessly distinguishes himself from those who write it. Johnson's friend and editor Arthur Murphy said *Rambler* 4 expresses Johnson's preference for the novels of Richardson over the recently published *Roderick Random* and *Tom Jones.* Modern novels, says

Johnson, portray 'an adventurer [who] is levelled with the rest of the world, and acts in such scenes of the universal drama, as may be the lot of any other man'. Hence, 'young spectators fix their eyes upon him with closer attention, and hope by observing his behaviour and success to regulate their own practices, when they shall be engaged in the like part.' Johnson acknowledges the Aristotelian position that 'it is justly considered as the greatest excellency of art, to imitate nature', but he takes the sophisticated view that 'it is necessary to distinguish those parts of nature, which are most proper for imitation. . . . If the world be promiscuously described, I cannot see of what use it can be to read the account; or why it may not be as safe to turn the eye immediately upon mankind, as upon a mirror which shows all that presents itself without discrimination.' Johnson would have heard with horror Stendhal's description of the novel as a mirror moving through the landscape on a freight train. He favours an analytical representation of human life that will serve as a training manual for those not yet skilled in dealing with the moral complexities of the real thing. Virtue and vice must be carefully distinguished, and there must be no admission for the argument of ironists like Swift that good and evil stem often from the same human sources:

> It is of the utmost importance to mankind, that positions of this tendency should be laid open and confuted; for while men consider good and evil as springing from the same root, they will spare the one for the sake of the other, and in judging, if not of others at least of themselves, will be apt to estimate their virtues by their vices. To this fatal error all those will contribute, who confound the colours of right and wrong, and instead of helping to settle their boundaries, mix them with so much art, that no common mind is able to disunite them.

The title of Bacon's framentary 'Colours of Good and Evil' may have played across Johnson's mind as he wrote this paragraph. In that work Bacon is engaged in sorting out the fallacies of rhetorical colours (or persuasives), and Johnson advises writers of fiction to spare readers that effort by plainly representing attractive virtue and repulsive vice. Johnson concludes with an affirmation of the role of Mr Rambler and his relationship with his audience written in terms of counsel for novelists: 'The Roman tyrant was content to be hated, if he was but feared; and there are thousands of the readers of romances willing to be thought wicked, if they may be allowed to be wits. It is therefore to be steadily inculcated, that virtue is the highest proof of understanding, and the only solid basis of greatness; and that vice is the natural consequence of narrow thoughts, that it begins in mistake, and ends in ignominy.'[13] At the risk of being unpopular Mr Rambler will demonstrate his greatness by recommending virtue, and, though Roman enough in his way, he will not buy followers by corrupting souls.

Although Johnson established the voice of Mr Rambler within a few weeks of beginning his periodical essays, he always retained some doubts

about his main character's commercial and social viability. Mr Rambler
is a speculatist, praised for his 'age, learning, abstraction, [and] virtue',
qualities that remove him from the concerns of domestic life. He is described as a 'wit', and his rivals are said to be at Agra or Ispahan, suggesting
an exotic, oriental life – distant, philosophical, and storied. In his own
voice, Mr Rambler tells the eight Eastern tales of wisdom and the similarly
magisterial eight allegories included in the *Rambler.* He is one of 'those
who have assumed the arduous province of preserving the balance of the
mental constitution' and, with more self-importance than Johnson could
countenance in his revision, 'of administering physick to the soul'. Like
the Hermit of Teneriffe and other seers in Johnson's writing, Mr Rambler
is a philosopher who rises above human experience in his thought but
thereby makes himself vulnerable to the criticisms of those who live and
suffer in the world. His limitations are the subject of the address of a
fictional correspondent, Philomedes ('laughter-loving'):

> Those who exalt themselves into the chair of instruction, and venture upon
> the presumptuous office of teaching others, very often without enquiring
> whether any will submit to their authority, have not sufficiently considered
> how much of human life passes in little incidents, cursory conversation,
> slight business, and casual amusements; and therefore they have endeavoured
> only to exhibit and to inculcate the severer, more difficult, and more awful
> virtues, without condescending to regard those petty duties or secondary
> qualities, which grow important only by their frequency, and which, though
> they are overlooked by the speculatist because they produce no single acts
> of heroism, nor astonish us by great events, yet are every moment exerting
> their influence upon us, and, as they are practiced or neglected, make the
> draught of life sweet or bitter by imperceptible instillations.[14]

Johnson wisely edited this sentence for the fourth edition and removed
the word 'speculatist', but even after revision the passage makes it plain
that Mr Rambler cannot understand everything that Johnson wished to
relate in his periodical essays.

Like the speaker of the *Vanity of Human Wishes*, Mr Rambler assumes a
sort of omniscience, occupying the hill of truth and citing Lucretius'
description of the privileged place, just as Bacon does in his essay 'Of
Truth'. The second time he quotes the famous proem of *De rerum natura*,
Book 2, however, it is in the ironic context of describing the garret, home
of the author. The fictional correspondent Hypertatus ('most above')
praises Mr Rambler's altitude, to his cost: 'when I read a composition,
I immediately determine the height of the author's habitation. As an
elaborate performance is commonly said to smell of the lamp, my commendation of a noble thought, a sprightly sally, or a bold figure, is to pro-
nounce it fresh from the garret; an expression which would break from
me upon the perusal of most of your papers, did I not believe, that you
sometimes quit the garret, and ascend into the cock-loft.'[15] Like Teneriffe,
the cock-loft is one of Johnson's Aonian mounts, and he delighted in

issuing pronouncements from on high. However, he always recognized the limitations of such sublime posturing, and much that he wishes to relate is beyond Mr Rambler's ken.

About sixty whole *Ramblers* and parts of others are from fictional correspondents, who are less impressive than Mr Rambler but are needed to address the aspects of human life that escape the sage. Many of these characters are female, and many of the males write on marital questions. Three of the four *Ramblers* actually written by others are by women (two by Elizabeth Carter and one by her good friend, Catherine Talbot). Although Mr Rambler successfully brings conventionally male subjects (like learning) to a female audience, his philosophical elevation makes him an unsuitable speaker on conventionally female issues, such as marriage and domestic life. He recognizes that 'the moralist, whose instructions are accommodated only to one half of the human species, must be confessed not sufficiently to have extended his views.' On domestic matters Mr Rambler is a listener rather than a speaker, the confidant of female correspondents whom Johnson invents to express his thoughts on the 'little incidents' of life. In Number 42 Euphelia ('well-loving' or 'good friend'), bored by her sojourn in the country, opens her heart to Mr Rambler in the following terms: 'I am no great admirer of grave writings, and therefore very frequently lay your papers aside before I have read them through; yet I cannot but confess that, by slow degrees, you have raised my opinion of your understanding. . . . I shall therefore chuse you for the confident of my distresses . . . though I never expect from you any of that softness and pliancy, which constitutes the perfection of a companion for the ladies: as in the place where I now am, I have recourse to the mastiff for protection, though I have no intention of making him a lap-dog.' A large, rough animal, 'too old to be much pained by hasty censure', a writer for whom 'whatever be [the] subject, melancholy for the most part bursts in upon [his] speculation', Mr Rambler is sometimes more like Boswell's seventy year-old Johnson than the forty-one year-old author of the *Rambler*.[16] Even before he was forty-one Johnson had some of Mr Rambler's qualities, but there is a distinction between his literary creation and himself that is too easily forgotten. Johnson himself had more 'versatility' (to recall Hawkins's word) than Mr Rambler. Remembering that the sage is one of many personae that Johnson created throws light on the breadth of his imaginative interests.

Apart from the various personae, there are other literary devices in the *Rambler*. Although many of these are consistent with the character of the main speaker, they further illuminate the range of Johnson's mind. The device that Johnson uses most in the *Rambler* is the old system of commonplaces or common topics, the mastery of which is recommended in classical treatises on the subject from Aristotle on. These stores of wisdom applicable to any subject gradually came in later works to include aphorisms, wise sayings, and even short pointed tales, as well as the sort of first principles that Aristotle had in mind when he spoke of topoi. Many of the great humanists with whom Johnson was spiritually allied wrote treatises on the stores of inherited wisdom passed down by the ancients and other writers. Erasmus's *Adagia* and his *De copia* are perhaps the grandest and greatest works of this sort, but all humanistic commentary is a form of topical treatment, critically tracing sources and making analogies. Bacon's *Essays* also are devoted to well-documented topics and make a critical use of existing material stored under their headings. Like Bacon, Johnson is critical of his inherited wisdom, even as he employs it to assemble his own work.

Despite scanty external evidence, it is clear that Johnson used his own collections of commonplaces in the construction of his *Ramblers*. Both Boswell and Hawkins saw his collections, which they refer to as 'Adversaria'; they reprinted small parts of them in their biographies, but the volumes subsequently disappeared, and all that remains of the six folio and one duodecimo notebooks are the printed excerpts. The printed extracts appear to be outlines for essays, studded occasionally with quotations that may have come from other parts of the volumes. Hawkins prints this interesting sketch:

Quid expedivit Psittacus
[Why did Psittacus – the parrot – prattle on?]

Reasons of writing, benevolence, desire of fame, vanity, hunger, curiosity to know the rate of a man's own understanding. Which most justifiable. All may be forgiven if not persisted in, but writing for bread most, *Rich talk without excuse*, Rosc[ommon]. . . .
The greatest writers have [written] for bread – Homer – Shakespear – Dryden – Pope. Fatui non famae – Degente de fatu et affame d'argent [not the fools of fame – patient of fame and eager for money].
Inconveniences of this life. To the public; the press is crouded with many books, yet this may diffuse knowledge, and leaves less room for vanity, sometimes it may choak the way to letters, and hinder learning but rarely. To themselves most inconven[ient,] seldom above want, endless labour, always a new work, subscriptions solicited, shameless importunity, meanness, patrons and encouragers to be got, wretched obsequiousness, companions of polite follies, vices, dedication, hateful flattery, utmost ambition or hope small place, youth of labour, old age of dependence. This place not often got, [John] Gay.[17]

Although Number 21 is the most relevant, parts of many *Ramblers* are suggested here, but the distaste for the life of writing in the social context of mid-century England is sharper in this note than it is any place in Johnson's published work. The fragment goes to show how Johnson tailored his thoughts and feelings to suit his audience and his chosen literary personae as well as how he built up his work from commonplaces that he had already modified to some degree. Johnson had been using such a system all along as a writer. When he was organizing loose notes into conventional political topics in his Parliamentary *Debates* or drafting *Irene* as a workout on philosophical topics, Johnson was learning the method that enabled him to write convincingly on almost any subject with remarkable speed. Johnson said that all his other works were wine mixed with water, but his *Rambler* was pure wine partly because in it he was working most fully, most critically, and most imaginatively with the already refined material of the commonplace tradition.

Each *Rambler* begins with a commonplace – a quotation in Latin or, much less often, in Greek, which serves as the theme or lesson of the composition. In fact, forthcoming numbers of the *Rambler* were advertised in places like the *Gentleman's Magazine* with the epigram on which Johnson was to dilate that day. His favourite sources are predictable: Horace, Juvenal, Ovid, and Vergil together account for 135 epigraphs, with Horace alone supplying more than half of these. After the quotation, which serves as a rubric for the the essay, Johnson often writes a summary of what has traditionally been said on the subject. An important part of the tone of the *Rambler* is a consciousness that these sayings are old and easy. Even in Number 2, when he is treating a theme that will return again and again in later *Ramblers,* Johnson conveys a sense that the topic has already been exhausted:

> That the mind of man is never satisfied with the objects immediately before it, but is always breaking away from the present moment, and losing itself in schemes of future felicity; and that we forget the proper use of the time now in our power, to provide for the enjoyment of that which, perhaps, may never be granted us, has been frequently remarked; and as this practice is a commodious subject of raillery to the gay, and of declamation to the serious, it has been ridiculed with all the pleasantry of wit, and exaggerated with all the amplifications of rhetoric. Every instance, by which its absurdity might appear most flagrant, has been studiously collected; it has been marked with every epithet of contempt, and all the tropes and figures have been called forth against it.[18]

The phrase 'amplifications of rhetoric' itself sounds patent or tired and is therefore suited to the tiredness that Johnson expresses. Embodying what he asserts, Johnson gives more summary treatment to even more common themes. Perhaps most replete with patent phrases is a paragraph in Number 143: 'Many subjects fall under the consideration of an author, which being limited by nature can admit only of slight and accidental diversities. All definitions of the same thing must be nearly the same. . . . Different poets describing the spring or the sea would mention the zephyrs and the flowers, the billows and the rocks; reflecting on human life, they would, without any communication of opinions, lament the deceitfulness of hope, the fugacity of pleasure, the fragility of beauty, and the frequency of calamity; and for palliatives of these incurable miseries, they would concur in recommending kindness, temperance, caution and fortitude.'[19] The four phrases beginning with 'the deceitfulness of hope' are rubrics for what moralists say about life and display themselves as rubrics; they parody rhetoric and its system of commonplaces. Although this is an extreme case, the resulting tone is present throughout the *Rambler*. Mr Rambler and many of his correspondents are late or belated philosophers wearily recounting the accumulated wisdom of their forerunners before going on to assemble works based on them.

Most *Ramblers* go on to exemplify the previously summarized maxims. In 143, for instance, Johnson presents pairs of classical and modern authors exhibiting a 'genealogy of sentiments', like the best sequences of illustrative quotations in the *Dictionary*. In fact, some of the comparisons in the *Rambler* may come directly from Johnson's reading for the *Dictionary*.[20] Although it can be impressive, this particular kind of exemplification tends to be ironic; it draws attention to the mechanism of Johnson's literary production and arranges his stock of literary material under rubrics he has already represented as time-worn.

In other essays, exemplification means the creation of narrative involving an allegory or a character with an allegorical name. For instance, the story of Polyphilus ('one with many loves') exemplifies the vanity of human wishes in a tale about a brilliant scholar who flies from one field of study to another without ever settling down to a fulfilling life or any useful work. Likewise, the story of Pertinax ('tenacious' or 'retentive') in Number 95 exemplifies the basic wisdom of the exhortation to know thyself in the story of a scholar who sacrifices religion and virtue to the allurements of learned success. Johnson may have modelled some of his exemplary characters on real people; the haughty, successful Prospero is said to be modelled on David Garrick, for instance. In taking models from life Johnson would have been living up to Mr Rambler's reputation as one of those 'who turn their speculations upon the living world'.[21] Yet, the level of abstraction and generalization is such in Johnson's exemplary stories that, like Bacon's *Apophthegms*, they usually read simply as amplifications of the epigram that initiated them; the stories are exemplary in the old moral sense rather than in the modern sense of providing historical evidence for speculative positions. Nevertheless, the *Rambler* does provide contemporary dress for the old maxims: the antiquary, the Grub Street hack, the county heir, and the city beauty help make up a set of stock characters with which Johnson can update received wisdom, much as he does in his imitations of Juvenal.

With all its reliance on existing stores of literary material, is there anything really new in the *Rambler*? Johnson shows some defensiveness about this obvious question not only in his sometimes parodic tone but also in his many statements concerning the permanence of moral truth and the fact that it was discovered by the first writers. For this reason, 'the excellence of aphorisms consists not so much in the expression of some rare or abstruse sentiment, as in the comprehension of some obvious and useful truth in a few words. We frequently fall into error and folly, not because the true principles of action are not known, but because, for a time, they are not remembered', and 'men more frequently require to be reminded

than informed.' However, a reminder is not simply a repetition, and
Johnson shows in many cases his sense that there is, despite the stability
of truth, a possibility of corruption in its transmission, which it behoves
him to address:

> the studies of mankind, all at least which, not being subject to rigorous
> demonstration, admit the influence of fancy and caprice, are perpetually
> tending to error and confusion. Of the great principles of truth which the
> first speculatists discovered, the simplicity is embarrassed by ambitious addi-
> tions, or the evidence obscured by inaccurate argumentation; and as they
> descend from one succession of writers to another, like light transmitted
> from room to room, they lose their strength and splendour, and fade at last
> in total evanscence.
>   The systems of learning therefore must be sometimes reviewed, complica-
> tions analised into principles, and knowledge disentangled from opinion.[22]

Johnson's particular subject here is literary criticism, where the elaborations of ambitious commentators more evidently require pruning than
the productions of more useful labourers in the vineyard of morality, but
in his handling of all topics Johnson adds an element of review and analyses
complications into principles. In his *Ramblers* on literary criticism Johnson
makes the basis of his analysis an ideal reader purified by time; likewise in
the essays on moral topics, the basis is a purified, ideal mind. In both cases
Johnson's criticism is profoundly affective, concentrating on the reaction
of a free, though generalized, agent to circumstances outside of itself.
These agents are impartial, objective observers, and Johnson constructs
them in order to reorganize received wisdom in the more modern shape
of empirical science. Hence, although he is perpetually indebted to his
forerunners, the epigraph for the whole *Rambler* is taken from the same
passage of Horace as the motto of the Royal Society: 'Nullius addictus
jurare in verba magistri' ('bound to make my declarations according to
the words of no master').

'Criticism,' Johnson says in Number 158, 'though dignified from the
earliest ages by the labours of men eminent for knowledge and sagacity;
and, since the revival of polite literature, the favourite study of European
scholars, has not yet attained the certainty and stability of science.' He
goes on to adduce passages and evaluate critical rules in light of the
empirical data of literature, which is registered chiefly as 'the pleasure of
the reader'. The reader in 'scientific' criticism is constantly reacting, and
the mind in 'scientific' morality is likewise constantly in motion, whether
it is responding to external or internal impressions and impulses. Because
it is the basis of moral science, the motion of the mind must be scientifically described. In Number 6 Johnson describes mental movement
succinctly: 'we desire, we pursue, we obtain, we are satiated; we desire
something else, and begin a new persuit.' These are 'the natural flights of
the mind' and Johnson writes about them as though they were a form of
physical motion expressible in the language of natural science. Johnson

describes the behaviour of the mind, therefore, according to an analogy which is metaphysical, not unlike the poetry of Donne or Cowley. The elaborate description of the soul in the beginning of Number 8 is worthy of either poet:

> It is said by modern philosophers, that not only the great globes of matter are thinly scattered thro' the universe, but the hardest bodies are so porous, that, if all matter were compressed to perfect solidity, it might be contained in a cube of a few feet. In like manner, if all the employment of life were crowded into the time which it really occupied, perhaps a few weeks, days, or hours, would be sufficient for its accomplishment, so far as the mind was engaged in the performance. For such is the inequality of our corporeal to our intellectual faculties, that we contrive in minutes what we execute in years, and the soul often stands an idle spectator of the labour of the hands, and expedition of the feet.[23]

The analogy in this passage is hard: consciousness is space, and deeds are matter. But since 'the soul always exerts her peculiar powers', spatial motion usually provides simpler terms for Johnson's descriptions of personal or interpersonal activity. For instance, Johnson analyses urban conformity this way in Number 138:

> In cities, and yet more in courts, the minute discriminations which distinguish one from another are for the most part effaced, the peculiarities of temper and opinion are gradually worn away by promiscuous converse, as angular bodies and uneven surfaces lose their points and asperities by frequent attrition against one another, and approach by degrees to uniform rotundity. The prevalence of fashion, the influence of example, the desire of applause, and the dread of censure, obstruct the natural tendencies of the mind, and check the fancy in its first efforts to break forth into experiments of caprice.

There is a reduction to principle in such descriptions that marks them as enthymemes in the moral science Johnson is perpetually discovering in the *Rambler*. He is discovering rather than constructing it because he believes the knowledge of morality is simple and available at all times to all people. He was accordingly contemptuous of the new constructions of schematic moralists, like Francis Hutcheson. Johnson's science of morality is a redescription of received truths in terms of the physical sciences. Rather than constructing something new, Johnson's moral science reduces given truths to their original simplicity: 'as the chemists tell us, that all bodies are resolvable into the same elements, and that the boundless variety of things arises from the different proportions of very few ingredients; so a few pains, and a few pleasures are all the materials of human life, and of these the proportions are partly allotted by providence, and partly left to the arrangement of reason and of choice.'[24]

Like the Latinate diction, which he adopted from 'natural philosophers' who are prominent in the *Dictionary* (Bacon, Boyle, Hale, and others),

Johnson's persistent metaphysical imagery in the *Rambler* links him with the seventeenth century. This does not mean that Johnson's view of the mind is reactionary or backward. In fact, his description of the mind resembles that offered by the forward-looking David Hartley, whose work on the 'associative' principles of mind Johnson owned and may have read when it came out in 1749. Whether he drew on old writers or new, however, Johnson made his description of mind his own in the course of writing the *Rambler,* and the same may be said of his 'philosophic' style.[25] This way of speaking is particularly appropriate to Mr Rambler, but it appears throughout the essays in the language of almost all the supposed correspondents. Moreover, it continued to be an important feature of Johnson's own voice in subsequent works, such as the Preface to Shakespeare.

Another characteristic of the *Rambler* that is proper to Johnson as well as his mask is its circle of literary reference. Mr Rambler's intellectual world bears Johnson's distinctive stamp, although it is largely conventional and predictable for a mid-century writer of philosophical moral essays. This is especially true of the classical references, both those in the epigraphs and those in the essays themselves. According to the editors of the Yale edition, there are 669 quotations or literary allusions in the *Rambler*; 406 are from classical writers, and Horace alone accounts for 103. Though Horace was important throughout Johnson's life of reading, he was also the favourite classical writer of the whole eighteenth century. The other classical authors who appear frequently were also extremely popular sources of quotation and allusion in Johnson's day; Juvenal, Ovid, Martial, Vergil, and Homer are all obvious choices for a periodical writer in 1750. The less frequently chosen writers are also mostly predictable. The lines about the 'hill of truth' from the proem to Book 2 of Lucretius, for instance, which appear twice in the *Rambler,* also served as the epigraph for *The World,* a periodical publication of a lighter, more polite cast, to which Chesterfield made frequent contributions. It is possible to feel there is something more characteristic about the quotations from the *Greek Anthology* and the citations of Boethius, partly because they were somewhat less obvious choices and partly because we know Johnson both read and translated passages from them throughout his life. The same might be said of Seneca, Pliny the younger, Euripides, and a few others. Even with its occasional reference to less familiar authors, like Macrobius, Prudentius, or pseudo-Pythagoras, the *Rambler*'s range of classical references is not strange or unique, but it may represent Johnson in the act of accommodating his individual interests to the task of addressing a general, educated audience. The same may be true of Johnson's references to other periods of literature. The number of continental neo-Latin writers is, as the Yale editors suggest, striking, yet the particular authors cited are among the most conspicuous of their time. Johnson makes the scholarly Pertinax ('the retentive one') retire with the obscure Smigleus, but Johnson himself is usually content to quote the renowned Scaliger, Grotius, de Thou, or Erasmus. Among English writers, too, Johnson's choices are not idiosyncratic. He concentrates on the seventeenth century, but he usually chooses his quotations from Milton, Bacon, Locke, and Hooker. The nearly contemporary writers in the *Rambler* are perhaps the most predictable of all – Pope, Swift, and Addison.

Its range of references gives the *Rambler* an air of learning but not overcurious scholarship. The remarkable fact that the Bible is referred to a tenth as often as Horace shows that Johnson designed that air of learning in a certain way; he did not just allow it to flow from his spontaneous associations. Yet the particular kind of allusiveness contained in the *Rambler* does have autobiographical meaning. As a whole, the essays convey a sense that the learning behind them was acquired long ago, much like the commonplaces they summarize. Despite the grand range of reference from classical to modern authors, this is literally true; Johnson did little fresh reading for the *Rambler*. Almost all his references can be traced to texts he read early in life, during his years at the *Gentleman's Magazine*, in his work on the Harleian Library, or in the first stages of work on the *Dictionary*. He confesses this in a way in *Rambler* 184: 'As every scheme of life, so every form of writing has its advantages and inconveniences, though not mingled in the same proportions. The writer of essays, escapes many embarrassments to which a large work would have exposed him; . . . he seldom . . . dims his eyes with the perusal of antiquated volumes, or burthens his memory with great accumulations of preparatory knowledge. A careless glance upon a favourite author, or transient survey of the varieties of life, is sufficient to supply the first hint or seminal idea, which enlarged by the gradual accretion of matter stored in the mind, is by the warmth of fancy easily expanded into flowers, and sometimes ripened into fruit.'[26] This 'confession' describes part of what in *Rambler* 2 Johnson called 'the pleasure of wantoning in common topicks' to which the whole *Rambler* series is simultaneously receptive and resistant.

In 1763 Johnson said to Boswell, 'Sir, in my early years I read very hard. It is sad reflection, but a true one, that I knew almost as much at eighteen as I do now.' Be this as it may, a great many of the writers Johnson cites in the *Rambler* were already favourites of his twenty years before. For example, Johnson is probably either remembering or reading in his notes from seventeen years before when he begins *Rambler* 127 with a brief discussion of the epigrams of Poliziano. When he proposed the edition of Poliziano in 1734, Johnson probably read Scaliger's biography of the poet, which he next cites. In Number 38 Johnson refers to Claudian's 'rustick', meaning his 'Old Man of Verona Who Never Left his Home Ground'. Johnson remarks that the farmer 'computes his time not by the succession of consuls, but of harvests', thus paraphrasing line 11 of the same twenty-two-line poem he referred to in his draft of *Irene* in 1735 and which he probably read in the edition of Claudian's works edited by Heinsius that he took to college with him in 1728. The next fragment that had occurred to Johnson in his draft of *Irene* also occurs in Heinsius' notes to Claudian's poem, but it does not show up in the *Rambler* until Number 203 when

Johnson quotes Martial's *Epigrams*, 10.47.3: 'Among Martial's requisites to happiness is *res non parta labore sed relicta*, an estate not gained by industry, but left by inheritance.'[27]

Johnson's early reading in a number of the other writers cited in the *Rambler* is documented by the existence of the books with dates of acquisition. His Melanchthon, Pliny, and Anacreon, for instance, still exist with pencil markings and dates of acquisition, showing that he read them long before quoting them in the *Rambler*. His earlier works testify to some of his other early reading in writers that appear in the *Rambler*. From the period of writing *Irene*, for example, Johnson took his reference to Richard Knolles's *Generall Historie of the Turkes*. Johnson's piece on epitaphs for the *Gentleman's Magazine* in 1739 and his reading in the *Greek Anthology* at that time or before obviously occurred to him when he invented Zosima, the correspondent in Number 12. In the next number he remembered a part of the *Memoirs of the Duchess of Marlborough*, which he had reviewed for the *Gentleman's Magazine* in 1742. In whatever way Johnson contributed to Robert James's *Medicinal Dictionary* (1743–5), it was probably while helping with that project that he read a biography of Aretaeus, the ancient physician who appears in *Rambler* 117. Johnson's work on the *Harleian Catalogue* (1743–5) also supplied him with stores that he used or used again in the *Rambler*. In Number 4, for instance, he cites Scaliger's *De re poetica* on Pontanus, and in Number 28 he brings in from the same source the epitaph of Pontanus that he had previously printed in number 4298 in volume 1 of the *Harleian Catalogue*. Here, he translates what there he had cited in Latin only.[28]

Examples, especially from the *Harleian Catalogue*, could be multiplied, but the point is that Johnson's reading and his range of reference, though vast, contain a strong element of return. He was constantly recycling his earlier studies in later work, and he often reread his favourite authors. At the very end of his life, for example, he did some Latin translations from the same Brodaeus edition of the *Greek Anthology* that had provided him with material in his essay on epitaphs in the *Gentleman's Magazine*. His contact with Euripides' *Medea* and certain odes of Horace can be documented over even longer stretches. Although Johnson's intellectual world continued to grow throughout his life, there was a shape and centre of gravity to it by about 1750 that remained largely unchanged. Moreover, Johnson's life of reading grew along the lines suggested early in his life when he imagined himself as a budding Latin poet-scholar, like the great humanists. There remained throughout his life an intellectual kinship with the likes of Poliziano, Scaliger, and Buchanan. The mixture of piety, moral allegory, epigram, poetry, scholarship, literary criticism, and biography found in the interests of a Renaissance humanist like Salutati persisted throughout Johnson's intellectual life, even though his drive to lead such a life was deflected by financial exigencies and the nature of the publishing world in which he lived.

The last really wide expansion of Johnson's reading is registered primarily in the *Dictionary,* and it is very directly reflected in the *Rambler* because Johnson was doing both projects at the same time. Like the *Rambler,* the *Dictionary* itself relies partly on earlier reading, as the many quotations from memory show. But Johnson did some heavy rereading for the *Dictionary,* and the inevitable deepening in his appreciation for certain authors is evident in the *Rambler.* Johnson had read Locke with Walmesley in Lichfield, for example, but both the *Dictionary* and the *Rambler* display a real intimacy with his works that came later. The *Educational Writings* are prominent in both works, as befits their mutual educational bent, but more curious inspection uncovers further connections. For instance, in *Rambler* 132, Johnson repeats a Lockean economic principle when he says, 'what is obtained by labour, will be of right the property of him by whose labour it is gained.' Part of the original appears in the *Dictionary* under 'his' where Johnson provides the illustrative quotation from Locke's *Second Treatise*: 'He that is nourished by the acorns he picked up under an oak in the wood, has appropriated them to himself: nobody can deny but the nourishment is *his*.' Locke's place in Johnson's thinking was solidified in the late 1740s, but an even greater presence is Bacon. He is directly quoted often, but at least as often he silently appears. Johnson's story of Nugaculus ('a nothing'), the dilettante scholar who is inquisitive to no good purpose, very closely follows Bacon's description of 'delicate learning' in the *Advancement of Learning*. As usual, Johnson begins *Rambler* 137 with a characteristic reminder of some received piece of wisdom: 'That wonder is the effect of ignorance, has often been observed. . . . Wonder is a pause of reason, a sudden cessation of the mental progress.' Johnson is remembering Bacon's *Valerius Terminus*: 'wonder: which is nothing else but contemplation broken off, or loosing it self.' To give one more of many possible examples, when Johnson cites the maxim of 'Alphonsus of *Aragon*, that dead counsellors are safest', he is imperfectly recalling Bacon's redaction of the saying in his *Apophthegms*: 'Alonzo of Aragon was wont to say of himself, that he was a great necromancer, for that he used to ask counsel of the dead; meaning of books.'[29]

Harmless industry might go on to find Johnson tracking and backtracking through the snowfields of favourite authors throughout his writing career. It is hard to resist this activity: the 'taedet' which Johnson uses to explain 'irksome' in his *Dictionary* is surely the same 'taedet' that appears in the epigraph to *Rambler* 171: 'Taedet coeli convexa tueri' ('Irksome it is to look on the bowl of the heavens'; *Aeneid* 4: 451). But enough. The point of such connections is to see that Johnson's intellectual empire has a certain shape, despite its vast expanse, and that there are certain authors that are prominent. The empire took its shape early, and even in the last period of great expansion – his reading for the *Dictionary* in the late 1740s – the formative years of Johnson's intellectual life exerted so great an influence that it was difficult for a new writer to rise up and reshape the existing world. By the age of forty, and probably much earlier, changes in Johnson's intellectual outlook depended mainly upon further reading of authors he already knew. Bacon's impact, so evident in the *Rambler*, was great partly because he was the sort of late humanist with whom Johnson had identified himself from an early age.

Unlike so many of Johnson's earlier works, the *Rambler* is not the product of a research programme but, like *The Vanity of Human Wishes*, the result of reflection upon vast research already done for other purposes. Unlike 'books', as Bacon describes them, the *Rambler* can teach the 'use of books'. It is a form of wisdom literature, like the *Vanity* and like *Rasselas*. As Walter Jackson Bate says, the *Rambler* 'may be described as the prose explication of *The Vanity of Human Wishes*'.[30] Rather than concluding in gnomic wisdom, like 'know thyself' or 'mens sana in corpore sano', the *Rambler* unpacks these nuggets, exemplifying them in allegorical tales and analysing them in the Latinate language of seventeenth-century natural philosophy. Although he should not be equated with Mr Rambler, and even though the round of reading in the whole *Rambler* is a selection from Johnson's wider researches, these 208 essays represent the full flowering of his literary identity. In later life he would read and write a great deal more, and his opinions on numerous subjects continued to change, but by the time he finished the *Rambler* Johnson's literary identity had an integrity and a centre that would hold together for the rest of his life. He was forty-three years old, neither early nor late to be in his full intellectual bloom. The identity he fashioned, however, is one that is often thought more appropriate to later life, and it left the real person plenty of room to grow into it and receive acknowledgement as the sage he had created.

11

Sermons

He that outlives a Wife whom he has long loved, sees himself disjoined from the only Mind that had the same hopes, and fears, and interest. . . . The continuity of being is lacerated. The settled course of sentiment and action is stopped, and life stands suspended and motionless till it is driven by external causes into a new channel.
Johnson to Thomas Lawrence, 20 January 1780

Despite its philosophical abstraction, the *Rambler* often reflects real events both in London and in Johnson's personal life, as James F. Woodruff has shown.[1] The coming of summer stimulates him to write on pastoral subjects or the vain wish for rural happiness; the opening of a new lottery impels the composition of a *Rambler* on the allurements of fortune; cardinal points in the Christian year evoke predictable responses; and Johnson's own birthday, of course, brings on a *Rambler* discussing the need for a periodic review and evaluation of one's life. There are also some more obscure connections. The *Ramblers* on Milton's prosody, for instance, may be Johnson's response to his embarrassing involvement in the attempt of an embittered Scot named William Lauder to discredit Milton by showing that he had plagiarized parts of *Paradise Lost* from neo-Latin sources.

Lauder's efforts began in scholarly letters to the *Gentleman's Magazine* in 1747 and culminated in the publication in 1749 of a malicious book, backed by the publishers of the *Rambler*, Payne and Bouquet. As a preface Johnson contributed material that he had written to advertise another of Lauder's efforts, a new edition of one of the 'sources' – Grotius's Latin poem *Adam Exsul.* Printed as an afterword was an advertisement Johnson had composed for a performance of Milton's *Comus* to benefit the poet's indigent granddaughter. Lauder's book was a subject of controversy in London, and Johnson was clearly identified as an anti-Miltonian. It was soon proven, however, that in citing Milton's 'sources' Lauder had interpolated lines from a Latin translation of *Paradise Lost.* Payne and Bouquet immediately made a public repudiation of their involvement with Lauder and issued new prefaces and postscripts for the book, which they then offered cut-rate as a curiosity. Johnson dictated to Lauder a confessional letter to the *Gentleman's Magazine*. Lauder appeared to accept the letter's unmitigated contrition, but at the last minute, without Johnson's knowledge, he inserted a couple of paragraphs excusing his crime. Like many other plagiarists and forgers, Lauder never understood how wrong his actions were. After his first failure, he justified his underhanded attack on Milton on the grounds that Milton had himself done something similar by having printers insert a prayer taken from Sir Philip Sidney's *Arcadia* in Charles I's *Eikon Basilike* before attacking the 'plagiarism' in *Eikonoclastes*. This charge, first made by Thomas Wagstaff in 1693, had not yet been properly examined, and it remained believable when Johnson credited it in his life of Milton nearly thirty years later. Milton's putative crime did not justify Lauder's, except in the eyes of die-hard Royalists. Johnson's *Life of Cheynel*, his exclusion of Milton's prose from the *Dictionary* (except 'On Education'), and his willingness to hear charges like Lauder's against Milton all suggest that Johnson's sympathies were Royalist. He adopted this attitude early in life, amidst tales of rebel atrocities in Royalist Lichfield, but Johnson was far from fanatical; he instantly repudiated Lauder when the forgery was exposed. Lauder himself never surrendered the cause, but by 1756 he had no supporters and went to Barbados where he died in poverty fifteen years later.[2]

Despite his efforts to clear himself, Johnson was still identified with Lauder as late as 1780 when Francis Blackburne attacked Johnson for aiding the forger before launching into a criticism of his life of Milton. In his own copy of Blackburne's book Johnson wrote, 'In the business of Lauder I was deceived, partly by thinking the man too frantick to be fraudulent.' In the light of the embarrassing situation that arose with the public detection of Lauder's fraud toward the end of 1750, it is remarkable that Johnson undertook at this time to criticize Milton's prosody in the *Rambler*. His friends were concerned for his reputation, as a letter from Catherine Talbot to Elizabeth Carter on 19 January 1751 shows: 'I was sorry the other day to see a *Rambler* (though a good one) upon Milton, because the author has been much censured for carrying his humanity and good-nature so much too far, as to assist that villainous forger Lauder in his Apology.'[3] His criticism of Milton at this dangerous time may be an indication that Johnson's natural rebelliousness was surviving middle age. The Lauder affair had excited a good deal of thoughtless, nationalistic bardolatry – just the sort of cant Johnson could never bear. Johnson's *Ramblers* on Milton, like his later biography, fully acknowledge the poet's greatness, while pointing out his relatively minor but potentially influential flaws. Using the language of literary criticism, Johnson was addressing the contemporary debate on Milton in a sort of code, saying, in effect, that he understood his error, but that he would not submit to demogoguery from either side.

In its second year the *Rambler* became shorter, somewhat less abstract, and more topical, probably because Johnson was concerned about sales. The print run was never more than 500 per copy in London, though there was a wide provincial distribution through reprints in other journals. In the later *Ramblers* there is an increase in the number of implicit allusions to Johnson's life beyond the ken of Mr Rambler. The work of the *Dictionary*, for example, is increasingly evident as the *Rambler* proceeds because of the growing number of essays on literary criticism and other philological matters. Johnson seems to be tuning up for his performance in the Preface to the *Dictionary* when he talks about the superiority of the classical to the modern languages in *Rambler* 169, the disparity between words and things in 152 and 168, the abuses of language in 202, and his effort to purify English of 'colloquial barbarisms' in 208. Some of the elegiac and pathetic gloom of the Preface also appears late in the *Rambler*. In 207, for example, Johnson can only be reflecting on his lexicographical work when he complains,

> When once our labour has begun, the comfort that enables us to endure it is the prospect of its end; for though in every long work there are some joyous intervals of self-applause, when the attention is recreated by unexpected facility, and the imagination soothed by incidental excellencies; yet the toil with which performance struggles after idea, is so irksome and disgusting, and so frequent is the necessity of resting below that perfection which we imagined within our reach, that seldom any man obtains more from his endeavours than a painful conviction of his defects, and a continual resuscitation of desires which he feels himself unable to gratify.[4]

By the time he wrote the Preface to the completed *Dictionary* in 1755, Johnson was more forgiving of himself: 'Yet these failures, however frequent, may admit extenuation and apology. To have attempted much is always laudable, even when the enterprize is above the strength that undertakes it.' He is reconciled to his feelings of shortcoming when he issues his famous envoy, but peace has come to him at great cost:

> In this work, when it shall be found that much is omitted, let it not be forgotten that much likewise is performed; and though no book was ever spared out of tenderness to the authour, and the world is little solicitous to know whence proceeded the faults of that which it condemns; yet it may gratify curiosity to inform it, that the *English Dictionary* was written with little assistance of the learned, and without any patronage of the great; not in the soft obscurities of retirement, or under the shelter of academick bowers, but amidst inconvenience and distraction, in sickness and in sorrow: and it may repress the triumph of malignant criticism to observe, that if our language is not here fully displayed, I have only failed in an attempt which no human powers have hitherto completed. . . . I may surely be contented without the praise of perfection, which, if I could obtain, in this gloom of solitude, what would it avail me? I have protracted my work till most of those whom I wished to please, have sunk into the grave, and success and miscarriage are

empty sounds: I therefore dismiss it with frigid tranquility, having little to fear or hope from censure or from praise.[5]

In the Preface to the *Dictionary*, as in the *Rambler*, Johnson reacts to events in his personal life in conventional language, but his feelings are real and powerful. 'In sickness and in sorrow' is a literate, allusive phrase, suggesting, ironically, the marriage service in the Book of Common Prayer. The gloomy reflections of the late *Ramblers* and the declarations of a painfully achieved stoicism ('frigid tranquility') in the Preface are expressions in a formal mode of the most painful single event in Johnson's personal life. His wife was seriously ill in the winter of 1752 and she died on 17 March, three days after publication of the final number of the *Rambler*. The cause of death was said to be opium addiction, but the drug had been prescribed to treat a variety of serious conditions over the course of several years. For some time she had been living in Hampstead with Mrs Desmoulins in a last effort to regain her health away from the dust and noise of the city. Elizabeth's death was not terribly sudden, but by all accounts Johnson was devastated. He wrote immediately to his old friend John Taylor who happened to be in London at the time and, according to what Taylor told Boswell, 'expressed grief in the strongest manner he had ever read'. This letter is unfortunately lost, but Johnson's note to Taylor on the next day is preserved; it begins, 'Let me have your Company and your Instruction – Do not live away from me. My Distress is great.' Johnson was nearly incapacitated for five weeks. He saw Tetty wrapped in a woollen shroud and laid in her coffin, but he did not go to the funeral in the suburb of Bromley, eighteen miles from the city. He was incapable of making the arrangements for a proper service in London. Hawkins reports, 'The melancholy which seized Johnson on the death of his wife, was not, in degree, such as usually follows the deprivation of near relations and friends: it was of the blackest and deepest kind.'[6]

After five weeks Johnson wrote prayers on the death of his wife. Recent commentators have agreed that these agonizing pieces focus on Johnson's fear and trembling rather than on the deceased. His wife's death was an occasion for Johnson to express remorse, beg forgiveness, and promise repentance, but there is nothing unusual in this. These prayers are representative of Johnson's style of piety, which is conventional in its concentration on the suppliant's trials and deeds. In his severest trial, Johnson displays acceptance of God's will and asks Him for strength to bear his sorrow well and use it wisely: 'Almighty and most merciful Father, who lovest those whom Thou punishest, and turnest away thy anger from the penitent, look down with pity upon my sorrows, and grant that the affliction which it has pleased Thee to bring upon me, may awaken my conscience, enforce my resolutions of a better life, and impress upon me such conviction of thy power and goodness, that I may place in Thee my own felicity, and endeavour to please Thee in all my thoughts, words, and actions.' In the second prayer Johnson specifically mentions resolutions that he made to

Tetty on her death bed and repeated, perhaps in written form, on her coffin. Readers of *Clarissa* were acquainted with the use of the coffin as a bearer of religious promises and exhortations, and to the pious such uses were not strange, except in the case of a physically healthy twenty-year-old like Clarissa. In 1760 Johnson admonished himself again 'to consult the resolves on Tetty's coffin'. It was certainly no disgrace to Tetty's memory that he used her death to encourage his own piety.[7]

More alarming than the apparent self-concern of the prayers is the guilt expressed in them. Johnson seems to look upon his bereavement as punishment for his failures in marriage. In a prayer he composed about a year later, on Easter, Johnson writes, 'grant that by true contrition I may obtain forgiveness of all the Sins committed and of all duties neglected in my union with the Wife whom thou hast taken from me, for the neglect of joint devotion, patient exhortation, and mild instruction.'[8] In this passage Johnson may also have cited a particular sin (the name of which is now indecipherable) as a cause of his bereavement, but in Boswell's transcription (which may or may not represent the state of the now lost manuscript) the phrase is rubbed out. It is impossible to know in what particulars Johnson felt remiss. He often expressed a grave sense of responsibility for the moral effect he might have on those under his influence, especially members of his household. He may have felt he simply had not spent enough time with his wife and been an insufficiently strong moral guide to his weaker partner. Perhaps Johnson felt that he had committed sins of a conjugal nature by being sexually importunate or even profligate. It is impossible to be sure of the particulars, but his guilt deepened Johnson's gloom.

One other disturbing element of Johnson's reaction to Tetty's death is Hawkins's suggestion, confirmed in a couple of prayers, that he feared an 'apparition of his departed wife [that] was altogether of the terrific kind, and hardly afforded him a hope that she was in a state of happiness.' In the small hours of 26 April 1752 Johnson wrote, 'O Lord, Governor of Heaven and Earth, in whose hands are embodied and departed spirits, if thou hast ordained the souls of the dead to minister to the living, and appointed my departed wife to have care of me, grant that I may enjoy the good effects of her attention and ministration, whether exercised by appearance, impulses, dreams, or in any other manner agreeable to thy government; forgive my presumption, enlighten my ignorance, and however meaner agents are employed, grant me the blessed influences of thy Holy Spirit, through Jesus Christ our Lord. Amen.' Johnson was not in the mad condition of Richardson's Lovelace after the death of Clarissa, but he suffered with a sensibility informed by some of the same assumptions and likewise aroused by guilt. A year later he observed the anniversary of Elizabeth's death with prayers, and continued to do so throughout his life. He was perpetually remorseful and perpetually conscious of her continuing though unknowable existence. Thirty years later, in 1782, he wrote: 'This is the day on which in 1752 dear Tetty died. On what we did amiss, and our faults were great, I have thought of late with more regret than at any former time. . . . I have now uttered a prayer of repentance and c[ontritio]n, perhaps Tetty knows that I prayed for her. . . . Perhaps Tetty is now praying for me. God, help me.'[9]

Thirteen months after Tetty's death, on Easter Day, Johnson wrote in his diary that he planned to 'seek a new wife' beginning the following day and 'to take my leave of Tetty in a solemn commendation of her soul to God'.[10] As befits an Easter Day resolve, this was probably a resolution to close his period of mourning, rather than a determination to propose marriage to a particular woman, for exhaustive research has been unable to find a very likely candidate.[11] Johnson knew a surprising number of women at this time: literary women like Elizabeth Carter, Catherine Talbot, Charlotte Lennox, and Hester Mulso; Lichfield ladies like the widow Mrs Desmoulins, Hill Boothby, Ann Hector, Molly Aston and her sister Elizabeth; and a few who fit into neither category, like Anna Williams. Although many of these women were unmarried in 1753, only Hill Boothby appears to have been the object of Johnson's aspirations. A month before Johnson's resolve, however, Boothby became the residuary legatee of her best friend and assumed the management of her household, including its six children. Johnson wrote to her in 1753 and in the succeeding few years of her life; she was the only woman with whom he ever kept up a regular correspondence. The surviving, later letters are written in terms of affection, but by then she was ill and dying, and some of the affection is consolatory. Still it is significant that he addressed her as 'My Sweet Angel' and 'Dear Angel'. In one of his letters Johnson refutes a rumour of his death with the Cartesian remark, 'I write therefore I am alive', and he adds, 'I am alive therefore I love Miss Boothby.' Hill Boothby died in 1756, and again Johnson was distraught. He wrote a prayer on the death of his correspondent, and the grief he felt over the death of Tetty continued. In the years from 1752 to 1756 Johnson's letters and diaries contain confessions of tears and lamentation, often expressed in the decent obscurity of a learned language. What he wrote to Thomas Warton on 21 December 1754 expresses a sadness from which Johnson, never remarrying, never fully emerged: 'You know poor Mr Dodsley has lost his Wife, I believe he is much affected. I hope he will not suffer so much as I yet suffer for the loss of mine. Ο Υμι' τι δ'ο'ιμι; θνῆτα γὰρ πεπόνθαμεν. [Alas. Why do I say Alas? We must submit to mortality.] I have ever since seemed to myself broken off from mankind a kind of solitary wanderer in the wild of life, without any certain direction, or fixed point of view. A gloomy gazer on a World to which I have little relation.'[12]

Although he made some later advances in the direction of eligible women, Johnson never again led a conjugal life; his household was peopled by human beings who had also been 'broken off from mankind' in one way or another. While Tetty was still alive, Anna Williams, an experimental subject in her father's electrical experiments, came to Gough Square to be conveniently situated for a cataract operation. The surgery failed; she was left totally blind; Johnson allowed her to remain in the house, and the two were housemates or neighbours for the next thirty years. At about the same time, Frank Barber, a freed slave from the Bathurst family, was placed under Johnson's protection; with some time off for adventures and schooling, he lived in Johnson's house until the death of his 'master', and became his principal legatee. Mrs Desmoulins also lived in Johnson's house for many years after the death of Tetty. Johnson moved around a good deal during certain periods after 1755, but, when he was settled in a house, he maintained his strange household. At Bolt Court he kept his spinster companions for many years together and almost to the very end of his life, although for most of his last twenty years he was a participant in the happier, wealthier, and more fertile domestic life of the Thrales. The breakup of that household was the tragedy of Johnson's old age.

Given the extreme sparsity of evidence, there has been an extraordinary amount of speculation on the nature of Johnson's private life, including his sex life, his religious life, and his psychic life in general. Such speculation suggests something about Johnson's folkloric identity, and the place he fills in the collective imagination of his society, but it tells us little about his real life. There is evidence that Johnson died with some unresolved feelings of guilt about his sexual conduct at a fairly early stage of life, probably while he was married.[13] As an unattached widower, he struggled with celibacy for a good part of his life. There is some evidence of affairs, flirtations, or amorous episodes in his later life but nothing definite. He clearly retained a courtly attitude toward women that inhibited possible sexual relations. He also had scruples about casual sexual contact with prostitutes and even, perhaps, about masturbation. In none of this was Johnson strange for his time. His domestic loneliness and his sexual deprivation, however, were facts of his life, the whole tenor of which might have been different if he had married and set up house with a suitable, intellectually accomplished woman such as Hester Mulso.

Naturally Johnson's private life affected his writing, but the connections are rarely direct. Johnson's awareness of genre, his mastery of commonplaces, and everything that today might be called his 'professionalism' complicate the relation between his private life and his life of writing. There is a personal presence in Johnson's writing, but he always concentrates on what it is proper, useful, and truthful to say to a given audience in a certain genre of literature. Unlike some writers, Johnson has no compulsion to express all aspects of his private life, at least not for others to read. Even his prayers submit to the prescribed forms and do what seemed to Johnson the requisite work of prayers. This is also true of Johnson's sermons, even the sermon he wrote for Elizabeth's memorial service, even though it contains a description of his own grief and a eulogy for his wife. Boswell and other biographers accept the story that John Taylor, who was supposed to give the sermon, was so put off by the exaggeration in the eulogy that the memorial service had to be cancelled. The story strains credibility. As the speaker of most of Johnson's surviving sermons, Taylor, who had just concluded a disastrous and embarrassing second marriage, frequently read things in the pulpit that were incongruous with his own life as 'the King of Ashbourne', and it is hard to believe that he balked at Johnson's eulogy.[14] Moreover, the passages in question make up a small portion of the sermon, and they are hedged around with confessions of Tetty's shortcomings and warnings about judging those on whom God has already passed final judgement.

While maintaining the voice of the minister, Johnson describes himself as 'he that has lately been separated from the person whom a long participation of good and evil had endeared to him; he who has seen kindness snatched from his arms, and fidelity torn from his bosom; he whose ear is no more to be delighted with tender instruction, and whose virtue shall be no more awakened by the seasonable whispers of mild reproof'. It is Johnson's own grief that is 'a total destitution of happiness, a sudden abruption of all . . . prospects, a cessation of all . . . hopes, schemes and desires', and it is his mind that has become 'a gloomy vacuity, without any image or form of pleasure, a chaos of confused wishes, directed to no particular end, or to that which, while we wish, we cannot hope to obtain; for the dead will not revive'. About two minutes of the sermon are devoted to qualities proper to Tetty, apart from her role as wife. Johnson touches lightly on her admirable intellectual powers and praises her charity, devotion, and kindness, as well as her patience and submission during her 'many months of languor, weakness, and decay'. Then he returns to the qualities of Tetty's mind: 'Yet, let it be remembered, that her wit was never employed to scoff at goodness, nor her reason to dispute against truth. In this age of wild opinions, she was as free from scepticism as the cloistered virgin. She never wished to signalize herself by the singularity of paradox. She had a just diffidence of her own reason, and desired to practise rather than to dispute.'[15] In making these remarks, Johnson is being personal, but he is also returning to one of his favourite topics: the vanities of the student or the temptations of the learned soul. For a moment, Johnson is not so much praising Tetty as admonishing his audience with an example like that of Pertinax in *Rambler* 95. This topic is so characteristic of Johnson's writing that its presence does not detract from the personal atmosphere of the eulogy. On the other hand, the passage shows the great extent to which Johnson displaces strong personal feeling in his writing in favour of his usual rhetorical topics.

In the rest of Elizabeth's funeral sermon Johnson is even more obviously supported by familiar topics. In general, his extreme concentration on these topics is what distinguishes Johnson's sermons from thematically similar *Ramblers*. Twenty-seven of his sermons have survived, but only two were published in his lifetime, one in 1745 and one in 1777, when each was written for a special occasion. The memorial sermon for Elizabeth was presumably written in 1752, but none of the other compositions can be dated.[16] It is reasonable to treat the other sermons at this point, however, because of their obvious similarity to the memorial sermon and their essential similarity to the *Rambler.*

The surviving, undated sermons, probably about half the number Johnson composed, were written for John Taylor and copied by him, sometimes with modifications to suit a particular audience or occasion. For Taylor and others Johnson produced sermons for the price of two guineas a piece. According to Hawkins, Johnson believed the fee bought the purchaser complete ownership of the work, and he never enquired after the future fate of his compositions. Like many of his other works, Johnson's sermons were jobs he did or commodities that he sold in the spirit of 'Quid Psittacus expedivit'. Modern expectations of originality in sermon writing were not unknown in the eighteenth century, but they were part of a long-standing debate about sermons that encompassed many carefully articulated positions. The practice of reading others' sermons was controversial, as it had been at least as early as the fourth century, and so was the practice of reading any prepared text from the pulpit. The methods of delivery varied, even among High Church preachers, from reading to recitation to extempore speaking; reading someone else's composition was one extreme in the range of acceptable possibilities. Hawkins denounced the practice in his biography, but Johnson apparently never felt uncomfortable about it.[17] Indeed, Johnson wrote a great deal that would eventually be spoken or printed by others without anything like proper attribution. He had no more compunction about writing a sermon for a preacher than he did about dictating a legal brief for Boswell, 'correcting' Samuel Madden's poem, adding a chapter to Mrs Lennox's *Female Quixote,* or writing parts of Robert Chambers's Vinerian Lectures.

Johnson did not distinguish sermons as a more personal sort of performance than other kinds of writing. In fact, he may have seen them as among the most impersonal kinds. Some of Johnson's diary entries indicate that he composed the sermons very speedily, a sign that he was depending upon formulas. In a letter to a young clergyman Johnson talked about his method: 'The Composition of sermons is not very difficult; the divisions not only help the memory of the hearer but direct the judgement of the writer; they supply sources of invention, and keep every part in its proper place.'[18] The 'divisions' refer to clear breaks between the points of exposition required by all the standard manuals of the day. Despite its usefulness, such standardization also has its drawbacks. Although there are passages in the sermons that closely resemble some of Johnson's most energetic writing in the *Rambler,* their diction is tamer, their grammatical structure is more rigid, and, in general, there is a lack of what Hawkins called 'versatility' in the writing. There is very little, if any, impersonation or irony in the sermons, for example. Although they are of some interest in themselves, Johnson's sermons may be most valuable for showing, by contrast, how much playfulness there is in his other writings.

As James Gray has observed, in the sermons 'recur ideas and themes familiar to readers of *Rasselas,* the *Idler,* and especially the *Rambler*: human vanity and the brevity of life, charity and revelation, domestic happiness, friendship and its laws, the peculiar temptations that beset the intelligent, the dangers of unrepentant forgetfulness, and the overwhelming need of an alert and wakeful conscience.' This particular constellation of topics marks the sermons as Johnson's own, but his treatment of them is adapted to the literary form of the sermon, as Johnson conceived of it. 'Sermons make a considerable branch of English literature', as Johnson observed upon the sale of his friend Beauclerk's great library, and he had many models from which to choose. As in his essays, Johnson took his models for the sermon from the century before his birth, again assuming his post as a late member of a rich tradition. James Gray concludes: 'Johnson was a late offspring of earlier and greater ages of the English pulpit . . . it is the seventeenth century and not his own century which provides the proper context.'[19]

The particular seventeenth-century tradition Johnson follows is generally High Church but mainly anti-sectarian, a tradition that favours the exposition of fundamental Christian beliefs in plain language, adapted to the minds and situations of the listeners. Taylor delivered some of the sermons at Ashbourne, but most were designed for an educated, politically powerful audience in Westminster where Taylor held several livings, including the rectorship of St Margaret's. Hence, in the extant sermons there is little sense of Johnson adjusting his intellectual caliber downward from the level of the *Rambler*. However, he did make changes in his stock of topics. Though he usually focuses on universal matters, like death, he devotes three sermons (23, 24, 26) and parts of others (notably 5) to the morality of political conduct, the responsibilities of governors, and the duties of those governed. Johnson's sermons have much in common with those of seventeenth-century London preachers whom he quoted frequently in the *Dictionary*: Sanderson, Hooker, Jeremy Taylor, John Wilkins, Tillotson, Stillingfleet, and South. Close connections have also been perceived to certain divines who were flawed from a strictly orthodox point of view, but evidently among Johnson's favourites, especially Samuel Clarke, William Law, and Richard Baxter. Although Clarke is mostly excluded from the religiously conservative *Dictionary*, his sermons are closest of all to Johnson's in tone and emphasis.

In paying attention to political responsibilities the sermons differ from the *Rambler*. A second point of difference is their relatively small number of literary allusions. They seem to reject allusiveness as a kind of gaudy and therefore inappropriate trope. It is particularly noticeable that, whereas the *Rambler* always begins with a classical quotation and sometimes cites the Bible later in the essay, the reverse is true of the sermons. Each begins with a biblical text, and classical allusions are uncommon. The exposition of the text very often begins, as in the *Rambler*, with an acknowledgement that the ground has been well covered by previous writers, but what Mr Rambler might have located in the aphorisms of Hippocrates (*vita brevis*), the preacher finds in Job: 'Man that is born of a woman, is of few days, and full of trouble.' Johnson goes on, almost seeming to preclude further discussion in his first paragraph: 'The position, contained in this sentence, neither requires, nor admits, proof or illustration; being too evident to be denied, and too clear to be mistaken. That life is of short continuance, and is disquieted by many molestations, every man knows, and every man feels; and the complaint, attributed to Job, in the history that is supposed to be the oldest book, of which mankind is in possession, has been continued, and will be continued, through all human generations with endless repetitions.' The rationale for proceeding, which comes in the next paragraph, justifies a great many of Johnson's sermons and much of his other moral writing: 'But truth does not always operate in proportion to its reception. What has been always known, and very often said, as it impresses the mind with no new images, excites no attention, and is suffered to lie unheeded in the memory.'[20]

As Johnson says in the *Rambler*, 'Men need more often to be reminded than informed', and this is most the case with the fundamental truths he expounds in the sermons. The truths appear in the sermons in a starker form than elsewhere in Johnson's writings, and the reminders usually pertain bluntly to the four last things. Sermon 10, for example, is devoted to exploding the fantasies we place between ourselves and the unavoidable fact that 'the common condition of man is not to live long.' Whereas in the *Rambler* these fantasies are given scope and body through their residence in named characters and specific hopes, in the sermons they are more clinically removed. Glances at the attractions of this world are rare and brief:

> To those, who procrastinate amendment, in hopes of better opportunities in future time, it is too often vainly urged by the preacher, and vainly suggested by a thousand examples, that the hour of death is uncertain. This, which ought to be the cause of their terrour, is the ground of their hope; that as death is uncertain, it may be distant. This uncertainty is, in effect, the great support of the whole system of life. The man who died yesterday, had purchased an estate, to which he intended some time to retire; or built a house, which he was hereafter to inhabit; and planted gardens and groves, that, in a certain number of years, were to supply delicacies to his feasts, and shades to his meditations. He is snatched away, and has left his designs and his labours to others.[21]

The inflexibility of the wisdom presented in the sermons, as well as its centrality to Johnson's writing, is best exemplified in Sermon 12, an exposition of Ecclesiastes 1: 14, 'I have seen all the works that are done under the sun; and behold, all is vanity and vexation of spirit':

> That all human actions terminate in vanity, and all human hopes will end in vexation, is a position, from which nature with-holds our credulity, and which our fondness for the present life, and worldly enjoyments, disposes us to doubt; however forcibly it may be urged upon us, by reason or experience.

Every man will readily enough confess, that his own condition discontents him; and that he has not yet been able, with all his labour to make happiness, or, with all his enquiries, to find it. But he still thinks, it is some where to be found, or by some means to be procured . . . he wears out life in efforts and pursuits, and perhaps dies, regretting that he must leave the world, when he is about to enjoy it.

The passage obviously invites comparison with the ending of *The Vanity of Human Wishes* where the soul 'makes the happiness she does not find'. However, the sermon asks the suppliant for greater resignation and requires of the reader less active engagement than the poem or any of Johnson's other works on the same theme. This is true of the sermons in general, as Paul Alkon has shown. To put it simply, they are more resolved than Johnson's other works on similar subjects.[22]

Despite its particular appeal to Johnson, the desire for learning, like all other kinds of worldly agitation, is controlled and contained when it appears in the sermons. Whereas the student in the *Vanity* is allowed to spread his dreams of scholarly conquest 'O'er Bodley's dome', the student in Sermon 8 is quickly confined to the proper attitude. Only a brief philosophical analogy, as rare in the sermons as it is common in the *Rambler*, registers Johnson's imaginative involvement in the desire:

Since no man can teach what he has never learned, the value and usefulness of the latter part of life must depend in a great measure upon the proper application of the earlier years; and he that neglects the improvement of his own mind, will never be enabled to instruct others. Light must strike on the body, by which light can be reflected. The disposition therefore, which best befits a young man, about to engage in a life of study, is patience in enquiry; eagerness of knowledge; and willingness to be instructed; a due submission to greater abilities and longer experience; and a ready obedience to those, from whom he is to expect the removal of his ignorance, and the resolution of his doubts.[23]

As he did in the memorial sermon for Tetty, Johnson attacks 'scepticism and captiousness' in Sermon 7 and 'scoffers and sophists' in Sermon 20. These are foibles of the learned that take on a very interesting form in the story of Pertinax in *Rambler* 95. Corruption there grows gradually on the retentive scholar; like Horace, who describes himself as 'parcus deorum' in the epigraph, Pertinax can only gradually return to intellectual health. In the sermons, however, everything is so accelerated that there is no invitation to imaginative sympathy:

The mind, long vitiated with trifles, and entertained with wild and unnatural combinations of ideas, becomes in a short time unable to support the fatigue of reasoning; it is disgusted with a long succession of solemn images, and retires from serious meditation, and tiresome labour, to gayer fancies, and less difficult employments.

> Besides, he that has practised the art of silencing others with a jest, in time learns to satisfy himself in the same manner. It becomes unnecessary to the tranquillity of his own mind to confute an objection; it is sufficient for him if he can ridicule it.
>
> Thus he soon grows indifferent to truth or falsehood, and almost incapable of discerning one from the other. He considers eternity itself as a subject for mirth, and is equally ludicrous upon all occasions.

In *Rambler* 95 Johnson actually impersonates the sceptic, composing the piece as though it were a letter from a correspondent, but here he is remote and unmoved. Pertinax does not get as absolutely depraved as the scoffers in Sermon 20; he falls gradually into the snare, and in the end he pulls back and recovers from his 'argumental delirium'. He moves between states of mind; there is oscillation for him, and, because Johnson extends sympathy to him, there is a play of attitudes for the reader. Truth is a straight path for Pertinax, but it is a path upon which he himself steps with some weight and some distinctive posture of movement. All this is lacking in the sermon. The scoffers are utterly lost: 'What delusion, what bigotry, is equal to this!' exclaims the preacher. Truth in this world is utterly severe: 'Let it be remembered, that the nature of things is not alterable by our conduct. We cannot make truth; it is our business only to find it. No proposition can become more or less certain or important, by being considered or neglected.'[24] Johnson is saying no more here than his seventeenth-century model preachers said. In a remark that Johnson quoted twice in the *Dictionary*, for example, Tillotson says, 'The truth of things will not *comply with* our conceits, and *bend* itself to our interest.' In almost all his other writing Johnson depends on fluctuations and multiplicities in the perception of truth for his literary effects, but this would be less visible without the example of his sermons. They provide a kind of writing degree zero in his rhetorical world that brings into focus his usual versatility and suggests the extent to which Johnson's appeal is located in fiction and subtle rhetorical effects.

1 View of Lichfield, drawn by C. Stanfield, engraved by E. E. Finden. Reproduced from *Graphic Illustrations of the Life and Times of Samuel Johnson, LL.D.* (London: J. Murray, 1837). (Courtesy of Vassar College, Special Collections.)

2   Michael Johnson, engraved by E. Finden. Repro-
duced from *Graphic Illustrations of the Life and Times of
Samuel Johnson, LL.D.* (Courtesy of Vassar College,
Special Collections.)

3 The Bishop's Palace, Lichfield, home of Gilbert Walmesley. (Hyde Collection, courtesy of Mary Hyde Eccles.)

4 Gilbert Walmesley. (Hyde Collection, courtesy of Mary Hyde Eccles.)

5   Elizabeth Jervis Porter, later Mrs Samuel Johnson. (Hyde Collection, courtesy of Mary Hyde Eccles.)

6   Edial, Johnson's academy near Lichfield, engraved by Charles J. Smith. Reproduced from *Graphic Illustrations of the Life and Times of Samuel Johnson, LL.D.* (Courtesy of Vassar College, Special Collections.)

7 Edward Cave, engraved by T. Worlidge from the painting by F. Kyte. Reproduced from the February 1754 issue of the *Gentleman's Magazine*. (Courtesy of Vassar College, Special Collections.)

8 Johnson about 1736, miniature by an unknown artist. (Hyde Collection, courtesy of Mary Hyde Eccles.)

9   Johnson in his late thirties, from the mezzotint by George Zobel. The
book in the picture is labelled *Irene*. (Courtesy of Professor Frank Ellis.)

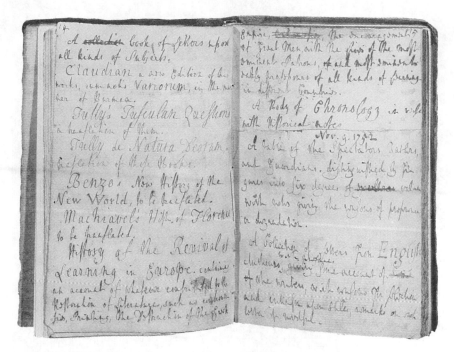

10 Johnson's 'Designs', pages 14–15 of a notebook containing prospective works, which Johnson gave to Bennet Langton towards the end of his life. Note especially the entry beginning at the bottom of page 14, 'History of the Revival of Learning in Europe. Containing an account of whatever contributed to the Restoration of Literature . . .' (see page 45). (Royal Library, Windsor Castle by permission of Her Majesty Queen Elizabeth II.)

11 *Robert Dodsley* by Sir Joshua Reynolds. (By permission of the Governors of Dulwich Picture Gallery.)

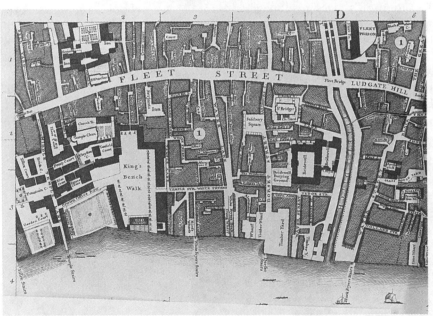

12 Johnson felling Thomas Osborne with a folio, the bookplate of Camden Morrisby, from the woodcut by Lionel Lindsay. (Courtesy of Vassar College, Special Collections.)

13 The Strand from Temple Bar to Fleet Ditch, Rocque's Map of London, 1746. Johnson's Court, Gough Square (just below the number 3 on top), and Bolt Court, Johnson's places of longest residence in London, are all shown here. (Detail, courtesy of the Print Collection, Lewis Walpole Library, Yale University.)

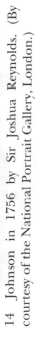

15 *William Strahan* by Sir Joshua Reynolds. (By courtesy of the National Portrait Gallery, London.)

14 Johnson in 1756 by Sir Joshua Reynolds. (By courtesy of the National Portrait Gallery, London.)

16 'John a Boot's Ass', 1762. Johnson is depicted on the far right with a weather vane stuck in his hat and holding a sign which says '300. Pr. Annum', indicating the amount of the pension he had recently been granted by Lord Bute (John a Boot). The figure of Johnson says, 'Least sad Poverty should fall upon my Head/Faith I write on either side for Bread.' The devil next to him says, 'Well said my little Weathercock thou art a Babe of my own.' (Courtesy of the Print Collection, Lewis Walpole Library, Yale University.)

17 'The Hungry Mob of Scribblers' by Alexander Mackenzie, 1762. Johnson is here first in line to receive the benefices of Lord Bute. (Courtesy of the Print Collection, Lewis Walpole Library, Yale University.)

18   Johnson in 1769 by Sir Joshua Reynolds. (Studio variant, Hyde
Collection, courtesy of Mary Hyde Eccles.)

19   *Hester Lynch Salusbury Thrale* by Richard Cosway. (Courtesy of
the Harry Ransom Humanities Research Center, University of Texas,
Austin.)

20   Johnson in 1775 by Sir Joshua Reynolds. (From the collection of
Loren and Frances Rothschild.)

21 *Walking up the High Street* by Thomas Rowlandson.
(Courtesy of the Print Collection, Lewis Walpole Library,
Yale University.)

22 No. 8, Bolt Court, engraved by
John Thomas Smith. Reproduced
from *Graphic Illustrations of the Life
and Times of Samuel Johnson, LL.D.*
(Courtesy of Vassar College, Special
Collections.)

23   Johnson about 1783 by John Opie. (By permission of the Houghton
Library, Harvard University.)

24   Johnson near the end of his life by Sir Joshua Reynolds. (Courtesy of Haverford College Library.)

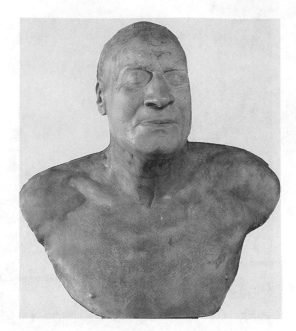

25 Johnson's death mask, after William Cumberland Cruick-shank. (Courtesy of the National Portrait Gallery, London.)

26 The bust of Johnson by Joseph Nollekens. (Lead cast, courtesy of the Board of Trustees of the Victoria and Albert Museum.)

12

The *Adventurer*

Strongly entwisted with human nature is the desire of exercising power, however that power be gained or given. Let us pity it in others, and despise it in ourselves.
Johnson to Hester Maria (Queeney) Thrale, 23 August 1783

About six months after the last number of the *Rambler* had been issued, one of its publishers, John Payne, engaged John Hawkesworth to take chief responsibility for producing a similar publication called the *Adventurer*. With at least two close associates running the periodical, it was inevitable that Johnson would eventually participate. He did not at first have a regular share in the publishing project, but he started making small contributions early on. Bishop Percy noted in his copy of Johnson's later *Idler*: 'Latin mottoes so readily occur'd to him on all occasions that Hawksworth, when writing the Adventurers, usually sent the Essays to him in MS for him to supply the mottos.' Anna Williams believed Johnson dictated some copy for his friend Bathurst, who may also have been involved at the inception of the publication. Later, Johnson dictated a whole issue to Warton. These contributions were easy for Johnson, and they interrupted neither his grief nor his lexicographical work. In times of stress, he could dictate more easily than write out his work, just as he had earlier dictated his translation of Le Grand's *Lobo* while he lay in bed almost incapacitated by melancholy. However, because his spirits were lifted by his resolution to seek another wife, because his other work was well in hand, or because he wished to help his friends, Johnson was soon drawn into actual composition; he contributed Number 34 for Saturday, 3 March 1753. Hawkesworth had begun the *Adventurer* in collaboration with someone else (either Bathurst or Bonnell Thornton), but, when he was left with the burden of producing nine consecutive numbers, he and his publisher struck a bargain with Johnson and his Oxford friend Thomas Warton. Johnson was to supply one fourth of the essays in Numbers 49–140. (The total number of issues had been predetermined to facilitate republication in four duodecimo volumes.) In the end Johnson provided two more than he had contracted for, a total of twenty-nine. Like the *Rambler*, the *Adventurer* was published anonymously, but in this case Johnson protected his anonymity carefully and admitted it frankly to no one except his dear Hill Boothby.[1]

In some later numbers of the *Adventurer*, Johnson rises to philosophic heights, but these essays, especially at the start, are less powerful and less volatile than the *Rambler*. This may be due to haste or want of energy, but Johnson may also have made a conscious decision to find a less lofty tone in which to address the public on serious subjects. Displaying a familiar topic in the bland colours of his sermons, Johnson begins *Adventurer* 120, 'The numerous miseries of human life have extorted in all ages an universal complaint.' *Adventurer* 45 is sufficiently mechanical to conform closely to notes in his 'Adversaria' located by Boswell, and other numbers seem unimaginatively to string together familiar quotations. Because of their unrefined state, however, these pieces are of biographical and intellectual interest. For instance, although it is facile, Number 58 is interesting because it clearly shows how readily Johnson could use his acquired literary stock and where he had his most plentiful resources. His earliest and his latest translations are from Horace, and the lines from Tibullus that he adds to Ode 1.6 in *Adventurer* 58 are the same lines that occurred to him as he lay dying in 1784:

> *Te spectem, suprema mihi cum venerit hora,*
> *Te teneam moriens deficiente manu.*

> Before my closing eyes, dear Cynthia, stand,
> Held weakly by my fainting trembling hand.[2]

Similarly, in *Adventurer* 107 Johnson recurs to his lifelong reading in the *Greek Anthology* and juxtaposes and translates successive declamatory epigrams from Book 9, which are among those that he translated into Latin in the winter of 1783–4 'to drive the night along' through his illness and sleeplessness. Although it was mechanically produced, *Adventurer* 107 presents pieces taken from the forefront of Johnson's lifelong treasury of reading and thereby provides a glimpse of him at his most unguarded and intellectually most habitual. First he gives the pessimistic view of human life rendered by Posidippus: 'Through which of the paths of life is it eligible to pass? In public assemblies are debates and troublesome affairs; domestic privacies are haunted with anxieties; in the country is labour; on the sea is terror . . . are you married? you are troubled with suspicions; are you single? you languish in solitude. . . . This choice only, therefore, can be made, either never to receive being, or immediately to lose it.' Then comes the 'contrary conclusion' of Metrodorus: 'You may pass well through any of the paths of life. In public assemblies are honours, and transactions of wisdom; in domestic privacy is stilness and quiet . . . are you married? you have a chearful house; are you single? you are unincumbered. . . . It will, therefore, never be a wise man's choice, either not to obtain existence, or to lose it; for every state of life has its felicity.'[3] Johnson does little with the juxtaposition here except to point out how differently the same object may at different times or by different sensibilities be viewed. The question of which is the wise man's choice came back to him, however, when he sought a subject for a longer moral essay. Dressed up in the robes of fiction, it became much more, but the argument of *Rasselas, or the Choice of Life* is essentially a brilliant amplification of this pair of epigrams.

For the most part, Johnson's translations of the Greek epigrams in *Adventurer* 107 are prosaic and literal. The one moment when he rises above that level is in the clause 'you languish in solitude.' A perfectly literal translation, much like the Loeb Library's, is 'you live still more lonely.' Conversely, the happiness of the unmarried state in the opposing epigram is only being 'unincumbered', although the Greek phrase is strictly parallel with the first and says literally, 'you live still more easily (or lightly).' The translations suggest the widower's concern with his loneliness. A stronger indication of the same self-concern appears in *Adventurer* 126, which Johnson devotes to attacking the unexamined opinion that solitude is either a pleasurable or an advantageous condition. The essay moves swiftly from discussing solitude in terms of rural retreat to a more general and abstract consideration of its usefulness in the higher activities of learning and piety. The thoroughness with which Johnson excludes its claims betokens a dissatisfaction with his own solitary state. There is a sort of disgust that suggests a fear of personal infection in Johnson's description of the solitary scholar who 'never compares his notions with those of others, readily acquiesces in his first thoughts, and very seldom discovers the objections which may be raised against his opinions; he, therefore, often thinks himself in possession of truth, when he is only fondling an error long since exploded.' There is likewise contempt in his description of solitary religious activity: 'Piety practised in solitude, like the flower that blooms in the desart, may give its fragrance to the winds of heaven, and delight those unembodied spirits that survey the works of God and the actions of men; but it bestows no assistance upon earthly beings, and however free from the taints of impurity, yet wants the sacred splendor of beneficence.'[4] The jejune piety of the solitary is almost pagan in Johnson's description, yielding to subordinate gods something like the smoke of a sacrificial fire.

Reflecting on his own 'gloom of solitude' may have led Johnson in *Adventurer* 131 to attack the 'pride of singularity' and the failure to attend to 'domestic affairs' that caused the downfall of the learned Sir Francis Bacon. As usual, Johnson does not express his feelings very directly in his writing. Number 137, however, reads like a confession. Like *Rambler* 208, this essay is valedictory; the speaker begins with a general reflection on the need regularly to recall and review one's own activities, and then assesses his own performance in this regard: 'Though I do not so exactly conform to the precepts of Pythagoras, as to practise every night this solemn recollection, yet I am not so lost in dissipation as wholly to omit it; nor can I forbear sometimes to enquire of myself, in what employments my life has passed away.' Then, suddenly, Johnson breaks into the confessional tone that he usually reserved for his diaries and private journals: 'Much of my time has sunk into nothing, and left no trace by which it can be distinguished, and of this I now only know, that it was once in my power and might once have been improved.' Then, swiftly, he is back on track, describing a somewhat desultory manner of life: 'Of other parts of life memory can give some account: at some hours I have been gay, and at others serious; I have sometimes mingled in conversation, and sometimes meditated in solitude; one day has been spent in consulting the antient sages, and another in writing Adventurers.'[5] This is not quite Johnson's personal voice; nor is it the voice of Mr Rambler, though the activities it describes are suitable to that character's intangible aesthetic life. A Mr Adventurer or T, as Johnson signed his contributions, never amasses himself into life in the pages of Johnson's contributions, but he nearly does so here.

In so far as he does exist, T is a character that resembles Johnson even more closely than Mr Rambler. T is less persistently philosophical than his predecessor; his language is easier; and he is less inclined to rise into allegory. As a writer, he is closer to his sources, less concerned or less able to summarize their overall meaning in the great scheme of things. Like all of Johnson's personae, T is interested in the lives of the learned, their vanities, and their ethical dilemmas. He is more concerned than the others, however, to offer an apology for scholarly work of the kind Johnson was doing at this time in his life. An aspect of the apology is Johnson's familiar emphasis on the importance of study. Mr Rambler had complained that the 'epidemical disease of the current generation is impatience of study', but T speaks in a less declamatory fashion on the same subject, having justified his approach with a quotation from Bacon's 'Of Study':

> Under the protection of so great a name, I shall, therefore, venture to inculcate to my ingenious contemporaries, the necessity of reading, the fitness of consulting other understandings than their own, and of considering the sentiments and opinions of those who, however neglected in the present age, had in their own times, and many of them a long time afterwards, such reputation for knowledge and acuteness, as will scarcely ever be attained by those that despise them.
>
> An opinion has of late been, I know not how, propagated among us, that libraries are filled only with useless lumber; that men of parts stand in need of no assistance; and that to spend life in poring upon books, is only to imbibe prejudices, to obstruct and embarrass the powers of nature, to cultivate memory at the expence of judgement, and to bury reason under a chaos of indigested learning.
>
> Such is the talk of many who think themselves wise.[6]

At least as early as the preface to the *Harleian Miscellany* Johnson was asserting the importance of intellectual history; the value of the 'lumber of libraries' is a constant theme in his essays and biographies. In his expression of these themes in the *Adventurer*, however, he puts greater emphasis on the use of intellectual history for the particular purpose of recovering the original meaning of literary texts. This is the theme of *Adventurer* 58 where Johnson adduces passages from Horace, Tibullus, and Ovid that require historical information in order to be appreciated. After a defence of the classics that survived the fall of Rome, 'preserved in the devastation of cities, and snatched up from the wreck of nations', Johnson articulates his emergent programme of literary scholarship:

> It often happens, that an author's reputation is endangered in succeeding times, by that which raised the loudest applause among his cotemporaries: nothing is read with greater pleasure than allusions to recent facts, reigning opinions, or present controversies; but when facts are forgotten, and controversies extinguished, these favourite touches lose all their grace; and the author in his descent to posterity must be left to the mercy of chance, without any power of ascertaining the memory of those things, to which he owed his luckiest thoughts, and his kindest reception.[7]

The rest of the essay provides commentary on passages that have become obscure or laments the loss of pleasure in passages that have outlived a knowledge of their historical context. The method is antiquarian, and the end of Johnson's enterprise is the pleasure and instruction of the reader, whose attention is the only means of survival for literary works.

Johnson's last *Adventurer*, Number 138, makes the importance of the reader clearer than anything he had written earlier. The writer is there levelled with the common man and sunk into a kind of bland mediocrity: 'Upon the whole,' Johnson concludes, 'as the author seems to share all the common miseries of life, he appears to partake likewise of its lenitives and abatements.' The reader, however, generalized and abstracted as the 'public' or 'mankind', assumes the seat of judgement. The author must 'be afraid of deciding too hastily in his own favour, or of allowing himself to contemplate with too much complacence, treasure that has not yet been brought to the test, nor passed the only trial that can stamp its value. From the public, and only from the public, is he to await a confirmation of his claim and a final justification of self esteem.'[8]

Historical criticism and Johnson's exaltation and abstraction of the reader are correspondent with one another because both acknowledge the effects of time on literature, and both are ways of repairing the damage. But even some of the beneficial effects of time on literary reputation must be opposed, as Johnson shows in his historical criticism of Vergil's pastorals in *Adventurer* 92. Here Johnson constructs an iconoclastic, inquiring reader named Dubio who recognizes Vergil's sources, asserts a predilection for the pieces that rest on knowable historical facts, and explodes the pretensions to greatness of those that time has left unintelligible. In Number

92 he uses the translations of Joseph Warton, but it was in a letter to his brother Thomas that Johnson most succinctly expressed his growing belief in the importance of historical context. The letter of 16 July 1754 thanks Warton for a copy of his recently published *Observations on The Fairy Queen of Spenser*, which is itself an important milestone in the growth of historical criticism in England. Johnson acknowledges this: 'You have shown to all who shall hereafter attempt the study of our ancient authours the way to success, by directing them to the perusal of the books which those authours had read.' As he goes on, however, Johnson suggests that he has been working along similar lines: 'The Reason why the authours which are yet read of the sixteenth Century are so little understood is that they are read alone, and no help is borrowed from those who lived with them or before them. Some part of this ignorance I hope to remove by my book which now draws towards its end.' Johnson's 'book' is his *Dictionary*, which was then substantially complete. No single English work of criticism, either practical or theoretical, could do more than the *Dictionary* to advance the cause of historical criticism. The *Dictionary* puts the English of all its sources in a historical context and simultaneously makes them the fashioners of that context, because it regards literary usage as the true test of meaning. It is only a slight overstatement to say that Johnson's book made the meaning of words equivalent to the history of words. The *Dictionary* provided historical spectacles for readers of English literature, and thereby greatly increased the dignity and prestige of its subject.[9]

When Johnson wrote to Warton in 1754 the publication date of the *Dictionary* was only nine months away. Johnson told Warton he needed to visit the 'Libraries of Oxford' before finishing. Most of the book was already in print, and all that remained for Johnson to do was the preliminary matter: the Preface, for which the *Plan* would serve as a draft, the Grammar, and the 'History of the English Language'. It was especially the last for which Johnson wished to do research in Oxford. Soon thereafter Johnson made his first visit to Oxford since his premature departure from Pembroke in 1729, twenty-five years earlier. He wrote back to his publisher in London that he had not found additional materials for his work in the Oxford libraries. This is only plausible because Johnson's research for the *Dictionary* was limited to printed works, and all those containing specimens of early English for his 'History' would have been available in London, most of them in his own collection. Although its early English collections were weaker before 1755, when it received the Rawlinson and Ballard bequests, Bodley and some other Oxford libraries already had manuscript materials that Johnson lacked in London. Although Johnson himself consulted manuscripts on occasion, the *Dictionary* was to be a quintessentially printed book, not only existing in print itself but composed only of other printed books.

The trip to Oxford in 1754 dramatizes the point that Johnson's professional life of writing for the London publishers cannot be taken as an accurate measure of his personal intellectual life. The Oxford libraries did not contribute to Johnson's *Dictionary*, but Johnson improved his personal knowledge of English in the time he spent there. Warton documented especially well Johnson's visits to Francis Wise, the Radcliffe librarian who lived three miles away in the village of Elsfield. As Warton reported, Wise was 'eminently skilled in Roman and Anglo-Saxon antiquities'. He had 'an excellent library; particularly, a valuable collection of books in Northern literature, with which Johnson was often very busy'. Johnson later referred fondly to Wise's 'nest of British and Saxon Antiquities'. Johnson's inquiries are not reflected in his 'History of English'; the work is neither carefully proportioned nor comprehensive. Like histories of Latin and Italian that he knew, Johnson's 'History' is composed almost exclusively of specimens. He covers the period from King Alfred to Henry VIII, but with scant attention to the earliest periods and a disproportionate display of material from the later periods, especially Sir Thomas More, whose biography Johnson was thinking of writing. Still, Johnson advanced the cause of Old English studies by printing a larger selection of the language than anyone had ever done before in a general dictionary or grammar. If the object of his research in Oxford was a precedent for his 'History', he, indeed would have found none.[10] In relegating almost all pre-Elizabethan English to his 'History', Johnson's *Dictionary* falls far short of the *OED*'s standard, but it does not promulgate the neo-classical prejudice against the 'Gothick' and the 'Teutonick' fostered by pundits of correctness and refinement, like Lord Chesterfield. Johnson's own curiosity about English, as his activity in Wise's 'nest of Antiquities' suggests, was still less inhibited.

In Oxford Johnson also took important steps towards a personal acquisition, which, unlike the full range of his linguistic interests, is plainly manifest in his *Dictionary*. Through the efforts of Warton and a few other friends, machinery was engaged to produce Johnson's honorary master of arts degree. The Latin degree, which was hand-delivered by the principal of St Mary Hall (now part of Oriel College), cites Johnson's achievements in the *Dictionary* and the *Rambler*. The lexicon especially receives high marks as 'a most useful work, adorning and stabilizing the national language'.[11] Johnson was deeply grateful for this honour and wrote an elegant Latin letter of thanks to George Huddesford, Vice-Chancellor of Oxford University. He pledged his fidelity to the university and in a surprisingly topical note deplored the ungrateful, unapprehended rascals who had recently published shameful, traitorous political verses in Oxford. The degree came in time for the publishers to place a distinguished 'A.M.' after Johnson's name on the title page.

Although Johnson did not enjoy the 'shelter of academick bowers' when he wrote his *Dictionary*, the accomplishment earned him honours therein, and his letter is all fealty to the institution. From the French Académie and from the Accademia della Crusca Johnson also received honours; lexicons were exchanged; and Johnson assumed a notable place in modern European letters. His social status also rose with the triumph, and Lord Orrery acted as his patron in presenting a copy of Johnson's book to the

Accademia. At about the same time, Johnson wrote his famous letter to the once prospective patron of the *Dictionary*, Lord Chesterfield. In Numbers 100 and 101 of the *World* Chesterfield had advertised the *Dictionary*. In an ironic postscript to Number 100 he had also suggested that he had some 'interest' in the project. However, parts of both numbers, approaching parody in their refinement and politeness, tend to trivialize Johnson's work. Johnson had addressed his *Plan* of the *Dictionary* to Chesterfield and played a polite game of flattery with him in that work. He had gone so far as to call him his Caesar, and Chesterfield had returned the compliment in the *World*. Support from the Earl had not, however, been forthcoming during the intervening nine years, from 1747 to 1754. In what has come to be called 'the celebrated letter' Johnson reflects on his supplicatory posture in the *Plan* and its ineffectualness: 'When I had once addressed your Lordship in public, I had exhausted all the Art of pleasing which a retired and uncourtly Scholar can possess. I had done all that I could, and no Man is well pleased to have his all neglected, be it ever so little.' He speaks of waiting in the lord's 'outward Rooms' and being repulsed, a scene which became the subject of a much publicized engraving, though Chesterfield denied that it could have happened. Johnson then directs at Chesterfield some of the vituperativeness that he elsewhere aimed at the general system of patronage. In a version of his analogy between the artist and Sisyphus in *Rambler* 3, Johnson says, 'Is not a Patron, My Lord, one who looks with unconcern on a Man struggling for Life in the water and when he has reached ground encumbers him with help.' Then, in the elegiac notes of the Preface to the *Dictionary*, he rejects Chesterfield utterly: 'The notice which you have been pleased to take of my Labours, had it been early, had been kind; but it has been delayed till I am indifferent and cannot enjoy it, till I am solitary and cannot impart it, till I am known and do not want it.'[12] Folklore has glorified this episode in Johnson's life, just as it has the episode in which Johnson felled Osborne with a folio when cataloguing the Harleian Library. Again, Alvin Kernan's interpretation of the letter as a 'declaration of independence for authors' and a repudiation of the *ancien régime* of patronage is correct; Johnson is being a modern author, making his living independently, and elevating his class. But again, Johnson is also claiming the rights of an older generation of scholars, like Erasmus and More, who retained some of the privileges of the monastery and whose learning put their souls, though not their lives, above courtliness.

Johnson's role in the social construction of authorship was complex, involving an unlikely mixture of marketplace economics with ancient, clerical status. One of the many complicating factors is that among Johnson's innumerable professional writing jobs were a great many dedications to patrons. He wrote a number of them in the years just before and just after the Chesterfield letter, including several for his friend Charlotte Lennox. He dedicated to the King, the Queen, the Prince of Wales, Lord Orrery, Lord Charlemont, the Duke of Newcastle, and the Houses of Parliament, and many other prospective patrons of the old order. 'Why I have dedicated to the Royal Family all round', Johnson told Boswell and boasted mildly of his 'readiness' in the genre. Johnson is never fawning, and in many of his dedications he comments frankly on the genre and its institutionalized disingenuousness, yet he is flattering in his somewhat harsh way and does the work of a suppliant author. The dedication 'To His Excellency Don Felix', the Italian ambassador, for Giuseppe Baretti's *Dictionary of the English and Italian Languages* (1760), for instance, begins: 'The acuteness of penetration into characters and designs, and that nice discernment of human passions and practices which have raised you to your present height of station and dignity of employment, have long shown you that Dedicatory Addresses are written for the sake of the Author more frequently than of the Patron; and though they profess only reverence and zeal, are commonly dictated by interest or vanity.' Johnson praises the addressee for being above the usual blandishments of a dedication, but he does so in a graceful, courtly and flattering way that does not altogether relieve him of the responsibility to flatter further. Another gambit that Johnson frequently employs is to comment on the appropriateness of the presentation of the particular work at hand to the addressee. This often gives him an opportunity to remark the inappropriateness of many dedications and thereby to imply the superiority of his flattery. A neat example is the dedication 'To His Royal Highness the Duke of York' for William Payne's *Elements of Trigonometry* (1772), which begins, 'They who are permitted to prefix the names of Princes to treatises of science, generally enjoy the protection of a patron, without fearing the censure of a judge.' The rest is easily deduced, but, as it does elsewhere, the gambit allows Johnson to focus on the work more than the person, or at least to praise the person mainly in terms of the work. The best examples of this strategy are the dedications for William Payne's *Game of Draughts* (1756) and Bishop Percy's *Reliques of Ancient English Poetry* (1765). In the latter, dedicated to Elizabeth, Countess of Northumberland, after the opening ploy Johnson says, 'But this impropriety, it is presumed, will disappear, when it is declared that these poems are presented to your LADYSHIP, not as labours of art, but as effusions of nature, shewing the first efforts of ancient genius . . . of ages that had been almost lost to memory, had not the gallant deeds of your illustrious ancestors preserved them from oblivion.'[13]

Except for the *Plan* of the *Dictionary*, Johnson never dedicated a work of his own to anyone, yet his ghost writing flatters 'the Royal Family all round'. Although his career as a writer was in many respects revolutionary, Johnson also spoke the language of the court. His extreme readiness as a writer made him almost a double agent, like earlier satirists such as Defoe and Swift, who could be difficult to place politically. A much simpler part in the reconstruction of authorship was played by Edward Cave, creator of the *Gentleman's Magazine* and Johnson's first patron of the new order. Johnson celebrated Cave's innovations in a biographical notice for the *Gentleman's Magazine* the month after Cave's death in January 1754. As the afterword to Johnson's second edition of his 'Life of Cave' proclaims, Cave invented 'a new species of publication' which made 'an epocha in the literary History of this Country'. The afterword particularly commends Cave for making his magazine a source of support for young writers. In summarizing Cave's character Johnson suggests how boldly revolutionary his efforts were: 'He was . . . a tenacious maintainer, though not a clamorous demander of his right. In his youth having summoned his fellow journeymen to concert measures against the oppression of their masters, he mounted a kind of rostrum and harrangued them so efficaciously, that they determined to resist all future invasions; and when the Stamp Officers demanded to stamp the last half sheet of the Magazines, Mr Cave alone defeated their claim, to which the proprietors of the rival Magazines would meanly have submitted.' Amidst his admiration and affection, however, Johnson carefully distinguishes Cave from the intellectuals he both nourished and harnessed: 'His mental faculties were slow. He saw little at a time, but that little he saw with great exactness.' Johnson lived most of his life on the support of new patrons like Cave, and after 1762, when he was granted a lifetime pension from the government, he enjoyed an older form of patronage. But his sense of his social identity as a writer was always both revolutionary and reactionary, tending to reject the claims of all kinds of patronage and to propel writers out of the class structure altogether, making them members of an older, monastic order or participants in what Paul Fussell in *Class* calls 'class X'.[14]

In 1755 aspirants to class X were less indemnified against economic failure than they are today. There was no academic position for Johnson, and he earned no royalties on his books. He may have been paid for the new preface that he wrote for the abridged version of his *Dictionary*, but he was not paid for sales of the derivative work, which came out and did well in 1756. Nor did he earn money on sales of the first edition or the second, which went into production the same year as the first. In fact, when the accounts were settled between the author and the publishers of the *Dictionary*, Johnson was found to be about £100 in arrears because of numerous advances. The publishers forgave him this sum, winning his undying gratitude, but, despite his international acclaim and his degree, Johnson was broke and looking for work. He did some miscellaneous work, some prefaces and dedications, for some of which he was paid.[15] He looked into doing a life of Sir Thomas More, and thought about starting a kind of literary digest of intellectual events in England and on the continent. He planned, as usual, to imitate a couple of great seventeenth-century learned works – the reviews of Le Clerc and Bayle, this time. Johnson did not follow through on this plan, however, nor did he sign a contract or produce much for a while. As a result, on 16 March 1756 Johnson was imprisoned for debt. Samuel Richardson speedily supplied six guineas, and Johnson was released, but he had already been galvanized into action because his note of thanks to Richardson included a copy of his edition of Sir Thomas Browne's *Christian Morals*, with a biography. He soon produced new proposals for the delayed edition of Shakespeare and made some contributions to a new periodical called the *Universal Visiter and Monthly Memorialist.*

These contributions, however, probably netted him nothing because they were gifts to the editor, Christopher Smart. Johnson came to Smart's aid when his increasing madness prevented him from fulfilling his obligations to the publication. The most interesting piece is a satire on the current state of authorship in England. It combines a kind of haggard lamentation for his own state with hostility towards the business of writing and publication. Johnson's main complaint is that there are too many authors, and many are unprepared for lives of literature: 'There is now no class of men without its authors from the peer to the thresher.' With so many writers, there can be few readers, and 'every man must be content to read his book to himself.' Johnson's modest proposal for this deplorable situation is to use authors in the army. They will be good soldiers, he says, because 'they are accustomed to obey the word of command from their patrons and their booksellers. . . . and if they should be destroyed in war, we shall lose only those who had wearied the public, and whom, whatever be their fate, nobody will miss.'[16]

In his 'Life of Sir Thomas Browne' Johnson also expresses some hostility to writers. He does not reject Browne's declaration that while it was circulating in manuscript his *Religio Medici* was given to a publisher without his knowledge, but he pauses to 'doubt the truth of the complaint so frequently made of surreptitious editions. . . . a strategem, by which an author panting for fame, and yet afraid of seeming to challenge it, may at once gratify his vanity, and preserve the appearance of modesty; may enter the lists and secure a retreat.' Johnson also laughs sardonically at the appearance of deference with which Browne and Kenelm Digby conducted their debate with each other: 'The reciprocal civility of authors is one of the most risible scenes in the farce of life. Who would not have thought, that these two luminaries of their age had ceased to endeavour to grow bright by the obscuration of each other.'[17] Because he was himself attacked for 'Brownisms', Johnson's moderate appraisal of Browne's style is interesting, as is his genial critique of Browne's remarks on Old English, but most of the biography is so highly derivative that Johnson's remarks on the life of writing must be read as gratuitous expressions of his own state of uneasiness and anger. With all his learning, after all his efforts on the *Rambler* and the *Dictionary*, after his degree from Oxford and his plaudits from the continent, he was living only days away from debtor's prison, and he needed work as much as all the other hack writers in the city.

13

The *Literary Magazine*

Life to be worthy of a rational Being must be always in progression; we must always purpose to do more or better than in time past. The Mind is enlarged and elevated by mere purposes, though they end as they begin by airy contemplation.
Johnson to Mrs Thrale, 29 November 1783

Despite his glowing description in the *Harleian Catalogue* of the *Acta Eruditorum Leipsiensia* and despite his proposals for the *Publisher,* a review meant to rival the learned, Leipzig journal edited by the great Mencken (an ancestor of the American lexicographer), Johnson's one attempt at full-time book reviewing was, like many of his works, a modest compromise with the London booksellers. In 1756 he became an editor, chiefly in charge of book reviews, for the newly created *Literary Magazine or Universal Review.*[1] The first number did not appear until May because Johnson was pretty seriously ill with some kind of cold or respiratory infection through the winter of 1755–6. His tenure as editor lasted only until July 1757. The periodical was doing poorly, but part of the reason for Johnson's resignation was an incident involving John Wilkie, the member of the publishing syndicate behind the *Literary Magazine* who was then due to take his turn in charge of the project. The incident is interesting because it shows the fierceness of Johnson's independence, the depth of his conviction about the importance of religion in education, and, incidentally, his feelings about his favourite beverage, tea.

Jonas Hanway included a brief dissertation on the evils of drinking tea in his complacent essay on local travel, *Journal of Eight Days Journey from Portsmouth to Kingston upon Thames . . . in Sixty-Four Letters: Addressed to two Ladies of the Partie* (1757). As a bit of advertising for his favourite charity, Hanway gratuitously assured his readers that the governors of the orphanage would protect their charges from such a pernicious habit. When Johnson reviewed the book, he took the occasion to chastise the educational practices of the orphanage:

I know not upon what observation Mr *Hanway* founds his confidence in the governors of the *Foundling Hospital,* men of whom I have not any knowledge, but whom I intreat to consider a little the minds as well as bodies of the children. I am inclined to believe irreligion equally pernicious with gin and tea, and therefore, think it not unseasonable to mention, that when a few months ago I wandered through the hospital, I found not a child that seemed to have heard of his creed or the commandments. To breed up children in this manner, is to rescue them from an early grave, that they may find employment for the gibbet; from dying in innocence, that they may perish by their crimes.[2]

In the midst of a funding crisis and therefore particularly sensitive to public opinion, the governors threatened legal action against the *Literary Magazine* if the anonymous reviewer did not publicly recant. (The governors were on fairly solid ground because they had in fact instituted religious instruction some months before, perhaps in response to an informal complaint that Johnson had registered during the visit he mentions.) The *London Chronicle,* edited by Wilkie, had reprinted Johnson's hostile review and was approached in the same manner by the offended governors. Wilkie issued a retraction, but J. Richardson, then in charge of the *Literary Magazine,* refused either to recant or to reveal the identity of his reviewer. Johnson's anonymous reply in the next issue of the *Literary Magazine* was legally sharp and forestalled the possibility of a suit. However, Johnson may have feared that when Wilkie took control of the *Magazine* he would no longer be protected. In any case, Johnson's response to Hanway's counter-attack was his last contribution to the *Magazine.*

Over the fifteen months that he spent editing the *Literary Magazine* Johnson reviewed thirty-nine books and wrote several opposition political editorials, in addition to a biography of Frederick the Great of Prussia and some smaller, miscellaneous pieces of writing. The editorials openly criticize the ministry's handling of foreign affairs, especially in prosecuting the Seven Years War, but the whole body of Johnson's work for the *Literary Magazine,* including the biography of Frederick, has a political cast. The book reviews also signal the beginning of an important new stage in Johnson's life as a reader and a critic. Like most other eighteenth-century book reviews, Johnson's more candidly and frankly rely on recapitulation and paraphrase than most modern reviews. Even when it is done openly, however, there is an art to paraphrase, and Johnson excelled at it. In a study of the thirty-nine books and Johnson's paraphrases of them Donald Eddy concludes, 'Johnson's "extracts" are generally much better written than the books he is quoting from, and it is amazing to see how successful he is in conveying an author's thoughts and information in so many fewer words than the originals.' Johnson showed this talent in earlier work on the *Gentleman's Magazine,* but he had recently honed his skill in the course of selecting from hundreds of books some 116,000 illustrative quotations for the *Dictionary.* The same terrific power of reading with attention that went into making the *Dictionary* also appears in the *Literary Magazine.* In fact, in his final assessment Donald Eddy compares Johnson's book reviews to the *Dictionary*: 'they constitute, collectively, a piece of writing which has more breadth and variety than anything else that ever came from Johnson's pen (with the obvious exception of the *Dictionary*).'[3]

Donald Eddy may be right about Johnson's book reviews, but it is remarkable how often scholars have had occasion to make statements of this kind about one or another of Johnson's relatively unknown literary productions. Johnson's works include a remarkable number of vast, generally unread tracts of writing: two volumes of Parliamentary debates, about two volumes of translations, a volume of book reviews, another of prefaces and dedications, another of early biographies, the *Harleian Catalogue*, a volume of sermons, and two volumes of the Vinerian law lectures. All this is in addition to the still largely neglected folios of the *Dictionary* and the often neglected volumes of notes to Shakespeare's works. Johnson's best-known works – *Rasselas*, the *Rambler* and *Idler*, the *Lives*, and a few English poems – constitute a relatively small part of what he wrote. Much of what Johnson produced is neglected because he composed it by editing, translating, extracting, and commenting, rather than by creating it in a wholly imaginative fashion. However, as Eddy and other students of the more obscure works have found, Johnson reveals his intellectual power in all of his compositions, and only by surveying the full range of his activities can his literary life be properly understood.

The thirty-nine books and pamphlets that Johnson reviews in the *Literary Magazine* are striking in their diversity: there are travel books, histories, works of religious and political controversy, books of literary criticism, manuals of practical divinity, a few works of speculative religion, histories of science, and several books on practical arts. A majority of the books were published by members of the syndicate behind the *Literary Magazine*, but Johnson had a good deal of freedom in making his selections. He reviewed some books by friends – works by Charlotte Lennox and Thomas Birch, and even, very briefly and modestly, his own edition of Sir Thomas Browne's *Christian Morals* – but personal interest was not his main criterion of selection.

One objective of the *Literary Magazine* was to become a guide for readers bewildered by the increasing fecundity of 'this age of writers'. To clear the overgrown paths of publishing Johnson proposes austere standards of evaluation based on the usefulness of books, the correctness of their method, and the candour or good intentions of their authors. He has the highest praise for truthful travel narratives and informative books on practical arts like *Collateral Bee-Boxes. Or, a New, Easy, and Advantageous Method of Managing Bees* by Stephen White (London, 1756) and *Experiments on Bleaching* by Francis Home (Edinburgh, 1756). Stephen Hales wins even higher commendation because he communicates to all a valuable procedure that might have made him more money if he had kept to himself *An Account of a Useful Discovery to Distill Double the Usual Quantity of Sea-Water* (London, 1756). The spelling reformer Charles Lucas earns less praise for his less useful *Essay on Waters* (London, 1756), and Jonas Hanway arouses Johnson's anger partly by giving useless, unfounded advice on the imaginary economic and physical evils of tea-drinking. Johnson interposes a disarming account of his own experience, in which Hanway evidently failed to see the humour: 'We shall now endeavour to follow [Hanway] through all his observations on this modern luxury; but it can scarcely be candid, not to make a previous declaration, that he is to expect little justice from the author of this extract, a hardened and shameless tea-drinker, who has for twenty years diluted his meals with only the infusion of this fascinating plant, whose kettle has scarcely time to cool, who with Tea amuses the evening, with Tea solaces the midnights, and with Tea welcomes the morning.'[4] The serious side of the passage is its ridicule of Hanway's calculations on the costs of tea-drinking and its depiction of Hanway's philanthropy as a prudish reduction in the small stock of innocent human enjoyment.

There is a political dimension to the discussion of tea because Hanway stresses the cost of importing it and implicitly justifies taxation. More obvious political interests underlie Johnson's decision to review several other books. At times political activism vies with Johnson's efforts to build a new literary-critical standard in the *Literary Magazine*, but there are also affinities between his politics and his criticism. His very first review, for example, concerns a reissue of *The History of the Island of Minorca* by John Armstrong (London, 1752). Minorca, ceded to the British in the Treaty of Utrecht (1713), was about to be a theatre in a world-wide war with France. At the conclusion of his review Johnson reflects on the value of the island to Britain: 'It is always good to consider the worst that can happen, and therefore I have amused myself with considering what we shall really lose by losing *Minorca*.' The book under review is useful and therefore valuable because it has provided Johnson with the economic and demographic information needed to draw this conclusion: 'If the distribution of empire were in my hands, I should indeed rather give up *Gibraltar*, the possession of which shall always keep us at variance with *Spain*, than *Minorca* which may be less invidiously retained. But I know not whether either is worth its charge, and by losing them, I am not sure that we shall suffer any thing more than that vexation which accompanies disgrace, and the pain of doing that against our will, which we should have been glad to do if no violence had compelled us.'[5] In the event, Minorca was lost by siege, and the ministry, which had inadequately defended Fort Mahon, blamed Admiral Byng for the 'disgrace' and punished him with death before a military firing squad.

In his reviews of four pamphlets issued while the trial was still in progress Johnson attacked the ministry's case against Byng and printed the full texts of relevant documents that had been tendentiously edited by the government-sponsored *London Gazette*. Such disclosure is Johnson's journalistic ideal in the *Literary Magazine*, and the basis of both his political and his literary work as its editor. Johnson explains the political importance of disclosure in the opening paragraph of 'Observations on the Present State of Affairs', which he wrote for the *Literary Magazine* as a sequel to the first number's broadly historical 'Introduction to the Political State of Great Britain'. After considering the history of the balance of power in Europe and the political effects of two centuries of exploration in the New World, Johnson pauses before discussing the recent inception of the Seven Years War and delivers this admirable journalistic credo:

> The time is now come in which every Englishman expects to be informed of the national affairs, and in which he has a right to have that expectation gratified. For whatever may be urged by ministers, or those whom vanity or interest make the followers of ministers, concerning the necessity of confidence in our governors, and the presumption of prying with profane eyes into the recesses of policy, it is evident, that this reverence can be claimed only by counsels yet unexecuted, and projects suspended in deliberation. But when a design has ended in miscarriage or success, when every eye and every ear is witness to general discontent, or general satisfaction, it is then a proper time to disentangle confusion and illustrate obscurity, to shew by what causes every event was produced, and in what effects it is likely to terminate: to lay down with distinct particularity what rumour always huddles in general exclamations, or perplexes by undigested narratives; to shew whence happiness or calamity is derived, and whence it may be expected, and honestly to lay before the people what inquiry can gather of the past, and conjecture can estimate of the future.[6]

Johnson here adjusts the view implicit in his Parliamentary *Debates*, where the highest ideal was 'science', and the particular issues under consideration were displayed as ramifications of basic, durable issues of government. In fact, in the first number of the *Literary Magazine* Johnson explicitly repudiates his *Debates*: 'We shall not attempt to give any regular series of debates or to amuse our Readers with senatorial rhetoric. The speeches inserted in other papers have been long known to be fictitious, and produced sometimes by men who never heard the debate, nor had any authentic information.' Johnson's new ideal is historical truth. He is not naive about the possibility of complete success, but he strives for truth in information: he prints many actual documents in the *Literary Magazine*, and he evaluates political and non-political works primarily on the amount of genuine information they contain. He understands the delusive potential of print, but his response now is not to adopt the Swiftian tactics of *Marmor Norfolciense*, which shows the unreliability of print, but rather to improve the veracity of the medium. Johnson's position is frankly anti-ministry; he is so indignant about the operations of the Europeans in the New World that he calls the Seven Years War 'only the quarrel of two robbers for the spoils of a passenger'.[7] Yet his overall stance, with its acceptance of the possibility that print may correctly inform a politically sentient populace, is inherently less rebellious and hostile than it was in the 1730s. As a supporter and protector of information Johnson is within the pale of a political world increasingly defined by the way it was reported in the medium of print.

Johnson is guilty of political bias in his judgements on the many political works that he reviewed, but he shows his integrity by judging non-
political books according to the same criteria of use and veracity. He
transfers his standards easily from the books to their authors: writers who
provide information are candid, and those who retail known facts as though
they were new or solicit credence for what they merely imagine are vain.
Satire is always more pleasing than panegyric, as Johnson later observed,
and his castigations of authorial vanity in the *Literary Magazine* are among
the most memorable parts of his writing. David Mallet, who defended the
ministry's handling of the infamous Byng affair, draws one of Johnson's
nicest condemnations: 'Of this pamphlet the eight first pages contain . . .
an exhortation to impartiality, and an encomium on the purity of his
own intention. When a man appeals to himself for what only himself can
know, he may be very confident of a favourable sentence. This author may
perhaps think as he writes, for there are men who think as they are bidden.'
Mallet, Johnson says in an elegant way, is a creature of the ministry and
only honest if he is mindless. As the editor of Lord Bolingbroke's *Works*
(1754), Mallet was already low in Johnson's estimation; some of his extreme hostility to the impious Bolingbroke fires Johnson's response to
Mallet. In the first edition of the *Dictionary* Johnson inserts a casual as-
persion of Bolingbroke under the word 'irony'. In his abridged edition of
1756 he exemplifies 'alias', a word in the vocabulary of criminal law, with
the phrase 'Mallet alias Malloch', referring to the writer's original Scottish
name and his general dishonesty.[8]

Throughout the *Literary Magazine*, Johnson is angry and indignant about
falsehood in contemporary politics, but he finds vain or idle speculation
on religious subjects even worse. Although he is careful to point out flaws,
Johnson gives generally favourable reviews to useful books of practical
religion, like Elizabeth Harrison's *Miscellanies on Moral and Religious Subjects* (London, 1756) and his own edition of Sir Thomas Browne's *Christian
Morals*. Religious works that are fundamentally speculative, however, draw
sharp criticism. For example, despite his respect for the correspondents,
Johnson is severe in his review of *Four Letters from Sir Isaac Newton to Doctor
Bentley. Containing Some Arguments in Proof of a Deity* (London, 1756).
Johnson's supremely hostile response, however, is reserved for Soame Jenyns
who compounded vanity with impiety by producing a book of religious
speculation that justifies the political status quo.

In 1742 when he began a forty-year career in Parliament (mostly representing the county of Cambridge), Jenyns was a supporter of the politically doomed Walpole. This did not endear him to Johnson (though his
view of Walpole was softening), but he became more odious in 1755 when
George II appointed him to the Lords Commissioners for the Board for
Trade and Plantations. On several political issues Jenyns did not differ
much from Johnson: both thought the Empire overextended both east
and west; both favoured the national militia, as opposed to a strictly professional, standing army; and both supported taxation of the American

colonies. But Jenyns was fundamentally a creature of the establishment and a seeker of preferment from mighty nobles like Chesterfield. To Chesterfield, for instance, Jenyns wrote simpering lines on his installation as a Knight of the Garter, including this nutrasweet couplet: 'See ev'ry friend to wit, politeness, love, / With one consent thy Sovereign's choice approve!' Jenyns's other poetry is also transparently conventional; he worked easily in the popular, courtly modes of the day, knocking out imitations of Pope's epistles, for instance. Although he tried more arduous tasks, notably a verse translation of Isaac Hawkins Browne's *De animi immortalitate*, his epitaph on Samuel Johnson provides a fair example of his easy, good-natured, insipid poetry:

> Here lies *Sam Johnson*: – Reader, have a care,
> Tread lightly, lest you wake a sleeping Bear:
> Religious, moral, generous, and humane
> He was; but self-sufficient, proud, and vain,
> Fond of, and overbearing in dispute,
> A Christian, and a Scholar – but a Brute.[9]

The work of Jenyns that aroused Johnson's wrath was *A Free Inquiry into the Nature and Origin of Evil.* In his religion, as in his politics, Jenyns held positions that were not incompatible with Johnson's. When he defended a later edition of the work against the attacks of Johnson and several others, Jenyns described intentions that Johnson found laudable in many other books: 'to reconcile the numerous evils so conspicuous in the creation, with the wisdom, power, and goodness of the Creator. . . . To ascertain the nature of virtue, and to enforce the practice of it . . . and lastly, to shew the excellence and credibility of the Christian revelation.' However, Jenyns achieves his ends by expounding a deterministic and pessimistic view of humanity, mixed with fatuous theodical speculation that blends the most thoughtless aspects of Hobbes, Mandeville, Bolingbroke, and Pope's *Essay on Man*. He divides the work into six letters: 'On Evil in General'; 'On Evils of Imperfection'; 'On Natural Evils'; 'On Moral Evils'; 'On Political Evils'; and 'On Religious Evils'. In the more specific chapters Jenyns exonerates God by dwelling on the inherent imperfection of man. Because man is imperfect, he must have an imperfect sort of government: 'All human government is the offspring of violence and corruption'; 'man can be governed by nothing but the fear of punishment'; 'a powerful army must be kept in pay to enslave the people, and a numerous clergy to decieve them.' What sounds at times like a prelude to denunciation, however, turns out to be an apology for the status quo. 'This necessity for evil in all government' gives 'weight and popularity' to the opponents of any government, but these are always 'ignorant wrong-headed people'; 'the wise man knows that these evils cannot be eradicated'; thus he submits cheerfully to the prevailing form of corruption. Likewise, all human religion must of necessity lack universality, authenticity, perspicuity, and policy; all must have 'corruption, with all that inundation of wickedness and misery which must flow from that corruption'.[10] So the wise man submits cheerfully to the prevailing form of religious corruption.

The political and ecclesiastical views in Jenyns are inimical to Johnson's personal spirit of criticism, inquiry, and opposition, and they are views that he considered dangerous to the public welfare, whether or not they were true. The mere fact that they could never be proven true or false and were therefore purely speculative is enough to damn Jenyns's opinions in terms of the criticism Johnson developed as book reviewer in the *Literary Magazine*. This comes out most clearly in Johnson's attack on Jenyns's more general chapters, which are filled with paraphrases of Pope's *Essay on Man* and invocations of hypostatic entities like the Great Chain of Being and the 'general system of things' which, if knowable, would resolve all our doubts about the true nature of present evil. Jenyns's confidence about the nature of what he acknowledges to be unknowable is the first object of Johnson's ire: 'This is a treatise consisting of six letters upon a very difficult and important question, which I am afraid this author's endeavours will not free from the perplexity, which has entangled the speculatists of all ages, and which must always continue while *we see* but *in part*. He calls it a *Free* enquiry, and indeed his *freedom* is, I think, greater than his modesty. Though he is far from the contemptible arrogance, or the impious licentiousness of *Bolinbroke*, yet he decides too easily upon questions out of the reach of human determination, with too little consideration of mortal weakness, and with too much vivacity for the necessary caution.' For merely recapitulating Pope and giving his readers nothing new, especially in the second letter, Jenyns is vain, by Johnson's standards, 'and yet', he says, 'how can vanity be gratified by plagiarism, or transcription? When this speculatist finds himself prompted to another performance, let him consider whether he is about to disburthen his mind or employ his fingers; and if I might venture to offer him a subject, I should wish that he would solve this question, Why he that has nothing to write, should desire to be a writer.'[11]

Johnson confesses himself in doubt about the Great Chain of Being and many other matters in Jenyns's treatise; he attacks Jenyns not for his opinions but for his 'presumptuous decision' especially concerning omnipotence: 'I do not mean to reproach this author for not knowing what is equally hidden from learning and from ignorance. The shame is to impose words for ideas upon ourselves or others.' Jenyns's error is not so much a fault of political science, philosophy, or religion as it is a writer's fault. Johnson shows this most entertainingly when he ridicules Jenyns's notion that there are species of beings intermediate between ourselves and God whose enjoyment of our personal woes explains the purpose of apparently senseless suffering in the great scheme of things. Using Jenyns's favourite device, the principle of analogy, Johnson imagines elaborations of his absurd solution to the problem of suffering: 'As we drown whelps and kittens, they amuse themselves now and then with sinking a ship, and stand round the fields of *Blenheim* or the walls of *Prague*, as we encircle a cock-pit. As we shoot a bird flying, they take a man in the midst of his business or pleasure, and knock him down with an apoplexy. Some of them, perhaps, are virtuosi, and delight in the operations of an asthma, as a human philosopher in the effects of an air pump. . . . Many a merry bout have these frolic beings at the vicissitudes of an ague, and good sport it is to see a man tumble with an epilepsy, and revive and tumble again, and all this he knows not why.' Johnson goes on in this vein until he depicts the 'pleasures' of watching 'the tossings and contortions of every possible pain exhibited together'. But his indignation at Jenyns's stupidity rests at last on his importunity as a writer addressing the public:

> One sport the merry malice of these beings has found means of enjoying to which we have nothing equal or similar. They now and then catch a mortal proud of his parts, and flattered either by the submission of those who court his kindness, or the notice of those who suffer him to court theirs. A head thus prepared for the reception of false opinions, and the projection of vain designs, they easily fill with idle notions, till in time they make their plaything an author: their first diversion commonly begins with an Ode or an epistle, then rises perhaps to a political irony, and is at last brought to its height, by a treatise of philosophy. Then begins the poor animal to entangle himself in sophisms, and flounder in absurdity, to talk confidently of the scale of being, and to give solutions which himself confesses impossible to be understood.[12]

Before he finished with Jenyns, Johnson praised a few of his particular tenets; he found his discourse on virtue sound, and he declared some of his statements about government worth repeating, but his vanity, his importunity, in short, his unjustified authorship, were what he could not forgive. Before finally dismissing Jenyns's imaginary beings, Johnson attacks authorial importunity in general: 'Many of the books which now croud the world, may be justly suspected to be written for the sake of some invisible order of beings, for surely they are of no use to any of the corporeal inhabitants of the world. Of the productions of the last bounteous year, how many can be said to serve any purpose of use or pleasure[?] The only end of writing is to enable the readers better to enjoy life, or better to endure it.'[13]

These critical criteria are as old and familiar as the phrase from Horace they recall: 'aut prodesse aut delectare'. But Johnson's context alters their meaning. The book review columns of a journal issued on the premise that the production of printed matter was increasingly unmanageable for readers provide a background in which 'use or pleasure' takes on new meaning. Speaking to potential buyers, Johnson emphasizes the criterion of use and associates it closely with the informative and the verifiable. He rejects the specious, the speculative, the idle, and the vain with such strictness and irritability that he curtails the range of works that might be commendable for their pleasurable qualities. The effect on Johnson's literary sensibilities of his fifteen months of reviewing for the

Literary Magazine are visible in the edition of Shakespeare, on which he resumed work during this period, in the *Lives of the Poets,* and in many of his famous, crotchety remarks about books in Boswell's records of his conversation. These years had a formative effect on the later Johnson who, reportedly, rarely read a book through. Johnson's impatience with fiction in supposedly historical narrative appears as early as his translation of Lobo, but in his work as book reviewer he generalized his preference for facts and useful knowledge in a way that is characteristic of his later criticism. In his fiftieth year Johnson is decidedly closer to the seventy-year-old critic who could complain about taking nothing solid away from the 'flowery labyrinth' of Akenside's verse than the thirty-year-old author of verse to 'a lovely thief' with a 'conscious hand' in 'To Eliza Plucking Laurel'.

14

The *Idler*

I know not any thing more pleasant or more instructive than to compare experience with
expectation, or to register from time to time the difference between Idea and Reality.
It is by this kind of observation that we grow daily less liable to be disappointed.
                                         Johnson to Bennet Langton, 27 June 1758

By early 1757 Johnson was doing very little work for the *Literary Maga-*
zine, although his reviews continued to appear through the July issue. As
always, he did various literary jobs for friends: prefaces and dedications for
Charlotte Lennox and John Payne, comments on the emerging antiquarian
work of Thomas Percy, and help of some kind with a pamphlet by Saunders
Welch, *Proposal to Render Effectual a Plan to Remove the Nuisance of Common*
Prostitutes from the Streets (London, 1757). How much money, if any, he
received for providing such assistance is unknown. But it is recorded that
Johnson was paid a guinea for writing the introductory article in the first
number of the *London Chronicle* (1 January 1757).[1] However, the main
project that Johnson now had in hand was his edition of Shakespeare. He
signed a contract with the publisher Tonson on 2 June 1756 which paid
him 250 sets of the eight-volume work. With a stake in the edition, he
became a kind of entrepreneur: he published proposals in the *Literary*
Magazine and sold subscriptions for two guineas apiece. To raise sales he
promised the edition by Christmas of 1757; his failure to meet the deadline had a disastrous effect. In June 1757, when his work for the *Literary*
Magazine was about over, Johnson borrowed £100 from Tonson, but in
September he needed another £26, and in February 1758 he required £40
to bail him out of debtor's prison, where he had landed for the second
time in his life. The arrest clearly stimulated activity; by spring 1758 two
volumes of Shakespeare were printed, but the project was still too far from
completion to boost sales and improve Johnson's cash flow. His entrepreneurial power in doubt, Johnson again signed with a publisher to

produce copy at regularly stated intervals for regular payment. The work
to which he committed himself this time was the lead article in a weekly
journal called the *Universal Chronicle.* Perhaps his dilatory progress on
Shakespeare was part of what incited Johnson to name his new, regularly
employed persona and the articles he produced the *Idler.* For each *Idler* he
received three guineas, enough to live on while he kept the larger, more
independent project on the back burner.

Because it takes up many of the same topics in roughly the same periodical format, the *Idler* invites comparison with the *Rambler.* However, the *Idler*
is obviously aimed at a wider audience than the *Rambler,* and Johnson altered
his work accordingly. To begin with, there is much less Latin and Greek
in the *Idler*: there are very few mottoes, and when classical authors appear
they are usually paraphrased, rather than quoted.[2] The allegorical characters in the *Idler* have English rather than Latin names: in the *Idler* we
hear from or about such people as Betty Broom, Tim Ranger, Molly Quick,
Dick Misty, and Polly Mohair, whereas in the *Rambler* we learn about
Quisquilius, Eugenio, Flavilla, Gelidus, and Gulosulus. As the reduced
presence of the classical languages suggests, the overall style of the *Idler* is
blunter and simpler than that of the *Rambler.* Although it is stylistically
lower than the *Rambler,* however, the *Idler* is not merely an inferior version
of its grandiloquent predecessor. Johnson does not merely simplify the
more august statements of the earlier work; indeed, he creates in the *Idler*
a language that is admirable on its own terms.

The stylistic distinction of the new series of essays is most evident in the
introductory sections of *Idlers* devoted to serious, moral subjects. Number
27, for example, begins with a moral injunction and a lament about its
neglect:

> It has been the endeavour of all those whom the world has reverenced for
> superior wisdom, to persuade man to be acquainted with himself, to learn
> his own powers and his own weakness, to observe by what evils he is most
> dangerously beset, and by what temptations must easily overcome,
>   This counsel has been often given with serious dignity, and often received
> with appearance of conviction; but, as very few can search deep into their
> own minds without meeting what they wish to hide from themselves, scarce
> any man persists in cultivating such disagreeable acquaintance, but draws
> the veil again between his eyes and his heart, leaves his passions and ap-
> petites as he found them, and advises others to look into themselves.

The pattern of composition resembles that in *Rambler* 165, but the earlier
voice is different:

> The writers who have undertaken the unpromising task of moderating de-
> sire, exert all the power of their eloquence, to shew that happiness is not the
> lot of man, and have by many arguments and examples proved the instability
> of every condition by which envy or ambition are excited. . . .
>   All the force of reason and all the charms of language are indeed necessary

to support positions which every man hears with a wish to confute them. Truth finds an easy entrance into the mind when she is introduced by desire, and attended by pleasure; but when she intrudes uncalled, and brings only fear and sorrow in her train, the passes of the intellect are barred against her by prejudice and passion; if she sometimes forces her way by the batteries of argument, she seldom long keeps possession of her conquests, but is ejected by some favoured enemy, or at best obtains only a nominal sovereignty, without influence and without authority.[3]

'To persuade man to be acquainted with himself' and 'to shew that happiness is not the lot of man' are equally conventional moral aims, stated with equal simplicity. The difference between the two pieces is in Johnson's analysis of the reception each truth receives. The *Rambler* erects a mind on the model of a medieval castle and fills the scene of its assault with allegorical abstractions: truth, fear, sorrow, prejudice, and passion all take roles in the scene, which begins to read like a chapter of Bunyan's *Holy War*. Such dramatization of mental and moral action is severely limited in the *Idler*. In the examples provided above, a veil is the only prop needed in the *Idler*, whereas the *Rambler* requires batteries, trains, passes, and a narrative of assault. The *Rambler*'s detailed, allegorical analysis of the human mind is impressive, but the *Idler*'s quicker, less monumental sketch is also appealing. As an image of self-deception, a refusal 'to cultivate disagreeable acquaintance' is representative of the *Idler*'s more social and less abstract psychology. Whereas the *Rambler* portrays the mind as a physical body under Newtonian inspection, the *Idler* sees it more simply as a social self.

The stylistic unit that reflects such differences and must be consistent with them is the persona of the essay series. Johnson is careful to establish the character of Mr Idler in the beginning of the series, and he does so with notably less consternation, hesitation, and self-consciousness than in his creation of Mr Rambler. The Rambler is a monitor set above his readers and largely inaccessible to them, despite the printer's regular invitation to correspondents, but the Idler seems intellectually and ethically within reach. In fact, author and reader are on a par from the start:

If similitude of manners be a motive to kindness, the Idler may flatter himself with universal patronage. There is no single character under which such numbers are comprised. Every man is, or hopes to be, an Idler. Even those who seem to differ most from us are hastening to encrease our fraternity; as peace is the end of war, so to be idle is the ultimate purpose of the busy.

There is perhaps no appellation by which a writer can better denote his kindred to the human species. It has been found hard to describe man by an adequate definition. Some philosophers have called him a reasonable animal, but others have considered reason as a quality of which many creatures partake. He has been termed likewise a laughing animal; but it is said that some men have never laughed. Perhaps man may be more properly distinguished as an idle animal; for there is no man who is not sometimes idle. It is at least a definition from which none that shall find it in this paper can be excepted; for who can be more idle than the reader of the *Idler*?[4]

Johnson never made a more genial approach to his readers. Only hints of
his philosophical outlook appear, as though they are vestiges of Mr Idler's
more vigorous youth, and latent cynicism about the nature of man is no
threat to the mellow tone.

Yet some fierce satire on man does break out in the *Idler*, especially in
the early numbers that touch on politics. One reason for the political
vituperation is that the character of Mr Idler allows Johnson to address
contemporary events more directly than he could as the philosophical Mr
Rambler. In Number 5, for example, Johnson remarks on the troop
movements in Britain in preparation for the widening war with France. He
appears at first to take up Mr Idler's particular concern with 'domestic
privacies' or 'diminutive history' by focusing on the feelings of the women
left behind. Soon, however, he launches a satirical suggestion that women
be allowed to follow the troops as auxiliaries. The masculine jollity of the
suggestion devolves into direct attacks on the ministry's handling of the
war reminiscent of Johnson's pieces in the *Literary Magazine*. He ridicules
specific episodes in the war, including the loss of Minorca, which he notice-
ably does not attribute to any failure of Admiral Byng's: 'Had Minorca
been defended by a female garrison, it might have been surrendered, as
it was, without a breach.' *Idler* 8 is a vicious and direct attack on the
cowardice of the British army (the professional assault army rather than
the home defensive militia that Johnson supported). Johnson maps out a
lengthy, insulting plan for training this army very gradually to face the
enemy. At first it will be safe to show them only 'shirts waving upon lines',
but 'In time it will be proper to bring our French prisoners from the coast,
and place them upon the walls in martial order. At their first appearance
their hands must be tied, but they may be allowed to grin. In a month they
may guard the place with their hands loosed, provided that on pain of
death they be forbidden to strike.'[5] The motivation for the troops to
overcome their fear is not loyalty or honour but the smell of roast meat
and tobacco.

The standing army was a conventional target of attack, but patriotism
was running high in 1758, and Johnson's anti-war satire must have seemed
radical to loyal followers of the government. Along with the *Idler*, Johnson
contributed five 'Observations' on politics to the *Universal Chronicle*. In
response to these pieces, at least one correspondent was deeply offended.
He assailed Johnson's 'pompous composition' and his 'inexcusable ignorance'. He bridled especially at Johnson's ridicule of a 'triumph' organized
in celebration of the battle of Louisbourg, a fort on the St Lawrence river
won by the British with the colonial militia in 1745 and then, to the
consternation of the colonists and others, returned to the French in 1748
with the Peace of Aix-la-Chapelle. Johnson calmly levelled his opponent
in a reply that recapitulates the commitment to veracity that made the
'triumph' and other empty displays of success so odious to him: 'I can
praise with truth, and hope, that there will never again be need of swelling
trifles into dignity, or of covering deficiency with splendid falshood.'[6]

Perhaps the fiercest satire in all of Johnson's works appears in the original *Idler* 22. On 9 September 1758, with operations against France going into full swing, Johnson published an anti-war fable in the form of a dialogue between a wise old vulture and its young. The old vulture teaches her young how to secure the 'more delicious food' of 'the flesh of man': 'When you hear noise and see fire which flashes along the ground, hasten to the place with your swiftest wing, for men are surely destroying one another; you will then find the ground smoking with blood and covered with carcasses, of which many are dismembered and mangled for the convenience of the vulture.' The innocent question of one of the vulture chicks in response to this direction leads to a telling moment in the satire: '"But when men have killed their prey", said the pupil, "why do they not eat it?"' Throughout the piece humans are at best bloodthirsty and irrational animals; at other times, they are merely inanimate meat. At the end of the essay, the old vulture relates the wisdom of a seer whom she used to visit in his eyrie on the Carpathian rocks:

> he had fed year after year on the entrails of men. His opinion was, that men had only the appearance of animal life, being really vegetables with a power of motion; and that as the boughs of an oak are dashed together by the storm, that swine may fatten upon the falling acorns, so men are by some unaccountable power driven one against another, till they lose their motion, that vultures may be fed. Others think they have observed something of contrivance and policy among these mischievous beings, and those that hover more closely round them, pretend, that there is, in every herd, one that gives directions to the rest, and seems to be more eminently delighted with a wide carnage. What it is that intitles him to such pre-eminence we know not; he is seldom the biggest or the swiftest, but he shews by his eagerness and diligence that he is, more than any of the others, a friend to vultures.'[7]

Issued in wartime, when prayers for the leaders were being offered in high places, this is a remarkably strong denunciation of the irrationality of war and the malignity of political and military commanders.

Johnson suppressed this essay in the collected edition of the *Idler* in 1761, but his reasons could not have been narrowly political because he retained many pieces that are just as critical of the ministry and the war. Johnson's objection to this piece is that it teaches the doctrine of human malignity, which, he once told Hester Mulso, he would not publish, although he believed it to be true. The fable makes man worse than Swift's Yahoos, and it shows that Johnson could entertain more deeply misanthropic views than those that appear in his published works. Perhaps the more permanent format of the collected edition impelled Johnson to reject *Idler* 22, whereas the ephemerality of the original publication in the *Universal Chronicle*, a sheet of newsprint, freed him to make the statement in the first place. In its bound form, the *Idler* resembles an instructional text, as Hannah More recognized in recommending it, along with most of

Johnson's other works, in her own educational manual, *Hints toward Forming the Character of a Young Princess*.[8] Although most of the changes Johnson made for the collected edition were stylistic, the package was wrapped up and sealed with both a Latin and a Greek motto announcing the moral value of the work. Such a package, dedicated to providing 'prudenti . . . consilio', was an inappropriate place for the expression of dangerous misanthropy.

The Greek motto for the collected *Idler* – χάρις μικροῖσι (for the sake of little things') – was equally suited to the periodical publication. In fact, the appropriateness of the *Universal Chronicle* to disquisitions on small, quotidian things makes for a sort of dynamic contrast between the author and his venue that is one of the main attractions of the *Idler*. To the appropriately petty subjects Johnson invariably brings his customary concerns and his penchant for thinking in general terms. For example, writing is a perpetual subject of Johnson's attention, and, adjusting to the stylistic register of the *Idler*, he discusses the newspaper: 'One of the principal amusements of the Idler is to read the works of those minute historians the writers of news, who, though contemptuously overlooked by the composers of bulky volumes, are yet necessary in a nation where much wealth produces much leisure, and one part of the people has nothing to do but to observe the lives and fortunes of the other.' Johnson satirizes journalists as spiders of literature whose cannibalism prevents them from cooperating to make a better product; then he parodies unreliable newspapers in a series of contradictory stories about a sea battle. There are tragic undertones in the garbled accounts that recall the Byng affair, but even here Johnson finds reasons for praising newspapers. It is genuinely a point of pride when the Idler says, 'All foreigners remark, that the knowledge of the common people of England is greater than that of any other vulgar.'[9]

As usual, Johnson's complaint is not about all writing, just all useless writing. He complained in the *Literary Magazine* about the growing volume of publication, and here he laments the fact that 'journals are daily multiplied without increase of knowledge. The tale of the morning paper is told again in the evening, and the narratives of the evening are bought again in the morning.' In *Idler* 30 the attack is sharper: 'No species of literary men has lately been so much multiplied as the writers of news. . . . In Sir Henry Wotton's jocular definition, "An ambassador" is said to be "a man of virtue sent abroad to tell lies for the advantage of his country"; a news-writer is "a man without virtue, who writes lies at home for his own profit". To these compositions is required neither genius nor knowledge, neither industry nor sprightliness, but contempt of shame, and indifference to truth are absolutely necessary.' Mr Idler keeps himself below the *Rambler*'s level of abstraction, but he deviates in a characteristically Johnsonian way from the subject of newspapers to the more general subject of truth. His concluding statement is less abstract but just as important and as memorable as anything said by his more philosophical predecessor: 'Among the calamities of war may be justly numbered the diminution of the love of truth, by the falsehoods which interest dictates and credulity encourages.'[10]

Although the *Rambler* is more responsive to contemporary events than it appears, the *Idler* provides our best glimpses of Johnson drawing the material of his work from daily London life before forming it along the lines of classical topics and ancient wisdom. *Idlers* 35 and 40 focus on the quotidian subject of newspaper advertising, making use of particular ads that Johnson must have seen. Advertisements are evil because they inflame the passions and, like hope and fear, prey on the human imagination. The Johnsonian position is easy to extrapolate, but his careful observation of such trivial pieces of printed language is nevertheless surprising: 'Promise, large promise, is the soul of an advertisement. I remember a "wash ball" that had a quality truly wonderful, it gave "an exquisite edge to the razor."' Turning trivia to another use, Johnson ridicules British cowardice in the Seven Years War when he brings to his readers' attention an ad for a raree show: 'A famous Mohawk Indian warrior'. Johnson comments drily, 'there are many true Britons that will never be persuaded to see him but through a grate.'[11]

As in the *Literary Magazine*, in *Idler* 40 Johnson mixes his political commentary with attacks on vain or useless authors: 'Every man that advertises his own excellence, should write with some consciousness of a character which dares to call the attention of the publick. He should remember that his name is to stand in the same paper with those of the King of Prussia, and the Emperor of Germany, and endeavour to make himself worthy of such association.' Since Johnson's estimation of these leaders is not high, his comparison diminishes both them and the self-advertisers. The irony continues into the next paragraph when Johnson continues an attack on 'this epidemical conspiracy for the destruction of paper' that he began in *Adventurer* 115: 'some regard is likewise to be paid to posterity. There are men of diligence and curiosity [read 'stupidity'] who treasure up the papers of the day merely because others neglect them, and in time they will be scarce. When these collections shall be read in another century, how will numberless contradictions be reconciled. . . .' Time has spoiled the tone of this passage because we really do value old newspapers now, and Johnson's disdain for the spread of publication is hard to understand in light of his many contributions to it. But the application of antiquarian methods to contemporary ephemera seemed odd to him, and the increased volume of publication was more and more to strike him as a threat to the integrity of literature. In *Adventurer* 115 he prophesied the end of such increase: 'General irregularities are known in time to remedy themselves. By the constitution of antient Aegypt, the priesthood was continually increasing, till at length there was no people beside themselves; the establishment was then dissolved, and the number of priests was reduced and limited. Thus among us, writers will, perhaps, be multiplied, till no readers will be found, and then the ambition of writing must necessarily cease.' This is not only prescient; it is also remarkably conservative in its exclusionary attitude. Such literary conservatism was becoming more and more characteristic of Johnson's stance. Increasingly, he praises books and encourages writers only when they have solid knowledge to contribute: 'The sequel of Clarendon's history, at last happily published, is an accession to English literature equally agreeable to the admirers of elegance and the lovers of truth; many doubtful facts may now be ascertained, and many questions, after long debate, may be determined by decisive authority.' This authority derives from Clarendon's personal experience of the history he relates, which is the antithesis of speculative imposture like that found in Jenyns's *Free Enquiry*. Those with solid information to impart should write, even if they have not sorted out all the details and organized everything into a regular series: 'Let it be always remembered that life is short, that knowledge is endless, and that many doubts deserve not to be cleared. Let those whom nature and study have qualified to teach mankind, tell us what they have learned while they are yet able to tell it, and trust their reputation only to themselves.'[12]

Part of the reason for Johnson's satirical writing in the *Idler* was certainly his disgust with the political situation: the beginning of the Seven Years War, the ministry's handling of the war, and George II's insistence on involving England in the politics of central Europe. But some of the satire directed at useless writers is related to a general bitterness Johnson felt about the lack of reward for all his literary work. After all his work on the *Dictionary* and all its success, he was meeting deadlines for the *Idler* to escape a third imprisonment for debt. In two *Idlers* he addresses the issue of imprisonment for debt and argues cogently for its unfairness and impracticality. The first of these was the original Number 23, which immediately followed the misanthropic *Idler* on the education of vultures. The two pieces, coming together, suggest a mood of extreme anger and hostility. Yet the piece on debtor's prison is very nicely controlled, pointing out the responsibility of creditors in the creation of insolvency and recurring to fundamental principles of law in such trenchant reminders as 'The end of all civil regulations is to secure private happiness from private malignity.'[13]

Equally finely controlled, despite their satire, are several *Idlers* devoted to literary criticism. The best example is the pair of consecutive *Idlers*, probably the two most famous, in which Johnson sketches out the life of Dick Minim, a critic who achieves eminence merely by mouthing the critical cant of his day. Having retired to Richmond to study the history of literary criticism, Minim returns retailing the best-known bromides extracted from Aristotle and Horace: 'that the chief business of art is to copy nature; that a perfect writer is not to be expected, because genius decays as judgment increases; that the great art is the art of blotting, and that according to the rule of Horace every piece should be kept nine years'. Minim characterizes modern writers in an equally compendious and thoughtless way: 'His opinion was, that Shakespear, committing himself wholly to the impulse of nature, wanted that correctness which learning would have given him', and so on. Some of Minim's opinions and positions are ones that Johnson himself expressed and held throughout his life; Minim's results are acceptable, but he is despicable because he has no method in his science but mere repetition. The absence of method leads sometimes to truths and sometimes to absurdities, such as Minim's discovery of the way sound echoes sense in two couplets of *Hudibras* about the 'glassy bubble' of honour, 'where one part crack'd, the whole does fly.' This line, says Minim, 'is "crack'd" in the middle to express a crack, and then shivers into monosyllables.' In fact, the description of the line is itself wonderful, but it is unfortunately applicable to any number of other lines and merely fantastic as a description of a reader's experience. Minim moves on from fancied associations between sound and sense to fancied physical responses to the verse of Milton. In Milton's description of his blindness Minim comes to feel 'an obscure sensation like that which he fancies would be felt from the sound of darkness'. The absence of method can lead anywhere and inevitably leads to more serious errors. In his final scene Minim is instructing an acolyte who resolves, in the cant of the day, 'to follow his genius, and to think how Milton would have thought', thus combining thoughtlessness with irreverence.[14]

Other cant positions that Johnson attacks in the *Idler* include the denunciation of 'hard words', 'the ravages of time on the ancient world', 'easy' poetry, the need of 'an art of memory', 'the harmonick system of the universe' (recurring to Jenyns), 'the evils of tea' (recurring to Hanway), and even, what he truly believed, the universal ignorance and error of mankind.[15] Though he may always have hated cant, Johnson at fifty demanded thought in writing and in individuals more loudly than ever. In particular he campaigned against thoughtlessness in books and issued warnings about the way in which such thoughtlessness was made more dangerous at the same time that it was revealed by the great increase in publication: 'One of the peculiarities which distinguish the present age is the multiplication of books. . . . It is observed that "a corrupt society has many laws"; I know not whether it is not equally true, that "an ignorant age has many books."' The danger is partly that readers will be unable to sift through the mass of material published to find what is valuable: 'the continual multiplication of books not only distracts choice but disappoints enquiry' and many writers 'claim the name of authors merely to disgrace it, and fill the world with volumes only to bury letters in their own rubbish'.[16] This represents a sentimental wish on Johnson's part for the cozier world of the Renaissance humanists, when less was printed, and the European intellectual world spoke a common, learned language. That was the world he saw himself entering as a late Latin poet-scholar before he went to London to make a living by plying his trade in a vulgar tongue. Yet Johnson avoids the cant of sentimentality, as he does every other sort of automatic thought. Moreover, he makes positive suggestions throughout the *Idler* that give his readers reason to believe he will go on reading and writing.

Just as it did at an earlier stage in his career, biography begins to emerge again in the *Idler* as the genre that Johnson can read and write with the most satisfaction. In *Idler* 84 Johnson describes biography in the most appealing terms and implies that it suits his own stage of intellectual development. He has lost his taste for fiction because he is past 'the time of life when fancy begins to be over-ruled by reason and corrected by experience', and therefore, 'the most artful tale raises little curiosity when it is known to be false.' This wish for truthfulness leads Johnson to recommend autobiography because 'the writer of his own life has at least the first qualification of an historian, the knowledge of the truth. . . . What we collect by conjecture, and by conjecture only can one man judge of another's motives or sentiments, is easily modified by fancy or by desire; as objects imperfectly discerned, take forms from the hope or fear of the beholder.' In Number 102, the last *Idler* before the envoy to the series, Johnson continues to lament that writers so infrequently write their own lives and urges others to do it for them: 'Nothing detains the reader's attention more powerfully than deep involutions of distress or sudden vicissitudes of fortune, and these might be abundantly afforded by memoirs of the sons of literature. They are intangled by contracts which they know not how to fulfill, and obliged to write on subjects which they do not understand. Every publication is a new period of time from which some encrease or declension of fame is to be reckoned. The gradations of a hero's life are from battle to battle, and of an author's from book to book.'[17] Johnson was suffering through just these 'vicissitudes of fortune' when he made this recommendation, and that makes it all the more significant that he could see the writer's life in heroic terms. The passage suggests how Johnson could go on writing with some degree of conviction, despite the fact that he was growing away from many kinds of literature. In particular, there is here an intimation of the spirit that possessed Johnson very late in life, when he could have lived without the money or the fame, to write his most delightful work, the *Lives of the Poets*.

15

Rasselas

Life is not long, and too much of it must not pass in idle deliberation how it shall be spent; deliberation which those who begin it by prudence and continue it with subtilty must after long expence of thought conclude by chance. To prefer one future mode of life to another, upon just reasons, requires faculties which it has not pleased our Creator to give us.

Johnson to Boswell, 21 August 1766

If there are signs in the *Literary Magazine, Adventurer,* and *Idler* that Johnson was growing hostile to fiction, how is it that he wrote *Rasselas,* his most popular work and his longest piece of fiction, in 1759, right in the midst of his work on the *Idler?* Part of the answer is that, like almost everything Johnson composed in English, *Rasselas* was a child of necessity. The work is not unmarked by Johnson's resistance to fiction, but he had to write it. In 1758 Johnson gave up the lease on his house in Gough Square, where he wrote the *Dictionary* and the *Rambler;* he was on the verge of spending several years without a settled place of residence. His household was broken up: Anna Williams was in her own lodgings, where Johnson went regularly for tea, and Frank Barber had enlisted in the navy. Things were not going well, but the crushing financial and psychological blow was the death of Johnson's aged mother in Lichfield in late January 1759. Towards the end, Johnson wrote to his mother, testifying to her goodness and begging her 'forgiveness of all that I have done ill, and all that I have omitted to do well'. Remorse, guilt, and grief are also evident in Johnson's other letters, prayers, and diary entries concerning his mother's death. He had seen so little of her for so many years that the loss was bound to immerse him in childhood feelings and reflections on his behaviour within the family. As part of an entry containing solemn prayers for his departed mother and for his own amendment, Johnson wrote, 'The dream of my Brother I shall remember.' This sounds like a pious admonition, and the dream of his deceased brother Nathaniel must have been frightening. Johnson clearly had a strong sense of duty, but he had never worked through his fierce competitiveness and rebelliousness as a son and brother. Hence he had failed in many filial duties, and he dwelt habitually on his failures when his mother's death engendered a flood of remembrance. This death was not nearly as shocking and debilitating as the death of his wife had been seven years before, but Johnson's mind worked powerfully upon itself in the aftermath. In *Idler* 44, shortly after the sorrowful event, he wishes paradoxically for an 'art of forgetfulness'. Though he does not mention himself in the piece, he was clearly feeling the effects of his own tenacious and punitive memory.[1]

The death of his mother brought Johnson in mind not only of past but also of present duties. There were expenses associated with her death, including the payment of her maid and other creditors. The primary expedient to which Johnson turned was, as usual, a literary project. On 20 January 1759 he wrote to William Strahan, proposing a deal for a small two-volume work to be entitled 'The Choice of Life' or 'The History of ____ Prince of Abissinia'. He suggested several alternative financial arrangements, including outright sale of the copyright for £75 per volume.[2] He said he would withhold his name, 'but expect it to be known'. He closed the letter with a plea, 'Get me the money if you can', meaning he wanted ready cash in advance. The bargain was quickly struck, and soon after his mother's death Johnson set to work. The book appeared in two volumes octavo on 20 April 1759. Although the initial reception was mixed, even among his friends, the work proved to be Johnson's most successful. By the end of the century there were fifty editions, including twenty foreign editions in six languages. Johnson told friends that he composed *Rasselas* in the evenings of one week, sent it off to the printer in pieces, and never read it over. This may be literally true of the composition, but there are many aspects of the work that Johnson had thought about for a long time. His eagerness to talk about the dispatch and carelessness with which he produced *Rasselas* is interesting, however. It suggests that Johnson continued to be impatient with fiction even as he wrote *Rasselas*. Johnson's hostility to the form was not disingenuous, for its ironic persistence in *Rasselas* explains some of the most puzzling features of the work.

Many of the books that supplied Johnson with background material for *Rasselas* were sources he had tapped when writing earlier works with oriental settings, especially *A Voyage to Abyssinia* and *Irene*. Johnson had kept up his interest in the East in his work on the Harleian Library and in his acquisition of books on Eastern languages and travel. He reread Knowles's huge *Historie of the Turkes* for the *Dictionary* and praised it elaborately in the *Rambler*. He chose some books on oriental subjects for review in the *Literary Magazine*, including Alexander Russell's *History of Aleppo*. Johnson used his knowledge of oriental places and customs to write numerous oriental tales in the *Rambler* and several in the *Idler*. All of these are moral fables and, as oriental apologues, they are miniature versions of *Rasselas*, especially

Ramblers 204 and 205, which tell the story of Seged, an oriental monarch who attempts to decree happiness. There are so many precursors of *Rasselas* in the *Rambler* and *Idler* that the editor of the Yale edition writes, 'To an observer of Johnson's entire canon, the conclusion is inescapable: the Great Moralist's work during his most fecund decade displays a repeated manipulation of the literary type which reached its amplest, most complicated flowering in the history of the prince of Abyssinia.' Johnson had gathered the props for nearly a lifetime; he had written small versions of the same kind of work; and he had earlier, especially in the *Rambler,* explored virtually all the particular moral topics that *Rasselas* clothes in oriental garb. Going even more deeply into his acquired literary stock, Johnson certainly drew on his lifelong knowledge of romance literature and his intimate acquaintance with the Bible for both thematic and ornamental purposes. Owen Ruffhead, an early critic, complained with some justice that 'the topics [of *Rasselas*] are grown threadbare.'[3]

With a lifetime of preparation behind him, it is not incredible that Johnson wrote *Rasselas* in the evenings of a single week. Given the speed of composition, the exigencies motivating him, and the extreme familiarity of the material, it is also not surprising that the work contains a vein of irony that undermines the possibility of reading it as a book, like most of its generic ancestors, with a final answer to the enduring questions of human life. What is less obvious is that Johnson wrote the work from the far side of a passion for fiction that had mostly run its course and was never unmixed with criticism. The form of the oriental tale itself had been used so much in Johnson's lifetime that employing it at all was a tacit acknowledgement that the compact between author and reader could include some laughter at the expense of the characters and the rest of the elements of the fiction.[4] On a literary scene with emergent, more realistic forms of fiction, the oriental tale was a self-conscious archaism that implicitly criticized fictionalizing, while demanding that it justify itself on moral and religious terms. Even a relatively unsophisticated work, such as Robert Dodsley's earnest *Oeconomy of Human Life* (1750), is arch about its putative origin in Brahminical sources. Writing later still, Johnson was more ironic about the artificiality of the oriental tale. Johnson referred to *Rasselas* in letters as 'a little story book' and 'my little book', suggesting an attitude toward the story confirmed by the small octavo format and his accounts of its rapid composition.

Johnson's ironic view of the genre manifests itself in various particular ways throughout his 'little book'. He does not subject Prince Rasselas to the humiliations of Lemuel Gulliver, but, like Swift, he is ironic in the presentation of his central character. (Though he has a genuine historical namesake, Rasselas is sometimes merely restless, just as Gulliver is sometimes merely gullible.) For example, in chapter 2 Rasselas observes the natural world and indulges himself in a vision of theodicy with particular attention to man's place in the invisible harmony. Speaking to the animals, he says they need not envy him, 'nor do I, ye gentle beings, envy your felicity; for it is not the felicity of man. . . . surely the equity of providence has ballanced peculiar sufferings with peculiar enjoyments.' This vision resembles the cant of Soame Jenyns more than the physico-theology of writers whom Johnson respected because it is facile and vain. Johnson indicates this, in case we were wondering, right away: 'With observations like these the Prince amused himself as he returned [to the palace], uttering them with a plaintive voice, yet with a look that discovered him to feel some complacence in his own perspicacity, and to receive some solace of the miseries of life, from consciousness of the delicacy with which he felt, and the eloquence with which he bewailed them.'[5] This vain self-congratulation cannot last, and it does not. Moreover, the prince's temporary complacency followed by disappointment sets the pattern for all of Rasselas's endeavours to find happiness. The reader may perceive the pattern early on in the story, but the character himself is ridiculously tardy in learning his lesson.

Irony also attends the other characters in the story, even Imlac, the Vergilian sage who guides Rasselas on his adventure of discovery. In chapter 10, when Imlac is in the midst of telling his life story, he waxes eloquent on the subject of poetry and delivers an oration on the superhuman qualifications of the true poet:

> But the knowledge of nature is only half the task of a poet; he must be acquainted likewise with all the modes of life. His character requires that he estimate the happiness and misery of every condition; observe the power of all the passions in their combinations, and trace the changes of the human mind as they are modified by various institutions and accidental influences of climate or custom. . . . He must divest himself of the prejudices of his age or country; he must consider right and wrong in their abstracted and invariable state; he must disregard present laws and opinions, and rise to general and transcendental truths, which will always be the same. . . . He must write as the interpreter of nature, and the legislator of mankind, and consider himself as presiding over the thoughts and manners of future generations; as a being superiour to time and place.
>
> His labour is not yet at an end: he must know many languages and many sciences.

There are elements of Imlac's dissertation that correspond closely with opinions that Johnson expresses elsewhere, particularly in the Preface to Shakespeare and the life of Milton. But Imlac's speech grossly overstates the case. With their perpetual awareness of the poet in a real, social world, Johnson's later Lives, which express a sensibility Johnson had mostly achieved by 1759, make a mockery of Imlac's exalted vision. However, the reader of Rasselas need only proceed to the succeeding chapter to come down to earth. The narrator begins, 'Imlac now felt the enthusiastic fit, and was proceeding to aggrandize his own profession, when the prince cried out, "Enough! Thou hast convinced me, that no human being can ever be a poet."'[6] Poetry, in this abstract sense, is not limited to verse, and

Johnson is saying, in part, that the story he is presenting to his own readers will not fulfil such high ambitions. No fiction can.

As Johnson describes it in the *Dictionary*, enthusiasm is partly compounded of vanity and delusion, whether it occurs in religious belief or in the serious area of literary performance. Hence, when Johnson calls Imlac's speech the product of an 'enthusiastic fit' he is warning his readers to regard it sceptically. In a sense, each choice of life and each answer to the characters' problems in *Rasselas* is a delusion that is momentarily credited and subsequently found to be deceptive. The credibility of each delusive answer fluctuates in this way because each is associated with a specious discourse containing truths that Johnson elsewhere recommends. This is true even of the 'projector' with his ill-fated plans for an aerial escape from the Happy Valley. He says, speciously, 'He that can swim needs not despair to fly: to swim is to fly in a grosser fluid, and to fly is to swim in a subtler. We are only to proportion our power of resistance to the different density of the matter through which we are to pass. You will be necessarily upborn by the air, if you can renew any impulse upon it, faster than the air can recede from the pressure.'[7] Despite the echoes of Robert Boyle's brilliant work on atmospheric pressure, 'The Spring of the Air', it is easy to predict a sudden collapse for such a windy philosopher, especially after we are told that the completion of the wings takes a full year. His flight, of course, is over in 'an instant'. Imlac's mistake is not much different from the aeronautic projector's because both think of their subjects abstracted from a consideration of the real elements in which we all live. Air is an element with real qualities to which flight must be specifically adapted, and the specific qualities of human lives also require specific adaptations of poetry.

Other good examples of discourses dissociated from real life are the speech of the stoic philosopher in chapter 18 and the cant of the speaker on the 'law of nature' in chapter 22. The stoic 'shewed, with great strength of sentiment, and variety of illustration, that human nature is degraded and debased, when the lower faculties predominate over the higher; that when fancy, the parent of passion, usurps the dominion of the mind, nothing ensues but the natural effect of unlawful government, perturbation and confusion; that she betrays the fortresses of the intellect to rebels, and excites her children to sedition against reason their lawful sovereign.' Rasselas's enthusiastic response heralds disaster. The prince regards the philosopher as a 'superiour being', employing precisely the phrase that Imlac had applied to the poet and indicating to the reader that he is equally incredible. After the satiric collapse of the philosopher's discourse, brought on by his despair over the sudden death of his only daughter, we see Rasselas in one of his least sympathetic moments. Having failed to revive the moralist with his own philosophy, 'The prince, whose humanity would not suffer him to insult misery with reproof, went away convinced of the emptiness of rhetorical sound, and the inefficacy of polished periods and studied sentences.'[8] It is left to the reader to conclude that the philosophy itself, as well as its spokesman, are ill suited to thrive in the real world.

As his answer to the problems of life is even grander and more assured, the talking-society philosopher in chapter 22 is even more obviously foolish. He tells Rasselas,

> The time is already come, when none are wretched but by their own fault. Nothing is more idle, than to enquire after happiness, which nature has kindly placed within our reach. The way to be happy is to live according to nature, in obedience to that universal and unalterable law with which every heart is originally impressed; which is not written on it by precept, but engraven by destiny, not instilled by education, but infused at our nativity. He that lives according to nature will suffer nothing from the delusions of hope, or importunities of desire: he will receive and reject with equability of temper; and act or suffer as the reason of things shall alternately prescribe.

He concludes with 'this simple and intelligible maxim, That deviation from nature is deviation from happiness.' Acting much like Rasselas after his own earlier observations on the perfect organization of nature, the speaker luxuriates in his own sensibility and 'the consciousness of his own beneficence'.[9] This behaviour shows the reader quite clearly how to regard his vain and fanciful answer to the problem of life, and even Rasselas sees that this is a specious performance, altogether out of touch with experience, the only test of truth.

As the commentary in the Yale edition of *Rasselas* shows, the intellectual pedigree even of this transparently delusive speech involves positions that Johnson sometimes recommends and which may be found in writers, like Cicero and Samuel Clarke, whom he admired, cited, and imitated. Like so many other Christian allegories, *Rasselas* sets its readers the task of sifting carefully through the various arguments, and it tests their ability to distinguish falsehood from truth. Yet this activity also is enclosed in irony because the tone of the whole story tells us that fictions do not contain truth any more than untested philosophies of motion and abstract philosophies of morality. The 'asperity of truth', to use Johnson's phrase, is incompatible with specious arguments, even when such arguments are compounded of truths. Johnson makes his tale, as he made all of his works, out of materials gathered in his reading, much of which he had early in life reduced to systems of topics or commonplaces. As early as the *Rambler* a certain weariness with the topics is evident, and *Rasselas* exposes them to a sharper critique by making them all elements of a fiction which is patently false. Johnson's most popular fiction solidifies his impatience with fiction as a part of his impatience with ideas and ideals. *Rasselas* inventories the various ways in which a person might fail to refute Berkeley or any other kind of idealism. Believing that the fiction of *Rasselas* or any other human invention can tell you the secret of life is one mode of such failure.

Moment to moment *Rasselas* is brilliantly written, but Johnson is consistent throughout the tale neither in his attitude towards the various ideas he entertains nor in his method. In the early chapters we are asked to consider choices of life as Rasselas observes them; then we see them embodied only in other characters; later there are debates about choices of life, the most famous of which is the debate on marriage. Debates in *Rasselas* are ironic because, unlike successful dialogues, they tend to show that compromise is impossible. Rasselas, usually more naive than Nekayah, suggests a wise compromise to the question whether an early or a late marriage better conduces to happiness; he receives a wiser rebuke from his sister: 'Flatter not yourself with contrarieties of pleasure. Of the blessings set before you make your choice, and be content. No man can taste the fruits of autumn while he is delighting his scent with the flowers of the spring: no man can, at the same time, fill his cup from the source and from the mouth of the Nile.'[10] Negative wisdom of this kind is more resounding in *Rasselas* than positive recommendations, but even the maxims of ignorance and error may be unreliable in the context of this fiction. Any statement involving the Nile is suspicious because it is a focal point of mystery and error, as Johnson pointed out in his *Voyage to Abyssinia* almost thirty years before writing *Rasselas*. Does a statement so grand and, from the literal point of view, so obvious, really apply to the question at hand? Is it not as foolish to say that there is no middle way as to say that there is?

Other changes in method occur toward the end of *Rasselas*. For a few chapters the plot thickens, and we hear the story of Pekuah's abduction. The visit to the pyramids is the last step in the group's exploration of vain attempts at human happiness. The pyramids are the type of all the other schemes of felicity. Expanding a classical critique of the pyramids, Johnson divests them of their contemporary social meaning and describes them as 'a monument of the insufficiency of human enjoyments' and 'that hunger of imagination which preys incessantly upon life'. The chapter concludes with a final denunciation of the vanity of human wishes: 'Whoever thou art, that, not content with a moderate condition, imaginest happiness in royal magnificence, and dreamest that command or riches can feed the appetite of novelty with perpetual gratifications, survey the pyramids, and confess thy folly!'[11] But there can be no finality in a work that rejects the possibility of finding truth in a work of fiction. The abduction of Pekuah is a rebuke to the satisfactory conclusiveness of the group's findings concerning the pyramids. Now there is real misfortune, not merely a philosophical acknowledgement that life is painful, deceptive, and surprising. Understanding is improved through suffering, but the incident goes nowhere in resolving the dilemmas posed by the book. The kidnapper turns out to be harmless because of his greed, ironically, and Pekuah is restored. Johnson abandons the device of narrative complication and returns to the earlier method of presenting characters who embody conventional answers to the questions of life.

The dominant new character of the final chapters of *Rasselas* is 'a man of learning', a familiar figure in Johnson's writing, akin to the student of

The Vanity of Human Wishes, Pertinax in the *Rambler,* and Johnson himself in the *Dictionary* and Γνῶθι Σεαυτόν. Nekayah responds to the man of learning, the Astronomer, with fresh enthusiasm: '"Surely," said the princess, "this man is happy"', but his story is a rebuke to Rasselas's decision to 'devote himself to science [knowledge], and pass the rest of his days in literary solitude'. Learning is the last earthly accommodation stripped from man in the allegory of Everyman, and the reader of *Rasselas* should expect the end of the book to be near when learning is also found to be deceptive. It is characteristic of *Rasselas* that learning turns out to be another form of fiction. The Astronomer believes that he both observes and controls the sky. Imlac analyses his madness in terms that describe both literary and psychological conditions:

> To indulge the power of fiction, and send imagination out upon the wing, is often the sport of those who delight too much in silent speculation. . . . He who has nothing external that can divert him, must find pleasure in his own thoughts, and must convince himself what he is not; for who is pleased with what he is? . . . the mind . . . feasts on the luscious falsehood whenever she is offended with the bitterness of truth. By degrees the reign of fancy is confirmed; she grows first imperious, and in time despotick. Then fictions begin to operate as realities, false opinions fasten upon the mind, and life passes in dreams of rapture or of anguish.[12]

The passage sounds like a condemnation of reading or theatre-going, as though it were a puritanical commentary on *The Female Quixote* by Charlotte Lennox, a book about a dreamy reader, to which Johnson contributed a chapter. All the discrete discourses, all the answers to life contained in *Rasselas* are as fictional as the Astronomer's imaginary control over the weather. In Johnson's way of thinking there is always a division between reality and our way of conceiving it or describing it. To forget this is madness.

As if to prove conclusively that our conceptions are mere fictions, Johnson proceeds to discuss the nature of the soul, a standard topic of human ignorance. Imlac's discourse focuses on relatively elementary questions concerning the immateriality and longevity of the soul, and he offers modest, orthodox solutions. Material versions of the soul are fictions; God only can destroy it, but human knowledge goes no further: '"That it will not perish by any inherent cause of decay, or principle of corruption, may be shown by philosophy; but philosophy can tell no more. That it will not be annihilated by him that made it, we must humbly learn from a higher authority."'[13] In *Rasselas* as in *The Vision of Theodore,* where philosophy or reason leaves off, religion begins. Henceforth in *Rasselas* fictions are forborne, and accordingly the tale ends. Without saying it directly, the final chapters – the discourse on the soul, the descent into the catacombs, and the intrusion of the old man – all impel the reader to draw an orthodox, pious conclusion: our hopes of happiness should focus on the next world rather than this.

The last chapter of *Rasselas* is subtitled 'The conclusion, in which nothing is concluded'. It begins with another allusion to an age-old mystery: 'It was now the time of the inundation of the Nile.' Like the nature of the soul, the flooding of the Nile is a topic of inevitable human ignorance, and its presence in the last chapter is an indication that nothing said now can be final and certain, despite its appearance at the end of the book. The main characters all form new wishes, and their only acquired wisdom seems to be the knowledge that 'none could be obtained.' Then they resolve to return to Abyssinia, but the fate of this resolve is left open to speculation or a sequel.[14] It is difficult to imagine a conclusion that is more determined to leave the reader in ignorance than this. If the ending says anything at all, it says that fiction is not the answer. The Johnson of the *Literary Magazine* who both decried and profited by growth in the publishing industry is certainly one with the author of *Rasselas*, a book that abjures fictions and fiction itself, while excelling at their creation.

At this stage in his life Johnson was not exactly a Prospero who could afford to break his magic wand and bury it certain fathoms in the sea. Yet *Rasselas* marked the end of his most productive decade, and there are indications in his life story that he turned away from art and focused more on living in the world. Like Imlac and the philosopher, Johnson entered 'the stream of life' and drifted about for a while. After writing *Rasselas*, he made an extended visit to Oxford in 1759, giving up his Staple Inn chambers; he returned to London, taking a flat in Gray's Inn before moving to more permanent though very slovenly quarters near Fleet Street. Frank Barber returned from the navy in 1760 and joined Johnson in this central City location, but the flat was not a scene of domestic regularity. Johnson's friend Charles Burney went there to snatch a relic for the benefit of an admirer but could find nothing to sanctify but bits of a straw broom. Another friend, William Fitzherbert, found the great writer without pen, ink, or paper.[15]

Johnson had not given up writing: the last *Idler* was published in April 1760, and the flow of miscellaneous pieces continued unabated. Johnson certainly still identified himself as a writer, but he was beginning to live more socially, and less than ever an aesthetic or artisanal life of writing. He began to attend meetings of organized benevolent societies, and he became a member of the Society for the Encouragement of Arts, Manufactures, and Commerce. He engaged in a civic debate over the design for a new bridge at Blackfriars, choosing, significantly, the more practical semi-circular over the more pleasing elliptical supports. He took writing commissions for worthy causes, such as the introduction to a report from the Committee for the Relief of French Prisoners of War.[16] At the age of fifty-one Johnson was not about to buy a topknot and start working as a stevedore because he was tired of fictions and weary of commonplaces, but for a while he wrote only casual and largely practical, short pieces of prose. By 1760 Johnson was past his most productive years as a writer and growing into a more public identity as a conversationalist; despite his poverty and his shabby quarters, he was enjoying an established reputation and becoming a participant in society rather than an observer of it.

In his civic identity Johnson expanded his range of interests and became a spokesman not only for writers but for all his fellow artists and artisans. In 1762 he wrote a preface for the Society of Arts Exhibition in which he discusses the exhibition in terms of publication; exhibiting artists, like publishing writers, are 'candidates for public notice' and admittedly 'desirous of praise'. He defends the cost of the exhibition to the public for the frank reason that it will allow 'Many Artists of great abilities . . . to sell their works for their due price'. In some of his other writing of the period Johnson goes even further and defends economic freedom for all. In a piece for the *British Magazine* in 1760, for example, he finds that economic freedom is the principal reason for the bravery of the English common soldiers: 'Whence then is the courage of the English vulgar? It proceeds, in my opinion, from that dissolution of dependance which obliges every man to regard his own character. While every man is fed by his own hands, he has no need of any servile arts: he may always have wages for his labour; and is no less necessary to his employer, than his employer is to him. While he looks for no protection from others, he is naturally roused to be his own protector.' This freedom leads to a certain 'insolence of the populace', but it is well worth the cost. In writing this piece Johnson kept in mind a section of the longest literary work he did at this time: a translation of part of Pierre Brumoy's three-volume history of the Greek theatre, commissioned by Charlotte Lennox. Johnson's Preface to Shakespeare may owe something to Brumoy's discourse on the ephemerality of comedy compared with tragedy, and his piece for the *British Magazine* recalls Brumoy's defense of Aristophanes' acrimony in terms of Greek society: 'the genius of independency naturally produces a satire more keen than delicate, as may be easily observed in most of the inhabitants of islands.'[17]

Still angry about the Seven Years War, Johnson also appreciated Brumoy's praise of the Greek polis, in which 'the poet . . . was not afraid of censuring the government for the obstinate continuance of a ruinous war.' About this time Johnson wrote his introduction to a report by the Committee on French Prisoners, a philanthropic group something like Amnesty International. Johnson hopes that charity to the enemy may 'soften the acrimony of adverse nations, and dispose them to peace and amity'. Johnson took this commission from Thomas Hollis, a republican and a sympathizer of American independence. Although Johnson and Hollis did not agree about everything, they had certain principles in common, including a Lockean belief in individual freedom and a hatred of colonialism. Johnson remained highly critical of Britain's colonial efforts in the Seven Years War even after the battle of Quebec, when opponents of the ministry could no longer complain about the ineffectiveness of the British military. Johnson's politics are evident in his long preface to *The World Displayed,* a collection of travel accounts published in twenty little volumes, less than six by four inches in size, obviously made for portable entertainment. As usual Johnson made sure the readers would take some moral instruction with their amusement. He calls the motivation of many missions 'the infection of enterprise', and he expresses indignation over the treatment of the natives encountered in the tales: 'we are openly told', he writes, 'that they had the less scruple concerning their treatment of the savage people, because they scarcely considered them as distinct from beasts; and indeed the practice of all the *European* nations, and among others of the *English* barbarians that cultivate the southern islands of *America* [the British West Indies] proves, that this opinion, however absurd and foolish, however wicked and injurious, still continues to prevail.' According to Johnson, the advances in navigation chronicled in *The World Displayed* merely gave 'a new world to *European* curiosity and *European* cruelty'.[18]

The one work Johnson performed during these years that belongs to the mainstream of his lifelong literary endeavours is an edition of the works of Roger Ascham. However, this book is weak evidence that Johnson pursued his old literary interests into this non-literary period because it is so perfunctory. Originally proposed in 1758, the work was done for James Bennett, an impecunious schoolteacher to whom the title page grants authorship. The biography is the only part that Johnson really worked at, and even there he limited himself to a single source. Still he praises Ascham highly and delights in contemplating that crucial moment of history on which so much of his own literary life focuses: '*Ascham* entered *Cambridge* at a time when the last great revolution of the intellectual world was filling every academical mind with ardour or anxiety. The destruction of the *Constantinopolitan* empire had driven the *Greeks* with their language into the interiour parts of *Europe*, the art of printing had made the books easily attainable, and *Greek* now began to be taught in *England*. . . . Learning was at that time prosecuted with that eagerness and perseverance which in this age of indifference and dissipation it is not easy to conceive.' Johnson's apology for Ascham is heartfelt. Contemporary writers and artists may have been Johnson's worldly colleagues, but the great scholars of the English Reformation were still his soul's companions: Ascham's 'philological learning would have gained him honour in any country, and among us it may justly call for that reverence which all nations owe to those who first rouse them from ignorance, and kindle among them the light of literature.'[19]

Writing about the impoverished Ascham in January 1762, Johnson may have reflected on his own lack of reward for kindling the light of English literature. In 1759 Edmund Burke, a rising political star, had concluded a review of *Rasselas* with a call for recognition of Johnson's contribution to English culture: he has 'employed a great part of his life in an astonishing work for the fixing the language of this nation; whilst this nation, which admires his works, and profits by them, has done nothing for the author.' Burke's appeal may have been the beginning of a long campaign that ended successfully in July 1762 with Johnson's reception of a lifetime pension of £300 per year. The *Dictionary* was certainly a work for which Johnson could reasonably have expected national recognition. After all, the Preface justly describes the state of the English language as an index of English glory, and the great book redresses an imbalance with rival France in a characteristically English, individualistic way. Christopher Smart was not the only one to praise the Englishness of the *Dictionary* when in 1756 he compared it to St Paul's Cathedral: 'each the work of *one* man, each the work of an Englishman'. A pension for Johnson under George II was unthinkable because Johnson had openly ridiculed the King and his ministers for years. When George III ascended the throne in 1760 Johnson joined in the general optimism surrounding the coronation of a truly English and more intellectual young man. His friends obviously saw that a pension might now be possible, and, in ways that may never be fully known, a concerted effort was made on his behalf. In the end, the King's minister Lord Bute extended the offer through an associate named Wedderbourne, who may have convinced Bute of the political expediency of pensioning an Englishman at a time when he was being criticized for partiality to fellow Scots like David Hume.[20]

Not only had Johnson been openly hostile to George II and doggedly critical of the King's ministry for many years, he had specifically satirized the corrupt use of pensions, most famously in his comment on 'pension' in the *Dictionary*: 'In England it is generally understood to mean pay given to a state hireling for treason to his country.' He also defined 'unpensioned' as 'Not kept in dependence by a pension' and illustrated it with four lines from Pope contrasting the Englishman's freedom with the venality of his French counterpart, Boileau. Undoubtedly Johnson took some pride in being, like Pope, 'Unplac'd, *unpension'd*, no man's heir or slave'. He therefore requested and received from Bute assurance that there were no political strings attached to the pension. Bute evidently repeated twice, 'It is not given you for anything you are to do, but for what you have done.' Once Johnson received this assurance, he took a night to consult with friends and sleep on his decision. The next day, despite the way he knew it would look to some people, Johnson accepted the King's offer. Perhaps it was not without some irony that Johnson had recourse to French in expressing his gratitude; he apparently said, 'I am pénétré with his Majesty's goodness.'[21] Johnson was tired of writing, and the pension gave him the opportunity to glide less anxiously down 'the stream of life', but he also sincerely and justifiably believed that he deserved the recognition and support of the pension.

Once the announcement was made, criticism followed. There were political cartoons, accusations of hypocrisy and inconsistency, and an embittered outcry even from his old friend Thomas Birch who complained that Johnson barely acknowledged the King's title to the throne. Johnson declined to answer these charges. He was conscious of the incongruity

that his attackers lampooned, but he also knew that they were envious and
that they did not deserve reward as much as he. It was midsummer. Johnson
continued to neglect the long-promised edition of Shakespeare and went
on holiday to Devon.

16

Shakespeare

When Shakespeare is demolished your wings will be full summed and I will fly You at Milton; for you are a bird of Prey, but the Bird of Jupiter.
Johnson to Charlotte Lennox as she approached completion of
Shakespear Illustrated, May 1753

As in *Rasselas*, in his subsequent work Johnson was confronted with the problem of reconciling his suspicion of fiction with the obvious fact that his present work might contribute to the falsehood that he deplored. He could have stopped writing in the face of this problem, and it may be one of the reasons, along with financial security, that his production diminished in later years. Writing was so essential to Johnson's civic identity, however, that stopping altogether would have been difficult. Requests came in from friends and publishers; promises had been made and would be made; and projects rising into being would evoke a renovation of hope and eagerness. But Johnson's changing attitude toward fiction affected his choice of projects. Although he set up a small chemical laboratory for himself, Johnson did not start writing useful treatises like those on bleach or distillation that had won his approval in the *Literary Magazine*, but he became increasingly apt to do work with a strong factual component: dictionary work, editorial work, biographical and historical work. The edition of Shakespeare (1765) and its revision (1773), Chambers's Vinerian Law Lectures, the revision of the *Dictionary* (1773), the *Journey to the Western Islands*, and the *Lives of the Poets* are the main works that Johnson composed after 1762. Although he also produced some important political pieces and a slackened but continuous stream of miscellaneous writing, mostly as favours for friends, his overall production was down, and he published very little writing that had a strong imaginative element.

Johnson's only substantial output of fictional works was a package of contributions to Anna Williams's *Miscellanies* (1766), but this included numerous poems that he had written earlier. The best poem in the group is 'The Ant', a paraphrase of Proverbs 6: 6 which he had drafted in 1752. The poem elevates the language of the King James Version into allegory and abstraction in much the same way that *The Vanity of Human Wishes* elevates Juvenal's language; in so doing, it shows in miniature Johnson's characteristic method of rendering received sentiments. Also for the *Miscellanies* Johnson produced a last fable about human wishes. *The Fountains* is a fairy tale. Wishes are granted: beauty, love, riches, wit, fortitude, and long life. They are found inadequate to happiness, and in the end the power of wishing is resigned in favour of a life that accepts 'the course of Nature'.[1] This is an anaemic composition, given the centrality of the myth in all of Johnson's writing, and it is so transparently fictional that it did not arouse in him the conflict between writing and a suspicion of fiction that underlies the ironies of *Rasselas*.

Much of Johnson's late work is literary criticism, and in this genre he reveals a growing uneasiness about the delusive potential of fiction in most writing. To lessen his qualms, Johnson's late literary criticism lays heavy emphasis on the real historical circumstances of the authors under consideration, taking account of their particular aims in writing, realistically including their financial aims. This emphasis excludes abstract, fictional standards of literary excellence, epitomized for Johnson in the strictures of Voltaire on Shakespeare in his *Appel à toutes les nations*.[2] In addition, Johnson values literature for its usefulness to the reader; pleasure is useful, but the paramount kind of use is moral instruction. The important work of fiction must be to inculcate general, moral truths, which have long been known but are often neglected. Finally, because criticism inevitably makes fictions about literary experience, Johnson adopts two procedures to mitigate their potentially delusive effects: he bends his own rhetorical structures more than ever to the task of imitating the literary experience under consideration, and he systematically employs a pattern of overstatement and contradiction as a way of zeroing in on a literary experience without importuning the reader with a competing or additional fiction of his own. Johnson did not perfect these methods until he wrote the *Lives of the Poets* in the late 1770s, but they are all visible in his edition of Shakespeare.

By the time the edition appeared in 1765 Johnson had been working on it, on and off, for twenty years. In 1745 he published his original proposals, consisting mostly of his *Observations on the Tragedy of Macbeth*, a good specimen of the kind of commentary he would provide. In his Preface to Charlotte Lennox's *Shakespear Illustrated* (1753), in his Proposals of 1756, and even in his fairly light piece of occasional verse, the *Drury-Lane Prologue* (1747), Johnson played seriously with key terms that would later appear in his Preface of 1765, particularly the essential word 'nature'. But his most important preliminary work was the *Dictionary*. In the late 1740s Johnson read the complete works of Shakespeare in Warburton's 1747 edition and marked out over 20,000 words, the meanings of which he found well illustrated in their Shakespearian contexts. Johnson says in the Preface to the *Dictionary* that he took 'the diction of common life' from Shakespeare; by arranging it and defining it, Johnson gave us, according to Bertrand Bronson, 'a diffused and unheralded [but] major work of Shakepearian scholarship'.[3] The edition of Shakespeare is not merely a spin-off from the *Dictionary*, but it belongs to the same series of projects on the history of learning – some completed and some only planned – that runs throughout Johnson's life from the proposed edition of Poliziano and the translation of Paolo Sarpi, through the *Harleian Catalogue* and the *Dictionary*, to Shakespeare and the *Lives of the Poets*.

Although Johnson always maintained a private conversation with classical learning, in his published works the trajectory of his drive to produce scholarship akin to that of his classicist idols is largely downward, from classical aspirations to merely English, and from vastly ambitious projects to more narrow achievements. In an important respect, however, especially at the end of his career, Johnson forged an ideal that is different from the one he increasingly failed to realize. Toward the end of his Preface to Shakespeare, Johnson brings his work into comparison with that of the immensely learned editors of the late Renaissance with whom he habitually compared himself, especially Joseph Scaliger. As usual Johnson's work suffers in the comparison, partly because he must work on the relatively new and still living language of English, whereas 'They are employed upon grammatical and settled languages, whose construction contributes so much to perspicuity, that Homer has fewer passages unintelligible than Chaucer.'[4] Nevertheless, Johnson does some of the work of his predecessors; his edition is a kind of variorum, retaining the prefaces and trenchant comments of important earlier editors, sometimes with comments upon them, as well as his own new notes.

In the wealth of his historical and philological information Johnson falls below the scholarly giants he mentions, but in some respects his economy is conscious, and his edition achieves less splendid but equally admirable ends. Johnson even finds support for his restraint in the pronouncements of his heroes. Citing Scaliger, Lipsius, and Pierre-Daniel Huet, he abjures 'conjectural criticism' and resists changing the readings offered by Shakespeare's original editors:

> Conjecture, though it be sometimes unavoidable, I have not wantonly nor licentiously indulged. It has been my settled principle, that the reading of the ancient books [primarily the First Folio, 1623] is probably true, and therefore is not to be disturbed for the sake of elegance, perspicuity, or mere improvement of the sense. For though much credit is not due to the fidelity, nor any to the judgement of the first publishers [Heming and Condell], yet they who had the copy before their eyes were more likely to read it right, than we who read it only by imagination.

Recounting exceptions to his rule and some history of his efforts, Johnson goes on, 'As I practised conjecture more, I learned to trust it less; and after I had printed a few plays, resolved to insert none of my own readings in the text. Upon this caution I now congratulate myself, for every day encreases my doubt of my emendations. Since I have confined my imagination to the margin, it must not be considered as very reprehensible, if I have suffered it to play some freaks in its own dominion. There is no danger in conjecture, if it be proposed as conjecture. . . . If my readings are of little value, they have not been ostentatiously displayed or importunately obtruded.' By the 'margin' Johnson means the foot of the page and the appendix, but the modern figurative meaning of the word makes sense too. Going even further, Johnson calls notes 'necessary evils' and talks about their 'refrigerating' effect on the reader, whose interaction with the text itself matters more than all that learning and scholarship can do.[5] Johnson's desire to present the naked text represents his arrival at a stage in his life when he wished to strip his own literary activity of its 'obtrusive', fictional qualities, or, at least, to confine those qualities to a space clearly marked off as marginal or fictional.

It is difficult to know precisely when Johnson was preparing the notes to his edition and arriving at the conclusions stated in his Preface. He was hard at work in 1757 when he wrote to Charles Burney predicting a March 1758 date of completion. Two volumes were printed by this time, and by 1761 six volumes were printed. The work displays a degree of layering and correction that makes dating it even harder while revealing that Johnson continued to revise previous work right up to the time of publication. Some later notes are wedged in between numbered notes by means of asterisks and obelisks; there is a substantial appendix with still later notes; and there are an unusual number of cancelled pages with authorial changes. Although the whole edition represents the accretion of some twenty years of intermittent work, in some respects the Preface reflects Johnson's state of mind at the particular time that he finally wrote it in 1765. Aspects of his mid-1760s mentality are revealed in anecdotes about Johnson derived from the trip to Devon of 1762. A number of these display Johnson's hardening, though not incurious, attitude toward the imaginary and the fictional.

Joshua Reynolds, Johnson's companion and guide on this trip to the painter's native county, insisted on pointing out the sublime view of Mount Edgcumbe and the sea. As Johnson later told Boswell, he could see that the prospect was noble, but he could not help being conscious of the nearby, though hidden, fleet and dockyards. As James Clifford properly points out, 'Any general ideas of sublimity, he thought, were apt to be undermined by specific ideas of labor and discontent.'[6] The real facts of the place prevented Johnson from yielding himself to the visionary landscape. Johnson also averred on this trip that he would gladly travel to the East Indies if he could witness the miraculous in the form of a trial by fire reported by a friend of his new friend Zachariah Mudge. Johnson insisted on hearing the account from the traveller; this was easier than going to China but a step in that direction; his expression of longing was a wish for firsthand experience of the incredible, without which he could not really believe. The trip to Devon also produced a story about Johnson witnessing the exposure of a Quaker's fiction about his divining rod. Johnson's response on that occasion is comparable to his sober report in the *Gentleman's Magazine* on the non-existence of the ghost said to have haunted Cock Lane in London earlier that year.

Another aspect of Johnson's behaviour reported in stories about the six-week holiday in Devon is his tendency on certain occasions to explosive overstatement. The best example is the story of how Johnson threw himself into a local political debate about whether or not the inhabitants of a new, dockyard town (now Devonport) would be allowed to use an aquaduct that served the established and competing town of Plymouth. Boswell's description of Johnson's behaviour is best: 'Johnson, affecting to entertain the passions of the place, was violent in opposition; and half-laughing at himself for his pretended zeal, where he had no concern, exclaimed, "No, no! I am against the *dockers*; I am a Plymouth-man. Rogues! let them die of thirst. They shall not have a drop!" '[7] Given Boswell's inclination to soften Johnson's extravagances, one ought to wonder whether Johnson half-laughed at himself or not. I would like to believe that he took the opportunity, since his opinion really was irrelevant, to throw himself into the fictional, extravagant identity, allowing his imagination, as it were, to play freaks in the margins. There are other indications of extravagance on the trip: the stories of vast eating, vast tea-drinking (seventeen cups in a row), one of vast drunkenness, and several of verbal excessiveness.

The quality of extravagance also shows up in some of Johnson's writing in the period just prior to the Preface. The close of the 'Life of Collins' (1763) is very pathetic in its presentation of the author's visit to the poet while he was languishing, mad, and near death, in an Islington room, clutching his only book: '"I have but one book," says Collins, "but that is the best."' The dedication for Percy's *Reliques of Ancient English Poetry* (early 1765) is among Johnson's most robust in that mode, and the final paragraph that he contributed to John Kennedy's *Complete System of Astronomical Chronology* (1763) is also overstated, especially if it is true, as Johnson claimed, that he never read the book: 'I have shewn, that the universe bears witness to the inspiration of its historian, by the revolution of its orbs, and the succession of its seasons; *that the stars on their courses fight against incredulity, that the works of God give hourly confirmation to the law, the prophets, and the gospel, of which one day telleth another, and one night certifieth another.*'[8] Exaggeration in this little piece is partly a matter of response to religious 'incredulity'; likewise, in the Preface to Shakespeare overstatement is a way for Johnson to handle his own literary incredulity and, finally, to express the truth of things in a form that is neither impotent nor unfaithful to the mixed, non-fictional, dockyard truth of things.

The Preface is an extravagant performance – exaggerated in its praise of Shakespeare, exaggerated in its condemnation of him and careless about reconciling its praise and blame into a coherent statement. Johnson allows himself to be contradictory, the way proverbial literature is contradictory, preferring statements that express a striking truth combined with others that present different but equally striking points of view. The perception underlying this method is that the welter of literary experience, especially the experience of a writer as various and life-like as Shakespeare, is not reducible to a theory or a coherent set of axioms.

The method of the Preface embodies Johnson's reluctance to form fictions of his own, except where they may evidently be seen as fictions. Correspondingly, the Preface asserts Shakepeare's superiority to fiction: 'This therefore is the praise of Shakespeare, that his drama is the mirrour of life; that he who has mazed his imagination, in following the phantoms which other writers raise up before him, may here be cured of his delirious extasies, by reading human sentiments in human language; by scenes from which a hermit may estimate the transactions of the the world, and a confessor predict the progress of the passions.' The natural quality purely laudable in Shakespeare is his truth to the heterogeneous state of life, his un-fictional, non-formal quality. Johnson's praise of this quality, as his frequent juxtaposition of the reader 'who has mazed his imagination' shows, reveals much about his own changing aesthetic sense. In fact, Johnson provides a sketch of his own aesthetic evolution when he discusses the state of learning in Shakepeare's England in terms of personal development: 'Nations, like individuals, have their infancy' when, precisely like Johnson, they love the romances of *Palmerin* and *Guy of Warwick.* The particular social conditions in which Shakespeare worked forced him sometimes to choose 'that incredibility, by which maturer knowledge is offended'. This 'maturer knowledge' is Johnson's, though he continued to acknowledge and to feel the power of more childish attractions, as he confesses when he declares, 'such is the power of the marvellous even over those who despise it, that every man finds his mind more strongly seized by the tragedies of Shakespeare than of any other writer.'[9]

Johnson's most elaborate demonstration of his attitude toward fiction occurs in his demolition of those old formalist rules of critical evaluation, the three unities. Derived from Aristotle's *Poetics* by Renaissance commentators and refined by the French theatre under the direction of Richelieu, *les trois unités* were supposed to ensure that the work of art would be a credible imitation of life. As Voltaire was merely the latest to have shown, Shakespeare does not even come close to following the rules: his dramatic action sometimes occupies years, whereas the rules limit it to a day, and his scenes sometimes shift thousands of miles, whereas the rules limit them to walking distance. English critics had complained about the unities before and used the example of Shakespeare to show their inadequacy. Even Dryden's *Essay of Dramatic Poesy* (1665), which honours critical rules, harshly criticized their stricter forms. On the other hand, in the blaze of fame surrounding his attack on the unities, it is forgotten that Johnson respectfully invoked them as late as the *Lives of the Poets* and his preface to Thomas Maurice's *Free Translation of the Oedipus Tyrannus of*

Sophocles (1779). The novelty of Johnson's attack and the source of its power is the view it takes of fiction. The underlying assumption of the unities is that the audience under some circumstances may believe the fiction presented on stage. The extreme version of this assumption is what Johnson attacks most vehemently. Anyone who employs the unities as a standard, he says,

> assumes, as an unquestionable principle, a position, which, while his breath is forming it into words, his understanding pronounces to be false. It is false, that any representation is mistaken for reality; that any dramatick fable in its materiality was ever credible, or, for a single moment, was ever credited. . . . Delusion, if delusion be admitted, has no certain limitation; if the spectator can be once persuaded, that his old acquaintance are Alexander and Caesar, that a room illuminated with candles is the plain of Pharsalia, or the bank of Granicus, he is in a state of elevation above the reach of reason, or of truth, and from the heights of empyrean poetry, may despise the circumscriptions of terrestrial nature.

Johnson proposes instead a model of affective criticism in which the reader is less susceptible to fiction, more mature, and equally conscious of the 'marginality' to life of artistic media, whether they consist of live performances or paper and ink: 'Imitations produce pain or pleasure, not because they are mistaken for realities, but because they bring realities to mind. . . . We are agitated in reading the history of Henry the Fifth, yet no man takes his book for the field of Agencourt. . . . A play read, affects the mind like a play acted. It is therefore evident, that the action is not supposed to be real.'[10]

As for Johnson's own fiction about Shakespeare, it takes shape in its infamous contradictory movements between extreme praise and extreme blame, and it is epitomized in its grand metaphors for the experience of Shakespeare. In summing up his first, encomiastic section, Johnson actually tells the reader he has been extreme before employing the predominant metaphor in his performance: 'These observations are to be considered not as unexceptionably constant, but as containing general and predominant truth. Shakespeare's familiar dialogue is affirmed to be smooth and clear, yet not wholly without ruggedness or difficulty; as a country may be eminently fruitful, though it has spots unfit for cultivation: His characters are praised as natural, though their sentiments are sometimes forced, and their actions improbable; as the earth upon the whole is spherical, though its surface is varied with protuberances and cavities.' As in the other grand metaphors of the Preface, Shakespeare is described as part of the natural world but so large a part that he is almost equivalent to the generalized abstraction Nature. This abstraction appears in a molecular form when Johnson contrasts the display of temporary customs in other poets with the exhibition of enduring human qualities in Shakespeare: 'The accidental compositions of heterogeneous modes are dissolved by the chance which combined them; but the uniform simplicity of primitive qualities neither admits increase, nor suffers decay.' Elemental simplicity is less conspicuous in the metaphorical life of the Preface, however, than more sensible comparisons of Shakespeare to the durable materials of visible nature: 'The sand heaped by one flood is scattered by another, but the rock always continues in its place. The stream of time, which is continually washing the dissoluble fabricks of other poets, passes without injury by the adamant of Shakespeare.'[11]

Like Milton, Johnson tried to create a language 'answerable' to his subjects. The grandeur of his language is an important indication of his response to Shakespeare, but so are its alternating pattern of praise and blame and its principal metaphor. The metaphor is most fully articulated in Johnson's defence of Shakespearian tragicomedy

> Shakespeare's plays are not in the rigorous and critical sense either tragedies or comedies, but compositions of a distinct kind; exhibiting the real state of sublunary nature, which partakes of good and evil, joy and sorrow, mingled with endless variety of proportion and innumerable modes of combination; and expressing the course of the world, in which the loss of one is the gain of another; in which, at the same time, the reveller is hasting to his wine, and the mourner burying his friend; in which the malignity of one is sometimes defeated by the frolick of another; and many mischiefs and many benefits are done and hindered without design.

In the next paragraph Johnson calls life 'this chaos of mingled purposes and casualties'. A similar description from the 'Life of Ascham' (1762) suggests that such a vision of things was on Johnson's mind at this time: determining the reasons for a biographical or historical event are difficult, Johnson says, because 'the inquirer having considered interest and policy, is obliged at last to omit more frequent and more active motives of human conduct, caprice, accident, and private affections.'[12] Johnson calls Shakespeare the poet of nature partly because he describes life in its unsorted, inexplicable reality. Metaphorically, he describes Shakespeare as nature, and his response to Shakespeare contains much of the variety and contour of the mixed condition of life: it moves from peaks of enthusiasm to valleys of condemnation, imitating in all its vicissitudes the natural variety of both Shakespeare and the globe.

When he is not creating a language 'answerable' to the experience of reading Shakespeare, Johnson tries to treat his subject as a real person inhabiting real financial, social, and educational circumstances. He simply reprinted Nicholas Rowe's biography of Shakespeare (1709) and so gave up the opportunity fully to entwine his prefatory criticism with biographical considerations, but his sense of the man engaged in literary business is evident in many of his notes throughout all eight volumes of the edition. For example, Johnson sometimes explains difficult or broken passages in Shakespeare by reference to the pressures, accidents, and temptations incident to a life of writing. His practice contrasts both with that of some earlier editors, who blamed rough spots in the text on interpolations of actors or mistakes of transcribers, and with that of romantic critics, like Samuel Taylor Coleridge, who decided a priori that every word in Shakespeare was as correctly placed as the stones in the Great Pyramid. Johnson's Shakespeare is a real writer who makes his own mistakes. For example, in act 5, scene 1, according to the First Folio, Hamlet reflects upon seeing a rustic carelessly toss a skull in the graveyard: 'This might be the pate of a politician, which this ass o'er-offices, one that would circumvent God, might it not?' Johnson remarks, 'In the quarto, for "over-offices" is, "over-reaches", which agrees better with the sentence: it is a strong exaggeration to remark, that an "ass" can "over-reach" him who would once have tried to "circumvent".' But Johnson explains the poorer rather than preferring the superior phraseology: 'I believe both the words were Shakespeare's. An authour in revising his work [from the text represented by the second quarto to the text represented by the First Folio], when his original ideas have faded from his mind, and new observations have produced new sentiments, casily introduces images which have been more newly impressed upon him, without observing their want of congruity to the general texture of his original design.' Similarly, in the very swift forgiveness offered by the King to Bertram in act 5, scene 3 of *All's Well that Ends Well* Johnson finds evidence of Shakespeare's writing habits: 'Shakespeare is now hastening to the end of the play, finds his matter sufficient to fill up his remaining scenes, and therefore, as on other such occasions, contracts his dialogue and precipitates his action. Decency required that Bertram's double crime of cruelty and disobedience, joined likewise with some hypocrisy, should raise more resentment . . . but Shakepeare wanted to conclude his play.' Johnson also explains the death of Falstaff fairly early in *Henry V* as the result of a professional dilemma: 'That he once designed to have brought Falstaff on the scene again, we know from himself; but whether he could contrive no train of adventures suitable to his character, or could match him with no companions likely to quicken his humour, or could open no new vein of pleasantry, and was afraid to continue the same strain lest it should not find the same reception, he has here for ever discarded him, and made haste to dispatch him, perhaps for the same reason for which Addison killed Sir Roger, that no other hand might attempt to exhibit him.' Not content with explaining the literary event in terms of the writer's problem, Johnson draws an admonition from his analysis: 'Let meaner authours learn from this example, that it is dangerous to sell the bear which is yet not hunted, to promise to the publick what they have not written.'[13]

Johnson returns frequently to the image of Shakespeare as a sort of merchant whose stock in trade consists of pieces of writing. Of an unexpected rhyme in *1 Henry VI*, for example, Johnson can only suspect, haplessly, he realizes, that 'this dialogue had been a part of some other poem which was never finished, and that being loath to throw his labour away, he inserted it here.' Other financial aspects of the writer's state also get attention. Remarking on the historically inaccurate praise of Somerset in *3 Henry VI*, for instance, Johnson writes, 'He was afterwards Henry VII. A man who put an end to the civil war of the two houses, but not otherwise remarkable for virtue. Shakespeare knew his trade. Henry VII. was grandfather to Queen Elizabeth, and the king from whom James inherited.'[14]

Such glances at patronage and the old order of literary finances are rare, however, and Johnson usually sees Shakespeare's social circumstances as much like his own. Although the fact that Shakespeare wrote 'what could be pronounced' on stage makes a big difference, Johnson imagines him in other respects to inhabit the imagination of a mid-eighteenth-century writer, focused on publication in printed media and remuneration calculated by the piece of completed work. In act 4, scene 4 of *The Winter's Tale*, Perdita's exclamation concerning the rustic garb of Florizel contains a conventional analogy between literary and biological creation:

> even now I tremble
> To think your father, by some accident
> Should pass this way, as you did: Oh the fates,
> How would he look, to see his work, so noble,
> Vilely bound up!

Johnson interprets the metaphor with too much specificity and brings Shakespeare into his own contemporary world of writing and publishing, hence revealing more about himself than his author: 'It is impossible for any man to rid his mind of his profession. The authourship of Shakespeare has supplied him with a metaphor, which rather than he would lose it, he has put with no great propriety into the mouth of a country maid. Thinking of his own works his mind passed naturally to the binder. I am glad that he has no hint at an editor.'[15] Although he was concerned with the business of producing plays for profit, Shakespeare gave less thought than Johnson to binders, editors, and printed works.

Although he is guilty of anachronism at times, Johnson presents Shakespeare as a real person by considering his professional concerns. He does so too by tracking down his allusions to contemporary issues and events. Shakespeare's fame rests on 'just representations of general nature', the permanent aspects of his works that alone remain after a hundred years have fretted away 'the advantages he might once derive from personal allusions, local customs, or temporary opinions'. Ephemeral effects are not absent in Shakespeare, however, and illuminating them lends the writer added historical reality. For example, in the second scene of *The Merchant of Venice*, 'the Count Palatine' is included in the list of Portia's suitors. Johnson comments, 'I am always inclined to believe, that Shakespeare has more allusions to particular facts and persons than his readers commonly suppose. The count here mentioned was, perhaps, Albertus a Lasco, a Polish Palatine, who visited England in our authour's time, was eagerly caressed, and splendidly entertained, but running into debt, at last stole away, and endeavoured to repair his fortune by enchantment.' To explain other obscure passages Johnson reminds his readers that in Shakespeare's time watches were very uncommon, that South Seas voyages were popular, that rushes were used instead of carpets, or that a traveller's tale was a common after-dinner entertainment. Johnson makes a general statement about his effort to restore the lost historical context of the plays in his comment on an anti-papal argument in *King John*: 'This must have been at the time when it was written, in our struggles with popery, a very captivating scene. So many passages remain in which Shakespeare evidently takes advantage of the facts then recent, and of the passions then in motion, that I cannot but suspect that time has obscured much of his art, and that many allusions yet remain undiscovered which perhaps may be gradually retrieved by succeeding commentators.'[16]

The part of Shakespeare's contemporary culture that Johnson was best prepared to retrieve was his language. To explain difficult words in Shakespeare, without emendation, Johnson brings in usages from many of the sixteenth- and seventeenth-century writers whom he cites in the *Dictionary*: Milton, Davies, Drayton, Donne, Jonson, Boyle, Wotton, Sidney, Peacham, and Hale. But Johnson did not rely on his *Dictionary* reading alone; he adds references from books of old ballads, including Percy's *Reliques*, from the works of Thomas More and Bishop Latimer, and from popular romances like *Guy of Warwick*. Although Johnson indulges his own interest in certain classical and neo-Latin writers, he is more careful than earlier editors, notably Warburton, to focus on English works that Shakespeare might have known. For example, Johnson reprints Warburton's citation of several lines of Juvenal's tenth satire as part of a gloss on Hamlet's phrase 'satirical slave', but he makes only one reference of his own to Juvenal. When he must have a classical allusion, Johnson often traces it to schoolbooks that were available to Shakespeare. For example, when Shakespeare gives Tranio a line from the Roman playwright Terence in *The Taming of the Shrew*, Johnson says, 'Our author had this line from Lilly [who cites it in his Latin grammar], which I mention, that it may not be brought as an argument of his learning.' In a note on *Othello* I.ii.13, which he later softened by means of a cancel, Johnson combats the tendency of Warburton's learned notes to elevate Shakespeare to a platonic world of books and scholars: 'All this learning . . . is, in this place, perhaps in many more, intrusive, ostentatious, and superfluous. There is no ground of supposing, that our author copied or knew the Greek phrase.'[17]

On many other occasions Johnson shows that Shakespeare's language comes not from high classical sources but from utterly non-canonical documents and even from the world of merely oral speech. For instance, on the same page that he prints his one reference to Juvenal, Johnson finds an allusion to the conspirator William Parry's letter of apology to Queen Elizabeth: 'This letter was much read at that time, and the authour doubtless copied it.' On other occasions Johnson explains Shakespeare's language by reference to the Midlands dialect of spoken English that the two shared to the degree that their difference in ages did not interfere. When Dogberry in *Much Ado* admonishes his posse, 'only have a care that your bills be not stolen', Johnson remarks, 'A "bill" is still carried by the watchmen at Lichfield', before going on to more learned explanations: 'it was the old weapon of the English infantry, which, says [Sir William] Temple, "gave the most ghastly and deplorable wounds". It may be called *securis falcata* [a hooked axe].' Purer in its use of Midlands English is Johnson's rumination on the Clown's lines at II.iv.51 of *As You Like It*: 'as all is mortal in nature, so is all nature in love mortal in folly.' Johnson says, 'This expression I do not well understand. In the middle counties, "mortal", from "mort" a great quantity, is used as a particle of amplification; as, "mortal tall", "mortal little". Of this sense I believe Shakespeare takes advantage to produce one of his darling equivocations. Thus the meaning will be, "so is all nature in love, *abounding* in folly.' But the Midlands fellowship of author and editor is most direct in Johnson's understanding of the name Iago calls Roderigo: 'A "quat" in the midland counties is a "pimple". . . . Roderigo is called a "quat" by the same mode of speech, as a low fellow is now termed in low language a "scab".'[18]

In numerous small instances Johnson suggests his sense of the historical Shakespeare plying his craft in a real world of temporary customs, opinions, and phraseology, but he also takes pains to locate the meaning of his poetry on an utterly permanent moral landscape. The ground he tends to diminish, though by no means to eliminate, is the intermediary ground of classical culture. In so doing, Johnson departs from the latest, neo-classical manifestations of humanistic culture in favour of something more profoundly conventional. Even if he did believe that 'the early writers are in possession of nature', to recall Imlac's pronouncements on poetry in *Rasselas*, Johnson did not like to give the impression that Shakespeare read them. Instead Johnson often finds the 'natural' sentiments in Shakespeare available in mottoes and other kinds of traditional wisdom. When the Duchess of Gloucester calls Mowbray a 'caitiff recreant' in act 1, scene 2 of *Richard II*, Johnson glosses the word by connecting 'slave', 'prisoner', and 'scoundrel', and he quotes the same line from the *Greek Anthology* about the dependence of morality on freedom that he had used under 'caitiff' in the *Dictionary* in 1755 and in his essay on epitaphs for the *Gentleman's Magazine* in 1740. Mottoes superadded to *Dictionary* entries on 'sage' and 'boot' also reappear in Johnson's edition of Shakespeare, and there are new ones as well. In *Coriolanus*, for instance, which is one of the most learnedly annotated plays, the protagonist says, 'Lest I surcease to honour mine own truth', and Johnson comments with a quotation from Pythagoras: πάντων δέ μαλις[τα] αἰσχύνεο σαῦτον ('you should feel shame most of all when alone').[19] Despite appearances to the contrary, Johnson is not connecting Shakespeare with the ancients. Rather, he is responding on his own terms to Shakespeare's meaning, filling it out, and reinforcing it. Because Johnson's literary resources were classical, this activity is sometimes identical in appearance, and perhaps in effect, to the adduction of classical 'sources' or 'parallels', but the difference of intention is still appreciable.

A reference to Pythagoras or the *Greek Anthology* is a shorthand expression of a permanent, Johnsonian truth, but Johnson more often writes these out longhand, thus avoiding altogether the middle ground of earlier literature in his depiction of Shakespeare as the poet of nature. Much more frequently than they do in the *Dictionary*, explanatory comments in the edition of Shakespeare blossom into the complete moral sentences of the *Rambler* and explicitly suggest the central myths of all of Johnson's writing. For example, Johnson draws his reader's attention to the song at *Cymbeline* IV.ii.269, 'Both the scepter, learning, physic, must / All follow this, and come to dust.' He had adduced it in the *Dictionary* under 'dust' to fairly obvious effect, but in the edition of Shakespeare he explicitly states the high moral import of the song: 'The poet's sentiment seems to have been this. All human excellence is equally subject to the stroke of death: neither the power of kings, nor the science of scholars, nor the art of those whose immediate study is the prolongation of life, can protect them from the final destiny of man.' Inevitable death is the topic again in Johnson's explication of Hotspur's famous speech ending 'time . . . Must have a stop' (*1 Henry IV* v.iv.82): 'Hotspur in his last moments endeavours to console himself. The glory of the Prince "wounds his thoughts", but "thought", being "dependent on life", must cease with it, and will soon be at an end. "Life", on which "thought" depends, is itself of no great value, being the "fool" and sport of "time"; of "time" which, with all its dominion over sublunary things, "must" itself at last "be stopped".' Johnson is paraphrasing, of course, but not merely so; he is also accommodating Shakespeare to his own rhetorical world, a place of timeless moral truths. His process of accommodation is more clearly visible in his explanation of a consolatory speech in *Measure for Measure*, beginning 'Thou hast nor youth, nor age' (III.i.32): 'This is exquisitely imagined. When we are young we busy ourselves in forming schemes for succeeding time, and miss the gratifications that are before us; when we are old we amuse the languour of age with the recollection of youthful pleasures or performances; so that our life, of which no part is filled with the business of the present time, resembles our dreams after dinner.'[20]

For the most part, the nature that Johnson finds in Shakespeare and explicates in the language of the *Rambler* consists of performances on a round of topics heavily treated throughout Johnson's own writing. To give one example of a famous topic, Johnson glosses Hamlet's remark 'to know a man well, were to know himself' by underlining the maxim, know thyself: ' ". . . no man can completely know another, but by knowing himself", which is the utmost extent of human wisdom.' Some of the topics in Johnson's Shakespeare are less conventional than this, but they are all compatible with Johnson's ethical world. It is not surprising, for example, that Johnson's gloss on 'perchance to dream' in Hamlet's most famous soliloquy gives full scope to the possibility of eternal punishment: 'If "to

die", were "to sleep, no more, and by a sleep to end" the miseries of our
nature, such a sleep were "devoutly to be wished"; but if "to sleep" in
death, be "to dream", to retain our powers of sensibility, we must pause
to consider, "in that sleep of death what dreams may come". . . . This fear
it is that gives efficacy to conscience, which, by turning the mind upon
"this regard", chills the ardour of "resolution", checks the vigour of "enterprise", and makes the "current" of desire stagnate in inactivity.' Other
passages that Johnson carefully explicates focus predictably on patterns
of guilt and sorrow which Johnson believed universal but which he also
experienced as conspicuous elements of his own inner life. As one final
example of Johnson finding a familiar, personal as well as general nature
in Shakespeare, consider *Much Ado about Nothing* I.iii.11–13 and Johnson's
comment:

> Don John. I cannot hide what I am: I must be sad when I have cause, and
> smile at no man's jests; eat when I have stomach, and wait for no man's
> leisure.

> This is one of our authour's natural touches. An envious and unsocial mind,
> too proud to give pleasure, and too sullen to receive it, always endeavours
> to hide its malignity from the world and from itself, under the plainness of
> simple honesty, or the dignity of haughty independence.[21]

There are places in his edition of Shakespeare where Johnson seems
merely moralistic; several of these involve the representation of women.
He complains about Juliet's impious jests, for example, and wonders if
'Shakespeare meant to punish her hypocrisy'. He also finds Desdemona
surprisingly culpable. When Iago says, 'She did deceive her father'
(III.iii.210), Johnson comments:

> This and the following argument of Iago ought to be deeply impressed on
> every reader. Deceit and falsehood, whatever conveniences they may for a
> time promise or produce, are, in the sum of life, obstacles to happiness.
> Those who profit by the cheat, distrust the deceiver, and the act by which
> kindness was sought, puts an end to confidence. The same objection may be
> made with a lower degree of strength against the imprudent generosity of
> disproportionate marriages. When the first heat of passion is over, it is easily
> succeeded by suspicion, that the same violence of inclination which caused
> one irregularity, may stimulate to another; and those who have shewn, that
> their passions are too powerful for their prudence, will, with very slight
> appearances against them, be censured, as not very likely to restrain them
> by their virtue.[22]

Such pedagogical moralizing is rare; more often Johnson openly acknowledges his own participation in the general, fallible human nature he
describes. It is significant, however, that several of these rarer pronouncements concern the behaviour of women.

One area in which Johnson readily acknowledges his fallibility is editing. He is hard on Warburton, but many of the cancelled leaves contain remarks on the Bishop that Johnson evidently found too severe upon reflection. Moreover, the lesson of humility that he draws from his editorial labours is general:

> I know not why our editors should, with such implacable anger, persecute their predecessors. Οἱ νεκροὶ μὴ δάκνουσιν, the dead it is true can make no resistance, they may be attacked with great security; but since they can neither feel nor mend, the safety of mauling them seems greater than the pleasure; nor perhaps would it much beseem us to remember, amidst our triumphs over the 'nonsensical' and the 'senseless', that we likewise are men; that *debemur morti*, and as Swift observes to Burnet, shall soon be among the dead ourselves.[23]

Ars longa, vita brevis. It is the oldest truth, but it is an important element of Johnson's honesty and his charm that he usually makes the first application of such truths to himself and his own activities.

17

Lectures on the English Law

The world is not to be despised but as it is compared with something better. Company is in itself better than solitude and pleasure better than indolence. Ex nihilo nihil fit, says the moral as well as the natural philosopher. By doing nothing and by knowing nothing no power of doing good can be obtained. He must mingle with the world that desires to be useful.

Johnson to Mrs Thrale, 21 June 1775

Johnson was thinking partly of himself when he praised Shakespeare's natural depiction of 'an envious and unsocial mind, too proud to give pleasure, and too sullen to receive it', but it was a self of an earlier date, one from which he was increasingly distancing himself, especially after the pension was conferred in 1762. He could still feel 'the dignity of haughty independence', but he was accepting a greater degree of dependence and enjoying in return greater social pleasure. The movement of his life was outward, into the social as well as the natural landscape. When he finished his edition of Shakespeare he wrote to Joseph Warton, declaring himself 'pleased that the publick has no farther claim upon me'. Free from the requirement of solitary endeavour to please the public, Johnson could lead a more social life. The trip to Devon cemented his friendship with Reynolds; he spent some time in Lincolnshire with Bennet Langton and his family; and he passed most of the summer of 1765 in Northampton-shire with Thomas Percy. In 1764 the famous Club was formed, engaging Johnson regularly to dine with numerous interesting, socially and intellec-tually challenging men, including Edmund Burke, Oliver Goldsmith, and Joshua Reynolds. Gradually the company expanded from its original nine to twenty in 1773 and to thirty-five in 1780. Over the years it included such notables as Garrick, Adam Smith, Sir William Jones, Gibbon, Sheridan, and Charles Burney.[1]

More important than his club life or his summer excursions, however, was the beginning in 1765 of Johnson's friendship with the Thrales, a prosperous, well-educated family, living very comfortably on the proceeds of the brewery left to Henry by his father in 1758. Johnson spent so much time in the 1770s at the Thrale estate in nearby Streatham that young Fanny Burney considered it his residence, although she noted that he retained his London apartment. Arthur Murphy, a close friend, editor, and biographer said that Johnson's intimacy with the Thrales 'contributed more than any thing else to exempt him from the solicitudes of life'. Johnson himself called Streatham 'home' beginning at least as early as 1767.[2]

In the years of social expansiveness following the pension Johnson also struck up the most famous, although not the closest, friendship of his life. On 16 May 1763 in Tom Davies's bookshop he met James Boswell, who that very evening began compiling notes on Johnson's appearance, behaviour, and, most of all, his conversation. Although Boswell's contact with Johnson was intermittent, his notes were full, and they enabled him to construct one of the most compelling and best-loved biographies ever written about anyone. Although it has helped to make Johnson one of the two or three best-known figures in English literature, Boswell's brilliant creation has also eclipsed certain aspects of Johnson, especially his writings. Johnson's conversation, as Boswell recorded it, is still better known than his own writing, although Johnsonian scholarship in this century has worked hard to redress that imbalance of attention. Scholarship has also revealed the extent to which Boswell's Johnson is a literary creation based on an incomplete experience of the man and a wish to portray him in a way that satisfied certain personal longings of the biographer. The Hercules of Toryism, the Jacobite royalist, the inflexible moralist, and the dictatorial Great Cham of literature in whom Boswell delights are approximations and caricatures of the real Samuel Johnson. Johnson is not the 'grand composition' that Boswell dubbed him in the dedication of the *Life*. On the other hand, much of what we know about Johnson is due to Boswell's relentless, if inevitably tinctured, observations and investigations of his hero, and it would be a mistake to discard his view altogether in an attempt to draw an accurate picture of the historical man.

One element of Boswell's nominal Johnson fell into place just before the publication of his Shakespeare in 1765 when Trinity College, Dublin, conferred on Johnson the degree of Doctor of Laws. John Hawkins maintained in his biography of Johnson that he was disrespectful of this honour and disliked being called 'Doctor' until Oxford granted him a similar degree ten years later. Boswell began calling Johnson 'Doctor' before the Oxford degree, and at some point Johnson ceased objecting to its use by friends and acquaintances. However, Boswell correctly reports that, even after he received the degree from Oxford, Johnson 'never . . . assumed his title of *Doctor*, but called himself *Mr Johnson*'. Only a couple of petty exceptions to this have been noted. He is merely 'Samuel Johnson' on the title page of his last major work, the *Lives of the Poets* (1779–81), which suggests that he recognized the artificial puffery of the laureate initials appended to his name on the title pages of the *Dictionary* and Shakespeare. Johnson used the title of 'Doctor' for academics and clerics, but he thought of himself as neither. Although he once had higher aspirations, Johnson considered himself and most other contemporary writers as unordained inhabitants of the real world working at a particular trade. Although they were redolent of venerable, medieval Salamancan or Palatine orders, the honorific titles had become ludicrously debased in Johnson's view. For example, he scoffs at the inappropriate application of the title of 'Doctor' a couple of times in the *Lives of the Poets*. He is particularly scornful of the 'man originally a comb-maker, but then known by the style of Doctor' who edited the third edition of Lyttelton's already scrupulously copy-edited history of Henry II of France: 'Something uncommon was probably expected, and something uncommon was at last done; for to the Doctor's edition is appended, what the world had hardly seen before, a list of errors in nineteen pages.' In his admiring life of Watts, Johnson said of this pious man's degree, 'Academical honours would have more value if they were always bestowed with equal judgment.'[3] It was thus partly humility and partly pride that impelled Johnson to forbear the famous title – partly his sense that he was a modern writer in a modern age and partly his lingering connection to a much older, nobler age of scholarship.

Johnson's letter to Dr Leland of Trinity College, Dublin, written in the vulgar language, unlike his Latin letter of thanks to Oxford for the A.M., acknowledges the honorary law degree in perfunctory, if not disdainful terms. On the other hand, although it may be merely coincidental, Johnson threw himself into the study of law at just this time, as though he were trying to justify the honour that had been conferred, or perhaps to take advantage of the title. On 26 September 1765 Johnson composed a prayer entitled 'Before the Study of Law': 'Almighty God, the Giver of wisdom . . . enable me, if it be thy will, to attain such knowledge as may qualify me to direct the doubtful, and instruct the ignorant, to prevent wrongs, and terminate contentions.' Two months later Johnson wrote a similar prayer entitled 'Engaging in Politicks with H—N'. William Gerard Hamilton, a Member of Parliament for whom Johnson may earlier have dictated a speech, was at this time looking for a successor to Edmund Burke, who had served as his aide for six years before rising to more illustrious public service. Johnson may have filled the post with a view to promotion later on, but the evidence of his work for Hamilton is sketchy. The only composition attributable to Johnson's engagement with Hamilton is 'Considerations on Corn', in which he advocates the legal status quo, including the 'bounty' (a form of price support) and excluding an intrusive governmental embargo. A more important immediate beneficiary of Johnson's legal studies was Robert Chambers, a lawyer whom Johnson visited frequently in Oxford from the mid-1750s until 1774, when Chambers joined the Supreme Court of Judicature in Bengal, India. Johnson's friendship with Chambers was longer and probably closer than his friendship with the less scholarly Boswell. Chambers was also, during this period of Johnson's social expansion, the centre of his Oxford society, and many of Chambers's University College colleagues became members of Johnson's circle. These included Herbert Croft, who contributed the biography of Edward Young to Johnson's *Lives of the Poets*, his good friend William Windham, and Europe's first great Sanskrit scholar, William Jones.[4]

In 1766 at the age of twenty-nine Chambers was accorded the daunting honour of succeeding William Blackstone, Britain's most influential legal scholar, to the recently established Vinerian professorship in English law. Constitutionally slow to write, Chambers faced both academic disgrace and substantial financial penalties for failure to produce the required sixty lectures per year. He actually incurred these penalties for 1766, and in October of that year, when his work on Shakespeare was finally published, Johnson went to his aid; he stayed in Oxford for a month to work with Chambers and prevent further embarrassment. The collaboration continued throughout the next half-year, with Chambers in London during most of the last month before the new deadline of 17 March 1767 and Johnson going to Oxford to be 'backstage' for the first few performances. In the winter of 1768–9, with the full sixty lectures still incomplete, Johnson spent two months with Chambers in Oxford, though his visit was prolonged by illness. The collaborative work probably came to an end no sooner than spring 1769, and may have lasted until the series of lectures was completed in the summer of 1770. Although it is difficult to say precisely what Johnson contributed, letters to Chambers and a few diary notes indicate that he was involved in the project in some way or other from start to finish. Judging by the prose style of the lectures, it appears that Johnson took a stronger hand in the theoretical and historical sections, in the introductory and concluding paragraphs of discrete sections and lectures, and in the overall logic and organization of the work, while depending upon Chambers for most of the particular knowledge of legal matters.[5]

Johnson undoubtedly learned some law in the 1760s; the effects of legal study are visible in his later political writings, in the briefs he dictated for Boswell, and in his recorded conversation. For the most part, however, Johnson's legal statements are more general than particular, and they are mingled with humanistic interests and intellectual predilections that were already integral to his way of thinking. The relatively small presence of legal particulars in Johnson's later writing is most readily assessed in his 1773 edition of the *Dictionary*. This was a major revision; Johnson made thousands of changes, and he used previously untapped literary sources, but he did not use much of the material employed in the Vinerian Law Lectures. Despite the wide range of legal sources quoted throughout the voluminous lectures, John Cowell's *Interpreter* (enlarged edition, 1727) remains far and away the main source of legal definitions in the revised edition of the *Dictionary*. Although the works of Edward Coke, for example, are cited on almost every page of the Lectures and there is very particular attention to Coke's *Commentary on Littleton*, there seems to be only one more quotation of Coke in the fourth edition of the *Dictionary* than in the first. The Lectures speak of Coke's *Commentary* as 'a work in which the student will find a great deal of sound legal learning thrown together with little method and much pedantry, but yet a work to which we may fairly apply the inscription of Apollodorus the painter on one of his performances, Μωμήσεταί τις μᾶλλον ἤ μιμήσεται. – "It will be easier to ridicule than to rival."' This sounds like Johnson; it is the kind of critical formula that he had at his fingertips, and he adapted it to the metaphysical school of poetry in his life of Cowley. But all that he adds to his *Dictionary* from Coke is an illustration of the legal sense of 'spinster'('a girl or maiden woman'): 'If a gentlewoman be termed *spinster*, she may abate the writ.'[6] Bracton, equally prominent in the Lectures, is equally rare in the *Dictionary*, appearing perhaps only under 'eyre' in both editions. Other sources of legal illustration seem to remain about constant between the editions: Thomas Blount (see 'esquire', 'barrister'), John Manwood (see 'thicket'), and Richard Hooker (*passim*), for example.

The fourth edition of the *Dictionary* also reflects little of the Lectures in its definitions and etymologies. Johnson did make a significant change in his etymological entry on 'captain'; providing a Latin derivative learned in his work on part 1, lecture 1, 'Of the Origin and Different Forms of Parliament': 'Those who held [lands] *in capite* or in chief, that is immediately under the king, were in the feudal law called *capitanei*, and as their tenure obliged them to serve the king in his wars with a certain number of followers or soldiers, the term which originally was applied only to a certain mode of tenure, acquired in time a signification wholly military, and he who leads a body of men in war is over a great part of Europe still called capitaneus (or captain) with the difference only of different terminations.'[7] But this sort of correspondence is rare. In most cases Johnson did not change his treatment of legal terminology when he revised the *Dictionary*. There are no changes in the entries on such words as 'headborough', 'tithingman', 'gavelkind', 'court', 'adjournment', and 'parliament', despite their special treatment in the Lectures. The fact that the Lectures exert so little influence on the *Dictionary* of 1773 suggests that the specialized knowledge of law in the Vinerian Lectures was not Johnson's province in the collaboration with Chambers. His studies in the English law necessarily engaged him in particulars, but what attracted him and stayed with him was mostly of a general nature.

Despite the fact that the Lectures engaged Johnson in a field that mattered deeply to him, his legal and political views are not clearly visible in them. Johnson concealed his part in writing the Lectures. Accordingly there are few if any expressions of personality or his personal point of view even on subjects that roused him to step out of his official character and speak *in propria persona* in equally public works, such as the *Dictionary* and the edition of Shakespeare. The excise is not described as a 'hateful tax', as it still was in the *Dictionary* of 1773, nor does discussion of the standing army arouse feelings about the 'barren talk of a brutal soldier', which he expressed in his notes on *1 Henry IV*.[8]

One observation that Johnson makes in both the edition of Shakespeare and the Lectures nicely shows the difference between the Lectures and Johnson's own performances, with respect to both personal expression and legal accuracy. In *3 Henry VI* Clarence alludes to the fact that the king has 'bestow'd the heir' of a rich estate on his 'new wife's son' (IV.i.56). Johnson comments, 'It must be remembered, that till the Restoration the heiresses of great estates were in the wardship of the king, who in their minority gave them up to plunder, and afterwards matched them to his favourites. I know not when liberty gained more than by the abolition of the Court of Wards.' The Vinerian Lectures present more detailed information on this law: 'And if the *heir female* of lands thus holden were unmarried and under fourteen at her ancestor's death the lord was guardian till she arrived at that age. And also by the Statute of Westminster II, c. 22, if the lord once got the wardship of her by the death of her ancestor before she was fourteen, he had a right to keep her in wardship till she were sixteen to tender convenable (i.e. suitable) marriage to her.... But this sort of guardianship being a kind of servile institution introduced among the Gothic nations to breed their youth to arms [male wards had to be instructed in chivalry]; it was deemed a great burden, and therefore is now abolished by the 12 Car. 2, c. 24.'[9] According to this information, Johnson was wrong on two counts in his note on *3 Henry VI*; it was twelve years after the Restoration that the law was abolished, and it was long in the domain of Chancery, not the Court of Wards and Liveries, which was not established until the thirty-second year of the reign of Henry VIII for the specific purposes that Johnson deplores. The edition of Shakespeare is more explicit emotionally and politically but not as accurate legally; nor did Johnson make any changes when he revised his Shakespeare in 1773. The details of legal precedent did not stay with him, but his sense of the fairness and the effects of the law did. Moreover, he could express this sense in his own works as he mostly dared not in his collaboration with Chambers.

Nevertheless, there are rare instances when the text of the Lectures behaves like the *Dictionary* in pausing awhile for moral admonition. For instance, having discussed the formerly crucial office of the coroner, the Lectures add, somewhat gratuitously, 'it may be justly feared that the laxity of principles lately introduced amongst us has produced much business for the coroner by making the dreadful act of self-murder more commonly perpetrated.'[10] In the *Dictionary* Johnson defines suicide as 'the horrid crime of destroying one's self', and in the illustration from *Clarissa* suicide is referred to as 'the most dreadful of all deaths'. The sentiment in the *Dictionary* and the Lectures is the same, and its expression is gratuitous in both cases.

Like their moral viewpoint, the political outlook of the Lectures is also occasionally discernible, and at moments Johnson's contribution to it seems apparent. Although they say nothing explicitly partisan, the Lectures stress the central position of the king in English law, and the interregnum is remarked with horror. The conventional rule of three (king, lords, and commons) is the model for government, and 'rebellions and civil wars are the greatest evils that can happen to a people.' Conventional social institutions are also prized, and the effects of rebellion on them is dreaded: 'Between the murder of King Charles the First and the Restoration, passed an interval in which many political experiments were made and as all reverence of ancient establishment was lost, the law was thrown open to the capricious innovations sometimes of enthusiasm and sometimes of licentiousness. . . . Among the freaks of those wild reformers was a law by which the office of celebrating marriage was transferred from the clergy to the civil magistrate.'[11] There follows a reference to Edmund Calamy (the younger), a figure well outside the circle of legal writers usually cited in the Lectures but whom Johnson knew well and had quoted in the *Dictionary*, despite his Nonconformist position. It is likely that Johnson, who was coming more and more to favour a strong king, put some of himself into this passage. Such criticism of the Protestant reformers of the interregnum is frequent throughout Johnson's work, no matter what his primary subject. His criticism of their legal innovation in the Vinerian Lectures, assuming he designed it, parallels his critique of their spelling innovations in his 'Grammar of the English Tongue'.

The political outlook taken by the Lectures, however, is hardly special to Johnson; it is conservative but neither extreme nor much particularized. Where Johnson may have made a stronger and more individual contribution to the Lectures is in its hallmark attention to the historical background of English legal institutions and English laws. Johnson's voice is most audible in the many passages that draw the reader (or auditor) to a careful examination of history, especially those passages that warn about the danger of determining confidently on the basis of insufficient historical evidence. The number of such passages is striking, especially in the earlier lectures, and it seems likely that these warnings about the nature of historical inquiry and perhaps the whole emphasis of the Lectures on strict inquiry, beginning with a strict inquiry into the history of law, is Johnson's most important contribution. This emphasis is very much a continuation of Johnson's contemporary concern with the fictions of intellectual writing and of his lifelong attention to matters of evidence. The following passage from the Lectures recalls Johnson's concerns in the Preface to *A Voyage to Abyssinia*, the review of the Duchess of Marlborough's *Memoirs*, the Harleian projects, the *Literary Magazine*, and edition of Shakespeare: 'In surveying the confusion of remote and obscure ages, we must be often content with slight hints and uncertain conjectures; and great care is to be taken that no man too hastily improve hints into systems, or imagine himself to know what he only guesses. Of the small information that laws and histories afford us, the dubiousness and darkness are sufficiently proved by remarking that they have been advanced in defence of opposite opinions, and that those who write in contradiction to each other can make a specious use of the same authority.'[12]

Such considerations cast doubt on the myth of an unbroken Saxon heritage of limited monarchy, and this has monarchical political implications, just as Johnson's accent on the 'Teutonick' roots of English in the *Dictionary* carried broad republican implications. But the politics of the passage are less direct and less important than the pedagogical point about responsible inquiry. The Lectures honour a strong king in their description of the various legal estates; they also focus much more on the institutional aspects of society and much less on personal and natural rights than their predecessor, William Blackstone's First Vinerian Lectures. Chambers's Lectures certainly did not appeal to the American founding fathers as did Blackstone's more constitutionally oriented *Commentaries*. Read against Blackstone, Chambers–Johnson is monarchical, at least in the sense that it stresses the necessity of government instead of the rights that government was instituted to protect. Yet, the Lectures do not often sound tendentious, and the warnings about the nature of history have their own separate validity. In many cases, the Lectures ask auditors both to withhold extravagant interpretation and to add historical context to their consideration of events of the past. There is a correction of Blackstone's politics implicit in such caution, but Johnson and Chambers may be looking for a niche in an already powerful tradition of lectures rather than attempting a political correction. Moreover, Blackstone was far from revolutionary; he explicitly opposed revolution; granted a strong king in his description of government; and, while agreeing with Locke's natural rights arguments in the abstract, specifically limited the possibility of applying them in reality.

Blackstone's most egregious flaw was occasional haste in his description of legal history. Although he genuflected to the darkness of distant times, for example, he was willing to refer to Parliamentary meetings as 'coeval with the kingdom itself'. Chambers Johnson is more careful. In discussing Magna Charta and whether or not it ensured cities and boroughs 'a right to send representatives to the Great Council', for example, the Lectures find the document inconclusive and warn against judging by the mere appearance of the matter in a very pedagogical manner:

It may not be improper in this place to caution young enquirers into the origin of government, against too great confidence in systematical writers or modern historians, of whom it may justly be suspected that they often deceive themselves and their readers when they attempt to explain by reason that which happened by chance, when they search for profound policy and subtle refinement in temporary expedients, capricious propositions, and stipulations offered with violence and admitted by compulsion and therefore broken and disregarded when that violence ceased by which they were enforced.

The passage is highly reminiscent of Johnson's remark in his 'Life of Ascham' when he gives up his inquiry into his Protestant subject's continued preferment under Queen Mary because it is lost in the inexplicable 'motives of human conduct, caprice, accident, and private affections'.[13]

The Lectures go on to advocate an awareness of the real social circumstances of Magna Charta and the meetings of the Great Council it occasioned:

> Our political historians too often forget the state of the age they are endeavouring to describe, an age of tyranny darkness and violence, in which perhaps few of the barons to whom the contrivance of this wonderful system of government is ascribed, were able to sign their names to their own treaties, and in which therefore there could be little foresight of the future because there was little knowledge of the past. When they thought themselves oppressed by the regal power, they endeavoured to set themselves free as a horse unbroken shakes off his rider; but when they had obtained a present relief, they went back to their castles and their tenants and contrived little for themselves and nothing for posterity.[14]

So much for the glorious myth of Magna Charta and its philosophical framers as the progenitors of modern political liberty.

Pedagogical warnings about tendentious historiography are more prominent in the Lectures than insinuations that a democratic imbalance in recent Parliamentary histories needs to be redressed. In discussing the history of the House of Commons the Lectures recognize the political sensitivity of the historical issue mainly in order to defuse it: 'Whether they had or had not a seat from the earliest ages in our legislative assemblies, is a question once agitated with so much ardour that it became a kind of test by which principles were tried, and every man was considered as a flatterer of despotism or friend of liberty, as he held one opinion or the other.'[15] The Lectures conclude that we have advanced beyond that state, and it is possible to acknowledge the late entry of the Commons into government without incurring an imputation of excessive monarchism. With some reservations, in view of the contrast with Blackstone, the lecturers should here be taken at their word.

The analysis of social history in the Lectures sounds most Johnsonian when it deviates not into politics but rather into a discussion of truths deriving from human nature and therefore visible in human institutions at all times and in all places. A passage on the origination of the Privy Council surveys mankind from China to Peru: 'The impossibility of conducting great affairs and adjusting the different motions of government, otherwise than by the united power of associated understandings, is so generally confessed that the despotic monarchs of the East are always surrounded by their viziers, and assemble their divans for frequent consultation. And the wild rovers of the American continent who pass the common course of their lives in the fishery or chase, almost without intercommunity of intelligence, yet call their old men, and their chiefs together, when there is fear of common danger or prospect of common advantage.' This is almost the 'pure wine' of the *Rambler*, as is the definitive opening sentence of the lecture 'Of Civil Rank, Order, and Precedence': 'Political society is that state of man in which some govern and others are governed; it therefore necessarily implies subordination, and ranks those of which it is composed in different degrees.'[16]

Johnson probably wrote or dictated such set pieces of philosophical definition to help organize and point Chambers's discussion of the intricacies of English law. Johnson may have acted first to get the tardy Chambers going on the right track, but Chambers was free to alter what he received from Johnson; it was certainly his task to fill in the material required by the 'outline' Johnson had given him. In order to do his part well Johnson had to learn some law, but he could concern himself most with writing problems that mainly required the rhetorician's ability to establish a certain point of view and maintain it throughout the treatment of law – a subject which is, as a Johnsonian clause in the introduction acknowledges, 'by its extent difficult to be comprehended or by its variety difficult to be methodized.' Moreover, his greatest service was probably in the beginning of the Lectures where the point of view needed most to be established, and where he could concentrate on general principles and on history, leaving the 'hard law' to Chambers. This was very much the view of Arnold McNair, KC: 'His interest lay rather in the social, moral and historical aspects of law, and we know that he had a special interest in feudal law, by no means confined to England, because the feudal system was the embodiment of a certain phase of European society and government.'[17]

McNair's view is consistent with my sense that Johnson took his intellectual bearings in every subject by reference to a European standard of learning, rather than one that was parochially English. In 1776, in a conversation with Boswell, which McNair recalls, Johnson argued.

'To write a good book upon [any trade], a man must have extensive views. It is not necessary to have practised, to write well upon a subject.' I mentioned law as a subject on which no man could write well without practice. JOHNSON. 'Why, Sir, in England, where so much money is to be got by the practice of the law, most of our writers upon it have been in practice; though Blackstone had not been much in practice when he published his "Commentaries". But upon the Continent, the great writers on law have not all been in practice; Grotius, indeed, was; but Puffendorf was not, Burlamaqui was not.'

If he was thinking of his own contributions to the Lectures at all here, Johnson was aligning himself, as he was most of his life, with a larger European milieu. Along with this identification went an interest in a philosophical view of any subject, one that transcends local details as well as ideology, which is a parochial version of theory. In his discussions concerning law with Boswell, Johnson disparages the 'formulary and statutary part' in favour of the 'rational and ingenious part'. Johnson's great exemplars in legal thinking remained the 'rational and ingenious' writers, Grotius, Pufendorf, Hooker, Selden, and many others who wrote mostly before law came to be dominated by precedents rather than principles. Though he studied English law during his collaboration with Chambers from 1766 to 1770, Johnson's intellectual priorities remained philosophical and historical, and his intellectual identity continued to be broadly European.[18]

18

Late Political Writings

Because it is difficult to distinguish Johnson's own view in the collaborative, educational project of the Vinerian Lectures, and because the Lectures themselves are not especially ideological, it is dangerous to conclude
that they represent a change in his political outlook. However, in the light
of later developments, it is reasonable to conclude that Johnson's work on
the Lectures reveals a strengthening of his conservative tendency to em-
phasize the importance of social institutions in government at the expense
of individual rights or, as they were frequently called in revolutionary
America and France, the 'rights of man'. Such conservatism is much more
evident in the late political pamphlets, which sometimes draw on the
Lectures, but the change in Johnson's political outlook is easily overestimated. Johnson was a hired pen on four occasions from 1770 to 1775,
but even in these paid political tracts his philosophical and historical view
of the institutions of government is predominant, and he retains his paramount interest in political issues with a strong moral dimension, such as
slavery. Johnson's politics really did move to the right after 1762, but the
alteration in his public political affiliation makes the change seem greater
than it was.

Before looking at the political writings themselves, it is reasonable to ask
why Johnson gave up the opposition stance that seemed so much to define
him politically in his youth and middle age. The answer is not simply that
the ministry bought him with a pension. He was ready to be enrolled;
though he needed assurances that he would owe no favours, he must have
realized that he would feel some obligation to his patrons. In fact, as early
as the *Dictionary* years, Johnson began showing a commitment to a mainstream political outlook that went beyond party affiliation but was implicitly

conservative. Still, what made him most willing to be associated with the ministry, which was predominantly Whig throughout the period, was the new king. King George III appealed to Johnson on several counts. There were temperamental similarities between the two, summed up in their mutual hatred of George II. More importantly, George III was deeply interested in arts and sciences and admirably accomplished in several of them. Among his many obsessive intellectual interests was book-collecting; he rebuilt the royal library and by 1811 had assembled 65,000 volumes, paying more attention, like Johnson, to printed works than to manuscripts. In 1762, the year of Johnson's pension, when he had been on the throne only two years, George bought for the recently created British Museum the Thomason Tracts, a collection of 35,000 items relevant to the study of the Civil War. The King further showed his respect for English intellectual life by commanding his agents never to bid against scholars attempting to obtain useful books at auction. He spent between £1500 and £3000 a year on his library, all from the Privy Purse, rather than national funds. His overall expenditure of £120,000 ranks George III with Lord Harley as one of the greatest book collectors of the century.[1]

Johnson himself was involved in the King's work of collecting and wrote a long letter of advice to his librarian, F. A. Barnard, in 1768 before his departure to the continent on a book-buying expedition. Like so many of his writings, this letter shows Johnson's intellectual identification with the larger community of Europe as it surveys the sorts of books likely to be found in various countries. The letter also suggests that Johnson may have done some purchasing either alongside or in competition with Barnard and his employer: warning Barnard to be careful, Johnson says, 'You remember how near we both were to purchasing a mutilated Missal at a high price.' Whether or not he was personally involved, Johnson certainly would have approved of the King's specialization in the acquisition of Bibles in as many foreign languages as possible; in 1766 he wrote a brilliant letter to William Drummond on the importance of these works. Johnson would also have approved the King's large collections of Shakespeare and of Samuel Johnson, including, eventually, the manuscript of *Irene*. Johnson met George III on at least one occasion, and appropriately the meeting took place in the King's library, which was located in the Queen's House, where Buckingham Palace now stands. The meeting occurred in February 1767 when Johnson was probably reading law for his work on the Vinerian Lectures. Boswell gave the event extensive coverage in his biography and top billing in his advertisements. According to Boswell, the meeting 'gratified [Johnson's] monarchical enthusiasm'.[2] It would be more accurate to say it gratified his interest in George III and the King's in Johnson.

Johnson and King George talked about books, libraries, writers, and writing, subjects in which they shared an interest but which Johnson obviously knew better. The King gathered information from Johnson on his speciality, as was his practice in talking with a great many of his subjects, high and low alike. According to Boswell, he also asked Johnson 'if he was then writing any thing', to which Johnson replied, 'he was not, for he had pretty well told the world what he knew, and must now read to acquire more knowledge. . . . Johnson said, he thought he had already done his part as a writer. "I should have thought so too, (said the King,) if you had not written so well." . . . When asked by another friend, at Sir Joshua Reynolds's, whether he made any reply to this high compliment, [Johnson] answered, "No, Sir. When the King had said it, it was to be so. It was not for me to bandy civilities with my Sovereign." ' Boswell says that the particular work the King suggested to Johnson, and which Johnson agreed to do, was 'the literary biography of this country'. But the genesis of the *Lives of the Poets* is more accurately traced to the wishes of a group of booksellers than to the King's injunction. As Alvin Kernan has shown in an important and expansive reading of Johnson's meeting with the King, Boswell may have intended to align Johnson and monarchy in the scene, but he has in fact provided an image of the writer achieving the highest possible status, a subject of equal if not superior interest to kings.[3] Whether or not Boswell's account is accurate, George III cared about books, and he elevated the status and dignity of scholars in England. For this alone, no matter what his party politics, he might have won Johnson's fealty.

Although he did not write the *Lives of the Poets* at the King's behest, his pension and the King's favour shifted Johnson's life as professional writer in the direction of the old manorial system of patronage. The underlying assumptions in the four pamphlets he wrote for his lord, however, come from deep down in Johnson's reservoir of thought where partisan politics are submerged in broader concerns. The first piece, *The False Alarm*, was written with characteristic dispatch on 10 and 11 January 1770 at the Thrales' house. Its purpose was to support the decision of Parliament to exclude from membership the duly elected but notorious Member from Middlesex, John Wilkes, who was imprisoned in mid-term on charges of seditious libel and obscenity. Wilkes had sought election largely as a way of solving his financial problems, since membership offered limited immunity from prosecution, but his supporters were much more idealistic republicans. Among them were the anonymous author of the *Letters of Junius*, and Horne Tooke, a linguistic projector who spawned a school of lexicography and language theory that was highly critical of Johnson's *Dictionary*. Boswell manoeuvred Johnson into dining with Wilkes, and, despite his reluctance to go the first time, he found the man good company.[4] The issue in the press, however, had little to do directly with Wilkes; for both sides it was a question of the power of Parliament in relation to the wishes of voters, or 'the people', as opposition speakers called them rather loosely, given the sexual and monetary limitations on the franchise in 1768.

Johnson's legal argument in *The False Alarm* is thoroughly consistent with the non-partisan, philosophical doctrine of Parliamentary rule in the Vinerian Lectures. He relies mainly on the constitutional fact that 'the

House of Commons has jurisdiction over its own members' and is therefore exempt in its determinations from the authority of other courts.
Furthermore, 'This exemption from the authority of other courts ... is
implied in the principles of government. If legislative powers are not co-
ordinate, they cease in part to be legislative, and if they be co-ordinate
they are unaccountable, for to whom must that power account, which has
no superiour?' The principles in this statement derive from the definition
of Parliament in the Vinerian Lectures as 'that legislative body consisting
of king, lords and commons in which is vested the supreme and absolute
government of this kingdom'. From the supremacy of Parliament the
'co-ordination' of its parts is deducible, and from that 'co-ordination'
the jurisdiction of each part over itself: 'The *privileges* of Parliament are,
for the most part, such as by political and almost by natural necessity are
comprised in the essence of a *supreme court*. Thus any question moved in
either House concerning their own conduct and procedure, is to be determined by the ancient usage of Parliament, of which the House in which
the question is moved must always be the judge. For the supreme court
would cease to be supreme if its conduct could be examined by any other
judicature, and the two Houses being co-ordinate are not amesnable either
to the other.' In a separate section on the House of Commons, the Lectures
likewise conclude, 'Their privileges are that they are their own judges. . . .
They decide the claims of candidates, and settle the rights of electors, and
expel such from their assembly as they judge unworthy to keep their
places.' This was not a point that the second Vinerian Lectures added or
emphasized because of current events. It was an accepted fact of English
government, and similar statements had already appeared in Blackstone's
Commentaries: 'the whole law and custom of Parliament has it's [*sic*] original
from this one maxim; "that whatever matter arises concerning either house
of parliament, ought to be examined, discussed, and adjudged in that
house to which it relates, and not elsewhere."'[5]

As the opposition had to admit, precedent as well as principle were on
Johnson's side. Johnson dwells on the logic, specificity, and 'science' of
the legal argument, while portraying the opposition view as the result of
ignorance, anxiety, and vulgar opinions. This is a rhetorical dichotomy
that Johnson began using as early as his praise of Father Lobo's veracity,
and his mastery of it is clear in the opening paragraph of the essay: 'One
of the chief advantages derived by the present generation from the improvement and diffusion of philosophy, is deliverance from unnecessary
terrours, and exemption from false alarms. The unusual appearances,
whether regular or accidental, which once spread consternation over ages
of ignorance, are now the recreations of inquisitive security. The sun is no
more lamented when it is eclipsed, than when it sets; and meteors play
their coruscations without prognostick or prediction.' Later in the piece,
Johnson further employs the rhetoric of empirical investigation to portray
the opposition as various kinds of enemies to science, including projectors
or speculatists: 'the opinion . . . that expulsion is only a dismission of the

representative [Wilkes] to his constituents . . . is plausible but not cogent. It is a scheme of representation, which would make a specious appearance in a political romance, but cannot be brought into practice among us, who see every day the towering head of speculation bow down unwillingly to grovelling experience.' When it becomes convenient, Johnson moves the study of government out of the natural sciences and into the realm of human sciences, such as philology and literary criticism. Like language and all other social institutions, governments are 'fabricks of dissimilar materials, raised by different architects, upon different plans. We must be content with them as they are. . . . Laws are now made, and customs are established; these are our rules, and by them we must be guided.'[6] Johnson could use this rhetoric for various purposes, but it embodies underlying assumptions which are broadly consistent with the deep, philosophical views of society that Johnson held all his life, no matter what the particular argument at hand and no matter whether the subject was law or language.

The opposition theorists are clever speculatists, like language reformers or framers of criticism's *trois unités*, but the people to whom they appeal are mere fools. In using this part of the rhetorical topic Johnson seems most to break with his political past. The vulgarity and gullibility of the rabble who follow the Wilkites is frequently mentioned, and towards the end of the essay Johnson directly attacks the lower orders of society:

As we once had a rebellion of the clowns, we have now an opposition of the pedlars. The quiet of the nation has been for years disturbed by a faction, against which all factions ought to conspire; for its original principle is the desire of levelling; it is only animated under the name of zeal, by the natural malignity of the mean against the great.

When in the confusion which the English invasions produced in France, the vilains, imagining that they had found the golden hour of emancipation, took arms in their hands, the knights of both nations considered the cause as common, and, suspending the general hostility, united to chastise them.

The whole conduct of this despicable faction is distinguished by plebeian grossness, and savage indecency

'The people' was not nearly as inclusive a political category of political discourse in the eighteenth century as it is in most countries today. In earlier 'patriotic' outbursts it is doubtful that Johnson was revealing a fundamentally different opinion of the political potential of the lower orders of society. Yet the change in his language is striking. Johnson also breaks with his political past by chastising the 'Tories, who being long accustomed to signalize their principles by opposition to the court, do not yet consider that they have at last a king who knows not the name of party, and who wishes to be the common father of all his people.'[7] During the reign of George II Johnson shared the custom of the Tories which he now renounces as a form of thoughtlessness.

Even more striking is Johnson's characterization of the increased availability of news as an enemy to peace. He looks back nostalgically on an

Arcadian past when Englishmen attended primarily to their corn, and he laments the fact that 'quiet and security are now at an end. Our vigilance is quickened, and our comprehension is enlarged. . . . The sphere of anxiety is now enlarged; he that hitherto cared only for himself, now cares for the public; for he has learned that the happiness of individuals is comprised in the prosperity of the whole, and that his country never suffers but he suffers with it, however it happens that he feels no pain.'[8] Throughout his career – in his Parliamentary *Debates* most directly but also in some other work for the *Gentleman's Magazine*, in the Harleian projects, in the *Dictionary*, and in the *Literary Magazine* – Johnson was among those who increased the information of the public and contributed to expanding 'the sphere of anxiety'. As early as *Adventurer* 115, however, he also displayed impatience with the exuberant increase in English publication, so his disgust with the proliferation of news, reactionary as it sounds, is consistent with some opinions he had expressed twenty years before.

Johnson's derision of the public derives from the controlling topic of the essay – the antagonism between speculative ignorance and experiential science – but the intention of the essay is not merely to combat pseudo-doxia, promote science, or clear the mind of cant. Johnson's rhetoric may reveal that his underlying intellectual beliefs have not changed, but the conservative shift and the political service are impossible to ignore. Johnson's politics, like those of More or Erasmus, are subordinate to deeper religious, moral, and intellectual convictions, which are expressed in the very forms of his language and undisturbed by most matters of party politics. Yet Johnson did lend his pen enthusiastically to the ministerial side. He may have done this without much discomfort because he believed that most matters of partisan politics were unimportant. Although he uses the point for rhetorical purposes in *The False Alarm*, Johnson probably believed the Wilkes affair really was trivial. As he usually could, Johnson found a classical tag to sum it up:

> Non de vi, neque caede, nec veneno,
> Sed lis est mihi de tribus capellis.[9]

(My suit is not about power, murder, or poisonous drugs, but rather about three little goats.)

The Patriot pursues many of the themes of *The False Alarm*. Johnson wrote it very rapidly in October 1774 as part of the election campaign of that year. (He also wrote campaign speeches for his friend Henry Thrale.) It is his most compendious political pamphlet, touching briefly on most of the issues that occupy him in the other pieces, and usually getting to the heart of the matter with great speed. As Donald Greene points out, one of the most effective strokes in the piece is the contrast between the noise surrounding the trivial Wilkes affair and the silence on the related but more important Grenville voting Act, which systematically reduced the likelihood that disputed elections to the House would be decided in a partisan fashion. The piece also reflects on the bankruptcy of the term 'patriot' and the way that recent political history had shifted the word away from its etymology to its current meaning as one who displays 'an acrimonious and unremitting opposition to the Court'.[10] There is no embarrassment for Johnson in the knowledge that he once exhibited the behaviour he now derides because his position depends mostly on a critique of linguistic usage. Moreover, he convicts his younger self of thoughtlessness only, and that, like most of the opposition's clamor, is relatively trivial.

On the really important political issues Johnson's critique reveals a consistency with his lifelong political commitments. In the ironic rhetoric of *The Patriot* the important issues are the matters in which one proves oneself 'to be not a Patriot', in an unironic sense of the word; defining his own position complexly, as different from a negation, also increased Johnson's comfort. Like other satirists, Johnson characteristically positions himself by virtue of his dissociation from a positively reprehensible view. Chief among the disqualifications for true patriotism is indulging the 'howling violence of patriotic rage' and urging the nation to go to war 'by aggravating minute injuries, or enforcing disputable rights of little importance'.[11] Johnson refers here to the opposition leaders who wanted England to go to war with Spain over the ownership of the Falkland Islands. He had treated that matter at length three years before in 1771 in the political pamphlet which most reveals his fundamental and unchanging politics: *Thoughts on the Late Transactions respecting Falkland's Islands*.

The pamphlet provides a full history of the islands, written from the same point of view that informs Johnson's *Political State of Great Britain* and his Preface to *The World Displayed*. The extensive colonization of the so-called New World is described as destructive to the native inhabitants and unhealthy in the long run for the overextended imperial nations. In the infatuation with adventurous enterprise, fantasy and fiction inevitably gained the sway over accuracy, good sense, and moderation. This was ludicrously so in the exploration and settling of the Falkland or Malvinas Islands. John Perceval, the second Earl of Egmont, is the protagonist of the islands' recent history. He was, according to Johnson, 'a man whose mind was vigorous and ardent, whose knowledge was extensive, and whose designs were magnificent; but who had somewhat vitiated his judgment by too much indulgence of romantick projects and airy speculations'. The opposition in Johnson's late pamphlets, as in so much of his writing on all subjects, is tainted with romanticism, or a tendency to view experience through the distorting lenses of abstract ideas. Given that romanticism is his fatal flaw, it is almost too good to be true that the man sent out by Lord Egmont to explore the Malvinas was Captain Byron, grandfather of the Romantic poet. Byron finds what Egmont hoped he would, and Johnson applies his nicest irony in describing the rose-coloured report:

He conceived the island to be six or seven hundred miles round, and represented it as a region naked indeed of wood, but which, if that defect were supplied, would have all that nature, almost all that luxury could want. The harbour he found capacious and secure, and therefore thought it worthy of the name of Egmont. Of water there was no want, and the ground, he described as having all the excellencies of soil, and as covered with antiscorbutick herbs, the restoratives of the sailor. Provision was easily to be had, for they killed almost every day an hundred geese to each ship, by pelting them with stones.

If Johnson's reader has not yet perceived the irony, he is rudely awakened in the next paragraph by the report submitted by the next Englishman to inhabit the place: 'He found, what he calls, a mass of islands and broken lands, of which the soil was nothing but a bog, with no better prospect than that of barren mountains, beaten by storms almost perpetual. Yet this, says he, is summer. . . . The plenty which regaled Mr Byron, and which might have supported not only armies, but armies of Patagons [native giants that Byron claimed to have seen], was no longer to be found. The geese were too wise to stay when men violated their haunts, and Mr MacBride's crew could only now and then kill a goose when the weather would permit.' The realistic MacBride was succeeded by the dogged Hunt who understood the undesirability of the place well enough 'that when he erected his wooden blockhouse he omitted to open the ports and loopholes' – the openings through which cannon and light arms would have been aimed. The garden fails, but some cattle endure, and so 'the garrison lived upon Falkland's Island, shrinking from the blast, and shuddering at the billows.'[12]

In November 1769 the Spanish arrive, to Hunt's surprise, and demand the surrender of the island. Complex negotiations are then punctiliously carried out among the various English and Spanish commanders. The Spanish force is obviously superior, and the English capitulate, after a suitable exhibition of courage and loyalty that is reminiscent of Johnson's account of the Byng affair. No one is at fault. The Spanish do not insult their conquered foes in any way, but they do impound the rudder of the frigate *Favourite* to ensure that the English remain on the island for the stipulated time of twenty days (lest they immediately seek reinforcements). Captain Maltby returns to England to tell the tale, and the English enter into diplomatic negotiations with the Spanish. Finding the Spanish inflexibly committed to their rights in the 'whole Magellanic region', the English prepare for war, eager to avenge the late entry of the Spanish into the Seven Years War, which had ended with the Peace of Paris only in 1763. Then, suddenly, diplomacy works: the King of France dismisses the minister who was encouraging the Spanish to go to war with England, and Spain backs down; Fort Egmont is restored, but the question of sovereignty over the islands remains open for future negotiations. Now the opposition at home still want war, and in Johnson's account they assume the romantic posture of Byron and the early explorers in the New World. They wish to avenge the honour of the English which has been insulted in various ways, including the Spanish detention of the *Favourite*'s rudder. Johnson elegantly goes with the grain of his opponents' arguments and allows the trivial complaint to be representative of their chivalric willingness to support with the utmost effort of war a claim that was never firm to begin with to a piece of land that has no value: 'If the rudder be to a ship what his tail is in fables to a fox, the part in which honour is placed and of which the violation is never to be endured, I am sorry that the *Favourite* suffered an indignity, but cannot yet think it a cause for which nations should slaughter one another.' Johnson's urbane tone reduces the incident to the scale of another story about a favourite, Thomas Gray's well-known 'Ode on the Death of a Favourite Cat, Drowned in a Tub of Gold Fishes'. The large inequality that Johnson establishes between the cause and the desired action of war is an extreme example of the truth with which he opens the essay: 'To proportion the eagerness of contest to its importance seems too hard a task for human wisdom. The pride of wit has kept ages busy in the discussion of useless questions, and the pride of power has destroyed armies to gain or to keep unprofitable possessions.'[13] This is a political version of Locke's widely accepted epistemological formula that belief should be proportioned to evidence. Although exact proportion in anything is 'too hard a task for human wisdom', Johnson proceeds to calculate the advantages and disadvantages of war so that sums of time, money, and blood will be contemplated instead of abstract ideals.

To show that war is a disproportionate response to the situation, Johnson not only dwells on the worthlessness of the property at stake but also on the horrors and the casualties of war. War is here much like the glass-furnace into which Locke invited idealists to put their hands before espousing their epistemology. Just as scathingly, Johnson writes:

> It is wonderful with what coolness and indifference the greater part of mankind see war commenced. Those that hear of it at a distance, or read of it in books, but have never presented its evils to their minds, consider it as little more than a splendid game; a proclamation, an army, a battle, and a triumph. ... The life of a modern soldier is ill represented by heroick fiction. War has means of destruction more formidable than the cannon and the sword. Of the thousands and ten thousands that perished in our late contests with France and Spain, a very small part ever felt the stroke of an enemy; the rest languished in tents and ships, amidst damps and putrefaction; pale, torpid, spiritless, and helpless; gasping and groaning, unpitied among men made obdurate by long continuance of hopeless misery; and were at last whelmed in pits, or heaved into the ocean, without notice and without remembrance. By incommodious encampments and unwholesome stations, where courage is useless, and enterprise impracticable, fleets are silently dispeopled, and armies sluggishly melted away.
>
> Thus is a people gradually exhausted, for the most part with little effect.[14]

Johnson goes on to suggest that the war is only promoted by demonic profiteers 'whose equipages shine like meteors and whose [satanic] palaces rise like exhalations', though they are merely 'vultures waiting for a day of carnage'. The whole passage makes as fierce an anti-war statement as the dialogue between the vultures in the original *Idler* 22, which Johnson published during the Seven Years War and found too virulent for republication in the collected edition. Even in comparison with anti-war passages published in recent times – during the latest Falklands crisis in 1982 or the war in the Persian Gulf in 1991 – Johnson's statement is extreme.[15] It is fuelled by Johnson's deepest beliefs and thereby exceeds his relatively superficial support of the crown and his correlative condemnation of the people.

Anti-war sentiments are part of Johnson's basic equipment for writing, just like the antithesis between scientific findings and vulgar opinion. But it must be confessed that in *Thoughts on Falkland's Islands* Johnson is almost as spirited in his condemnation of the rabble as of war. In concluding the piece, Johnson describes the rabble as the overflowing of the city's sewers and as an infestation of lice, though he saves his nastiest barbs for their leaders. Even in an age of mud-slinging and name-calling in political campaigns, it is difficult to imagine any political writer printing anything sharper than what Johnson says at the very close of his pamphlet: 'From the present happiness of the publick the patriots themselves may derive advantage. To be harmless though by impotence obtains some degree of kindness; no man hates a worm as he hates a viper; they were once dreaded enough to be detested, as serpents that could bite; they have now shewn that they can only hiss, and may therefore quietly slink into holes, and change their slough unmolested and forgotten.'[16]

One test of the depth of Johnson's anti-war sentiment is his willingness to retain it in a situation which he thought called for military action, the insurgency of the American colonists. In *Taxation No Tyranny*, his paid political response to the Resolutions and Address of the American Congress in 1774, Johnson is true to his anti-war, humanist heritage. However, because his side has decided on force, he is gentler, even self-deprecating in his wishes to avoid it: 'Men of the pen have seldom any great skill in conquering kingdoms, but they have [a] strong inclination to give advice. I cannot forbear to wish, that this commotion may end without bloodshed, and that the rebels may be subdued by terrour rather than by violence; and therefore recommend such a force as may take away, not only the power, but the hope of resistance, and by conquering without a battle, save many from the sword.' Elsewhere Johnson uses the grammar of prayer to wish again: 'Since the Americans have made it necessary to subdue them, may they be subdued with the least injury possible to their persons and their possessions.'[17]

Although his antagonism to war had to be muted in *Taxation No Tyranny*, the pamphlet gave him a clear opportunity to be vociferous about another of his deep, unchanging political convictions. A central irony of the American position was that they demanded liberty and talked constantly about freedom, while condoning institutionalized slavery on a large scale. Johnson's most memorable comment on the irony appears toward the end of the pamphlet when he is dealing with American arguments that a reduction of liberty in the colonies will lead to a correspondent loss of liberty at home: 'If slavery be thus fatally contagious, how is it that we hear the loudest yelps for liberty among the drivers of negroes?' Johnson takes advantage of the irony frequently in his handling of 'patriotic' American rhetoric about liberty, but this is only one of several means he employs to reduce the seriousness of the American threat and belittle the whole enterprise. He uses other racial contrasts to the same end, imagining, for example, a similar rebellion in Cornwall. From the hypothetical he moves more easily into the thoroughly fictional and ends by ridiculing the American threat in terms of a mock-heroic poem, Addison's 'Battle of the Pygmies and Cranes', the same Latin work he had translated as a schoolboy. Johnson also explicitly backs the emancipation of the slaves and a scheme to give them the British support and protection which their masters spurn.[18] This fantasy of establishing 'a simple form of government' for an African-American nation is meant, by comparison, to trivialize the American republic; it does not indicate that Johnson was an early Black nationalist or even an especially progressive thinker, but it is an expression of his fundamental opposition to slavery, which, like his opposition to bloody battle, is a legacy of European humanism.

Johnson has room in *Taxation No Tyranny* to dilate on the topics of slavery, freedom, and war, but the underlying argument of the piece, like that of *The False Alarm*, is constitutional and may be found in the Vinerian Lectures. The most relevant section is part 1, lecture 15, 'Of the Government of Ireland and the American Provinces', but a principle stated in the previous lecture, 'Of Aliens', is also important: 'As every one that is born in the king's dominions has from birth a right to protection, he is supposed to incur from his birth the duty of allegiance.' Lecture 15 articulates the principle with respect to colonies and finds, for example, 'that a greater or a less degree of obedience has generally been required from colonies in proportion to the assistance and protection which the parent societies have been able or willing to afford them.' Johnson applies this principle to the American question, and frequently reminds his audience of the pains England took to defend the colonies from the French in the Seven Years War. Among the forms of obedience and cooperation that government requires from those it defends is payment of taxes. The specific question of whether or not Americans owe taxes to the British comes up in the Lectures, and the answers given there provide the outline of Johnson's remarks in the later pamphlet. Like the pamphlet, the Lectures recur to the most basic principles: 'The *moral* part of this question is in my opinion easily decided, no man has a right to any good without partaking of the evil by which that good is necessarily produced; no man has a right to security by another's danger, nor to plenty by another's labour, but as he gives something of his own which he who meets the danger or undergoes the labour considers as equivalent. No man has a right to the security of government without bearing his share of its inconveniences.' In *Taxation*

No Tyranny Johnson is similarly fundamental, and he arrives at such incontrovertible statements as 'They who are subject to laws, are liable to taxes' and 'Of every empire all the subordinate communities are liable to taxation, because they all share the benefits of government, and therefore ought all to furnish their proportion of the expence.' In fact, Johnson builds his whole argument around the necessity of acknowledging a basic fact of government – a piece of received wisdom that he encloses in quotation marks, although it is not a citation: ' "the supreme power of every community has the right of requiring from all its subjects such contributions as are necessary to the public safety or public prosperity." '[19]

Such statements are self-evident, if one accepts the concept of government as a social compact in which ruler and ruled both agree to certain restrictions on their freedom. Johnson supports this realistic, historical framework of government in opposition to the imaginary 'state of nature' on which the colonists build their self-evident truths. Unlike the social world, the 'state of nature' does not really exist; therefore any attempt to apply its principles in the real world stems from 'the madness of independence' and 'the delirious dream of republican fanaticism'. Furthermore, it is only logical that 'no province can confer provincial privileges on itself; they may have a right to all which the King has given them; but it is a conceit of the other hemisphere, that men have a right to all which they have given themselves.' The proper evaluation of the situation depends upon an understanding of history and of the real acts and decisions of the explorers and colonists of America. Johnson provides some of this social history, and here again he is true to one of his deepest convictions, the evils of imperial colonization. Of the efforts of Columbus to find patronage for his explorations, for example, Johnson says, 'nor has any part of the world yet had reason to rejoice that he found at last reception and employment.'[20]

In sober truth, Johnson argues, immigrants to the New World voluntarily chose disenfranchisement for practical reasons, like financial gain, and it is disingenuous of them now to reclaim the rights they traded for their own profit and convenience:

> By his own choice he has left a country where he had a vote and little property, for another, where he has great property, but no vote. But as this preference was deliberate and unconstrained, he is still 'concerned in the government of himself'; he has reduced himself from a voter to one of the innumerable multitude that have no vote. He has truly 'ceded his right' [citing the American arguments again], but he is still governed by his own consent; because he has consented to throw his atom of interest into the general mass of the community. Of the consequences of his own act he has no right to complain; he has chosen, or intended to chuse, the greater good; he is represented, as himself desired, in the general representation.
>
> But the privileges of an American scorn the limits of place; they are part of himself, and cannot be lost by departure from his country; they float in the air, or glide under the ocean.[21]

The airy, the imaginary, the romantic, in brief, the fictional is the realm of American claims and American notions of government, whereas conventional British notions are based on fact and experience. Johnson found this opposition between the real and the ideal operating in a great many of the intellectual debates of his time, and, whether the issue was politics or language, he always aligned himself with history, experience, and fact.

Johnson concludes *Taxation No Tyranny*, as he did *Thoughts on Falkland's Islands*, with some political invective that cannot be comfortably assimilated to his underlying humanistic assumptions. Indeed, Johnson's remarks are so satirical that Lord North's ministry, fearful of creating ill feeling, cut several pages of them, even after Johnson had toned them down himself. Like much of the hostility in the pamphlet, Johnson's vituperation at the end is directed as much against British supporters of the American 'usurpation' as it is against the Americans themselves; this is probably what worried the ministry. Everything that Johnson said is not known because neither a manuscript nor a complete set of proofs survives. However, Johnson commented on the revisions he was obliged to accept in a note to his publisher William Strahan on 1 March 1775: 'I am sorry to see that all the alterations proposed are evidence of timidity. You may be sure that I do [not] wish to publish, what those for whom I write do not like to have published. But print me half a dozen copies in the original state, and lay them up for me. It concludes well enough as it is.'[22]

No record of these copies exists, though Johnson asked Strahan to send him one by mail and also one to Elizabeth Aston in Lichfield. The second request suggests the spirit in which Johnson may have written parts of *Taxation No Tyranny* and parts, perhaps, of all the late political pamphlets. The Astons, including his beloved Molly, were 'violent Whigs' whom Johnson had always delighted affectionately to bait. He may have sought playfully to vex his old friend with this pamphlet, especially with the attacks on Whigs at the end, when he had Strahan send it to the Astons just ahead of his own journey to the Midlands. Obviously Johnson did not write the work principally for his friends, but he is indulging a habit of argumentation in the pamphlet that is characteristic of his consciously excessive behaviour in conversation. The signal that Johnson is taking off into the realm of overstatement and satire is the hypothetical framework of the remarks. At the end of the piece Johnson is imagining what might happen in the future, after an armed conflict between the colonies and England:

> If by the fortune of war they drive us utterly away, what they will do next can only be conjectured. If a new monarchy is erected, they will want a king. He who first takes into his hand the scepter of America should have a name of good omen. William has been known both as conqueror and deliverer, and perhaps England, however contemned, might yet supply them with another William [Pitt, that is, as Greene points out]. Whigs indeed are not willing to be governed, and it is possible, that King William may be strongly inclined to guide their measures; but Whigs have been cheated, like other mortals,

and suffered their leader to become their tyrant, under the name of their
Protector [i.e. Cromwell, the Lord Protector]. . . .
   Their numbers are at present not quite sufficient for the greatness which,
in some form of government or other, is to rival the ancient monarchies; but
by Dr Franklin's rule of progression, they will in a century and a quarter be
more than equal to the inhabitants of Europe. When the Whigs of America
are thus multiplied, let the princes of the earth tremble in their palaces. If
they should then continue to double and to double, their own hemisphere
will not long contain them. But let not our boldest oppugners of authority
look forward with delight to this futurity of whiggism.[23]

Whatever Johnson went on to say here, he undoubtedly continued in the
vein of unbridled but also somewhat playful attacks on 'whiggism'. Plenty
of Johnson's friends were Whigs, and Whigs were important in the government for whom Johnson was writing. He knew better than to categorize
them all as dangerous revolutionaries. In these paragraphs of prophetic
enthusiasm (which turn out to be more prophetic than he could have
wished) Johnson is enjoying his extravagance and taunting his political
jousting partners new and old. The ministry, who had more serious business to conduct and could ill afford to alienate important allies, were
evidently not amused. Quite possibly it was Johnson's extravagance that
liberated him from further assignments, and quite possibly he was glad.
Throughout Johnson's varied and voluminous political writings there is a
rebellious streak that often ends in satire and overstatement. Part of his
political attitude is an unwillingness to do what he is bidden or to withhold what he has been asked to censor. With a part of his mind that never
changed or mellowed Johnson may very well have meant to tell Strahan
what his accidental omission of a 'not' has him saying in the letter of 1
March 1775, and it is quite possible that he did 'wish to publish, what
those for whom I write do not like to have published'.
   Although Johnson produced his political pamphlets with such remarkable speed that they occupied very little of his time, politics were on his
mind throughout the early 1770s. His influential friends William Strahan
and Henry Thrale even made efforts to get Johnson a seat in Parliament
where they imagined he would be an awesome spokesman on behalf of
the King. Lord North was evidently interested at first but then demurred
because, reports have it, 'he was afraid that Johnson's *help* . . . might have
been sometimes *embarrassing* . . . that, like the elephant in the battle, he
was quite as likely to trample down his friends as his foes.' This was in
1771 before the rampage at the end of *Taxation No Tyranny*, but Johnson
had already shown how difficult he was to control. An Irish clergyman
named Maxwell left a recollection of Johnson's political character that
tends to vindicate North's fears and confirm the spirit Johnson shows in
the pamphlets: 'This excellent person was sometimes charged with abet-
ting slavish and arbitrary principles of government. Nothing in my opinion could be a grosser calumny and misrepresentation; for how can it
rationally be supposed, that he should adopt such pernicious and absurd

opinions, who supported his philosophical character with so much dignity, was extremely jealous of his personal liberty and independence, and could not brook the smallest appearance of neglect or insult, even from the highest personages?'[24] There are indications in notes by Hester Thrale and in Johnson's remarks to Burke that he really would have liked the chance to perform in public, instead of being merely behind the scenes assisting other speakers – Robert Chambers, the Vinerian lecturer, the MP William Hamilton, and candidate Henry Thrale – but it was not to be, and he may never have made a public speech in his life.

Despite his engagement in politics and law, there were large vacancies in Johnson's time; his prayers and meditations accordingly are full of self-lacerating exhortations to get busy. These intensify greatly at the beginning of each year, on his birthday, and around Good Friday. The prayer at the beginning of the new decade is representative:

> Almighty God by whose mercy I am permitted to behold the beginning of another year, succour with thy help, and bless with thy favour, the creature whom thou vouchsafest to preserve. Mitigate, if it shall seem best unto thee, the diseases of my body, and compose the disorders of my mind. Dispel my terrours and grant that the time which thou shalt yet allow me, may not pass unprofitably away. Let not pleasure seduce me, Idleness lull me, or misery depress me. Let my remaining days be innocent and useful. Let me perform to thy glory and the good of my fellow creatures the work which thou shalt yet appoint me. . . .

'Diseases of body' and 'disorders of mind' plagued Johnson most of his life, and his relief from them was only intermittent. He once contemplated writing a 'history of [his] melancholy', but even at the thought of it, he noted, 'I know not whether it may not too much disturb me.'[25] If Johnson carried out his plan, no record remains, and he surely would have burned the document along with the other private diaries he disposed of in that manner shortly before his death. We know much more about his incessant physical ailments, including the rheumatism that beset him in the early 1770s, and his moral struggles to order himself – to rise early, to do regular amounts of reading and other work, to attend church, and to expel vagrant fantasies of sexual exploits or other 'vanities' from his mind. The history of his melancholy would presumably have entered into the life of Johnson's fancy. One of the differences between Johnson and many later writers is that they would have considered such inner life suitable for public presentation, whereas Johnson considered it a highly private subject; he rarely mentions it in his own journals and only in the decent obscurity of a learned language. One famous example is his cryptic reference on Easter 1771 to 'de pedicis et manicis insana cogitatio' ('an unhealthy thought concerning manacles and shackles').

One aspect of Johnson's melancholy was the debility that resulted from having a highly active imagination, the freaks of which he severely condemned. Occupying his mind with useful and innocent thoughts was therefore important to Johnson for a mixture of psychological and moral reasons. He wrote to Boswell in 1771, 'Whatever philosophy may determine of material nature, it is certainly true of intellectual nature, that it *abhors a vacuum*: our minds cannot be empty; and evil will break in upon them, if they are not pre-occupied by good.' Johnson sometimes busied his mind with computation or chemistry, but his main sources of relief from the disturbing vagaries of his undirected fancy were travel, reading, composing verse (mostly in Latin), and other kinds of literary work. Political writing engaged him fully on occasion, but he needed more regular duties. He set himself tasks of reading in the early 1770s: so many lines per day or so many chapters per week of the Greek Bible and other works.[26] The two main literary projects that Johnson undertook in this period also provided steady activity for his mind of a kind which, unlike imaginative composition, tended to suppress his fancy.

Right around the start of the decade Johnson began revising his edition of Shakespeare. He had a collaborator, George Steevens, who took charge of the project, and both editors enlisted the occasional help of numerous scholars, including Richard Farmer, Thomas Warton, Thomas Percy, Hawkins, and Goldsmith. Because it includes such varied critical commentary, along with editorial comment on existing notes, the revised Shakespeare, which appeared in 1773, is sometimes called the 'first variorum'. Although Johnson's work on the revision was certainly less than Steevens's, he went over the whole text and made some 486 changes in his notes. True to the variorum quality of the edition, he commented on his own earlier remarks: he softened his attacks on Warburton; he retracted some of his conjectures and advanced some others; he corrected or added to his earlier philological and historical comments. Bits of autobiography are visible in the content of the remarks; his legal studies, for example, show themselves in his recollection of an anecdote about Lord Coke's cat-like legal balance, undoubtedly picked up in his work with Chambers. Another comment registers life at the Club by recalling his having heard Edmund Burke 'commend the subtility of discrimination with which Shakespeare distinguishes the present character of Timon [of Athens] from that of Apemantus, whom to vulgar eyes he would now resemble' since Burke's recent rise to fame.[27] The work on the revision was therapeutic, occupying Johnson's mind with details, and allowing him to register the daily passage of time.

The similar but greater task of this period was Johnson's revision of his *Dictionary*. It occupied him steadily for over a year, beginning in the late summer of 1771. On 29 August he wrote to Bennet Langton, 'My summer wanderings [in the Midlands] are now over, and I am engaging in a very great work the revision of my Dictionary from which I know not at present how to get loose.' Having refused to go even so far as Oxford during the year, Johnson wrote to Taylor in Ashbourne on 6 October 1772, announcing his intention to visit Lichfield the following week: 'I am now within a few hours of being able to send the whole dictionary to the press, and though

I often went sluggishly to the work, I am not much delighted at the conclusion.' Johnson knew the work was good for him, and his journal shows that during this period he was often in relatively good spirits; he was a little more pleased with himself; he was better in mind and body than usual, and he even completed his scheme of reading the Greek Bible. About 1774 Johnson sought additional regular and methodical work when he volunteered to revise Chambers's *Cyclopedia.* He said he liked 'that *muddling* work', and he was grieved that the job went to someone else. Some muddling work to do was vital to Johnson; it punctuated and de-marcated his time, which otherwise would be filled in disturbing ways by his fancy. When he acquired an expensive watch in 1768, Johnson had the dial inscribed with a reminder of death from the New Testament (St John 9: 4), νὺζ γὰρ ἔρχεται – 'the night cometh [when no man may work]'. The saying may have been as conventional on watches as certain verses were on wedding rings, but the time-piece so inscribed is an appropriate symbol of Johnson's need to fill his time with work.[28]

In his year of labour on revising the *Dictionary* Johnson had the help of at least one of his former amanuenses, V. J. Peyton, and probably another, William Macbean. As Allen Reddick's recent study suggests, the amanuenses may have had a good deal of responsibility in the early stages of assembling the fourth edition out of materials left over from the first, but Johnson had the final say, and he rejected many of the changes pro-posed by his employees. Throughout the fourth edition Johnson himself trimmed old and added new material for the sake of both philological and extra-philological purposes. He abridged some of the long illustrative quo-tations from encyclopedias and technical dictionaries in order to make room for 2500–3000 new quotations that further his moral and religious purposes.[29]

Johnson improved the religious value of his book, but, despite the addition of some new writers and the increased prominence of some, like William Law, who are marginal in the first edition, the intellectual char-acter of the 116,000 quotations remains fundamentally the same. Johnson also made changes to definitions, etymologies, and especially to the ordering of the senses under each word. Arthur Sherbo counted about 700 changes in the letter M alone, and, although Reddick has shown that various parts of the *Dictionary* were revised to varying degrees, the changes in M are fairly representative of what Johnson did overall. Many of the changes are minor, however, and Johnson was tinkering and correcting roughly ac-cording to his original scheme, rather than making radical changes. Fortunately for scholars, some of Johnson's copytext for the fourth edition was lost, never printed, and recovered some years later to be placed even-tually in the British Library. Johnson had hurriedly to make a new revision for these pages, mostly of the letter B. Comparisons among these lost changes, other changes that Johnson made for the fourth edition, and the few he made for a revision that was printed posthumously all suggest that he revised in an extempore and ready way rather than according to a blueprint. Looking at the same text on two different occasions, Johnson made different minor corrections in one instance than he did in the other. The same pattern emerges in Johnson's revision of Shakespeare and its occasional dependence upon the *Dictionary*.[30] Working from these findings, Allen Reddick has proposed looking at the *Dictionary* as a fluid, changing text rather than as the monument, like St Paul's, that most readers have perceived in Johnson's imposing volumes. If the fixity and stability of print and binding will not allow us to see the *Dictionary* in this way, we should nevertheless appreciate the flexibility and the improvisational readiness of the mind that created it. Like almost everything Johnson wrote, the fourth edition of the *Dictionary* is further evidence of what Hawkins called his versatility as well as of his better-known philosophical and monumental qualities.

During his months in Lichfield and environs in the fall of 1772 Johnson wrote frequently to Mrs Thrale. It was a depression year in England, and the mercantile Thrales were under considerable pressure. Johnson entered fully into the family problems; he had financial suggestions, and may have shared in some of the financial investments. He grew closer to the household and even achieved a place in the good graces of Mrs Thrale's mother shortly before her final illness. His constant solicitude for her and Mrs Thrale during the illness deepened his intimacy with the mistress of the household. In the ensuing years Johnson shared more of his inner life with Mrs Thrale than he did with anyone else. He may even have intimated to her his deepest fears and his most vagrant longings. Early June 1773 is the probable time of his writing to her, from his room at Streatham to hers, the famous letter, written in French, in which he invites her to lock him in, if only she will visit twice a day with her key. He describes her power over him in terms of 'l'esclavage que vou[s] sçavez si bien rendre heureuse' ('the slavery you well know how to make happy'). This passage has stimulated speculation about the possibility that some kind of erotic masochism was part of Johnson's relationship with Mrs Thrale. Such speculation draws support from references in Johnson's diary to manacles, Mrs Thrale's mention of Johnson's 'roving wishes', and an item sold at auction in 1823 described in Mrs Thrale's handwriting as 'Johnson's Padlock'. However, the language of freedom and bondage is highly conventional in the sort of courtly wit that Johnson's letter displays; he had used the same convention in a Latin poem to Mary Aston many years before, and at least one other letter of his in French shows that he used that language for courtly purposes. Walter Jackson Bate perceptively describes the letter as 'self-defensive, ironic, coy, disguising complaint under the appearance of excessive courtesy and self-abasement, and filled with signals asking for reassurance that he was not in the way but rather a cherished member of the family'. Johnson may be mimicking the complex pose that he strikes, but he is not doing so coolly. He was an emotional person, the most 'sensible', or feeling, man his wife had ever met. His readiness to weep; his liability to explosive anger followed by remorse; his financial, verbal, and physical extravagances all suggest his emotional nature. Mrs Thrale, for her part, shows a great capacity to deal successfully with such a character, and she evidently valued his friendship highly enough to soothe him, when that was required, with a whole heart. A couple of years later Mrs Thrale could refer to the jest about manacles in a jocular way by reference to her 'Iron Dominion'.[31] 'Scolding' and 'huffing' on both sides were a feature of Johnson and Mrs Thrale's relationship, one that they laughed about and elaborated in fictions about themselves. A jest so expanded by fancy and extended over years has meaning, of course, but there is no convincing evidence that it was realized in anything beyond polite behaviour and a kind of country-house theatrical life.

19

A Journey to the Western Islands of Scotland

The use of travelling is to regulate imagination by reality, and instead of thinking how things may be, to see them as they are.

Johnson to Mrs Thrale, 21 September 1773

One of Mrs Thrale's suggestions to Johnson in her response to his famous letter in French was that he accept Boswell's frequently repeated invitation to tour Scotland. Mrs Thrale's mother died in late May with Johnson at the bedside. On 6 August 1773, with his place at home secure, Johnson set out for Scotland. On 11 August he reached Newcastle in company with Robert Chambers and stayed at the house of the Vinerian professor's mother. On 14 August he joined Boswell in Edinburgh, and the two were off on a jaunt of nearly two months covering numerous towns and islands, up the east coast past Aberdeen, west beyond Banff, Inverness, and Loch Ness, around the isles of Skye, Coll, and Mull, before returning via Glasgow and the Boswell family seat of Auchinleck to Edinburgh on 9 November. Both Johnson and Boswell kept journals, and both published books about the tour. Within a few months of his return to England, probably in early 1774, Johnson put together *A Journey to the Western Islands of Scotland* from his notes and from letters written along the way to Hester Thrale. The book was officially published early in 1775. In deference to his friend's wishes, Boswell did not bring out his more personal version of the story until 1785, the year after Johnson's death. Except in his treatment of seats of learning, on which he regarded himself as specially qualified to report, Johnson's belief that the success of travel books depends upon their novelty guides him in his choice of subjects. He concentrates on his experiences in Skye and the other Hebrides because they were less travelled, and he conscientiously omits descriptions of very well-known places like Glasgow and Edinburgh. He is conscious of his literary predecessors, Martin Martin, whom he may have read as a child, and Thomas Pennant, whose *Tour in Scotland* had run to three editions between 1771 and 1774, including a second part in 1774 entitled *Voyage to the Hebrides*. In this regard, Johnson's book, like his whole sense of things, is utterly different from Boswell's. Johnson wrote about a place where others had been, whereas Boswell described his own inimitable experience and his unique companion. In an important sense, Boswell had no predecessors. Johnson could never feel that way.[1]

Early in his journey Johnson wrote to Mrs Thrale, 'You have often heard me complain of finding myself disappointed by books of travels, I am afraid travel itself will likewise end in disappointment.' There were exciting moments for Johnson on his trip, but he displays a sense throughout the *Journey*, even in the description of the Hebrides, of having come too late to make any striking discoveries. He was late not only because others had been there before, but also because what would have been most interesting was now gone. In particular, Johnson finds missing from even the remotest corners of Scotland the traditional, oral society of bards and chiefs celebrated in folklore and artificially revived in the Ossian poems published by James Macpherson in the early 1760s. Johnson speaks directly of his lateness soon after arriving in Skye: 'We came thither too late to see what we expected, a people of peculiar appearance, and a system of antiquated life. The clans retain little now of their original character, their ferocity of temper is softened, their military ardour is extinguished, their dignity of independence is depressed, their contempt of government subdued, and their reverence for their chiefs abated. Of what they had before the late conquest of their country, there remain only their language and their poverty. Their language is attacked on every side.' In one sense, Johnson is late by less than thirty years because many of the lamentable changes in Scottish society resulted from the failed rebellion of 1745 and the subsequent Parliamentary Acts of 1746 and 1748 which forbade traditional dress and other distinguishing features of the Highlanders' life.[2] However, Johnson's sense of lateness in the Hebrides is also related to his general sense of his own intellectual lateness in the history of literature, imagination, and faith. Johnson was acutely aware of living in a post-romantic, post-miraculous, and late humanistic time. In response to this awareness, whether he is contemplating religion or traditional Highlands society, Johnson mixes urbane acceptance with irritable re-examination of the situation.

Unlike the majority of his works, which originated behind the scenes in London bookshops, Johnson apparently conceived the *Journey* in a wilderness reverie which he discloses as part of his narrative:

I sat down on a bank, such as a writer of Romance might have delighted to feign. I had indeed no trees to whisper over my head, but a clear rivulet streamed at my feet. The day was calm, the air soft, and all was rudeness, silence, and solitude. Before me, and on either side, were high hills, which by hindering the eye from ranging, forced the mind to find entertainment

for itself. Whether I spent the hour well I know not; for here I first conceived the thought of this narration.

The story is too good to be true. The conventional romantic setting for
literary conception resembles the framework of dreaming in *The Vision of
Theodore*. The confining hills of *Rasselas* are also suggested in Johnson's
description, and, as soon as his habitual literary setting is in place, Johnson's
perpetual theme occurs to him:

> The phantoms which haunt a desert are want, and misery, and danger; the
> evils of dereliction rush upon the thoughts; man is made unwillingly ac-
> quainted with his own weakness, and meditation shews him only how little
> he can sustain, and how little he can perform. . . . Whoever had been in the
> place where I then sat, unprovided with provisions and ignorant of the
> country, might, at least before the roads were made, have wandered among
> the rocks, till he had perished with hardship, before he could have found
> either food or shelter. Yet what are these hillocks to the ridges of Taurus,
> or these spots of wildness to the desarts of America?

The theme of *The Vanity of Human Wishes* even brings with it some
'phantoms' and a quick survey of the globe. The contrast between this
passage and what he wrote to Mrs Thrale about the same moment further
suggests that Johnson fabricated it according to his favourite literary con-
ventions: 'I looked round me, and wondered that I was not more affected,
but the mind is not at all times equally ready to be put in motion.'[3]

The *Journey* never fully devolves into a homily on the weakness and
infirmity of man, but in his ode on the Isle of Skye Johnson shows that
the Hebrides evoked in him such melancholy thoughts. Johnson's Latin
ode begins with a description of the island as a pastoral refuge, but it
soon turns into a confession of human weakness and a hymn to almighty
God ('Rex summe, solus tu regis arbiter'). As it does in the Skye ode, the
romantic setting in the *Journey* turns out to be ironic. In his sober and
rational evaluation of everything romantic and fabulous, in his insistence
on presenting a world abandoned by the gods, and in his refusal to tempt
his reader with the allurements of fiction, Johnson makes the book a
lesson in humbly seeing things as they are. Although readers may have
started the book hoping for romantic tales and scenes in which their
imagination can expatiate, by the end they must be prepared to accept the
frigid tranquillity of Johnson's farewell to the Hebrides: 'Of these Islands
it must be confessed, that they have not many allurements, but to the
mere lover of naked nature. The inhabitants are thin, provisions are scarce,
and desolation and penury give little pleasure.'[4]

Before one gets to the frigid ending, much of the fun of reading the
Journey is in finding out if Johnson will ever indulge in the allurements of
fancy which are all about him. The trip resembles the journey in *Rasselas*,
as Bertrand Bronson has suggested. Johnson in Scotland is much more
like the rational and experienced Imlac than the gullible young prince,

but he feels the attractions of romance. The tension is most frequently played out in Johnson's attitude to the lost, feudal world of the Highlanders. He describes their former condition, sometimes with regret, sometimes even with an infusion of nostalgia. This is particularly so in his musings on the unfair laws against bearing arms imposed by the English conquerors:

> That dignity which they derived from an opinion of their military importance, the law which disarmed them, has abated. An old gentleman, delighting himself with the recollection of better days, related, that forty years ago, a Chieftain walked out attended by ten or twelve followers, with their arms rattling. . . .
>
> It affords a generous and manly pleasure to conceive a little nation gathering its fruits and tending its herds with fearless confidence, though it lies open on every side to invasion, where, in contempt of walls and trenches, every man sleeps securely with his sword beside him; where all on the first approach of hostility come together at the call to battle, as at a summons to a festal show. . . .
>
> This was, in the beginning of the present century, the state of the Highlands. Every man was a soldier, who partook of national confidence, and interested himself in national honour. To lose this spirit, is to lose what no small advantage will compensate.[5]

In his description of the hospitable Laird of Coll Johnson likewise glows with admiration for the good old days:

> Wherever we roved [on the Isle of Coll] we were pleased to see the reverence with which his subjects regarded him. He did not endeavour to dazzle them by any magnificence of dress: his only distinction was a feather in his bonnet; but as soon as he appeared, they forsook their work and clustered about him: he took them by the hand, and they seemed mutually delighted. He has the proper disposition of a Chieftain, and seems desirous to continue the customs of his house. The bagpiper played regularly . . . and he brought no disgrace upon the family of *Rankin*, which has long supplied the Lairds of *Col* with hereditary musick.

The scene obviously appealed to Johnson, and he recreates it with imaginative sympathy; the detail of the handclasp and the glance at the lineage of the bagpiper especially suggest Johnson's willingness to participate in the feelings of his subject, at least temporarily. Boswell reports Johnson's sympathy rising to greater heights when 'One night, in Col, he strutted about the room with a broad sword and target, and made a formidable appearance; and, another night, I took the liberty to put a large blue bonnet on his head. His age, his size, and his bushy grey wig, with this covering on it, presented the image of a venerable *Senachi*' (the official oral historian of a clan).[6] Boswell's images of Johnson imitating the heroic Highlanders are broadly dramatic, almost vaudevillean, but Johnson's subtly sympathetic descriptions of the noble people provide a factual basis for Boswell's more colourful images.

Unlike Boswell, Johnson sometimes criticizes the feudal system of the clans by extolling, for instance, the advantages of a centrally administered legal system. He is especially keen in his analysis of the advantages of standard currency, although this vastly hastened the demise of the feudal system. A primary reliance on oral communication is an aspect of traditional society that supports non-standard exchange and legal systems, and, for all its allure, Johnson is generally contemptuous of it. One of his reasons for defending the tacksman, the middleman between the laird and the peasants, is that he increases communication: 'Without intelligence man is not social, he is only gregarious; and little intelligence will there be, where all are constrained to daily labour, and every mind must wait upon the hand.' In addition, Johnson takes his usual position on the advantages of written over orally transmitted information in a section devoted to his pursuit of the extinct bards:

> As there subsists no longer in the Islands much of that peculiar and discriminative form of life, of which the idea had delighted our imagination, we were willing to listen to such accounts of past times as would be given us. But we soon found what memorials were to be expected from an illiterate people, whose whole time is a series of distress; where every morning is labouring with expedients for the evening; and where all mental pains or pleasure arose from the dread of winter, the expectation of spring, the caprices of their Chiefs, and the motions of the neighbouring clans; where there was neither shame from ignorance, nor pride in knowledge; neither curiosity to inquire, nor vanity to communicate. . . . Books are faithful repositories, which may be a while neglected or forgotten; but when they are opened again, will again impart their instruction: memory, once interrupted, is not to be recalled. Written learning is a fixed luminary, which, after the cloud that had hidden it has past away, is again bright in its proper station. Tradition is but a meteor, which, if once it falls, cannot be rekindled.[7]

Johnson is sceptical about the existence of the bards and the extemporaneous poetry they are supposed to have created. He describes his confidence crumbling when he discovers the popular memory confused between the bard and the senachi. But this is disingenuous; throughout the *Dictionary* Johnson denigrates unwritten speech as 'merely oral', and he arrived in the Highlands predisposed to doubt the veracity, if not the reality, of the bards. Johnson denies the traditional singers even their ability to recite genealogies with accuracy, and he derides the hereditary assignment of the offices: 'The history of the race could no otherwise be communicated, or retained; but what genius could be expected in a poet by inheritance? . . . if they were ignorant, there was no danger of detection; they were believed by those whose vanity they flattered.' This line of reasoning leads to a stern rejection of the authenticity of Macpherson's Ossian poems, but its motivations are deeper than a wish to penetrate that recent literary hoax. Johnson's rejection of Ossian is just one expression of his general contempt for merely oral language. The linchpin of his argument against Macpherson is that the author will not present the manuscripts upon which he foolishly claimed to have based his 'translation'. Johnson maintains correctly that Macpherson had no manuscripts and inaccurately that Erse was never written at all until the seventeenth century. He is off by a century but close enough to support his point, if one grants his unwarranted assumptions that an unwritten language can never achieve the polish required for fine poetry and that oral tradition cannot preserve a poem of any great length.[8]

Johnson claims to have looked for evidence of the traditional preservation of Ossianic material and found none, but he was not very receptive. For him, belief in the existence of this poetry without hard evidence is another example of human ignorance and error. Johnson forgives the credulity of the Scottish because they are affected by national feeling, but he will not forgive his English audience: 'To be ignorant is painful; but it is dangerous to quiet our uneasiness by the delusive opiate of hasty persuasion. . . . If we know little of the ancient Highlanders, let us not fill the vacuity with *Ossian*. If we have not searched the *Magellanick* regions, let us however forbear to people them with *Patagons*.'[9] Johnson refers to Captain Byron's romantic fancy, which was an instance of imaginative irresponsibility that he combated in his pamphlet on the Falkland Islands. To a degree, all such fancies have a collective identity for Johnson, even though his empiricism commits him to examining each one independently.

Among the other phantoms that Johnson encounters in the *Journey* are second sight, the fabulous depth of Loch Ness, the two giant stones at Coll, the Brownie, and the *genius loci* at Iona. Johnson shows very little interest in miraculous physical objects, so he quickly dismisses most of these marvellous items. In the physical world of the Highlands he sometimes finds a terrifying sublimity, but he resists being strongly impressed. He insults Scottish storms with a comparison to English weather and Scottish mountains with a comparison to the Peak District of Derbyshire. Where he is impressed by physical objects, he tends to use the impression to naturalize the fabulous, rather than the other way around. For example, 'castles afford another evidence that the fictions of romantick chivalry had for their basis the real manners of the feudal times.' In the one instance when Johnson gets close to the genuinely unknown, he launches into a lecture on the importance of accurate measurement. On the coast of Mull the party descends into Mackinnon's Cave with insufficient illumination. Johnson notes his observation of a 'square stone, called, as we are told, *Fingal's Table*', a reference to the Ossianic world, and then he goes on, unmoved: 'If we had been provided with torches, we should have proceeded in our search, though we had already gone as far as any former adventurer, except some who are reported never to have returned; and, measuring our way back, we found it more than a hundred and sixty yards, the eleventh part of a mile.' Although Johnson often mentions the importance of measurement for travellers, he reserves his longest discussion of it for juxtaposition with his most nearly strange encounter with the landscape. He avers that the failure to bring proper instruments is a cause of error, but the more frequent causes are excitement and the consequent unwillingness to note things down right away. Failures in measurement, he concludes, engender the romance of the unknown. Boswell reports Johnson's scepticism in the cave, and reflects, 'As, on the one hand, his faith in the Christian religion is firmly founded upon good grounds; so, on the other, he is incredulous when there is no sufficient reason for belief; being in this respect just the reverse of modern infidels, who, however nice and scrupulous in weighing the evidences of religion, are yet often so ready to believe the most absurd and improbable tales of another nature, that Lord Hailes well observed, a good essay might be written *Sur la credulité des Incredules*.'[10] A good essay on Johnson, as Boswell implies, must switch the terms and discuss the incredulity of this believer.

In his evaluation of metaphysical wonders Johnson is less strict than in his approach to the supposedly marvellous in nature. He is, for example, much more inclined to credit second sight in human beings than any-thing miraculous in the physical world. With second sight, as with ghosts, Johnson is afraid to determine against a phenomenon that is well attested, especially when that determination might suggest a knowledge of the supernatural which is presumptuous:

> Strong reasons for incredulity will readily occur. . . . It is a breach of the common order of things, without any visible reason or perceptible benefit. It is ascribed only to people very little enlightened; and among them, for the most part, to the mean and the ignorant.
>
> To the confidence of these objections it may be replied, that by presuming to determine what is fit, and what is beneficial, they presuppose more knowledge of the universal system than man has attained; and therefore depend upon principles too complicated and extensive for our comprehension; and there can be no security in the consequence, when the premises are not understood; that the Second Sight is only wonderful because it is rare, for, considered in itself, it involves no more difficulty than dreams . . . that a general opinion of communicative impulses, or visionary representations, has prevailed in all ages and all nations; that particular instances have been given, with such evidence, as neither *Bacon* nor *Boyle* has been able to resist . . . and that where we are unable to decide by antecedent reason, we must be content to yield to the force of testimony.

Johnson concludes, 'There is against it, the seeming analogy of things confusedly seen, and little understood; and for it, the indistinct cry of national persuasion, which may be perhaps resolved at last into prejudice and tradition. I never could advance my curiosity to conviction; but came away at last only willing to believe.'[11]

If we view the *Journey* as a story about Johnson's curiosity and its potential advance to conviction, the climax of the book is on Icolmkill at the remains of the monastery of Iona. The editor of Shakespeare understandably entertains the attractions of 'classic ground' when passing the seat of

Macbeth, but Johnson also had some special preparation for his response to Iona. As a seat of ancient, apostolical religion, Iona is a counterpoint that completes Johnson's frequent complaints about 'the tumult and violence of Knox's reformation' in Scotland. As a seat of learning, it is also of special interest to Johnson, and his response is elevated by the platform of remarks made earlier in Aberdeen, where he thought of Hector Boethius and fifteenth-century learning, and in St Andrews, 'where that university still subsists in which philosophy was formerly taught by Buchanan, whose name has as fair a claim to immortality as can be conferred by modern latinity, and perhaps a fairer than the instability of vernacular languages admits.' Most of what Johnson sees in Scotland is local or national, and, though he laments the wholesale emigration by which the old Scottish nation was being destroyed, he is also critical of the old national order. Humanistic learning and catholic religion, however, transcend nationality, and Johnson responds to them with uncritical loyalty. These communities of learning and faith comprise Johnson's true nationality. It is telling that his climactic sentence about Iona uses for comparison a description of national feeling, but the 'nation' is not England: it is literally Athens and, by expansion, Europe, since the foe at Marathon was Asian Persia:

> We were now treading that illustrious Island, which was once the luminary of the *Caledonian* regions, whence savage clans and roving barbarians derived the benefits of knowledge, and the blessings of religion. To abstract the mind from all local emotion would be impossible, if it were endeavoured, and would be foolish, if it were possible. Whatever withdraws us from the power of our senses; whatever makes the past, the distant, or the future predominate over the present, advances us in the dignity of thinking beings. Far from me and from my friends, be such frigid philosophy as may conduct us indifferent and unmoved over any ground which has been dignified by wisdom, bravery, or virtue. That man is little to be envied, whose patriotism would not gain force upon the plain of *Marathon,* or whose piety would not grow warmer among the ruins of *Iona!*[12]

This passage is particularly exclamatory and emotional in view of the extent to which Johnson has applied 'frigid philosophy' throughout his travels. When he examines the remains of castles, the supposed graves of kings, and other phenomena Johnson is studiously logical and 'philosophical', both stoical and scientific. He frequently uses 'philosophic' words like 'conglobate' and 'succedaneous' to describe what he has seen, but, even when he does not, his frigidity is apparent. Johnson's studiously objective description of the fabled women of Skye provides a good example of his 'frigid philosophy':

> The ladies have as much beauty here as in other places, but bloom and softness are not to be expected among the lower classes, whose faces are exposed to the rudeness of the climate, and whose features are sometimes contracted by want, and some times hardened by the blasts. Supreme beauty

is seldom found in cottages or work-shops, even where no real hardships are suffered. To expand the human face to its full perfection, it seems necessary that the mind should cooperate by placidness of content, or consciousness of superiority.

This physiognomic theory verges on a parody of the philosophical and becomes almost Swiftian in the last sentence, even though it relies on accepted contemporary beliefs. In other instances Johnson's philosophical approach is less obtrusive than it is on the traditionally subjective topic of beauty. But the point is that his enthusiasm in Iona is striking and the only real instance of such warmth in the whole *Journey*. It occurs here because an element of intellectual and spiritual patriotism moves Johnson to excesses that he resists while the ground he treads is merely Scottish or, for that matter, merely English. Significantly, Boswell, whose aptitude for nationalistic transport was infinitely greater than Johnson's, could do no better in his own description of their arrival at Iona than to quote Johnson's rare passage in full.[13]

It would be interesting to find that once Johnson had broken through his reserve and become ecstatic he was then generally more able to advance curiosity into conviction. But this is not the case. As soon as he leaves the subject of transcendent intellectual and spiritual identity, Johnson's scepticism returns. In the Graveyard of the Kings he is not able 'to sooth his imagination with the thoughts that naturally rise in places where the great and powerful lie mingled with the dust'. One question to the guide and 'his delight is at an end'; he must conclude, '*Iona* has long enjoyed, without any very credible attestation, the honour of being reputed the cemetery of the Scottish Kings. It is not unlikely, that, when the opinion of local sanctity was prevalent, the Chieftains of the Isles, and perhaps some of the *Norwegian* or *Irish* princes were reposited in this venerable enclosure. But by whom the subterraneous vaults are peopled is now utterly unknown. The graves are very numerous, and some of them undoubtedly contain the remains of men, who did not expect to be so soon forgotten.' 'Men, who did not expect to be so soon forgotten' could be any men, and Johnson is back in his philosophical mode. On the way south Johnson is caught in a storm so strong that he confesses to hearing 'the rough musick of nature', and he finds some appeal in the 'sullen dignity of the old castle' at Auchinleck, but, allowing for Johnson's wish to express his genuine gratitude for hospitality received throughout the trip, his response to the college for the deaf in Edinburgh is more robust than it is to either of those distinctly Scottish experiences. The educational project seems truly heroic to Johnson, and it moves him to an exclamation that also sums up his feelings about the Western Isles: 'after having seen the deaf taught arithmetick, who would be afraid to cultivate the *Hebrides*?'[14]

In a footnote to his *Tour to the Hebrides* and again in his *Life* Boswell reported the judgement of Robert Orme that the *Journey* contains 'thoughts, which, by long revolution in the great mind of Johnson, have been formed and polished – like pebbles rolled in the ocean!'[15] This is certainly true of the antagonism between report and reality that persists throughout. But almost all of Johnson's writing gives the impression that it is composed of thoughts long revolved. One reason for this is that the sea of Johnson's mind is an arm of common European culture where the thoughts he expresses were revolving for some centuries before his birth. As there is a profound conventionality in Johnson's story of the trip north, there is ever a striking novelty in Boswell's version. Like a fashion photographer, Boswell is constantly posing his subject. Contrasts please him: the defender of civilized, urban life disputing with the 'naturalist' Monboddo; the stoical sage with a Highland beauty on his lap; the High Churchman among the Presbyterian men of learning; and the arch-Tory confronting the arch-Whig, Boswell's father. Even better than a contrast, however, is a surprising affinity: as the scene in the King's library is a focal point in the *Life*, Johnson's contact with Highlanders who were involved in the rebellion of 1745 is central in the *Tour*. The meeting with Flora MacDonald on Skye is important, but a real climax occurs when Johnson occupies for a night the bed on which the poor wandering prince slept. Johnson's reception at the home of the Duke of Argyll also receives careful attention, as does the charming episode in which Lady Eglinton, discovering that she was married one year before his birth, declares that she will adopt the Great Cham. A much more romantic artist than Johnson, Boswell was bent on hero-worship, and one way that he aggrandizes Johnson is by getting him as close as possible to royalty.

Boswell is forever making Johnson's life into a fairy tale about the ugly duckling or Cinderella, and he obviously had more influence than anyone in creating the Johnson of folklore. Not only did Boswell's fiction catch on, it inspired further elaborations. In 1786, for example, one year after it was published, Boswell's book became the subject of a series of satirical sketches by Thomas Rowlandson. These ten prints, especially the one of Johnson and Boswell 'walking up the High Street' in Edinburgh, have shaped the public image of Johnson. This image, twice removed, at least, from the historical figure, was powerful enough in the nineteenth century to stimulate Sir Walter Scott, among others, to use the *Tour* as a lattice on which to grow more folklore about Johnson. In Scott's notes (1831) Johnson's confrontation with old Lord Auchinleck is heated, his Jacobitism intensified, and by misquotation his 'table talk' is increased. Yet, it is important to remember that the mythical Johnson already existed at the time of the journey, for Boswell accurately reports the appearance in a Glasgow newspaper (14–21 October 1773) of an article stating, 'We are well assured that Dr Johnson is confined by tempestuous weather to the isle of Sky. . . . Such a philosopher, detained on an almost barren island, resembles a whale left upon the strand. The latter will be welcome to every body on account of his oil, his bone, &c. and the other will charm his companions, and the rude inhabitants, with his superior knowledge and wisdom, calm resignation, and unbounded benevolence.'[16]

However gigantic Johnson was in Boswell's or in the public eye, in his own estimation he remained a man of depressingly human proportions. He wrote to Mrs Thrale from Skye: 'I cannot forbear to interrupt my Narrative. Boswel, with some of his troublesome kindness, has informed [the Macraes], and reminded me that the eighteenth of September is my birthday. The return of my Birthday, if I remember it, fills me with thoughts which it seems to be the general care of humanity to escape. I can now look back upon threescore and four years, in which little has been done, and little has been enjoyed, a life diversified by misery, spent part in the sluggishness of penury, and part under the violence of pain, in gloomy discontent, or importunate distress.' Johnson found time on Skye to enter in his diary a similar reproach, 'when I consider my age, and the broken state of my body, I have great reason to fear lest Death should lay hold upon me, while I am yet only designing to live. But,' he added, 'I have yet hope.'[17]

Along with his familiar literary topics and his humbling, troublous sense of self, Johnson carried to the Hebrides his affection for Mrs Thrale and a few other friends. He was as nervous about news from Streatham as Boswell was about news of his family in Edinburgh. Johnson wrote the longest letters of his life to Mrs Thrale while on this journey, and he also composed a Latin ode to her on Skye, which he sent a little later from Inverary, very decorously enclosed in a letter to her husband Henry. The ode itself is a polite celebration of the Thrale family circle, with Hester in the centre, but affection and something of the pathos of the playful letter in French shine through: 'Sit memor nostri, fideique merces / Stet fides constans' ('Keep the memory of me, as a reward for my faithfulness, and let faithfulness be steadfast').[18]

Johnson blamed Boswell for the pair's need to hurry back to Edinburgh for the opening of the court sessions, but he too was in a hurry to get home. He wished to be with the Thrales, and he was very eager to see Robert Chambers before his departure for India. Fearing that he would miss his dear friend, Johnson wrote from Skye, 'If I am detained from you by insuperable obstructions, let this be witness that I love you, and that I wish you all the good that can be enjoyed through [the] whole of our Existence.'[19] Fortunately, Chambers displayed his usual dilatoriness, and Johnson was able to see him again. To do so, he left for Oxford after only a weekend in London; his correspondence throughout this period is dotted with indications of how dearly he felt the impending loss of this friend. Johnson missed Chambers, as he missed his 'dear, dear Bathurst'. Although he had close friends his own age, it was for a group of younger men and the younger Mrs Thrale that Johnson had the warmest feelings: Thrale most of all, then Langton, Chambers, and Boswell in particular, but also young George Strahan, Beauclerk, and William Bowles. The affection was partly fatherly, and these literate young people, to whom Johnson entrusted many of his manuscripts and much of his reputation, supplied the place of children for him.

Whether they were younger or not, many of Johnson's friends confirmed their friendship with him during a journey. The last and best to do so was Mrs Thrale, with her husband and Johnson's godchild Queeney. In the summer of 1774 the party went to North Wales to inspect a recently inherited estate, and the bond of travelling companionship was doubled because the group stayed some time with Johnson on his home ground before journeying west to the place of Hester Thrale's origins at Bodvil Hall, near Pwllheli on the Lleyn Peninsula. In Wales Johnson preceded Pennant, who did not make his tour until 1780, and his diary of the trip shows some signs that he was preparing to write another travel book. There are intricate and sensitive descriptions of the landscape that suggest similar passages in the *Journey*. In one place, Johnson finds 'not the tranquillity but the horrour of solitude, a kind of turbulent pleasure between fright and admiration'. Elsewhere he records an experience that he might have adapted as the inspiration for the volume when 'The gloom, the stream, and the silence generate thoughtfulness.' There is also an adventure in a cave that might have paralleled his passage in the *Journey* on Mackinnon's Cave. Moreover, Johnson was so impressed by Caernarfon Castle that he noted, 'it surpassed my Ideas.' Yet Johnson wrote to Boswell after the trip, 'Wales is so little different from England, that it offers nothing to the speculation of the traveller.' This conclusion, though hasty, may be the reason why Johnson did not write up his Welsh journal, and it suggests that he needed the element of speculation in a travel book, although he was committed to subjecting speculation perpetually to the test of experience. Much as he might have approved of merely useful books of the sort he lauded in the *Literary Magazine* on bleach or salt water, Johnson's own literary endeavours thrive on the interplay of the imaginative and the factual.[20]

In 1775, a year after his return from Wales and two years after the Hebridean journey, Johnson went with the Thrales to Paris. This trip was as long as his journey north and perhaps filled Johnson's mind with as many impressions. Unfortunately, only half of his journal of the expedition remains, and he never planned to publish a report on such a well-known itinerary. But some of his notes are interesting. We know that he viewed the King and Queen at dinner, and visited a great many palaces, libraries, monasteries, and a zoo. The mythical Johnson has accrued to himself so much animal imagery that it is pleasing to have even his brief descriptions of large and strange creatures: 'Rhinoceros. . . . The skin folds like loose cloath doubled, over his body, and cross his hips, a vast animal though young, as big perhaps as four Oxen. The young Elephant with his tusks just appearing. The brown Bear put out his paws.'[21]

Johnson's opportunities for contact with the world of learning, which he had managed to locate even in North Wales, were abundant in Paris. He vastly increased his appreciation of painting and sculpture and particularly delighted in a gallery of greats, mingling, as was proper to Johnson's mind, artists and scholars: 'Michael Angelo, drawn by himself, Sir Thomas

Moore, DesCartes, Bochart, Naudaeus, Mazarine'. Johnson also saw a vast number of books in many grand places, including the King's library, the library of the Sorbonne, and that of Saint-Germain-des-Prés. He noted the dates of incunabula, printing styles, and unusual books, like a Gutenberg Bible. In these great libraries Johnson was at home, and he further accommodated himself by reading, usually in familiar Latin books, as he did on all his travels. Bumping along in a coach in Wales, crossing a Hebridean channel, or sitting in the cell of a French Benedictine monastery, Johnson could by reading enter his intellectual homeland in a moment. He carried this wonderful capacity with him in his mind at all times, but he also bore his inexorable sorrows. On a given day, in an extravagantly lavish mansion, Johnson is overwhelmed with 'a profusion of wealth and elegance' and says definitively, 'This house struck me.' But another day, on a similar occasion, he is too sad for the images to penetrate, and his deepest sorrows return to view: 'The sight of palaces and other great buildings leaves no very distinct images, unless to those who talk of them and impress them. As I entred [the Palais-Bourbon] my Wife was in my mind. She would have been pleased; having now nobody to please I am little pleased.'[22]

20

The *Lives of the Poets*

---

*If I had money enough what would I do. Perhaps, if You and Master did not hold
me I might go to Cairo, and down the Red Sea to Bengal, and take a ramble in India.*
Johnson to Mrs Thrale, 11 July 1775

Before his trip to France and for a little while afterwards, Johnson was
dreaming of wider and wider excursions. He was in high hopes of visiting
Italy with the Thrales in the spring of 1776, but the trip was cancelled
because of the sudden death of yet another of the Thrales' children (they
lost seven of eleven, and three in one year). After this disappointment,
Johnson's opportunities for travel diminished, and even his fantasies were
restricted by poor health, financial constraints, and his commitment to
one last literary project, *Prefaces Biographical and Critical to the Works of the
English Poets* (1779–81), better, though less accurately, known as the *Lives
of the Poets.*[1]

In 1775, before going to France, Johnson published his last political
pamphlet, *Taxation No Tyranny*. Shortly thereafter he received an honorary
Doctor of Laws degree from Oxford. Lord North had recommended the
honour to the Vice-Chancellor of the University, and upon receipt of the
award Johnson wrote an elegant Latin letter of acceptance. This was
the last benefit conferred on Johnson through government intervention.
With his fixed pension of £300 dwindling with inflation, Johnson petitioned
the Lord Chamberlain in April 1776 for a residence in Hampton Court:
'I hope', wrote Johnson, 'that to a man who has had the honour of vin-
dicating his Majesty's Government, a retreat in one of his houses, may be
not improperly or unworthily allowed.' Johnson had quite recently moved
from Johnson's Court to nearby Bolt Court, and there he stayed because
the request was respectfully denied for want of space. Johnson applied to
the government once more; very near the end of his life he requested
funds to permit his winter stay in an Italian monastery; he was again

officially denied, and Lord High Chancellor Thurlow's offer to mortgage Johnson's pension for ready cash came too late to be attractive. Although the ministry made many changes in *Taxation No Tyranny* and did not want Johnson around as a loose cannon in Parliament, there is no evidence that he had seriously displeased anyone and was neglected as a result. Still, his financial situation worsened in the late 1770s; he was not lavishly supported by the government; nor did he have much purchase in high places (the 'infidel pensioner' Hume had £400 a year). Except for one visit to Rochester and one to Salisbury, his travels shrank permanently to an annual trip to the Midlands, an occasional trip to Oxford, and visits to the Thrales in Streatham and Brighton.[2]

He was not in dire financial straits, but it was probably helpful for Johnson to do some paid literary work at this time. Among his other expenses were his liberal benefactions to the people of his household and to Lichfield kith and kin. However, it is unlikely that he received much for the odd pieces of poetry and prose that he produced in the 1770s. He revised the life of Zachariah Pearce, the Bishop of Rochester, for the front matter of his posthumously published *Commentary with Notes on the Four Evangelists* (London, 1777). He wrote a prologue for a play called A Word *to the Wise* by Hugh Kelly, a dedication for Charlotte Lennox, a preface for Baretti's *Easy Phraseology* (London, 1775), perhaps a sermon for John Taylor, a preface for William Shaw's *Analysis of the Galic Language* (London, 1778), and another for Thomas Maurice's *Free Translation of Sophocles* (London, 1779). Johnson turned out most of these pieces with very little effort, but at about the same time he exerted himself more strenuously in some occasional pieces which he wrote on behalf of William Dodd.

Johnson had met Dodd only once, in 1750, when he was a popular young minister who cut a dashing figure and preached before large, mixed audiences, on such 'shocking' and provocative texts as 'If a man look on a woman to lust after her'.[3] Dodd was predictably involved in London high society and enjoyed the distinction of serving as tutor to Chesterfield's son, a position that the Earl's famous letters on breeding (1774) stamped with a seal of the highest social approval. He apparently used his position for good and charitable ends, though he was not immune to vanity. Unfortunately, Dodd was financially incapable of maintaining his place in society, and he attempted to buoy himself up by forging a bond for £4200 in his tutee's name. He was convicted on 22 February 1777, sentenced to death, and executed on 27 June. In an attempt to save himself, Dodd applied to Johnson for rhetorical help. He did not want Johnson to intercede for him; he certainly knew more highly placed persons; but there was no one like Johnson for writing power. Johnson agreed to help and, among other things, secretly wrote Dodd's 'Speech to the Recorder of London', his application of clemency to the King, 'The Petition of the City of London to his Majesty, in favour of Dr Dodd', which was signed by 20,000 people, and 'The Convict's Address', a sermon which Dodd delivered in Newgate Prison on 6 June 1777.

The sermon is the longest and most important of these performances, but the whole group is interesting from a literary point of view because they show Johnson at a kind of authorial extreme, impersonating a doomed, penitent man. Dodd's situation was for Johnson an image of the human condition, and he used appeals to morality like those in his other sermons and the *Rambler*: 'A little time for recollection and amendment is yet allowed us by the mercy of the law. Of this little time let no particle be lost.' Johnson did not altogether yield to the temptation of equating Dodd's state with everyone's. There is an analogy, but an equation would be fiction. The best evidence of Johnson's insistence upon seeing the convict's case as special is his treatment of the proper behaviour at execution. Johnson recommends that convicts not try to die with a show of bravery because 'We ought not to propagate an opinion, that he who lived in wickedness can die with courage.'[4] Johnson's own unabashed fears of death are consistent with what he expresses on Dodd's behalf, but the special case of the convict is not forgotten. It would have been easy to press the analogy; Johnson prefers the reality.

By the time of Dodd's execution Johnson was already launched on the *Lives of the Poets*. On 3 May 1777 he wrote to Boswell, 'I am engaged to write little Lives, and little Prefaces, to a little edition of the English Poets.' Shortly before that, on 29 March, Johnson had agreed for £300 to provide prefaces for an edition of the English poets to be undertaken by a coalition of 'almost all the booksellers in London'. The edition was quintessentially a booksellers' project, with the special purpose of reasserting the copyrights held in London against the 'invasion' of Martins at Edinburgh. The publishers originally planned to begin with Chaucer, but the wish or the capacity to protect more recent copyrights, under the Statute of Anne (1709), advanced the starting point to Milton. The edition was never intended to be 'little', but Johnson's note to Boswell and the small fee he accepted (£100 more than he asked) suggest that the design called for short prefaces. By late summer the poets to be included had been named, and the edition was in press, where it would remain, in part, until sixty-eight small octavo volumes were produced: fifty-six of the works of the poets, ten of prefaces, and two for the index. Johnson proposed including the works of no more than five poets other than those named by the booksellers: Watts, Blackmore, Pomfret, Thomson, and Yalden. These additions made for relatively small changes in the scheme, and Johnson was so little involved in the publication of the poetry itself that he complained to the principal publisher John Nichols that 'your Edition . . . is very impudently called mine.'[5]

Johnson's main contribution to the vast project was his expansion of the 'little Prefaces'. He began gathering material at once from learned correspondents, like James Farmer of Cambridge; he researched the project during his summertime visit to Oxford, and in Ashbourne, in the third week of October 1777, he finished 'Cowley', his favourite of the *Lives*.[6] He continued writing intermittently over the next three to four years, and his work exceeded the expected size and date of completion by so much that his individual treatments could not be bound in preliminary to each of the poets but had to be printed in separate volumes. In the first printing of the *Works of the English Poets* (1779), there were only four volumes of *Lives*, the full ten not appearing until two years later. Also in 1781 the *Lives* were printed separately in four large octavo volumes, and they have enjoyed consideration as an independent production ever since. This is somewhat delusive, however, and the genesis of the *Lives* as prefaces to be inserted before the various sections of the *Works of the English Poets* should be remembered.

Each of Johnson's prefaces is divided into three parts: the biography of the poet, an account of his character, and a criticism of his works, with an emphasis on the poetry included in the *Works of the English Poets*. The distinctness and the proportion among the parts of the prefaces vary, though not as much as the number of words or pages allotted to each: from 300 words for John Pomfret or Richard Duke to a whole volume for Pope. The prefaces to Pope, Dryden, Milton, Addison, Cowley, and Swift make up over half of what Johnson wrote in the three to four years of work on the project. (The life of Savage was a redaction of his 1744 biography, and the longish biography of Young was contributed by Herbert Croft.) In a rough way, Johnson proportions the size of his preface to the size of the writer's contribution to the edition. The critical statements he makes also display a reaction that can be calculated in terms that are nearly arithmetical. However, Johnson's critical judgements reflect his own interest rather than the prominence of the author in the edition: quite simply, the more words in Johnson's response, the richer his experience of the poetry. Moreover, it is richness of experience that matters more than the proportion of beauties and faults in a poet. Hence, the voluminous though often censorious treatment of the metaphysical poets is a much higher recommendation than the studiously short response to Swift: 'In the Poetical Works of Dr Swift there is not much upon which the critick can exercise his powers. They are often humorous, almost always light, and have the qualities which recommend such compositions, easiness and gaiety. They are, for the most part, what their author intended.' Johnson carries on methodically to consider Swift's language, but the whole is as dismissive as his treatment of Waller's 'sallies of occasional flattery': 'Of these petty compositions, neither the beauties nor the faults deserve much attention.'[7] The lack of proportion, however, between Swift's large contribution to the *Works* and Johnson's thin treatment makes the criticism of Swift's *oeuvre* much sharper than similarly worded criticisms of smaller collections of poetry.

Although Johnson speaks about the quality of his experiences in his critical judgements, the prefaces are formulaic enough to make their relative quantities important and conspicuous. In making the vast number of quick critical judgements included in the *Lives*, Johnson appears to have configured himself as a sensitive machine, set to register in a limited

number of terms a wide range of similar experiences. (Boswell was reacting to this quality of the *Lives* when he suggested that they provide the
materials for a Linnaean or Aristotelian 'code'.) The formal matrix of
these judgements is Dryden's definition of poetry as 'a just and lively
representation of human nature', a combination of Aristotle's notion that
poetry is an imitation of nature and Horace's precept that it should either
please or instruct. A slight work calls forth a faint version of the definition,
as when Johnson dismisses Milton's *Comus* as 'inelegantly splendid, and
tediously instructive'.[8] *Comus* is unsuitably lively and merely just, in Dryden's
terms; in Horace's, it pleases a little and instructs poorly. However, when
Johnson comes a few paragraphs later to *Paradise Lost*, the critical machinery heats up and comes to life.

As he prepares for the transition, Johnson says, 'Those little pieces may
be dispatched without much anxiety; a greater work calls for greater care.'
He then spends fifty-seven paragraphs on *Paradise Lost*, not only applying
conventional criteria of excellence, like Horace's and Aristotle's, but re-
stating them and implicitly re-evaluating them in light of the tremendous
experience of Milton's epic: 'Poetry is the art of uniting pleasure with
truth, by calling imagination to the help of reason. Epick poetry undertakes to teach the most important truths by the most pleasing precepts,
and therefore relates some great event in the most affecting manner. . . .
Before the greatness displayed in Milton's poem all other greatness shrinks
away.' After praising the design or plot, Johnson discusses other Aristotelian
elements – the characters, the probable and the marvellous, the machinery,
the episodes, and integrity or wholeness of the work. As he always does,
especially in considering the greatest poets, Johnson finds faults and points
them out: 'The want of human interest is always felt. *Paradise Lost* is one
of the books which the reader admires and lays down, and forgets to take
up again. None ever wished it longer than it is. Its perusal is a duty rather
than a pleasure.' There are faults in the quality of instruction and in the
design as well, but one cannot conclude that Johnson was ambivalent
about the importance of the poem. The magnitude and energy of Johnson's
treatment of the poem are decisive, as he indicates in the last paragraph
of his critique: 'Such are the faults of that wonderful performance *Paradise
Lost*, which he who can put in balance with its beauties must be considered
not as nice but as dull, as less to be censured for want of candour than
pitied for want of sensibility.'[9]

'Sensibility' here means the capacity for perception and response, and
in this sense Johnson develops a physics of critical sensibility in the *Lives*.
His reaction to the poetry under consideration is a mathematically
dependable indication of the poetry's force. Moreover, this scientific registration of critical response is part of an overall physicality, with its attend-
ant empiricism, that appears in all parts of Johnson's *Prefaces Biographical
and Critical*. What distinguishes the prefaces written from 1777 to 1781
from Johnson's earlier critical and biographical writing is an even greater
and more radical emphasis on empirical truth. Johnson continues his

lifelong interest in the learning of his biographical subjects, the telling
details of their domestic lives, and their moral characters; he is as judicious
as ever in discussing both the defects and the beauties of their writing; but
the concern for historical truth is greater in the *Lives* than anywhere in
Johnson's literary criticism.

In some respects, the best preparation for reading the *Lives* is not
Johnson's earlier criticism and biography but rather the *Journey to the Western
Isles*. In both works Johnson examines traditions – folktales, popular beliefs, received opinions, and all the various kinds of unexamined information passed on by word of mouth that obscure historical truth. With the
same sort of scepticism that he applied to the tales of second sight or the
fabulous beauty of the maidens of Skye, Johnson approaches the tales
about Milton's achievements as a teacher, Waller's trip to Bermuda, William
King's undergraduate feats of reading, or the pranks said to have been
played with Dryden's corpse. In a way, Johnson is again imitating his
intellectual idols, humanists like Joseph Scaliger who undertook to correct
the historical facts in classical texts and commentaries. In any case, Johnson
is extending his tendency toward empiricism, which was always strong, and
battling against the prevalence of fiction in the related areas of biography,
poetry, and criticism. It is a small episode in Johnson's life, but a little
experiment he recorded in his Annals in 1777, when he was just beginning the *Lives*, suggests his frame of mind at the time. He took the trouble
to shave the hair off a place on his arm simply to see how long it would
take to grow back.[10] He was testing his own vitality, as he ran tests on his
mind late in life. Likewise, he never retreated intellectually from the real
world of experience. In fact, he sought contact with the real, empirical
state of things even more boldly in his last years; this is apparent in the
great work of the *Lives* and in his trivial depilatory exercise.

Johnson begins many of his prefaces by saying how little is known of
the subject. When he says this, Johnson is usually referring to a dearth of
firsthand, recorded information. 'Dryden' opens in typical fashion: 'Of
the great poet whose life I am about to delineate, the curiosity which his
reputation must excite will require a display more ample than can now be
given. His contemporaries, however they reverenced his genius, left his
life unwritten; and nothing therefore can be known beyond what casual
mention and uncertain tradition have supplied.' Johnson has many strat-
egies for dealing with 'uncertain tradition', but he rarely ignores it. Indeed, one of the pleasures in reading the *Lives* is hearing Johnson react
to the many fables about writers that he records, and there is pleasure in
the fables themselves. One way that Johnson reacts to stories about authors
is to test their probability on reasonable grounds, to test them, that is,
against what is likely to have been the case, given the constant of human
nature. In 'Prior', for example, Johnson both reports and doubts the tale
that Prior really wounded Dryden by publishing *The City Mouse and the
Country Mouse*, a parody of Dryden's *Hind and the Panther*:

There is a story of great pain suffered and of tears shed on this occasion by Dryden, who thought it hard that 'an old man should be so treated by those to whom he had always been civil'. By tales like these is the envy raised by superior abilities every day gratified: when they are attacked, every one hopes to see them humbled; what is hoped is readily believed, and what is believed is confidently told. Dryden had been more accustomed to hostilities than that such enemies should break his quiet, and if we can suppose him vexed it would be hard to deny him sense enough to conceal his uneasiness.

The story is probably false because Dryden, like other people with similar experience in such a situation, would either have been immune to the attack or have hidden his feelings. Moreover, human nature is inclined to be credulous in such a case, and that contributes to Johnson's scepticism. Johnson similarly reasons from general principles in his evaluation of the problem of Congreve's place of birth: 'it was said by himself that he owed his nativity to England, and by everybody else that he was born in Ireland.' Johnson leaves the question undecided and adds: 'To doubt whether a man of eminence has told the truth about his own birth is, in appearance, to be very deficient in candour; yet nobody can live long without knowing that falsehoods of convenience or vanity, falsehoods from which no evil immediately visible ensues, except the general degradation of human testimony, are very lightly uttered, and once uttered are sullenly supported.'[11]

If Johnson's acute awareness of the human proclivity to embrace convenient falsehoods does not preclude 'candour' (meaning geniality), it comes close. Hence, Sprat's story about Cowley's inability 'to retain the ordinary rules of grammar' is 'an instance of the natural desire of man to propagate a wonder'. As his treatment of this tale about grammar suggests, Johnson is most secure in exploding myths concerning areas of his own experience or expertise. The tales of Milton's exalted pedagogy, for instance, are brought to the test of the bitter reality that Johnson himself faced as a schoolmaster:

> It is told that in the art of education he performed wonders, and a formidable list is given of the authors, Greek and Latin, that were read in Aldersgate-street by youth between ten and fifteen or sixteen years of age. Those who tell or receive these stories should consider that nobody can be taught faster than he can learn. The speed of the horseman must be limited by the power of the horse. Every man that has ever undertaken to instruct others can tell what slow advances he has been able to make, and how much patience it requires to recall vagrant inattention, to stimulate sluggish indifference, and to rectify absurd misapprehension. . . .
>
> Of institutions we may judge by their effects. From this wonder-working academy I do not know that there ever proceeded any man very eminent for knowledge.[12]

Johnson was critical of Milton's emphasis on the sciences in elementary education, and that may have something to do with his overall response to the 'wonder-working academy', but an autobiographical impetus is present in the force of the denunciation. Throughout the *Lives* Johnson is particularly confident in evaluating stories of pedagogy and study. His own experiences as a teacher, as a student, and a 'hard reader' make him sceptical about reports of great feats of reading. William King, for example, 'is said to have prosecuted his studies with so much intenseness and activity that, before he was eight years standing, he had read over and made remarks upon twenty-two thousand odd hundred books and manuscripts.' This stimulates Johnson to do some arithmetic of the kind he used to project his own schemes of reading: '[King's] books were certainly not very long, the manuscripts not very difficult, nor the remarks very large; for the calculator will find that he dispatched seven a day, for every day of his eight years, with a remnant that more than satisfies most other students.'[13]

'Pope' is the longest chapter in the *Lives* partly because Johnson was aware of so many traditional stories about him. Johnson mainly appeals to reason to cast doubt on these tales. In his examination of Pope's presentation of himself in his published letters, however, he employs a variety of tactics. Exhibiting both his tendency to suspect fiction in almost anything published as well as his general view of human nature, Johnson's exposure of Pope's disingenuousness in his letters is one of the most brilliant passages in all of his biographical writings. He begins by proposing a revised, rational view of the personal epistle as a literary genre:

> It has been so long said as to be commonly believed that the true characters of men may be found in their letters, and that he who writes to his friend lays his heart open before him. But the truth is that such were the simple friendships of the *Golden Age*, and are now the friendships only of children. Very few can boast of hearts which they dare lay open to themselves, and of which, by whatever accident exposed, they do not shun a distinct and continued view; and certainly what we hide from ourselves we do not shew to our friends. There is, indeed, no transaction which offers stronger temptations to fallacy and sophistication than epistolary intercourse.

Johnson then lays bare the various elements of Pope's representation of himself in his letters, focusing especially on his image of himself as careless about worldly things. He concludes by juxtaposing the false image, which reason has suspected, to historical realities proved by reliable testimony:

> When Pope murmurs at the world, when he professes contempt of fame, when he speaks of riches and poverty, of success and disappointment, with negligent indifference, he certainly does not express his habitual and settled sentiments, but either wilfully disguises his own character, or, what is more likely, invests himself with temporary qualities, and sallies out in the colours of the present moment. His hopes and fears, his joys and sorrows, acted

strongly upon his mind, and if he differed from others it was not by carelessness. He was irritable and resentful: his malignity to Philips, whom he had first made ridiculous and then hated for being angry, continued too long. Of his vain desire to make Bentley contemptible, I never heard any adequate reason. He was sometimes wanton in his attacks, and before Chandos, Lady Wortley, and Hill, was mean in his retreat.[14]

Appeals to direct experience, such as the one Johnson makes at the end of this paragraph, become more and more prominent as the biographies advance chronologically. Johnson was in a position to investigate many of the stories about Pope because he knew so many people who lived at Pope's time, but the tenacity of his pursuit is striking nevertheless. Even when an embroidered tale does not directly concern the subject of his biography, Johnson is compelled to expose it. When he comes to Pope's *Epistle to Bathurst*, for example, Johnson cannot forbear to discuss the historical model for this figure, one Kyrl, and the true manner in which he appeared to give such vast sums to charity from his comparatively modest holdings. It turns out that he skilfully and honestly solicited the help of other wealthy people in making donations, which is not a very startling discovery, but Johnson must unmask the fiction. He provides the reason and his source: 'Wonders are willingly told and willingly heard. . . . This account Mr Victor received from the minister of the place [Ross, Victor's home], and I have preserved it, that the praise of a good man, being made more credible, may be more solid. Narrations of romantick and impracticable virtue will be read with wonder, but that which is unattainable is recommended in vain: that good may be endeavoured it must be shewn to be possible.'[15]

Ben Victor is one of many obscure residents of Grub Street whom Johnson used as sources for firsthand information about his subjects. He made some written enquiries while preparing the *Lives*, but very often he relied on oral testimony. He preferred this form of investigation, as he suggests in a letter concerning a legal matter in the Midlands: 'To do business by letters is very difficult, for without the opportunity of verbal questions much information is seldom obtained.' To give one small example, for information on Pope's learning Johnson interviewed a man named Dobson whom the poet engaged to translate the *Essay on Man* into Latin. (Dobson informed Johnson that Pope knew '"More than I expected."') In most cases, however, Johnson did not engage in investigations at all but simply recalled firsthand information that he had gathered over the years. In discussing the historical occasion of the *Rape of the Lock*, for instance, he takes up the tradition that the poem reconciled the real Baron and Beauty, Robert Lord Petre and Arabella Fermor, along with the families and friends who had entered the feud: 'Whether all this be true, I have some doubt; for at Paris, a few years ago, a niece of Mrs Fermor, who presided in an English Convent, mentioned Pope's work with very little gratitude, rather as an insult than an honour; and she may be supposed to have inherited the opinion of her family.'[16]

Despite his distrust of loose traditions and tales, Johnson puts a great deal of faith in fixed traditions of testimony, if he has had personal contact with the line of descent. Yet he knows that even this kind of information has its liabilities and that biography, like every other human enterprise, is imperfectible. In a great passage on biography itself, Johnson acknowledges the way in which the truth in this genre must be traduced for the sake of its sources:

> The necessity of complying with times and of sparing persons is the great impediment of biography. History may be formed from permanent monuments and records; but Lives can only be written from personal knowledge, which is growing every day less, and in a short time is lost for ever. What is known can seldom be immediately told, and when it might be told it is no longer known. The delicate features of the mind, the nice discriminations of character, and the minute peculiarities of conduct are soon obliterated; and it is surely better that caprice, obstinacy, frolick, and folly, however they might delight in the description, should be silently forgotten than that by wanton merriment and unseasonable detection a pang should be given to a widow, a daughter, a brother, or a friend. As the process of these narratives is now bringing me among my contemporaries I begin to feel myself 'walking upon ashes under which the fire is not extinguished', and coming to the time of which it will be proper rather to say 'nothing that is false, than all that is true.'[17]

The Horatian ode to which Johnson refers is about the dangers of writing on the recent Roman civil war, and it suggests the deep feelings of kinship that he had for his subjects. But he was no closer to his subjects than to his sources, most of whom were members of the London book trade. Much of the material for the *Lives* comes from the likes of John Nichols, the powerful principal publisher, and from closer, more readily accessible acquaintances, like Johnson's landlord in Bolt Court, the printer Edmund Allen. About his sources Johnson is studiously respectful, where he is not actually celebratory or elegiac, and his acknowledgements contribute very significantly to an autobiographical element that is stronger in the *Lives* than in any of Johnson's other works.

Johnson reviews his own life in the *Lives*, in part, by mentioning so many of the people he knew. By bringing in these sources Johnson extends the sphere of primary evidence in his book, and he recalls the social worlds that he inhabited throughout his lifetime. He mentions his father, 'an old bookseller', for example, as a source of information about the popularity of Dryden's *Absalom and Achitophel* (1681), and later he remembers his anecdotes about the preaching habits of Sprat and Burnet, adding, 'This I was told by my father, an old man, who had been no careless observer of the passages of those times.' Johnson's childhood friend Andrew Corbett is his source of information on Addison's schoolboy pranks, and a story in 'Fenton' comes from Johnson's cousin Cornelius Ford, 'a clergyman, at that time too well known, whose abilities, instead of furnishing convivial merriment to the voluptuous and dissolute, might have enabled him to excel among the virtuous and wise.' Other old acquaintances who receive notice as oral sources of information or opinion for Johnson are his wife Elizabeth, Samuel Madden, Mr Ing, 'a gentleman of great eminence in Staffordshire', old Mr Lewis (a Russell Street bookseller), Warburton, Langton, Lintot (the son of Bernard, the famous publisher), Jonathan Richardson, Jr (son of the painter), Richard Savage, Robert Dodsley, 'Mr Boswell', John Hawksworth, 'the late learned Mr [Samuel] Dyer', George Steevens and Jacob Tonson, the younger, 'a man who is to be praised as often as he is named'. There are references to Mrs Thrale's opinions, but they are decently referred to 'a lady, of whose praise [Young] would have been justly proud'. His old amanuensis Robert Shiels receives tribute as the real author of Cibber's *Lives of the Poets*: 'His life was virtuous, and his end was pious.' Goldsmith, in supplying most of the life of Parnell, also provides Johnson with an opportunity to praise his late friend, 'a man of such variety of powers and such felicity of performance that he always seemed to do best that which he was doing'. Hawkesworth, a biographer of Swift, to whom Johnson imparted his scheme for the life 'in the intimacy of our friendship', is 'a man capable of dignifying his narration with so much elegance of language and force of sentiment'. Even Joseph Warton, an estranged friend, is saluted as 'the learned author of the *Essay on the Life and Writings of Pope*; a book which teaches how the brow of criticism may be smoothed, and how she may be enabled, with all her severity, to attract and to delight'. Johnson also bows to past acquaintances and friends when he pauses in the life of Shenstone to hail Pembroke College, 'a society which for half a century has been eminent for English poetry and elegant literature'. But most elaborately and fondly, Johnson cites his old friend Gilbert Walmesley as his source of information about Edmund Smith, and, as he speaks of Walmesley, a couple of other close friends pass before Johnson's mind and receive their final tribute from him:

> Of Gilbert Walmsley, thus presented to my mind, let me indulge myself in the remembrance. I knew him very early; he was one of the first friends that literature procured me, and I hope that at least my gratitude made me worthy of his notice.
> He was of an advanced age, and I was only not a boy; yet he never received my notions with contempt. He was a Whig, with all the virulence and malevolence of his party; yet difference of opinion did not keep us apart. I honoured him, and he endured me. . . .
> At this man's table I enjoyed many chearful and instructive hours, with companions such as are not often found: with one who has lengthened and one who has gladdened life; with Dr James, whose skill in physick will be long remembered; and with David Garrick, whom I hoped to have gratified with this character of our common friend: but what are the hopes of man! I am disappointed by that stroke of death, which has eclipsed the gaiety of nations and impoverished the publick stock of harmless pleasure.[18]

This casual kind of celebration is extended to other artists in Johnson's circle, and the whole work of the *Lives* has an element of reprise. In his life of Rowe, for instance, Johnson cannot touch on *The Fair Pentitent* and its villain Lothario without paying tribute to the creator of Lovelace, the fictional son of Lothario: 'The character of Lothario seems to have been expanded by Richardson into Lovelace, but he has excelled his original in the moral effect of the fiction. . . . It was in the power of Richardson alone to teach us at once esteem and detestation; to make virtuous resentment overpower all the benevolence which wit, elegance, and courage naturally excite, and to lose at last the hero in the villain.' Occasionally, Johnson's narrative brings in a source of information whom he must censure rather than praise. These cases are rare, and there is usually a mellow quality to Johnson's remembrance of earlier acquaintances, which he does not allow to infiltrate his criticisms of the poetry. But Johnson cannot remember his employer in the Harleian projects without recalling his ugliness: 'Osborne was a man entirely destitute of shame, without sense of any disgrace but that of poverty. He told me, when he was doing that which raised Pope's resentment [selling cheap copies of Pope's *Iliad*], that he should be put into *The Dunciad*; but he had the fate of Cassandra. I gave no credit to his prediction till in time I saw it accomplished [in the *New Dunciad*]. The shafts of satire were directed equally in vain against Cibber and Osborne; being repelled by the impenetrable impudence of one, and deadened by the impassive dulness of the other.'[19]

In addition to his recollections of old friends and acquaintances, other elements of autobiography arise for Johnson in the *Lives*, especially as he speaks about his contemporaries. In 'Lyttelton', for instance, the very last of the prefaces, Johnson reviews his own political evolution while describing the politics of his subject. Johnson says that Lyttelton's juvenile *Persian Letters* 'have something of that indistinct and headstrong ardour for liberty which a man of genius always catches when he enters the world, and always suffers to cool as he passes forward.' As G. B. Hill notes, Lyttelton lived to oppose the appeal of the American Stamp Act, and Johnson's progress from the days of *Marmor Norfolciense* to those of *Taxation No Tyranny* is somewhat similar. Lyttelton's political opinions are much more clearly a matter of public record than Johnson's, but the biographer may have been describing himself when he reviewed his subject's record in Parliament: 'He opposed the standing army; he opposed the excise; he supported the motion for petitioning the King to remove Walpole.' There is a double sort of recapitulation here because Johnson not only read the accounts of Lyttelton's behaviour in Parliament, he also wrote some of them.[20]

In addition, Johnson met Lyttelton in the neighbourhood of Stourbridge on his visits to his cousins, and, according to Bishop Percy, the two were early antagonists in 'colloquial disputes'. To this early antagonism, Percy attributes the 'grudging' character of Johnson's life of Lyttleton. Perhaps. But 'Lyttelton' is no more grudging than many of the other prefaces, and if Johnson is severe in some respects, he is whole-hearted in his praise of

Lyttelton's *Observations on the Conversion of St Paul,* one of the handful of contemporary works which he quoted in the *Dictionary.* Johnson is captious about Lyttelton's political career partly because he was equally hard on himself in reviewing his own similar past actions and opinions. There is greater acrimony in his description of Akenside's youthful political ardour: 'Whether, when he resolved not to be a dissenting minister, he ceased to be a Dissenter, I know not. He certainly retained an unnecessary and outrageous zeal for what he called and thought liberty – a zeal which sometimes disguises from the world, and not rarely from the mind which it possesses, an envious desire of plundering wealth or degrading greatness; and of which the immediate tendency is innovation and anarchy, an impetuous eagerness to subvert and confound, with very little care what shall be established.' Johnson denounced this vein of idealism earlier in *The Patriot,* but, when the passage takes flight after the dash, it may be impelled by a characteristically stern autobiographical reflection, the same kind of reflection that led to his description of himself in college as 'mad and violent': 'I thought to fight my way by my literature and my wit; so I disregarded all power and all authority.'[21]

The *Lives* provide a last view of Johnson's politics because he is obliged to treat the major events that occurred in the lifetimes of his subjects: the Civil War, the Glorious Revolution, the collapse of the Tory Party upon the death of Queen Anne, the South Sea Bubble, Marlborough's rise during the War of the Spanish Succession, Prince Frederick's separation from the court, the removal of Walpole, and the Seven Years War all loom large in the background of Johnson's *Lives.* He gives most attention to the episodes most affecting writers – the rise and fall of great patrons – and he makes distinctions among the various rulers of England on the basis of their capacity for understanding poetry and poets. But his view of history does not often seem narrow. Admittedly, royalism and conservatism are evident in the *Lives:* Johnson wrote to Mrs Thrale after sending the Lives to George III, 'If the King is a Whig, he will not like them; but is any King a Whig?'[22] Nevertheless, the long historical view in the *Lives* usually gives prominence to Johnson's non-partisan humanistic political commitments. For example, his hatred of war and his suspicion of those who wage it are unabated. As ever, he is realistic to the point of cynicism about government patronage and favours, and throughout he detests the persistent difference between high-minded political rhetoric and the mean political motives it often conceals.

Johnson is habitually incredulous concerning systematic or idealistic politics. Likewise, he tends to despise literature that is written to rule and does not depend upon or reflect actual experience. As a form of writing that was largely divorced form experience, pastoral poetry represents the kind of literature that Johnson found most distasteful. Moreover, because almost all the poets in the *Lives* performed in this genre, Johnson has occasion to denounce pastoral in almost every preface. His criticism of Milton's *Lycidas* provides the most famous example: 'In this poem there is no nature, for there is no truth; there is no art, for there is nothing new. Its form is that of a pastoral, easy, vulgar, and therefore disgusting: whatever images it can supply are long ago exhausted; and its inherent improbability always forces dissatisfaction on the mind.' Johnson's most trenchant and frequent objection to pastoral in the *Lives* is its falsehood, and his settled antipathy to the form is not merely a matter of critical bias; it is an extension of his impatience with political falsehood and with any writing that is not based on experience and fact. This is an impatience that Johnson may have had all his life, but he started to display it in its mature form in 1756 in his reviews for the *Literary Magazine*. Johnson probably agreed with Dryden, as he cited him in the *Dictionary*, that '*Fiction* is the essence of poetry', but his demand for truth in writing, especially late in life, was stronger than his love of poetry. Hence, he cannot abide poetry that merely exhibits the essence of poetry, or is merely fictional:

> Where there is fiction, there is no passion; he that describes himself as a shepherd, and his Neaera or Delia as a shepherdess, and talks of goats and lambs, feels no passion. He that courts his mistress with Roman imagery deserves to lose her for she may with good reason suspect his sincerity. [Hammond] produces nothing but frigid pedantry.

> By the help of such easy fictions and vulgar topicks, without acquaintance with life and without knowledge of art or nature, a poem of any length, cold and lifeless like [Prior's *Ode to the Queen*] may easily be written on any subject.

> In this question [of Edmund Smith's *Phaedra*], I cannot but think the people in the right. The fable is mythological, a story which we are accustomed to reject as false, and the manners are so distant from our own that we know them not from sympathy, but by study: the ignorant do not understand the action, the learned reject it as a school-boy's tale; *incredulus odi*. What I cannot for a moment believe, I cannot for a moment behold with interest or anxiety.

> To select a singular event, and swell it to a giant's bulk by fabulous appendages of spectres and predictions, has little difficulty, for he that forsakes the probable may always find the marvellous. And it has little use: we are affected only as we believe; we are improved only as we find something to be imitated or declined. I do not see that [Gray's] *Bard* promotes any truth, moral or political.[23]

The principle in all these judgements is quite simple. As Johnson states it in 'Addison', 'The rejection and contempt of fiction is rational and manly', or as he says in 'Gay', 'the mind is repelled by useless and apparent falsehood.' Even more absolutely in 'Cowley' he says, 'the basis of all excellence is truth.' This is a general principle for Johnson and not merely a reaction to pastoral concocted for other reasons; he applies it to poetry of all kinds. His preference for fact over fiction is what makes *Eloisa to Abelard* his favourite among Pope's poems: 'The heart naturally loves truth. The adventures and misfortunes of this illustrious pair are known

from un-disputed history. . . . So new and so affecting is their story that
it supersedes invention, and imagination ranges at full liberty without
straggling into scenes of fable.' The principle is operative again in Johnson's preference for Dryden's over Pope's *Ode for St Cecilia's Day*: 'Dryden's
plan is better chosen; history will always take stronger hold of the attention than fable: the passions excited by Dryden are the pleasures and
pains of real life, the scene of Pope is laid in imaginary existence. Pope
is read with calm acquiescence, Dryden with turbulent delight; Pope
hangs upon the ear, and Dryden finds the passes of the mind.'[24]

Johnson's rejection of fiction is also evident in his responses to philosophical poetry, another realm of fanciful ideals. For example, Johnson
will not pass over the moral epistle called 'The Characters of Men' without
exploding Pope's notion of the 'ruling passion': 'Of any passion thus
innate and irresistible the existence may reasonably be doubted. . . . to the
particular species of excellence, men are directed not by an ascendant
planet or predominating humour, but by the first book which they read,
some early conversation which they heard, or some accident which excited
ardour and emulation.' Experience rather than nature shapes life in
Johnson's view, but his hostility to the 'ruling passion' and other kinds of
determinism, such as astrology, is not merely philosophical: 'this doctrine
is in itself pernicious as well as false; its tendency is to produce the belief
of a kind of moral predestination or overruling principle which cannot be
resisted: he that admits it is prepared to comply with every desire that
caprice or opportunity shall excite, and to flatter himself that he submits
only to the lawful dominion of Nature in obeying the resistless authority
of his "ruling Passion".' Johnson was always against innate ideas, any form
of determinism, and anything else that might depreciate moral freedom,
without which there could, in his orthodox view, be no morality. But in
the *Lives*, where he discusses and implicitly recommends the inherently
fictional world of poetry, his intolerance of fiction is more literal and
absolute than anywhere else in his works. The paradox occurs to him in
his treatment of Waller's panegyrics: 'Poets, indeed, profess fiction, but
the legitimate end of fiction is the conveyance of truth; and he that has
flattery ready for all whom the vicissitudes of the world happen to exalt
must be scorned as a prostituted mind that may retain the glitter of wit,
but has lost the dignity of virtue.'[25]

It is in defence of truth in fiction, as well his own authorial class, that
Johnson so roundly denounces Dryden's panegyrical dedications. One of
these, Johnson says, is written 'in a strain of flattery which disgraces genius,
and which it was wonderful that any man that knew the meaning of his
own words could use without self-detestation. It is an attempt to mingle
earth and heaven, by praising human excellence in the language of religion.' As it often does for Johnson, fiction in Dryden's panegyric violates
religious truth. In fact, the one kind of poetry that Johnson rejects as
steadily as pastoral throughout the *Lives* is devotional poetry. He explains
why such poetry must fail in 'Waller':

Contemplative piety, or the intercourse between God and the human soul, cannot be poetical. Man admitted to implore the mercy of his Creator and plead the merits of his Redeemer is already in a higher state than poetry can confer. . . .

Of sentiments purely religious, it will be found that the most simple expression is the most sublime. Poetry loses its lustre and its power, because it is applied to the decoration of something more excellent than itself. All that pious verse can do is to help the memory and delight the ear, and for these purposes it may be very useful; but it supplies nothing to the mind. The ideas of Christian Theology are too simple for eloquence, too sacred for fiction, and too majestick for ornament; to recommend them by tropes and figures is to magnify by a concave mirror the sidereal hemisphere.

Hence, even the devotional verse of Watts, whom Johnson admires more than any man in the *Lives*, must fail: 'his devotional poetry is, like that of others, unsatisfactory. The paucity of its topicks enforces perpetual repetition, and the sanctity of the matter rejects the ornaments of figurative diction. It is sufficient for Watts to have done better than others what no man has done well.'[26]

Johnson's demands on poetry are so severe that one wonders if he had not actually lost his taste for it by the time he wrote the *Lives*. He is remarkably censorious throughout, considering that his publishers must have looked on his prefaces as invitations to the reading public. He evidently considered much of English poetry puerile fiction and all of it beneath the dignity of religion. Yet, in a middle world, beyond the childish realm of pastoral verse and beneath the sphere of religious devotion, there is a place for poetry in Johnson's conception – a place with historical bearings and an anchorage in experience. Perhaps the best indication of poetry's middle state in Johnson's latest conception is his frequent description of it in terms of landscape, and for this reason also the *Journey to the Western Isles* is good preparation for reading the *Lives*. Poetry is a world of intellectual experience in which Johnson travels and records his impressions, and it is his impressions that matter, even when the poetry is defined by the botanical or geographical shape it takes. In his famous contrast between Pope and Dryden in 'Pope', for instance, Johnson is describing his reception of the two experiences when he writes, 'Dryden is sometimes vehement and rapid; Pope is always smooth, uniform, and gentle. Dryden's page is a natural field, rising into inequalities, and diversified by the varied exuberance of abundant vegetation; Pope's is a velvet lawn, shaven by the scythe, and levelled by the roller.' The great extent to which Johnson was seeing literature as the reader's experience is suggested again in the rhetorically similar, but negative, account of reading Swift: 'the peruser of Swift wants little previous knowledge; it will be sufficient that he is acquainted with common words and common things; he is neither required to mount elevations nor to explore profundities; his passage is always on a level, along solid ground, without asperities, without obstruction.' 'The great source of pleasure is variety': Swift's views provide less pleasure than those of Pope or Dryden, and it is very much a pleasure of diversified observation that Johnson seeks both from travel and from poetry. This is nowhere clearer than in the tribute he pays to the durable pleasures of reading Dryden: 'Works of imagination excel by their allurement and delight; by their powers of attracting and detaining the attention. That book is good in vain which the reader throws away. He only is the master who keeps the mind in pleasing captivity; whose pages are perused with eagerness, and in hope of new pleasure are perused again; and whose conclusion is perceived with an eye of sorrow, such as the traveller casts upon departing day.'[27]

The kinds of landscape to which he compares them suggest that the artificiality of Pope and the magnificence of Milton are both less inviting to Johnson in the long run than the pleasures of Dryden. Johnson's implicit preference for Dryden at this stage of his life is part of his increasing insistence on historical truth and a kind of fiction firmly anchored in experience, as though he had arrived, like the older Wallace Stevens, at the philosophical position that reality is the most august form of the imagination. His view of authors and authorship, readers, and the act of reading are all affected by this realism. Johnson studiously removes romantic fictions from the popular conception of authors, just as he removes mythology from the conception of poetry. The reality of authors is shown perhaps most ironically in their deaths, a part of the *Lives* that Johnson polished into homiletical form.[28]

Death comes to Johnson's poets, as it does to others, while they are in the midst of living and often when they are about to enjoy the fruits of their labours. There is an abruptness in Johnson's accounts of the end that makes it particularly hard for us to imagine that some genius or guiding light was directing the course of an author's life or that it was, in Keats's phrase, 'a life of allegory'. The death of Halifax is characteristically sudden and prosaic: 'At the queen's death he was appointed one of the regents; and at the accession of George the First was made earl of Halifax, knight of the garter, and first commissioner of the treasure. . . . More was not to be had, and this he kept but a little while; for on the 19th of May, 1715, he died of an inflammation of the lungs.' Equally typical is the sudden death of Ambrose Philips: 'Having purchased an annuity of four hundred pounds, he now certainly hoped to pass some years of life in plenty and tranquillity; but his hope deceived him: he was struck with a palsy, and died June 18, 1749, in his seventy-eighth year.' A few deaths more spectacularly illustrate the vanity of human wishes, such as Otway's choking to death on a piece of bread he begged in his indigence. Some too are more carefully crafted and supported by literary models: the death of Pope, for example, precipitated by his over-refined taste for potted lamprey, follows accounts of deaths by Suetonius and Juvenal.[29] Whatever the manner of death and whether the description is elaborate or curt, however, Johnson naturalizes rather than canonizes his subjects in their deaths.

He accomplishes a similar naturalization and demythologization by dwelling perpetually on printing histories, contractual arrangements, and schemes for achieving fame as the real backgrounds of literary works, rather than anything psychological or transcendental. In describing modes of composition, too, Johnson is eager to eliminate anything extraordinary. He ridicules Milton's submission to a vernal muse and his notions about the influence of climate on writing. Although Johnson himself found the period from Easter to Whitsuntide particularly fruitful, he will not invest such accidents with the trappings of belief. In fact, he laughs at the account of Milton's sudden bursts of poetic creativity: 'These bursts of lights and involutions of darkness, these transient and involuntary excursions and retrocessions of invention, having some appearance of deviation from the common train of Nature, are eagerly caught by lovers of a wonder. Yet something of this inequality happens to every man in every mode of exertion, manual or mental. The mechanick cannot handle his hammer and his file at all times with equal dexterity; there are hours, he knows not why, when "his hand is out."' Johnson contemns both the promulgators of fictions about authorship and authors who convince themselves that there is something extraordinary about writing. Johnson finishes his character of Gray, for example, by reporting, 'he had a notion not very peculiar, that he could not write but at certain times, or at happy moments; a fantastick foppery, to which my kindness for a man of learning and of virtue wishes him to have been superior.'[30] Johnson is not simply measuring other authors by his standard; he is demanding that they be thought of realistically, naturally, and historically from birth to death, even in the performance of their art.

Since authors are ordinary people in Johnson's *Lives*, we should expect readers to be so too. Reading in the *Lives* is naturalized as a kind of perception, the kind we employ when travelling over a landscape, but the 'common reader' whom Johnson often invokes as the arbiter of literary merit is so stripped down to the essentials of perception that this abstraction passes out of the natural world. The reader is the one key element in literary transactions that Johnson idealizes, but the fact that he accomplishes this by depriving this figure of qualities, rather than by superadding them, makes Johnson's reader largely consistent with the rest of the critical apparatus in the *Lives*. For example, when Johnson takes up the notion that Pope's verse is 'too uniformly musical', he says, 'I suspect this objection to be the cant of those who judge by principles rather than perception.' To have perception without principles is something that Johnson might admit to be humanly impossible, even in his most empirical mood. Yet as a figure of perfection Johnson's common reader has neither principles of criticism nor learning, and in these deficiencies finds power. After blasting most of Gray's work as unnatural, 'glittering accumulations of ungraceful ornaments', Johnson turns at last to the *Elegy in a Country Church-yard*: 'In the character of his *Elegy* I rejoice to concur with the common reader; for by the common sense of readers uncorrupted with literary prejudices, after all the refinements of subtilty and the dogmatism of learning, must be finally decided all claim to poetical honours.' All real readers inevitably accumulate 'literary prejudices', but Johnson's common reader sheds them, along with an interest in the kinds of 'temporary and local' manners that made Butler's *Hudibras* popular for a while. As he did in the Preface to Shakespeare and some other earlier writings, Johnson does not in the *Lives* work hard to forge an apotheosis of the common reader as an allegorical representative of the judgement of time. He creates instead a reader who is pure perception. Such a reader is as unreal as an allegorical figure, but the ideal reader's minimalism suggests the radically empirical frame of mind Johnson was assuming and recommending late in life.[31]

Reduced to a naked sensibility, Johnson's reader registers pleasure more directly and more exclusively than a more sophisticated or more fully delineated reader might. The importance of such immediacy to literary success is the underlying subject in Johnson's discussion of Cowley's language: 'The diction, being the vehicle of the thoughts, first presents itself to the intellectual eye; and if the first appearance offends, a further knowledge is not often sought. Whatever professes to benefit by pleasing must please at once. The pleasures of the mind imply something sudden and unexpected; that which elevates must always surprise. What is perceived by slow degrees may gratify us with the consciousness of improvement, but will never strike with the sense of pleasure.' On the same theory, Prior's *Solomon* fails: 'Tediousness is the most fatal of all faults; negligences or errors are single and local, but tediousness pervades the whole: other faults are censured and forgotten, but the power of tediousness propagates itself. He that is weary the first hour is more weary the second; as bodies forced into motion, contrary to their tendency, pass more and more slowly through every successive interval of space.'[32] Such philosophical analogies are as rare in the *Lives* as they are common in the *Rambler*. Being so stripped down, however, Johnson's ideal reader is suited to a physics of reading.

Because he is learned and sophisticated, Johnson differs from his common reader, but he shies away from displaying his distinctive intellectual features, such as his expert knowledge of classical and neo-Latin poetry, and his uncommon predilections. On the fundamental question of pleasure in reading Johnson frequently defers to the common reader. Such deference is evident, for example, in the last, weary paragraph of 'Akenside': 'To examine such compositions [Akenside's odes] singly cannot be required; they have doubtless brighter and darker parts: but when they are once found to be generally dull all further labour may be spared, for to what use can the work be criticised that will not be read.' Johnson does not often shrink himself to this skeletal sort of reading, but the primacy of the demand for pleasure is apparent throughout the *Lives*. Finally, it is pleasure that Johnson registers in reacting fully and richly to a poet, and the absence of pleasure results in a perfunctory or brief response. Throughout the *Lives* Johnson takes the Horatian criteria of pleasure and instruction more literally and directly than ever. In its final refinement, his criticism achieves also a kind of reduction to basic principles. The kind of courage implicit in this reduction is evident in the ways that Johnson similarly refused the anodyne attractions of sophistication and fiction in his experience of the last years of his life.

21

Final Years

Age is a very stubborn Disease.

Johnson to Mrs Thrale, 18 September 1777

Among all the other things it meant to him, in his later years especially, Johnson's writing was a test of his vitality, and he could regard his literary production in the same clinical light that he regarded evidence of his physical energy. In his diary for 20 April 1778, Johnson wrote out his annual, Easter Day self-examination with his usual severity: 'My health has indeed been very much interrupted. My nights have been commonly not only restless but painful and fatiguing. My respiration was once so difficult that an asthma was suspected. I could not walk but with great difficulty from Stowhill to Greenhill' (two places in Lichfield). He follows his account of his physical state with an assessment of his intellectual condition: 'I have written a little of the lives of the poets, I think, with all my usual vigour. I have made sermons perhaps as readily as formerly. My memory is less faithful in retaining names and, I am afraid, in retaining occurrences.' Johnson says these things not by way of complaint but as admonitions to himself, and he blames his degeneration, just as he blamed his involuntary nervous tics and twitches on his own bad habits: 'Of this vacillation and vagrancy of mind I impute a great part to a fortuitous and unsettled life, and therefore purpose to spend my time with more method.' Johnson never achieved such method, of course, and three years later his Easter assessment included the note, 'Sometime in March [1781] I finished the lives of the Poets, which I wrote in my usual way, dilatorily and hastily, unwilling to work, and working with vigour, and haste.'[1] As always, the laudable fact that he persevered to the conclusion of a large and admirable work is merely another occasion for reflecting on his reprehensible habits. In moments of serious, moral self-examination Johnson was inveterately severe on himself to the end of his life, and he seems never to have allowed his professional successes to mitigate that severity.

Johnson wrote some of the first *Lives* in Lichfield and others at the Thrales', but most of the work was done in his own home in Bolt Court. He kept himself there within reach of his own books and within shouting distance of many Grub Street contacts who could supply the kind of information he most valued. Towards the end of his work the confinement was bothersome, especially as the summer of 1780 slipped away, and his annual trip to the Midlands was in jeopardy. In July of 1780 Johnson wrote to Mrs Thrale in Brighton:

> I stay at home to work, and yet do not work diligently, nor can tell when I shall have done, nor perhaps does any body but myself wish me to have done, for what can they hope I shall do better? Yet I wish the work was over, and I was at liberty. And what would I do if I was at Liberty? Would I go to Mrs Aston and Mrs Porter, and see the old places, and sigh to find that my old friends are gone? Would I recal plans of life which I never brought into practice, and hopes of excellence which I once presumed, and never have attained? Would I compare what I now am with what I once expected to have been? Is it reasonable to wish for suggestions of Shame, and opportunities of Sorrow.[2]

Johnson worked through the summer and winter of 1780–1 and only left London for a short trip to Brighton before finishing the *Lives*. Despite his facility in writing, Johnson felt the agonies of the task, but he never romanticized them. He understood the tricks his mind played to escape its labour, and he coolly unmasked its fictitious suggestions of a better life elsewhere, even as he felt their power. He revised the *Lives* lightly in 1782 for the second edition, which appeared the next year; he wrote one more dedication; and he occasionally helped friends and acquaintances with their literary projects, but his work as a publishing writer was all but over in 1781. He went on reading and writing, however, pursuing literature and keeping busy with books, almost as he had before he became a professional writer; in fact, he was engaged with many of the same writers and works – mostly Greek and Latin – that had attracted him in his early years.

In his retirement from professional writing, especially after publishing the celebrated *Lives*, Johnson enjoyed a higher degree of fame than he had ever known before. His company was sought by fashionable as well as learned people. He was the centre of the new Essex Head Club, though he missed many more meetings than he attended, and a prominent member of the Royal Academy. Although he did not achieve the recognition among noblemen that Boswell thought he deserved, Johnson met many of the high, rich, and famous. He was even once visited by Mrs Siddons, the most popular and alluring actress of the day, and on more than one occasion he had offers of financial support from wealthy admirers. He enjoyed public life, and he appreciated his fame. Remarking on his house full of gifts, he wrote to Mrs Thrale, 'Attention and respect give pleasure, however late, or however useless. But they are not useless [rousing himself from melancholy], when they are late, it is reasonable to rejoice as the day declines, to find that [it] has been spent with the approbation of mankind.'[3] Still, Johnson was careful to preserve his liberty, and he rejected the offers of financial assistance. His life continued to centre on a few friends, and the great sorrow of his final years was his loss of so many of them. In the context of these losses, Johnson produced many of his last compositions. The rest he wrote as a stay against loneliness, out of a need to be intellectually active, or as trials of his mental strength.

Johnson's greatest grief began with the death of an old friend, but ended in the loss of the person he loved the best. The death of Henry Thrale on 4 April 1781 is one of the few external events that Johnson recorded in his diary – a work intended wholly as a record of his own mind, body, and soul, as the last sentence in the entry on Thrale indicates:

> At night I was called to him, and found him senseless in strong convulsions. I staid in the room except that I visited Mrs Thrale twice. About five (I think) on Wednesday morning he expired. I felt almost the last flutter of his pulse, and looked for the last time upon the face that for fifteen years had never been turned upon me but with respect or benignity. Farewel. May God that delighteth in mercy, have had mercy on thee.
> I had constantly prayed for him some time before his death.
> The decease of him from whose friendship I had obtained many opportunities of amusement, and to whom I turned my thoughts as to a refuge from misfortunes, has left me heavy. But my business is with myself.

Johnson was absolutely on his honour to tell the perfect truth in his diary, as he shows in his parenthetical hesitation about the time of death and the scrupulous mention of his two trips outside the sickroom. His surprising past perfect tense in wishing God's mercy on Thrale registers his belief that God's judgement on the dead is immediate and so would already have occurred by the time he was writing. It is also honest of Johnson to note right away the loss of his own pleasure entailed in his friend's death. He echoes the sentiment in his first consolatory letter to Mrs Thrale: 'I am not without my part of the calamity. No death since that of my Wife has ever oppressed me like this.' Johnson continued writing every other day for a while and testified again to his share of grief: 'I feel myself like a man beginning a new course of life. I had interwoven myself with my dear Friend.'[4]

As the closest friend of the widow, an executor of the estate (and minor legatee), and as guardian, or godfather, of some of the surviving children, Johnson continued to be involved with the family for three more years. However, his intimacy with Mrs Thrale, perhaps the greatest pleasure in his life, gradually waned and was finally extinguished by her remarriage. She was forty years old in 1781, and, despite the shocks of many deaths in her family, still healthy; she had recently loved to swim among the breakers at Brighton and was proud of being on rough days the only woman in the surf. Johnson was seventy-two and quickly growing infirm. For comfort and confidence Mrs Thrale turned to younger people than Johnson, especially after the shattering death a year later of yet another child. One of those on whom she relied was the singer and music teacher Gabriele Mario Piozzi, a man just about exactly her own age. Soon the two fell in love, and by late 1782 their intimates knew they were to be married. Johnson was not among them. He noted in his diary at Brighton on 19 December 1782, 'Mistress, sorrowful', but he was not made privy to the reason, which was the cold reception that her announcement of marital intentions had received from her closest friends and family members. Johnson probably never saw Mrs Thrale again, though he continued writing warmly and frequently for another year and a half. He knew in 1782 that he had been displaced in her affections, but he did not know of her marriage plans until 30 June 1784, when she sent him a note begging his 'parental' permission along with a public announcement of the marriage directed to all the guardians of the children. Johnson wrote back in fury:

> If I interpret your letter right, you are ignominiously married, if it is yet undone, let us once talk together. If you have abandoned your children and your religion, God forgive your wickedness; if you have forfeited your Fame, and your country, may your folly do no further mischief.
>
> If the last act is yet to do, I, who have loved you, esteemed you, reverenced you, and served you, I who long thought you the first of human kind, entreat that before your fate is irrevocable, I may once more see you. I was, I once was, Madam, most truly yours.

Mrs Thrale was spirited in her reply to this brutal letter and exhibited an aggressive loyalty to her second husband. Johnson wrote a final letter to his 'mistress' on 8 July 1784. He quit the relationship with 'one sigh more of tenderness' and offered his blessings with something a little above frigid tranquillity: 'I wish that God may grant you every blessing, that you may be happy in this world for its short continuance, and eternally happy in a better state. And whatever I can contribute to your happiness, I am ready to repay for that kindness which soothed twenty years of a life radically wretched.'[5]

The final break with Mrs Thrale put an end to Johnson's most interesting correspondence with the mother and, for the most part, ended his most charming correspondence with the daughters of the family. As well as providing important biographical information, Johnson's letters contain passages of superior literary merit. Many of them can be read as small *Ramblers*, and those to the Thrale children comprise a system of educational and moral instruction adapted to the young. Johnson suggested how easily these letters are assimilated to the rest of his writing in a letter to Mrs Thrale about her daughter Hester Maria (Queeney): 'I have a mind to look on Queeny as my own dear Girl, and if I set her a bad example, I ought to counteract it by good precepts, and he that knows the consequences of any fault is best qualified to tell them. I have through my whole progress of authorship honestly endeavoured to teach the right, though I have not been sufficiently diligent to practice it, and have offered

Mankind my opinion as a rule, but never proposed my behaviour as an example.' One example here must suffice to display the general tone and the elegance of Johnson's letters to the young girl. In July of 1780 he addressed Queeney as 'My dear Charmer', and imagined her at Brighton:

> You, dear Madam, I suppose wander philosophically by the Seaside, and survey the vast expanse of the world of waters, comparing as your predecessors in contemplation have done its ebb and flow, its turbulence and tranquillity to the vicissitudes of human life. You, my Love, are now in the time of flood, your powers are hourly encreasing, do not lose the time. When you are alone read diligently, they who do not read can have nothing to think, and little to say. When you can get proper company talk freely and cheerfully, it is often by talking that we come to know the value of what we have read, to separate it with distinctness, and fix it in the memory. Never delight your self with the dignity of silence or the superiority of inattention. To be silent or to be negligent are so easy, neither can give any claim to praise, and there is no human being so mean or useless, but his approbation and benevolence is to be desired.[6]

The advice is both general and specifically directed to Queeney, who evidently tended to be cool. The tone of the letter is more than avuncular and suggests a kind of courtly civility that was already antique at the time. Such courtliness marks Johnson's relations with the Thrales to the end. His letters to Mrs Thrale often allude to lines from Restoration comedy, and in his relationship with her Johnson may have inhabited the kind of lost, seventeenth-century world that surfaces, albeit ironically, in the more romantic, swash-buckling scenes of the *Life of Savage*.

As part of his courtly service to Mrs Thrale, Johnson produced not only many hundreds of letters but numerous occasional poems, sometimes as jests and sometimes as tributes for his mistress and her little girls. Almost all of these pieces are trite, but even in the most trite of them Johnson sometimes weaves his familiar themes. Characteristic is his little extempore poem on hearing Queeney deliberate in 1780 about whether or not to wear a new hat to a dinner party:

> Wear the gown, and wear the hat,
>   Snatch thy pleasures while they last;
> Hadst thou nine lives like a cat,
>   Soon those nine lives would be past.

Johnson wrote a couple of more intimate pieces to Mrs Thrale in the decent obscurity of Latin, but his most polished performance as her courtier is a translation of a poem first printed in the supplement to the *Greek Anthology* and popularly known as 'Anacreon's Dove'. Mrs Thrale noted in *Thraliana* for 15 January 1778, 'Mr Johnson told me today that he had translated Anacreon's Dove, & as they were the first verses that struck him when a Boy; so says he they continue to please me as well as any Greek

Verses now I am Three score.' The poem is mostly spoken by a dove or
pigeon belonging to the poet Anacreon. The eloquent creature brings the
beautiful listener vows of amorous servitude. Johnson departs from his
text somewhat to direct these 'Vows to Myrtale the fair; / Grac'd with all
that charms the heart'. The original poem directs them literally to
'Bathyllus, the boy who has recently become the lord and master of all'.
Ignoring the gender of the words was conventional, but 'all that charms
the heart' is a particularly soft and gentle translation of κρατοῦντα καὶ
τύραννον ('ruler and master', l. 10). The dove goes on to explain how she
does not prefer freedom to the pleasure-filled life as the slave of Anacreon:

> Now the generous bowl I sip
> As it leaves Anacreon's lip,
> Void of care, and free from dread
> From his fingers snatch his bread,
> Then with luscious plenty gay
> Round his chamber dance and play.
>
> (31–6)

Here again Johnson has softened the poem but also embroidered it by
using 'with luscious plenty gay' for πιοῦσα ('having drunk or drunk',
l. 30). The dove is a type of Tinkerbell, alluring its listener with tales of
a world elsewhere inhabited by a poetic, unruly spirit. Mrs Thrale says
Johnson dictated the poem to her. The role he assumed in doing so was
courtly as well as learned, civilized and erotic in an elaborately formal way.
Fashioning himself as a court poet for the Thrales, focusing his attention
on his mistress, yet establishing an exalted place of honour for himself,
Johnson realized, in a way, the ambition to be a kind of courtly poet that
he had entertained early in life at Pedmore and Walmesley's palace. Even
in his last letter to Mrs Thrale, Johnson was playing the courtier. In giving
her his final piece of advice he recalled the attempt of the Bishop of St
Andrews to prevent Queen Mary from going to England and her destruction: 'The Queen went forward. – If the parallel reaches thus far; may
it go no further. The tears stand in my eyes.'[7] Although the courtly mask
was artfully constructed and self-consciously maintained, Johnson's feelings were real.

   None rivalled Hester Thrale, but there were a few others to whom
Johnson directed courtly verse. In one effort, for example, he transforms
a portrait of Lady Mary Wortley Montague into Roman sculpture and
celebrates her as 'Minerva, cast in Virtue's mould'. He wrote a song for
Fanny Burney and several Latin verses to his doctor and friend Thomas
Lawrence, a past president of the Royal College of Physicians. The best of
these comprises an ode urging Lawrence to rise from his grief over the
departure of his son to foreign shores. It contains some parts of the myth
that Johnson was writing and rewriting all his life. In the poem Learning
deserts the sufferer, and he languishes, like man in *The Vanity of Human*

Wishes, in a tedious dark night: 'Per caeca noctis taedia turbidae . . .
Torpesque languescisque. . . .'[8] Like the *Vanity* and the Skye ode, this poem
concludes by ordering the listener to have faith in God and leave to Him
the government of worldly things.

Johnson's most important late poem was also written for a medical
doctor, and it uses some of the same artifices as the ode to Lawrence, but
Johnson's elegy 'On the Death of Robert Levet' is in common English and
suited in every other way to the humbler circumstances of its subject. Both
the speaker and the subject labour and suffer in the shadowy darkness
that invests so many of Johnson's poetic landscapes. In the opening Johnson
quickly sketches the 'clouded maze of fate', as it appeared to him towards
the end of his life:

> Condemn'd to hope's delusive mine,
>   As on we toil from day to day,
> By sudden blasts, or slow decline,
>   Our social comforts drop away.

Johnson keeps the focus on Levet for the rest of the poem, but he views
him explicitly in 'affection's eye' (9), and there is a lingering sense of his
own suffering as he traces the physician on his daily rounds through
'misery's darkest caverns' (17), the homes of the poor where Levet practised
his empirical, unlearned, entirely clinical sort of medicine. Levet's quotidian
existence, 'the toil of ev'ry day' (24), is what Johnson praises, and in so
doing he intimates the nature of the loss he has suffered. When he exalts
Levet, it is not with a reference to anything classical but to the humbler
biblical parable of the talents, a story to which Johnson was almost constantly recurring in his sermons, prayers, and meditations:

> His virtues walk'd their narrow round,
>   Nor made a pause, nor left a void;
> And sure th' Eternal Master found
>   The single talent well employ'd.
>   (25–8)

Levet died very suddenly at home in Bolt Court. In a letter to Margaret
Strahan, Johnson described Levet as 'suddenly snatched away', and he
wrote to Dr Lawrence, 'Our old friend Mr Levet, who was last night
eminently cheerful, died this morning.'[10] Johnson describes the suddenness of Levet's death in a third way in the last stanza of the poem:

> Then with no throbbing fiery pain,
>   No cold gradations of decay,
> Death broke at once the vital chain,
>   And free'd his soul the nearest way.
>   (33–6)

Here sudden death is a consolation that suggests ascension and salvation. The 'vital chain' is life in terms of Johnson's first definition of it in the *Dictionary*, 'Union and co-operation of soul with body'. The periphrasis of the poem recalls the plight of those still confined in 'hope's delusive mine', like chained prisoners, and the release of Levet's soul 'the nearest way' (36) is a reminder that the speaker's 'comforts drop away' (4). The 'throbbing fiery pain' (33) and 'cold gradations of decay' (34), which Levet did not feel, must be referred to the speaker as well, and overall there is a remarkable degree of echo, both in sound and sense, between the first stanza and the last. Partly by means of this effect, Johnson manages to encompass in his elegy the qualities of a very public poem, like an epitaph, and those of a much more personal expression of grief. The poem is remarkable for being both a memorial to Levet and an expression of Johnson's own state of mind.

Johnson never described his domestic situation in Bolt Court as happy, but it was essential to filling his days. He wrote to Mrs Thrale late in 1778, when they were still on intimate terms, 'We have tolerable concord at home, but no love. Williams hates every body. Levet hates Desmoulins and does not love Williams. Desmoulins hates them both. Poll loves none of them.' Bad as this sounds, it got worse as the household gradually broke up. Polly Carmichael, whom Johnson characterized bluntly as a 'stupid slut', may have been no great loss, but when Levet died Johnson described his home in more dismal terms: 'This little habitation is now but a melancholy place, clouded with the gloom of disease and death. Of the four inmates one has been suddenly snatched away, two are oppressed by very afflictive and dangerous ilness; and I tried yesterday to gain some relief by a third bleeding from a disorder which has for some time distressed me.' In the spring of 1783 the Lichfield widow Mrs Desmoulins moved away, and Johnson wrote to Queeney Thrale, 'I have only one sick woman to fight or play with instead of two, and there is more peace in the house.' Toward the end of that summer, the blind spinster Anna Williams died, and Johnson wrote to Reynolds, 'Your kind attention has done all for me that it could. My Loss is really great. She had been my domestick companion for more than thirty years, and when I come home I shall return to a desolate habitation. I hope all her miseries are past.'[11]

When Johnson wrote this, he was visiting a relatively new friend, the poet William Bowles, who lived near Salisbury. On this last trip to a new place Johnson saw Stonehenge for the first time and discussed the puzzling monument with Edmund Burke, who had also just seen it for the first time. Johnson evidently viewed the place with the same kind of inquisitive scepticism that he brought to Mackinnon's Cave on his Hebridean travels. Although his intimacy with Mrs Thrale had diminished greatly by this time in 1783, the final breach had not yet occurred and Johnson was still writing his best letters to her: 'I told [Burke] that the view had enabled me to confute two opinions which have been advanced about it. One that the materials are not natural stones, but an artificial composition hardened

by time. . . . The other opinion . . . is that it was erected by the Danes.'
Johnson then tells how Bowles showed him the knobs and hollows holding
the structure together without mortar. These things proved to him that
the people who built Stonehenge were both ingenious enough in their
handling of stone not to need artificial rock, and that, unlike the Danes,
they did not have the use of mortar. Johnson concludes with his own opinion of Stonehenge and a nice observation showing the spectrum of his
taste in architecture: '[Stonehenge] is in my opinion to be refered to the
earliest habitation of the Island, as a Druidical monument of at least two
thousand years, probably the most ancient work of Man upon the Island.
Salisbury Cathedral and its Neighbour Stonehenge, are two eminent monuments of art and rudeness, and may show the first essay, and the last perfection in architecture.'[12]

Johnson struck up a few new friendships late in life. No one had quite
the vivacity of Boswell, but he was only occasionally available, and William
Bowles, though a very different person, gave Johnson the similar pleasure
of conversation with a younger intellectual admirer. Johnson also revived
to some degree his old friendship with Bennet Langton and spent a couple
of happy weeks with him and his large family in Rochester. When Thomas
Lawrence gave up medicine after a stroke in 1782, Johnson became the
patient of Dr Richard Brocklesby and confided in him with candour and
fondness. When Edmund Allen died, Johnson explicitly asked John Nichols
to fill his place. Johnson had known Nichols for a long time, but he
sought greater intimacy with him very late in life, especially after Nichols
published his *Anecdotes of William Bowyer*: 'Though I have not given you
any amusement, I have received amusement from you. . . . I had the luck
to borrow Mr Boyer's Life a book so full of contemporary History, that a
literary Man must find some of his old friends. I thought that I could now
and then have told you some hints worth your notice, and perhaps we may
talk a life over. I hope, we shall be much together, You must now be to
me what you were before, and what dear Mr Allen was besides.' Johnson
had much of the 'universal and minute literary information' ascribed to
him by Boswell, and he did give Nichols 'hints', as the later nine volumes
of *Anecdotes* about the London book world show. One of Johnson's last
public contributions to literature was a letter to Nichols, which he published in the *Gentleman's Magazine* for December 1784, revealing the names
of the anonymous authors of the *Ancient Universal History*, an immense Fleet
Street project undertaken early in the century. Johnson had the information in the form of a handwritten note from an Oxford don named Swinton;
his transmission of the document to Nichols was the last of his many
contributions to literary history.[13] It is fitting that Johnson's last publication involved the *Gentleman's Magazine*, the most important vehicle of his
early career, and fitting too that he contributed information concerning
a publishing project that joined the learned and the commercial worlds of
book production because such a combination is representative of his whole
career as a writer.

Although Johnson reached out to new friends and some new topics in his last years, his attention centred on his oldest circle of friends and gradually withdrew itself from the world altogether to rest uncomfortably on himself and his approaching death. He paid some attention to politics in his last years. He responded with some alarm to the crisis of power in the younger Pitt's ministry and generally opposed innovations that would weaken the central authority of government. After some hesitation he was, for example, with many Whigs in opposing the motion for reform brought forward by Pitt in 1783 to increase equality of representation in Parliament. He wrote to Taylor in Ashbourne:

> An equal representation can never form a constitution because it can have no stability, for whether you regulate the representation by numbers or by property, that which is equal today, will be unequal in a week.
>   To change the constituent parts of Government must be always dangerous, for who can tell where changes will stop. A new representation will want the reverence of antiquity, and the firmness of Establishment.

A little later Johnson lamented the 'tumult in government', particularly because it came 'at a time when . . . the King and parliament have lost even the titular dominion of America, and the real power of Government every where else'. Though his political interest contracted conservatively to questions of stability and control, Johnson occasionally showed some of the penchant for incisive and cynical political observation that made him a kind of radical earlier in life. He adds to this lament about England's lost power, 'Thus Empires are broken down when the profits of administration are so great, that ambition is satisfied with obtaining them, and he that aspires to greatness needs do nothing more than talk himself into importance.' His wish for a more heroic public life, like his desire for a more courtly social world, grew somewhat stronger in his final years, but Johnson never forgot that life was lived in 'domestic privacies'. His last letter to Robert Chambers in Calcutta sums up his feelings nicely: 'The state of the Publick, and the operations of government have little influence upon the private happiness of private men, nor can I pretend that much of the national calamities is felt by me; yet I cannot but suffer some pain when I compare the state of this Kingdom, with that in which we triumphed twenty years ago. I have at least endeavoured to preserve order and support Monarchy.'[14]

Late in 1783 Johnson began suffering from dropsy and from increasingly painful asthma. He was confined to the house for 129 days before pronouncing himself recovered on 21 April 1784. He took opium for his cough, as was common, but he was frightened of taking it in great amounts because it often kept him up at night, made him sleepy during the day, and 'subjected [him] to the tyranny of vain imaginations'. Especially when death was imminent, Johnson wanted his faculties in order; he felt he needed every lucid moment to work out his salvation as well as he could.

During his sleepless nights of opium and coughing, Johnson tried to make good use of his God-given talents and to keep his mind active with trials of its strength. Declaring himself recovered, he wrote to Mrs Thrale, 'When I lay sleepless, I used to drive the night along, by turning Greek epigrams into Latin.'[15] He did about a hundred of them during his illness, returning to a book that he read in most of his life and rediscovering such gems as the epitaph for Zosima that he had praised in his essay on epitaphs for the *Gentleman's Magazine* in 1740 and some verses that he had turned into English for the *Adventurer* in the 1750s.

Many of the poems in the *Greek Anthology* are epitaphs; they belong to a vein of wisdom literature that reminds readers of the inevitable approach of death or the inability of mortals to make sense of life. Johnson gravitates to the most ironic verses, rendering into Latin such harsh little pieces as the 'Wisdom of Glycon', which the Loeb edition faithfully translates as 'All is laughter, all is dust, all is nothing, for all that is cometh from un-reason.' Johnson's choice of material may have been part of a preparation for death by contemning worldly life, but translation of any kind was always good exercise for his mind. It is most striking that he so frequently returned to his all-time favourites. He spent some nights turning Boethius into Greek, though the results do not survive, and he translated all of Sallust's *Catiline*.[16]

In 1782 Johnson began the study of Dutch to test his mental strength in much the same way that he always tested his physical strength at Brighton by trying to draw water from the deep well at the Thrales' seaside home. Johnson was always testing himself, but the most famous of his mental tests is his composition of a pair of Latin distichs on the night of his stroke. He described the incident in a letter to Mrs Thrale on 19 June 1783:

> In the afternoon and evening I felt myself light and easy, and began to plan schemes of life. Thus I went to bed and in a short time waked and sat up as has been long my custom, when I felt a confusion and indistinctness in my head which lasted, I suppose half a minute; I was alarmed and prayed God, that however he might afflict my body he would spare my understanding. This prayer, that I might try the integrity of my faculties I made in Latin verse. The lines were not very good, but I knew them not to be very good, I made them easily, and concluded myself to be unimpaired in my faculties.

This famous trial is only a small example of what Johnson was doing intellectually throughout his final years. Translation suited him because the activity is more continuous than it is in original composition and because, like his self-examination after the stroke, it entails a twofold process of understanding and interpreting, of absorbing and rendering. Perhaps he was instinctively drawn to the physical trial of releasing and drawing the water bucket at the deep well in Brighton for similar reasons. The element of comment and criticism, the activity of response as well as statement, was always essential to Johnson's idea of intellectual engagement.[17]

Johnson's speech was permanently weakened by his stroke, and towards the end of the year in which it occurred his long confinement for illness began. Although he recovered in the spring of 1784, Johnson justly feared his health would not last, and he prepared for a farewell visit to the Midlands. In Boswell's company he went to Oxford in June where he helped advance the posthumous publication of a late friend's edition of Xenophon and urged on a prospective edition of the Greek poet Oppian. Later in the summer he went to Ashbourne and in September to Lichfield. He visited Edmund Hector, his step daughter Lucy Porter, and Elizabeth Aston, but he also said goodbye to the environs of his childhood, to the memories of his family, and, in an important sense, to his life. He wrote his last original poem in Lichfield in the autumn of 1784, a meditation on a stream in which he bathed as a child. It begins,

> Errat adhuc vitreus per prata virentia rivus,
> Quo toties lavi membra tenella puer;
> Hic delusa rudi frustrabar brachia motu,
> Dum docuit blanda voce natare pater.

> (Still the glassy stream winds through the green field
> Where often as a boy I bathed my young limbs.
> Here I was balked by awkward arms, inept,
> While my father sweetly taught me to swim.)

The poem ends with a wish for the longevity of the stream and of his friend Hector's stream of life. The image and the concern with death are conventional; the poem might have been written at any time in Johnson's life, but it is particularly poignant as a last, parting poem. It places its speaker in a retrospective position on the bank, almost beyond life, looking back into its movement. The speaker sees his movement in life as an awkward, childish struggle, and he remembers fondly the disembodied voice of his parent. Johnson does not excessively indulge this late vision, which a modern reader might compare to some of the scenes in Bergman's film *Wild Strawberries*. For better or worse, he hastens into largely formulaic lines on the 'cursus ... indefessa perennis' ('the stream, unwearied for ever') and closes smartly with a classical allusion that winks knowingly at his friend Hector. The poem is a milder sort of penance than the long walk from Lichfield to Uttoxeter that Johnson made to expiate a childhood act of filial impiety. He stood in the rain bareheaded on that occasion to make up for having refused to keep his father's bookstall one day fifty years before.[18] Though he was now more comfortable with his past, Johnson was feeling valedictory, and he was eager to review and settle his memories of parents and friends. One of his last acts in life was to arrange for the placement of an inscribed stone to be laid over the graves of his mother, father, and brother in the middle aisle of St Michael's church.

Johnson's condition worsened as the weather in Lichfield freshened, and his doctor suggested he return to London late in October. Johnson replied, 'I am not afraid either of a journey to London or a residence in it. . . . In the smoky atmosphere I was delivered from the dropsy, which I consider as the original and radical disease. The town is my element, there are my friends, there are my books to which I have not yet bidden farewell, and there are my amusements. Sir Joshua told me long ago that my vocation was to publick life, and I hope still to keep my station, till God shall bid me *Go in peace.*' Johnson returned to London on 16 November, having stopped in Birmingham for a last visit with Edmund Hector. On his way to town he translated one last ode from Horace, 'Spring's Return', a bittersweet contrast between rejuvenation in nature and the finality of man's death:

> Her losses soon the moon supplies,
> But wretched man, when once he lies
> Where Priam and his sons are laid,
> Is naught but ashes and a shade.[19]

Johnson knew he was going to London to die, and he was always frightened of death and judgement, but there is a kind of morbid cheerfulness in the poem that suggests his sadness may have been mingled with excitement and a wish to spirit himself up for the performance of his last tasks.

After this last piece of classical translation, Johnson spent what literary energy he had left on Latin prayers and meditations. He made the final arrangements for a stone to be laid over the grave of his departed wife. He paid debts and wrote a codicil to his will, in which he distributed his Lichfield property to hometown kith and kin, books to his friends and doctors, and most of his money to Frank Barber. He reviewed his private papers, destroyed many of them, including two quarto volumes of diaries, and gave some, like his translations from the *Greek Anthology*, to Bennet Langton. He actively sought to prolong his life, treating his body with his usual roughness. He had often called for bleedings late in life, and, as the dropsy advanced, he called for lancing and letting. He went so far as to lance himself, and he seems to have been extremely anxious not to give any appearance of accepting death voluntarily and therefore impiously. Speaking of his illness to one friend, he declared, 'I will be conquered; I will not capitulate.'[20]

Though he was rough on his body toward the end, Johnson was careful with his mind and avoided clouding his faculties with drugs. He prepared himself for the final judgement with prayers and meditations. In October in Lichfield he was clearly thinking through the problems of his own salvation when he sketched some outlines of a book about prayer and another on the nature of religious scepticism. Although he rarely expressed his religious doubts because he feared promulgating them, Johnson was intensely sceptical and enquiring intellectually, and he struggled against applying his critical faculties with disastrous results to the truths of the Christian faith. On 5 December 1784 he took communion for the last time and composed a prayer especially for the occasion: 'Almighty and most merciful Father, I am now, as to human eyes it seems, about to commemorate for the last time, the death of thy son Jesus Christ, our Saviour and Redeemer. Grant, O Lord, that my whole hope and confidence may be in his merits and in thy mercy: forgive and accept my late conversion, enforce and accept my imperfect repentance. . . . Have mercy upon me and pardon the multitude of my offences. Bless my Friends, have mercy upon all men.'[21] By 'conversion', as the editors of Johnson's prayers note, Johnson does not mean a change in religion but a change in his state 'from reprobation to grace', such as he achieved in acknowledging his sins and becoming absolved of them in the act of communion. The resolution and piety of this prayer preclude other features of Johnson's writing and obscure his literary voice. Yet, even in this last piece of writing, in his final attempt to be at peace before death, there is at least one characteristic note: 'as to human eyes it seems' is the kind of parenthetical hesitation and reflection on his own statements that Johnson exhibited in a lifetime of strictness about truth. Even *in extremis* he will not admit the seeming truth without questioning it, remarking it, and showing thereby that restless activity of mind that he exhibited throughout his writing and that ended only with his death on 13 December 1784.

Shortly before his death Johnson was visited by Joshua Reynolds, who took a mould for the death mask. The pre-eminent artist of his day had painted Johnson's portrait four or five times, and several other artists contributed to the preservation of his image.[22] His bust was modelled by Nollekens, and he was the subject of numerous topical sketches. Johnson's body was interred in Westminster Abbey while Reynolds and Burke attended the coffin. James Boswell, who had been preparing a more elaborate form of preservation for twenty years, soon immortalized Johnson in his *Tour to the Hebrides* (1785) and then, most magnificently, in the *Life of Samuel Johnson, LL.D.* (1791). By then there had already been several other biographies, including Sir John Hawkins's.

Through the efforts of Boswell and others, Johnson quickly became a part of his nation's folkloric life. He achieved in some respects the magnitude of a figure like Socrates whose historical life is overshadowed by his life in the fictional accounts of students and admirers. Unlike Socrates, however, Johnson wrote, and his most important legacy is his writing. His collected works first appeared in 1787, and there were numerous printings thoughout the nineteenth century. In this century Yale University Press has undertaken a comprehensive collection of his works, although editing the *Dictionary* is outside their scope, and there is still truth in Boswell's comment that 'we shall in vain endeavour to know with exact precision every production of Johnson's pen.' Individual works and selections of his works have been printed, edited, and reprinted much more often, and Johnson has kept the presses as busy in recent years as he did while he lived. In fact, if one includes works of criticism and commentary as well as biographies and editions, Johnson is now responsible for the production of many more pages per year than he ever was as a living writer. Simply listed, with no more than a bare bibliographical description, the books and articles spawned by Johnson to the year 1969 take up 250 tightly printed pages. Those published between 1970 and 1985 occupy another 100 pages. If he could, how would Johnson react to such fecundity? One clue is in his reaction to Boswell's news that a hostile anthology called *Deformities of Dr Samuel Johnson* (Edinburgh, 1782) had been printed in ironic imitation of the earlier *Beauties of Johnson*. Johnson calmly wrote to Boswell in March 1782, 'The Beauties of Johnson are said to have got money to the collector; if the "Deformities" have the same success, I shall be still a more extensive benefactor.'[23]

In addition to enjoying the satisfaction of extensive benefaction to writers, printers, and publishers, Johnson would now be concerned about the effect of his works being so widely dispersed and discussed. Most readers of Johnson today cannot share the religious convictions that were most important to him. However, Johnson's strength of mind, his restlessness in inquiry, and the beauty of his performances will continue to be inspiring and to produce the beneficial effects of inspiration as long as reading remains the principal means for individuals to participate in the conversation of culture. With or without the huge body of commentary that they have attracted, the works of Samuel Johnson offer English readers almost unparalleled access to the full historical range of European intellectual life. That the view of these riches runs through the world of details we know about his person and his life, especially his later life as London's Great Cham, is an alluring fact that should no longer beguile us out of achieving the higher satisfactions of reading Johnson's work. In order to do this, however, it should no longer be necessary to ignore the facts of Johnson's life and the placement of his work in a real political and economic situation. For the past fifty years formalist criticism has worked hard to free literary experience from the distractions of historical and biographical facts. The cause was worthy, but the job is now sufficiently complete, and it is safe once more to resituate a writer's works in their historical context where they may be most richly and fully appreciated. No writer's work needed liberation more than Johnson's, and no one's will benefit more from a properly considered repatriation.

Notes

Preface

1 *Life* 1: 73 and see Boswell, *Notebook*, 7–8.
2 *Journey*, 123–4.
3 London *Times*, 9 January 1981; the recent book is Allen Reddick, *The Making of Johnson's Dictionary 1746–1773*, 195 n. 2.
4 Allodoli, 'Poliziano e Johnson', 459; I realized it was propaganda after reading Natalie Zemon Davis, 'Rabelais among the Censors (1940s, 1540s)', *Representations* 32 (1990), 1–32.

Chapter 1   Lichfield

1 Throughout this chapter I rely heavily on Aleyn Lyell Reade's astonishing eleven volumes on Johnson's family and early life, *Johnsonian Gleanings*. I am similarly dependent upon James Clifford's *Young Sam Johnson*. On Johnson's watch see *Yale* 1: 20 and Hawkins, *Life of Samuel Johnson*, 408. Johnson refers the story about *Absalom and Achitophel* to 'my father, an old bookseller' (*Lives*, 'Dryden', 109). The Whigs' attempt in 1710 to impeach an outspoken Tory parson was the focal point of an immense pamphlet war in which some items sold as many as 100,000 copies. The reference may be to the pamphlets as a group or specifically to the longer publication, *The Tryal of Dr Henry Sacheverell* (London: Jacob Tonson, 1710); see Geoffrey Holmes, *The Trial of Doctor Sacheverell* (London: Eyre Methuen, 1973), and F. F. Madan, *A Critical Bibliography of Dr Henry Sacheverell*, ed. W. A. Speck (Lawrence, Kansas: University of Kansas Libraries, 1978).
2 On the Derby Library see Reade, *Johnsonian Gleanings* 10: 182. Johnson's note is at *Yale* 1: 7.
3 Johnson at Ulinish, *Life* 5: 246.
4 Clifford, *Young Sam Johnson*, 7; Johnson, *Yale* 1: 4.
5 *Letters* 2: 304–308 (no. 463); *Yale* 1: 201.

6 Annals, *Yale* 1: 7.
7 Ibid., 14 (twice); Mrs Thrale, *Johnsonian Miscellanies* 1: 163; *Vanity*, ll. 40–1, *Yale* 6: 93.
8 *Johnsonian Miscellanies* 1: 153–4.
9 On Johnson's scrofula see John Wiltshire, *Samuel Johnson in the Medical World*, 13–21; the smallpox is recorded in a later diary, *Yale* 1: 176.
10 On the early appearance of symptoms see Reade, *Johnsonian Gleanings* 10: 84. For a diagnosis see T. J. Murray, 'Dr Samuel Johnson's Movement Disorder', *British Medical Journal*, 1 (1979), 1610–14. On the the nature of the disease see Oliver Sacks, *The Man who Mistook his Wife for a Hat and Other Clinical Tales* (1985; rpt New York: Perennial Library, 1987), and Shapiro et al., 'The Symptomology and Diagnosis of Gilles de la Tourette's Syndrome', *Journal of the American Academy of Child Psychiatry*, 12 (1973), 702–23. These authors warn against the misdiagnoses of the symptoms as resulting from 'psychological conflict over inhibited aggression' adding up to 'obsessive–compulsive neurosis, hysteria ... and schizophrenia' (703). Just such misdiagnoses have been common in twentieth–century biographies of Johnson. Also see John Wiltshire, *Samuel Johnson in the Medical World*, 29–34. In my treatment of this question I draw on notes added to his copy of Mrs Piozzi's *Anecdotes* by the late James Day, a distinguished professor of classics who diagnosed his own condition as Tourette's syndrome and compared his case with Johnson's. The episode with Hogarth is at *Life* 1: 146–7.
11 Johnson, *Yale* 1: 17 and 20–1.
12 Annals, *Yale* 1: 19; Hector is quoted in Hawkins, *Life of Samuel Johnson*, 6.
13 Hector, ibid., 7; on Tourette's syndrome see Shapiro et al., 'Symptomology and Diagnosis', 704 and *passim*; Johnson's reading, *Life* 3: 285; his mother's remark, *Yale* 1: 14.
14 Johnson's attitude to his teachers, *Johnsonian Miscellanies* 1: 164; parental authority, ibid., 1: 162; his father, *Yale* 6: 342.
15 Hunter, *Life* 1: 44; Reade, *Johnsonian Gleanings* 3: 133–4.
16 Hawkins, *Life of Samuel Johnson*, 2n., 7; *Lives*, 'Fenton', 13; Reade, *Johnsonian Gleanings* 3: 153.
17 On Samuel Lea, *Life* 1: 50.
18 Johnson at Stourbridge, Reade, *Johnsonian Gleanings* 3: 159, and *Johnsonian Miscellanies* 2: 208.
19 Lines 25–8, *Yale* 6: 3–4.
20 Clifford makes the connection to Herrick (*Young Sam Johnson*, 77).
21 Hector in *Complete English Poems*, 182; 'Friendship', ll. 21–4, *Yale* 6: 70–2 (with Hector's readings inserted).
22 'Integer vitae', *Yale* 6: 73–5; Boswell, *Notebook*, 19; 'Festina Lente', *Yale* 6: 15.
23 *Iliad*, ibid., 17–21; Πυγμαιογερανομαχια, ibid., 21–7. I am heavily indebted here to Isobel Grundy, *Samuel Johnson and the Scale of Greatness*, 5–6 and *passim*.
24 Annals, *Yale* 1: 24–5 and 18; *Life* 1: 57 (twice) and 445.
25 Reade prints the list with commentary, *Johnsonian Gleanings* 5: 213–29.
26 *Lives* 'Smith', 75; Clifford, *Young Sam Johnson*, 96; Greene, *Politics*, 65–6.
27 Ford, *Johnsonian Miscellanies* 1: 155; Boswell, *Life* 3: 66 and 24; Burney, ibid., 24 n. 2.
28 See G. B. Hill, *Letters* 1: 83–4.
29 Mrs Carless, Clifford, *Young Sam Johnson*, 95; 'To a Young Lady on Her Birthday', *Yale* 6: 36; 'An Epilogue to *The Distrest Mother*', ibid., 37–8.

Chapter 2 Oxford and Birmingham

1 Hawkins, *Life of Samuel Johnson*, 16; Taylor, Boswell, *Correspondence*, 103; Johnson on Jorden, *Life* 1: 59–61, 272.

2 Greene, *Politics*, 60; account, *Life* 1: 74; 'rude and violent', Clifford, *Young Sam Johnson*, 121; Hawkins, *Life of Samuel Johnson*, 16.

3 *Yale* 6: 29–36.

4 *Yale* 6: 30, 28; Fleeman makes the connection to Milton in *Complete English Poems*, 230.

5 'The Student', *Yale* 6: 72–3; J. Husbands, *A Miscellany of Poems by several Hands* (Oxford: Leon. Lichfield, 1731), A2r.

6 Boswell, *Life* 1: 70; reading schemes, *Yale* 1: 27; Hawkins, *Life of Samuel Johnson*, 11.

7 Boswell, *Life* 1: 68–9.

8 William Law, *A Serious Call to a Devout and Holy Life* (London: William Innys, 1729), 401, 153, 262–4; Law, *Remarks upon a Late Book, entituled The Fable of the Bees* (London, 1724); see *Life* 1: 68 and 4: 286–7 n. 3, where Johnson calls Law 'no reasoner'.

9 James Gray, 'Arras/Hélas! A Fresh Look at Johnson's French', in Paul Korshin (ed.), *Johnson after Two Hundred Years*, 79–96; Johnson's soliloquy, *Life* 1: 73 and Boswell, *Notebook*, 7–8; Bate, *Samuel Johnson*, 98–9.

10 Hector, Boswell, *Correspondence*, 91; Johnson on Cheyne, *Life* 3: 26–7; George Cheyne, *The English Malady* (1733; facsim. rpt Delmar, New York: Scholar's Facsimiles, 1976), 11 and *passim*; Johnson's new book, Reade, *Johnsonian Gleanings* 8: 109.

11 *Yale* 1: 29.

12 Boswell, *Correspondence*, 87.

13 Throughout this section I rely heavily on Joel J. Gold, both his introduction and notes to volume 15 of the *Yale Edition of the Works of Samuel Johnson* and his article 'Johnson's Translation of Lobo', *PMLA*, 80 (1965), 51–61. On Warren see Joseph Hill, *The Book Makers of Old Birmingham* (Birmingham: Shakespeare Press, 1907), 39–45. English works on Abyssinia are treated by Donald M. Lockhart, '"The Fourth Son of the Mighty Emperor": The Ethiopian Background of Johnson's *Rasselas*', *PMLA*, 78 (1963), 516–28. The politics of Johnson's Lobo are remarked by Greene, *Politics*, 66–72.

14 *Yale* 15: 3–4 and 86–8.

15 For the comparisons between Le Grand and Johnson I am indebted to Gold, 'Johnson's Translation of Lobo'; 'The circumstances...', *Yale* 15: 176.

16 'At a distance', ibid., 47; 'In the province...', ibid., 46 and n. 2.

17 'Dieu...', ibid., 56 n. 4; 'shakes...', ibid., 58 n. 7; 'no real grounds ...', ibid., 40; *The Shortest Way*, Hill, *The Book Makers of Old Birmingham*, 49.

18 Gold, *Yale* 15: lv–lvi; 'About the same time...', ibid., 239; on Johnson's humanistic anti–colonialism see Greene, *Politics*, 66–72.

19 *Yale* 15: 144.

20 Ibid., xxvi, citing Herman Liebert, 'Dr Johnson's First Book', *Yale University Library Gazette*, 25 (1950), 28.

Chapter 3   *Irene*

1 *Letters* 1: 6 (no. 3).
2 Clifford, *Young Sam Johnson*, 152; Mrs Porter's remark, *Life* 1: 95; see the treatment of 'sensible' in the *OED* and Jane Collier, *The Cry* (London: R. and J. Dodsley, 1754), 1: 77–8. On the subject in general see Janet Todd, *Sensibility: An Introduction* (London: Methuen, 1986).
3 Clifford, *Young Sam Johnson*, 163.
4 Edial described, Reade, *Johnsonian Gleanings* 6: 37; Johnson's unsuitability for teaching posts, ibid., 30, and *Life* 4: 407–8 n. 4.
5 Johnson's curriculum, *Life* 1: 99–100; his advertisement, Reade, *Johnsonian Gleanings* 6: 44; *Gentleman's Magazine* 6: 360, 428.
6 *Lives*, 'Milton', 36; *Life* 1: 96 n. 1.
7 Cited with commentary by David Nichol Smith, 'Johnson's Irene', *Essays and Studies by Members of the English Association*, 14 (Oxford: Clarendon Press, 1929), 35–54; rpt, Oxford *Poems*, 234. Also see Bertrand H. Bronson, 'Johnson's "Irene": Variations on a Tragic Theme' (1944), rpt in *Johnson Agonistes and Other Essays*, 100–55. I am indebted to these two essays in my treatment of *Irene* and to 'The Mighty Moral of Irene' by Marshall Waingrow, in F. W. Hilles and Harold Bloom (eds), *From Sensibility to Romanticism*, (New York: Oxford University Press, 1965), 79–92.
8 Act 5, scene 13, ll. 10–15; *Yale* 6: 216–17.
9 Johnson, Oxford *Poems*, 353; *Cl. Claudiani Quae Extant*, ed. Nicolaus Heinsius, 2 vols (Amsterdam: Elzevir Press, 1665), 2: 862; Martial 10.47; Petronius, Loeb edition, ed. M. Hazeltine and E. H. Warmington (London: Heinemann, 1969), 422–3.
10 Demetrius and Aspasia, *Yale* 6: 219–20; Aspasia, Oxford *Poems*, 366; act 4, scene 2, ll. 120–3 (*Yale* 6: 177).
11 Bronson, 'Irene', 119, 120, 123; Johnson, Oxford *Poems*, 372.
12 Ibid., 372, 375
13 Draft, ibid., 375; Bronson, 'Irene', 133; Greene, *Politics*, 72–80.
14 Dryden, *Aureng-Zebe*, ed. Frederick M. Link (Lincoln, Nebraska: University of Nebraska Press, 1971), 4.1.33–44.
15 Bronson, 'Irene', 137, 142.

Chapter 4   London

1 Reade, *Johnsonian Gleanings* 6: 59–60, and *Letters* 3: 320, both cited in Clifford, *Young Sam Johnson*, 165–7.
2 *Thraliana* 1: 189 and Herman W. Liebert (who cites this passage), 'Portrait of the Author: Lifetime Likenesses of Samuel Johnson', 49–50.
3 For information on the Sarpi project I am indebted to Thomas Kaminski, *The Early Career of Samuel Johnson*, 8–9 and 67–76.
4 *Life* 4: 381–2 and see plate 10.
5 On the Tridentine Council, see Carl Theodor Mirbt, *Encyclopedia Britannica*, 11th edn (New York, 1911), 27: 247–50. Eisenstein, *The Printing Press as an Agent of Change* (Cambridge: Cambridge University Press, 1980), 145–7.

6   Hawkins, *Life of Samuel Johnson*, 40; Boswell, *Life* 1: 112.
7   For the background of 'Ad Urbanum' see *Johnsonian Miscellanies* 1: 377 and Kaminski, *Early Career*, 17. The poem is at *Yale* 6: 40–3.
8   Εἰς τὸ τῆς ΕΛΙΣΣΗΣ, *Yale* 6: 44–5; 'To a Lady', ibid., 43.
9   *Yale* 6: 61–2 and 63.
10 *Letters* 1: 15 (no. 6); for information on Johnson's earnings, I rely on J. D. Fleeman, 'The Revenue of a Writer'.
11 Boswell, *Life* 1: 118; for a view of the poem as primarily 'an excercise of talent' see W. J. Bate, *Samuel Johnson*, 171–5; against Bate, see Geoffrey Finch, 'Johnson's "Sincerity" in "London"', *Papers on Language and Literature*, 17 (1981), 353–62. 'Johnson drank so deep . . .', Edward A. and Lillian D. Bloom, 'Johnson's *London* and the Tools of Scholarship', *Huntington Library Quarterly*, 34 (1971), 115–39, 115. Also see their 'Johnson's *London* and its Juvenalian Texts', ibid., 34 (1970), 1–23.
12 *Lives*, 'Dryden', 300. In this summation and throughout my commentary on *London* I am indebted to Edward A. and Lillian D. Bloom, 'Johnson's "Mournful Narrative": the Rhetoric of "London"'.
13 Thomas Stanley, *The History of Philosophy, Containing the Lives, Opinions, Actions and Discourses of the Philosophers of every Sect*, second edn (London: Thomas Bassett, 1687), 12–13.
14 The line citations are to *Yale* 6: 45–61, although capitalization of many nouns in the existing manuscript lines and in many earlier printings would serve better to illustrate my point about Johnson's abstractions.
15 *A General Index to the first Twenty Volumes of the Gentleman's Magazine* (London, 1753), reprinted by L. F. Powell in 'An Addition to the Canon of Johnson's Writings', *Essays and Studies*, 28 (1942): 38–41.
16 *Gentlemen's Magazine* 12: 410.
17 *Commons Journals* XXIII: 148. Throughout this section I am indebted to Benjamin Beard Hoover, *Samuel Johnson's Parliamentary Reporting*, both for historical information and for interpretive insights.
18 *Gentleman's Magazine* 8: 283.
19 Ibid., 12: 228, 230, 233–4 successively.
20 Ibid., 11: 621 and 467.
21 Ibid., 11: 417, 5, 520, and 13: 522 successively.
22 Although my emphasis differs somewhat, I am indebted to Isobel Grundy's incisive treatment of the *Debates* in *Samuel Johnson and the Scale of Greatness*, 34–61.
23 On the Playhouse debates, see Hoover, *Parliamentary Reporting*, 12, citing *Gentleman's Magazine* 5: 777, 6: 365, 405, and 447.
24 *Yale* 10: 69–73.
25 The first account, *Gentleman's Magazine* 11: 633; the debate, ibid., 11: 672. The reason that some of the MPs may have wanted the manuscript can be inferred from unsubstantiated accusations made later that the paper was written by a Member, but Johnson does not dignify their motives.
26 The debate, ibid., 11: 672–3, 675; *Marmor, Yale* 10: 35–7.
27 *Gentleman's Magazine* 11: 676; Grundy precedes me in comparing this passage and Imlac's speech in *Rasselas*.
28 *Debates in Parliament* 1: 38–40. The King apparently agreed to try Meres, but unfortunately there is no record of the proceedings in the *English Reports* of the King's Bench (*Commons Journals* XXIII: 549).

29 *Lords Journals* 27: 107–8; Astley, the publisher of the *London Magazine*, also had to appear, but neither was jailed. Also see Hoover, *Parliamentary Reporting*, 30.
30 *Gentleman's Magazine* 13: 63, 68–70.
31 Ibid., 117 and 125.
32 Pitt, ibid., 131; Howe, ibid., 134; Heathcote, ibid., 135; Hoover, *Parliamentary Reporting*, 139; Robert Giddings, 'The Fall of Orgilio: Samuel Johnson as Parliamentary Reporter', 101.
33 *Gentleman's Magazine* 13: 181; I am indebted to Isobel Grundy's treatment of this passage in *Samuel Johnson and the Scale of Greatness*, 56.
34 *Johnsonian Miscellanies* 1: 379.
35 *Gentleman's Magazine* 12: 691, 123, and 13: 674.
36 Pulteney, ibid., 12: 63; Pitt, ibid., 13: 303; Cornwall, ibid., 12: 175 and 14: 8; Bishop of Oxford, ibid., 13: 698 and 14: 3. On the *Beaux' Stratagem* see *Life* 2: 461 and n. 3.
37 Shippen, *Gentleman's Magazine* 12: 461; Chesterfield, ibid., 12: 670; Cornbury, ibid., 13: 175.

Chapter 5 Early Biographical Writings

1 The 'Considerations' were not published until 1787; *Gentleman's Magazine* 57: 555–7.
2 *Letters* 2: 230 (no. 349). In the letter Johnson advocates sale of the copyright for a fourteen-year period; additional possible sales of seven-year periods; and retention of copyright in the estate of the author until thirty years after his death. By these rules he envisions the private ownership of copyrights for about fifty years, after which time they will probably need notes and therefore need to be public property for redaction to be feasible financially. Also see *Life* 2: 259.
3 John Brett was the publisher of *Marmor*, as he was of *Common Sense*, one of the journals on which Cave, with Johnson's help, heaped abuse in the Grub Street wars of the day. See Kaminski, *Early Career*, 59.
4 The description is Arthur Murphy's, included in *Johnsonian Miscellanies* 1: 371. Also see *Life* 1: 163–4. On Johnson's marital difficulties see Reade, *Johnsonian Gleanings* 6: 121–3.
5 *Letters* 1: 22–4 (no. 12); Clifford, *Young Sam Johnson*, 228 and n. 18.
6 *Life* 1: 133–4.
7 *Letters* 1: 19 (no. 9); Reade, *Johnsonian Gleanings* 6: 87.
8 *Life* 4:127 and 494–6.
9 Crousaz, *A Commentary on Mr Pope's Principles of Morality*, 59; Lives, 'Pope', 365; cf. 181–94.
10 *Commentary*, 152–3, 144, and 109n. successively.
11 *Commentary*, 3n., 37–8n., 124n., and 40n. successively. The exception, in which Johnson praises du Resnel, is *Commentary*, 78.
12 Ibid., 312; *Yale* 7: 65 and n. 3, citing Lives, 'Pope', 338; to Gower, *Life* 1: 133–4 (above, p. 70).
13 A recent article argues persuasively that Johnson's contributions to James's work were modest: the dedication, the revised 'Boerhaave', 'Alexander', and

the opening sections of 'Actuarius' and 'Aegineta'. See OM Brack and Thomas Kaminski, 'Johnson, James, and the *Medicinal Dictionary*', *Modern Philology*, 81 (1984), 378–400. On errors in *Savage*, see Kaminski, *Early Career*, 188–9, who relies in part on Clarence Tracy's edition. I take Johnson's remark to Boswell from Robert Folkenflik, *Samuel Johnson, Biographer*, 53, citing *Life* 3: 344. I am indebted to this excellent study throughout my treatment of Johnson's biographical writings.

14 Kaminski, *Early Career*, 53.
15 *Early Biographical Writings*, 82–3.
16 Ibid., 49–51.
17 *Life of Richard Savage*, 93.
18 *Early Biographical Writings*, 58 and 37.
19 Perhaps the only biography of a non-literary man after the early 1740s is Johnson's 'Memoirs of the King of Prussia' (*Literary Magazine*, 1756). The closest Johnson gets to a biography of a woman is his 'Review of *An Account of the Dutchess of Marlborough*'. See Folkenflik, *Samuel Johnson, Biographer*, 221–6 for a summary of Johnson's biographical work. 'Boerhaave' appeared in the *Gentleman's Magazine* 9: 37–8, 72–3, 114–16, 172–6; I cite *Early Biographical Writings*, 33. Fussell treats 'Boerhaave' in *Samuel Johnson and the Life of Writing*, 101–9. Boswell's description of Johnson is at *Life* 4: 425 (also see 1: 462 and 472).
20 *Oratio Academica in Memoriam Hermanni Boerhaavii* (Leiden, 1738). See Kaminski, *Early Career*, 54.
21 *Early Biographical Writings*, 27, 29, and 30 consecutively. See Greene, *Samuel Johnson's Library*, 39, for Johnson's collection of Boerhaave.
22 *Rambler* 114, *Yale* 4: 242; *Early Biographical Writings*, 32, 35.
23 *Early Biographical Writings*, 96 (*Gentleman's Magazine* 12: 356). Folkenflik identifies Johnson's subjects in these biographies as Christian stoics (*Samuel Johnson, Biographer*, 67).
24 'Sydenham', *Early Biographical Writings*, 193–4; Kaminski, *Early Career*, 158–61; *Lives*, 'Pope', 261.
25 *Barretier*, *Early Biographical Writings*, 171, 174. (I am again indebted to Kaminski, *Early Career*, 113–14.) Zachariah Williams, the father of Johnson's close friend Anna, attempted a solution to the longitude problem, which Johnson wrote up and had published for him in 1755 – *An Account of an Attempt to Ascertain the Longitude at Sea* (London: R. Dodsley, 1755).
26 Robert James's *Medicinal Dictionary* provides examples.
27 *Savage*, 140, 125.
28 Ibid., 125–6.
29 Ibid., 102. For my sense of *Savage* as ironic comedy I am indebted to Paul Fussell, *Samuel Johnson and the Life of Writing*, 258–64, and Alvin Kernan, *Samuel Johnson and the Impact of Print*, 79.
30 *Savage*, 31. On legal language in *Savage* see William Vestermann, 'Johnson and the *Life of Savage*', *English Literary History*, 36 (1969), 359–78.
31 *Savage*, 31, 140; published account, *Select Trials for Murders . . . at the Sessions-House in the Old Bailey*, 2 vols (London, 1734–5), 2: 246, cited in the introduction by Timothy Erwin to *The Life of Savage* (1727; rpt Los Angeles: William Andrews Clark Memorial Library, 1988), vi. On indeterminacy in readers' responses to *Savage* see Paul K. Alkon, 'The Intention and Reception of Johnson's *Life of Savage*', *Modern Philology*, 72 (1974), 139–51.
32 *Savage*, 135.

33 Ibid., 3, 74 (twice).
34 Ibid., 103; also see 58.
35 'In his lowest State . . .', ibid., 99; dedications, 28; 'Voice of the People', 72; free press, 49.

Chapter 6   Miscellaneous Prose

1 Johnson's remarks on Psalmanazar, Clifford, *Young Sam Johnson*, 239–40, citing Thrale and Tower; Psalmanazar, *An Historical and Geographical Description of Formosa* (London, 1704), 26.
2 *Minor Lives*, ed. Edward L. Hart (Cambridge, Mass.: Harvard University Press, 1971), 342–4. I follow Clifford and Kaminski in using this anecdote about Boyse at this stage of the biography.
3 Apart from poems that he had clearly written earlier, in the early 1740s Johnson published only an epitaph on Claudy Philips, a musician, a Latin translation of a poem by Pope, and a prologue for Garrick's play *Lethe*. See Kaminski, *Early Career*, 155. *Monarchy Asserted*, Yale 10: 85–6. I am indebted to Greene's introduction, ibid., 74–9.
4 Ibid., 89–90.
5 *Gentleman's Magazine* 12: 89 and 149 consecutively; in this paragraph I draw on Kaminski, *Early Career*, 148–53.
6 Amazons, *Gentleman's Magazine* 11: 202–3; *Idler* 87, Yale 2: 272.
7 *Gentleman's Magazine* 12: 128–9.
8 Ibid., 10: 593 and 595. Writing on Pope's epitaphs in 1756 Johnson again described the best subject as 'Domestick virtue, as it is exerted without great occasions or conspicuous consequences in an even unnoted tenor . . .' – *Universal Visiter* (1756), 207–19, reprinted in *Lives*, 'Pope', 412.
9 *Gentleman's Magazine* 10: 595 and 596.
10 *Jests, Gentleman's Magazine* 11: 477–9; *Acta Diurna*, ibid., 10: iii–viii; *Cryptographia*, ibid., 12: 135. For my sense of the canon during the early 1740s I have relied most heavily on Thomas Kaminski, David Fleeman, O. M. Brack, and Donald Greene. David Fleeman's bibliography, a professional lifetime in the making, is expected soon. OM Brack's forthcoming *Shorter Prose of Samuel Johnson* will also do much to establish the Johnsonian canon, and it will take into consideration some of Donald Greene's extensive unpublished attributional work. Both Brack and Fleeman consider the attribution of *Cryptographia* doubtful.
11 'Foreign Affairs', *Gentleman's Magazine* 12: 54 and 11: 556 – Kaminski makes the attribution, *Early Career*, 145.
12 *Gentleman's Magazine* 11: 670, 12: 223 and 167 consecutively.

Chapter 7   The Harleian Library

1 *Gentleman's Magazine* 12: 112.
2 Oldys copies his own marginalia, *Catalogus Bibliothecae Harleianae*, vol. 3, no. 159. He also cites his own *British Librarian*, e.g. vol. 3, no. 6917. Oldys's MS on London libraries, *Notes and Queries*, 2nd Series, XI (8 June 1861), 441.

3   A memorandum of 1715 from Humphrey Wanley estimates the cost of the
     library to the founder, Robert Harley, at £4,573. After Robert's death, his
     brother Edward pursued extensive projects of acquisition, raising the total of
     printed books from about 12,000 to about 50,000 including forty-two incunabula
     printed by Caxton. For a full account of the growth of the library see *The Diary
     of Humphrey Wanley*, ed. C. E. Wright and Ruth C. Wright, 2 vols (London: the
     Bibliographical Society, 1966). The British government bought the manu-
     scripts in 1753 and joined them with the Cottonian collections in the newly
     formed British Museum. Throughout this section I frequently rely on Kaminski,
     Early Career, 174–84, and 'Johnson and Oldys as Bibliographers: An Introduc-
     tion to the Harleian Catalogue', *Philological Quarterly*, 4 (1981), 439–52.

4   See Archer Taylor, *Book Catalogues: Their Varieties and Uses* (Chicago: Newberry
     Library, 1957), and *British Book Sale Catalogues 1676–1800*, edited by A. N. L.
     Munby and Lenore Coral (London: Mansell, 1977).

5   *Bernard's Catalogue* is *Catalogus librorum manuscriptorum, Angliae et Hiberniae*
     (Oxford, 1697); no. 483 in Greene, *Samuel Johnson's Library*. 'Account', rpt,
     Catalogus Bibliothecae Harleianae 1: 2, 3–4, 5, and 6 consecutively. For Johnson
     on the importance of Northern studies, also see 'Foreign Books', *Gentleman's
     Magazine* 12: 391.

6   'Account', [1]. C. E. Wright and Ruth Wright, editors of the Wanley *Diary*, say
     the descriptions of the books are 'most inadequate' (1: lxxix). Thomas Kaminski
     has evaluated the bibliographical quality of the work more carefully, and he
     also sees the job as pedestrian, 'Johnson and Oldys as Bibliographers'. Although
     Kaminski is reliable, there may be a wider range of reference than he suggests.
     Hearne's edition of Robert of Gloucester's *Chronicle*, for instance, and Nicolson's
     Historical Libraries are often cited.

7   *Catalogus Bibliothecae Harleianae* 1: nos 158, 160, 161, 173 and 189.

8   Ibid., 2: nos 12131–76, 11345, 11339, 11337, and 11493.

9   Ibid., 1: no. 2976.

10   Ibid., 1: no. 704.

11   See OM Brack, *Bred a Bookseller: Samuel Johnson on Vellum Books, A New Essay*
     (Los Angeles: Samuel Johnson Society of Southern California, 1990). In his
     forthcoming five-volume work, *Shorter Prose of Samuel Johnson*, Brack identifies
     a number of other descriptions in the *Catalogue* as probably written by Johnson.
     On Johnson's proposed history, see above, p. 45. 'Account', *Catalogus Biblio-
     thecae Harleianae* 1: 3; G. B. Hill identifies the 'great English critic' as Bentley
     (*Life* 1: 153 n. 7).

12   *Catalogus Bibliothecae Harleianae* 2: no. 12532 and 1: no. 6346.

13   Reuchlin, ibid., 2: no. 15328; Hemmerline, ibid., 3: no. 1447 (cf. 3: no. 1017);
     Vechiettus, ibid., 1: no. 6336.

14   De Thou, ibid., 1: no. 6426 (cf. 1: no. 992); Piccolomini, ibid., 1: no. 6434;
     Nichols, ibid., 1: no. 2954.

15   Pontanus, ibid., 1: no. 4298 (see *Yale* 3: 157 for Johnson's translation).

16   Scapula, ibid., 2: no. 15096; Doletus, ibid., 2: no. 15130; Stephanus, 2: no.
     15094. On the lugubrious complaints of many lexicographers see Paul Korshin,
     'Johnson and the Renaissance Dictionary', *Journal of the History of Ideas*, 35
     (1974): 300–12.

17   Postell, *Catalogus Bibliothecae Harleianae* 1: no. 6701 and 2: no. 15373; Pococke,
     ibid., 1: no. 818 – see dissertation 10 in Johnson's Lobo (*Yale* 14: 42 n. 4);
     Sambucus, ibid., 1: no. 6211.

18 *Le Voyage*, ibid., 2: no. 11,786 (cf. 2: 11,519); Chrysoloras, ibid., 2: no. 15392.

19 Reference books: he used at least Hearne's edition of Robert of Gloucester's *Metrical Chronicle* and Nicolson's *Historical Libraries* in both. The same editions that Johnson used are listed in *Catalogus Bibliothecae Harleianae*, 3: no. 4077 and 1: no. 7516. In his *Handlist* (1984) Fleeman traces only one of his books definitely to the Harleian Library, but agreement between books that Johnson is known to have owned and some of those in the *Harleian Catalogue* is suggestive. *Acta Eruditorum*, see Greene, *Samuel Johnson's Library*, 25–6, and *Life* 1: 284–5 n. 4. Johnson wrote the proposals for such a work, *The Publisher*, which only ran to four numbers, from late 1744 to early 1745 (Hazen, *Johnson's Prefaces and Dedications*, 193–5).

20 *Life* 1: 154; Kernan, *Samuel Johnson and the Impact of Print*, 256; Poggio, see R. P. Oliver, 'Giovanni Tortelli', in *Studies presented to D. M. Robinson II* (1953), 1257–71, cited by Rudolf Pfeiffer, *History of Classical Scholarship, 1300–1850* (Oxford: Clarendon Press, 1976), 55 n. 3.

21 Donald Greene, 'Johnson and the "Harleian Miscellany"', *Notes and Queries* (July 1958), 304–6.

22 *Harleian Miscellany* 3: 170; *Life* 1: 471.

23 On the publishing history of the *Miscellany* see R. M. Wiles, *Serial Publication in England before 1750* (Cambridge: Cambridge University Press, 1957), 244–5; William B. Todd and Peter J. Wallis, 'Provincial Booksellers c. 1744: The *Harleian Miscellany* Subscription List', *The Library*, 29 (1974), 422–40; and John Feather, *The Provincial Booktrade in Eighteenth-Century England* (Cambridge: Cambridge University Press, 1985), 24 and 29. Johnson, *Harleian Miscellany* 1: ii, vi, iv consecutively. On the politics of the *Miscellany*, see Mark Goldie, 'The Revolution of 1689: Pamphlets and the Allegiance Controversy', *Bulletin of Research in the Humanities*, 83 (1980), 473–564, and Olivier Lutaud, 'Tradition de Révolution: "From Penn to Paine..."' (Conservateurs de révolution et révolutionnaires par tradition)', in *Vivante tradition, sources et racines: évolution de quelques formes et forces en littérature et civilisation anglaises* (Paris, 1982), 178–89.

24 Johnson's projects: *Life* 1: 188 and David Fleeman, 'Some of Dr Johnson's Preparatory Notes for his Dictionary, 1755', *Bodleian Library Record*, 7 (December 1964), 205–10; *Observations*, Yale 7: 10 n. 3; 35, 43 (Camden), and 30.

25 Hickes, *Linguarum Veterum Septentrionalium Thesaurus* (Oxford, 1703) 1.1.231; *Observations*, Yale 7: 3.

Chapter 8   Johnson's *Dictionary*

1 On Johnson's financial state, see Kaminski, *Early Career*, 196; on his application to Smalbroke, see Clifford, *Young Sam Johnson*, 285; on speculation concerning his services on behalf of the Pretender, ibid., 288.

2 On life in Gough Square, see Clifford, *Dictionary Johnson*, 15–28. On the contract for the *Dictionary*, see E. J. Thomas, 'A Bibliographical and Critical Analysis', 17. I rely on Thomas throughout this section and on Sledd and Kolb, *Dr Johnson's Dictionary: Essays in the Biography of a Book*.

3 Allen Reddick, *The Making of Johnson's Dictionary 1746–1773*, 42–5. I am indebted to Reddick's account of Johnson's method.

4 E. J. Thomas analysed the extant books that Johnson used for finding quotations and discovered that of the 27,077 marked passages 17,523 actually appear in the *Dictionary* ('A Bibliographical and Critical Analysis', 188–92). It is possible that the amanuenses helped in the collection as well as the copying of quotations. Macbean contributed some etymological comments and some definitions, even signing his name to at least four ('mounc', 'salubrious', 'scale', and 'sorn').

5 *Plan*, Oxford *Works* 5: 21.

6 *The World*, no. 100 (28 November 1754); (rpt in the four volume edition (London: R. and J. Dodsley, 1755), 3: 267.

7 On Latinate words, see E. L. McAdam, 'Inkhorn words before Dr Johnson', in *Eighteenth-Century Studies*, ed. W. H. Bond (New York: Grolier Club, 1970), 187–206. On Germanic roots, see my 'Johnson's *Dictionary* and the "Teutonick" Roots of the English Language', in *Language and Civilization*, 2 vols, ed. Theresa Kirschner (Berne: Peter Lang, 1991), 1: 19–34.

8 Preface, par. 67; *Plan*, Oxford *Works* 5: 20 and 13. The best book on English lexicography before Johnson remains DeWitt Starnes and Gertrude Noyes, *The English Dictionary from Cawdrey to Johnson* (Chapel Hill: University of North Carolina Press, 1946). For a complete account of Johnson's 'brandings' see Harold B. Allen, 'Samuel Johnson and the Authoritarian Principle in Linguistic Criticism' (diss., Univ. of Michigan, 1940).

9 See Jürgen Schäfer, *Documentation in the OED* (Oxford: Oxford University Press, 1979).

10 Preface, paragraphs 57 and 92.

11 Chambers, *Cyclopedia*, 4th edn, 2 vols (London, 1741), 1: xxv, and *Considerations Preparatory to a Second Edition* (n.p., n.d.), 4; Preface, par. 72.

12 Locke, *An Essay concerning Human Understanding*, ed. P. H. Nidditch (Oxford: Clarendon Press, 1975), 720; Preface, paragraphs 17, 45, and 75 successively. On seventeenth-century linguistic reform, see James Knowlson, *Universal Language Schemes in England and France 1600–1800* (Toronto and Buffalo: University of Toronto Press, 1975).

13 Preface, par. 28.

14 For the best treatment of this element in the *Dictionary*, see William K. Wimsatt, *Philosophic Words* (New Haven: Yale University Press, 1948).

15 See my *Johnson's Dictionary and the Language of Learning*, 234.

16 In the miscellaneous correspondence to the *Gentleman's Magazine* for September 1744 there is a piece entitled 'On Hell's Torments etc, a Specimen of a supplemental article to Chambers's *Dictionary*'. If this piece is by Johnson, it suggests that he entertained in 1744 the criticism of Chambers's *Cyclopedia* that is implicit in the way he presents the field of knowledge in the *Dictionary*. For the manuscript note, see 'A Short Scheme for compiling a New Dictionary of the English Language', reprinted in *The R. B. Adam Library relating to Dr Samuel Johnson and his Era*, 3 vols (Buffalo: privately printed for the author, 1929); see my *Johnson's Dictionary and the Language of Learning*, 11–19.

17 For a fine analysis of the tale, see Richard Schwartz, 'Johnson's "Vision of Theodore"', *New Rambler* C, 14 (1973): 31–9.

18 See my *Johnson's Dictionary and the Language of Learning*, 62.

19 Ibid., 62; Locke, *An Essay concerning Human Understanding*, 581. See Gwin Kolb and Ruth Kolb, 'The Selection and Use of Illustrative Quotations in Dr Johnson's *Dictionary*', in Howard Weinbrot (ed.), *New Aspects of Lexicography* (Carbondale: University of Illinois Press, 1972), 61–72.

20   *Catalogus Bibliothecae Harleianae* 3: A2v.
21   'To Daniel Wray', MS Bodleian 1012, fol. 208. See DeMaria, 'The Politics of Johnson's *Dictionary*', *PMLA*, 104 (1989), 65.
22   See Richard Ashcraft, *Revolutionary Politics and Locke's Two Treatises of Government* (Princeton: Princeton University Press, 1986).
23   Above, p. 92.
24   Clifford, *Dictionary Johnson*, 120, citing Mrs Chapone's *Posthumous Works* (London, 1807), 1: 72–4.
25   See DeMaria, 'The Politics of Johnson's *Dictionary*', 65, where I have inadvertently misquoted Johnson as writing, 'Bolingbroke was a pious man'.
26   Thomas, 'A Bibliographical and Critical Analysis', 100–6; *Yale* 1: 52.
27   Prayers, *Yale* 1: 41 and 50.
28   'It is gone', *Life* 2: 203–4 n. 3. For the story of the fourth edition and the unprinted work, see Allen Reddick, *The Making of Johnson's Dictionary*. I draw here on my earlier conclusions in *Johnson's Dictionary and the Language of Learning*.

Chapter 9   *The Vanity of Human Wishes*

1   See Nicholas Hudson, *Samuel Johnson and Eighteenth-Century Thought*, 46.
2   *The Correspondence of Robert Dodsley 1733–64*, ed. James E. Tierney (Cambridge: Cambridge University Press, 1988), 18–19 and 97–8.
3   Johnson revised the *Vanity* for the fourth edition of Dodsley's *Collection* (1755); he contributed other poems to the first edition of 1748.
4   *Yale* 6: 90–1 and *Life* 2: 15.
5   Lipking, 'Learning to Read Johnson: *The Vision of Theodore* and *The Vanity of Human Wishes*'. Richard Schwartz likewise calls *The Vision of Theodore* 'a kind of epitome or précis of [Johnson's] total statement as essayist, poet, biographer, travel writer, dramatist, and writer of sermon and parable': see 'Johnson's "Vision of Theodore"', *New Rambler* C, 14 (1973), 31–9.
6   On the Greek and Latin sources of Juvenal, see E. Courtney, *A Commentary on the Satires of Juvenal* (London: Athlone Press, 1980); *Rambler* 66, *Yale* 3: 349; on the connection between *Rambler* 66 and the *Vanity* see Fussell, *Samuel Johnson and the Life of Writing*, 177.
7   The manuscript is published as Appendix 3 in *Complete English Poems*.
8   Line 353; Johnson's poem also has many qualities foreign to odes, and what the eighteenth century called 'Pindarick' is not altogether consistent with what is found in Pindar. The poet's presentation of himself and his presumed audience are in Johnson and Pindar radically different. See Sitter, 'To *The Vanity of Human Wishes* through the 1740s'. On 'observation', see Isobel Grundy, *Samuel Johnson and the Scale of Greatness*, 158–62.
9   For material in the *Dictionary* relating to the pains of scholarly life, see my *Johnson's Dictionary and the Language of Learning*, 132–6 and 210–12.
10   *All the Works of Epictetus* (London, 1758), ii.
11   Dodsley, *The Preceptor* 2: 528–9 and 518.
12   *Yale* 6: 272, ll. 49–50. The translation by Arthur Murphy included in *Yale* 6 seems poor to me; better is John Wain's translation in Donald Greene's anthology, *Samuel Johnson* (Oxford and New York: Oxford University Press, 1984), 28–30. But truer to the text is the anonymous prose translation filed with the

manuscript in the Beinecke Rare Books and Manuscript Library. It renders the passage, part of which is cited above, as, 'Nor does the mind, watcher from a high tower, marvel at amassed wealth or assume wide honors, itself its own judge, but seeing as its own kingdom, the blessings of a life gently spent, shudders at the regions wrapped far and wide in silence, where empty forms and fleeting shades and thin shapes of things flit through the void.'

Chapter 10   The *Rambler*

1   Cited from William Shaw's *Memoirs* by James Clifford, *Dictionary Johnson*, 8. See Brack and Kelley, *Early Biographies*, 159.
2   Sledd and Kolb, *Johnson's Dictionary*, 107.
3   Hawkins, *Life of Samuel Johnson*, 196; on Johnson and doctors, see John Wiltshire, *Samuel Johnson in the Medical World*; Johnson on Bathurst, Clifford, *Dictionary Johnson*, 33, citing *Johnsonian Miscellanies* 1: 390, 158, and 204.
4   Hawkins, *Life of Samuel Johnson*, 228–30.
5   See the *Student* 2 (1751), 260–9, 290–4, and 331–4; reprinted in *Early Biographical Writings*, 389–406.
6   Hawkins, *Life of Samuel Johnson*, 230–1.
7   I am indebted for this insight to Richard Schwartz, 'Johnson's "Mr Rambler" and the Periodical Tradition', *Genre*, 7 (1974), 196–204.
8   *Yale* 4: 204 (see above, p. 101).
9   Ibid.; *Yale* 1: 43; Bacon, *Works*, 4 vols (London, 1740), 4: 488.
10 *Yale* 3: 3.
11 Ibid., 13.
12 Ibid., 14.
13 Ibid., 21, 22, 24, and 24–5 consecutively.
14 Mr Rambler's rivals, *Yale* 5: 121; the oriental tales, ibid., 3: xxvi, n. 6; characterizations of Mr Rambler, ibid., 3: 253 and 4: 12, reading the first edition.
15 Ibid., 4: 264.
16 Nos 44 and 100 were by Carter; no. 30 by Talbot and no. 97 by Richardson. Parts of three other *Ramblers* (10, 15, and 17) were by Hester Mulso, David Garrick, and Joseph Simpson respectively. 'The moralist . . .', *Yale* 3: 184; Euphelia, ibid., 3: 227; characterizations of Mr Rambler, ibid., 4: 216.
17 Hawkins, *Life of Samuel Johnson*, 238n.
18 *Yale* 3: 9. For the repetition of the theme in the *Rambler*, see number 41, n. 1 (*Yale* 3: 221).
19 *Yale* 4: 395.
20 'Genealogy of sentiments', *Dictionary*, Preface, par. 67. Johnson was reading Charles Aleyn and Prior as well as Crashaw and Pope for the *Dictionary*; hence, he may have drawn these two comparisons in *Rambler* 143 from notes for the *Dictionary*.
21 *Yale* 3: 268.
22 'The excellence of aphorisms . . .', *Yale* 5: 160; 'men more frequently . . .', ibid., 3: 14; 'the studies of mankind . . .', ibid., 5: 66.
23 'Criticism . . .', ibid., 5: 75–6; 'we desire . . .', ibid., 3: 35; 'It is said . . .', ibid., 41.
24 Ibid., 4: 365 and 3: 359–60 consecutively.

25 See William K. Wimsatt, *Philosophic Words* and *The Prose Style of Samuel Johnson*.
26 *Yale* 5: 201.
27 Johnson to Boswell, *Life* 1: 445; 'Old man of Verona', see above, p. 37 and n. 9; Martial, *Yale* 5: 293.
28 Aretaeus, *Yale* 4: 264; Pontanus, above, p. 102.
29 *Rambler* 132, *Yale* 4: 334; Bacon, *Works* 2: 426; *Rambler* 137, *Yale* 4: 360; Bacon, *Valerius Terminus*, *Works* 1: appendix, 72; Alonzo, *Yale* 4: 96 and Bacon, *Works* 3: 276.
30 *Yale* 3: xxviii.

Chapter 11 Sermons

1 Woodruff, 'Johnson's *Rambler* and Its Contemporary Context', *Bulletin of Research in the Humanities*, 85 (1982), 27–64.
2 My information on the 'Lauder affair' comes from Clifford, *Dictionary Johnson*, 57–70. The evidence needed for a proper evaluation of Wagstaff's charge was not gathered until this century. For a summary of problem see *The Complete Prose Works of John Milton*, vol. 3 (New Haven: Yale University Press, 1962), 152–9.
3 Johnson's marginalia, Fleeman, *Preliminary Handlist* (1984), no. 26; Talbot, cited by Woodruff, 'Johnson's *Rambler*', 42 n. 21, from *A Series of Letters between Mrs Elizabeth Carter and Miss Catherine Talbot*, ed. Montagu Pennington, 4 vols (London, 1809), 2: 3–4.
4 On the printing history of the *Rambler* see Woodruff, 'Johnson's *Rambler*', and Roy M. Wiles, 'The Contemporary Distribution of Johnson's *Rambler*', *Eighteenth-Century Studies*, 2 (1968), 155–71; *Rambler* 207, *Yale* 5: 311.
5 Preface, paragraphs 72 and 94.
6 *Life* 1: 238; *Letters* 1: 61 (no. 41); Hawkins, *Life of Samuel Johnson*, 280.
7 Commentators on Johnson's prayers, Clifford, *Dictionary Johnson*, 103; prayers, *Yale* 1: 44–5 and 71.
8 Ibid., 51.
9 Hawkins, *Life of Samuel Johnson*, 281; prayers, *Yale* 1: 46–7 and 319.
10 Ibid., 52.
11 See Donald F. Hyde and Mary Hyde, 'Dr Johnson's Second Wife' (1953), rpt in Hilles, *New Light on Dr Johnson*, 133–52. Through this section I rely on this very interesting article.
12 To Boothby, *Letters* 1: 118 (no. 78); to Warton, ibid., 90 (no. 56).
13 See F. A. Pottle, 'The Dark Hints of Sir John Hawkins and Boswell', in Hilles, *New Light on Dr Johnson*, 153–62.
14 *Yale* 14: xxx–xxxiii.
15 Ibid., 266, 267, 269 successively.
16 My discussion of the sermons is indebted to the *Yale* volume (edited by James Gray and Jean Hagstrum) and to James Gray's subsequent study *Johnson's Sermons*. An attempt at dating the sermons appears in Maurice Quinlan's *Samuel Johnson: A Layman's Religion* (Madison: University of Wisconsin Press, 1964).
17 On modes of delivering sermons, see Gilbert Burnet, *A Discourse of the Pastoral Care* (1692). I am grateful to Gerard Reedy for help with this subject. Hawkins, *Life of Samuel Johnson*, 347n.

18 On Johnson's method of composition, see Gray, *Johnson's Sermons*, 9; *Yale* 1:
    276, 277, 279; and *Letters* 3: 312 (no. 704).
19 Gray, *Yale* 14: xxx, xlv, li–lii; *Life* 4: 105.
20 *Yale* 14: 159 (cf. *Yale* 14: 237).
21 Ibid., 113, 112.
22 Ibid., 127; Paul Alkon, *Samuel Johnson and Moral Discipline*, 195–201.
23 *Yale* 14: 90.
24 Sermons, ibid., 221–3; Pertinax, *Yale* 4: 148.

Chapter 12   The *Adventurer*

1   Both Percy and Boothby are cited by L. F. Powell in his introduction to the
    Adventurer, *Yale* 2: 327 n. 5 and 323 respectively. For the publication history
    of the *Adventurer* I rely on Powell. Arthur Sherbo argues that Johnson wrote
    all the mottoes for the *Adventurer*; see 'Translation of the Mottos and Quota-
    tions in the *Adventurer*' in *Samuel Johnson, Editor of Shakespeare*.
2   *Yale* 2: 466, 377 and n. 7.
3   'To drive the night along', letter no. 954; the epigrams, *Yale* 6: 327–8; *Ad-
    venturer*, *Yale* 2: 443–4.
4   ζῆς ἔτ' ἐρημότερος, 9.359.6; ζῆς ἔτ' ἐλαφρότερος, 9.360.6; Loeb edition of
    The Greek Anthology, ed. W. R. Paton, 5 vols (London: Heinemann, 1917), 3:
    192–3; *Yale* 2: 474–5.
5   Ibid., 487–8.
6   Ibid., 412.
7   Ibid., 372.
8   Ibid., 496–7.
9   *Letters* 1: 81 (no. 53). Alvin Kernan suggests that Johnson's *Dictionary* had a
    major role in creating 'literature', in the modern sense of that word: see *The
    Death of Literature* (New Haven: Yale University Press, 1990) and *Samuel Johnson
    and the Impact of Print*.
10 Warton, *Life* 1: 273 and 275 n. 4; Wise's 'nest', *Letters* 1: 109 (no. 72); Johnson's
    study of More, ibid., 112–13 (no. 75). The closest available thing to Johnson's
    own history was in James Greenwood, *An Essay towards a Practical English
    Grammar* (London, 1711).
11 *Life* 1: 281.
12 *Letters* 1: 95–6 (no. 61).
13 Johnson on his dedications, *Life* 2: 225; 'To Don Felix', Hazen, *Johnson's
    Prefaces and Dedications*, 7–8; 'To the Duke of York', ibid., 152; dedication to
    Percy's *Reliques*, ibid., 167.
14 *Early Biographical Writings*, 409–10; Fussell, *Class, A Guide through the American
    Status System* (1983; rpt New York: Ballantine Books, 1984), pp. 212–23.
15 He received three guineas for the preface to *Rolt's Dictionary of Trade and
    Commerce*, Fleeman, 'The Revenue of a Writer', 213.
16 *Universal Visiter and Memorialist*, 1 (April 1756): 162, 165–6.
17 *Early Biographical Writings*, 419 and 421.

Chapter 13   The *Literary Magazine*

1   *Acta Eruditorum* and the *Publisher*, above, p. 105 and n. 19. For information on Johnson's role in the *Literary Magazine* I rely on Donald D. Eddy, *Samuel Johnson, Book Reviewer in the Literary Magazine: or, Universal Review 1756–1758*. Also see Donald Greene, 'Johnson's Contributions to the Literary Magazine', *Review of English Studies*, new series, 7 (1956), 367–92.

2   *Literary Magazine* 2: 166. For information on this episode I rely on Ruth K. McClure, 'Johnson's Criticism of the Foundling Hospital and its Consequences', *Review of English Studies*, new series, 27 (1976), 17–26. Also see Clifford, *Dictionary Johnson*, 177.

3   Eddy, *Samuel Johnson, Book Reviewer*, 87 and 94.

4   'This age of writers', *Literary Magazine* 1: iv; 'hardened tea-drinker', ibid., 2: 162.

5   Ibid., 1: 13–14.

6   *Yale* 10: 185–6.

7   'We shall not attempt . . .', *Literary Magazine* 1: iii; 'only the quarrel . . .', *Yale* 10: 188. I am indebted to Greene's introductions to the pieces in *Yale* 10.

8   On Mallet, ibid., 253; *Lives*, 'Mallet', 9 n. 6; and *Life* 2: 128.

9   Jenyns to Chesterfield, Soame Jenyns, *Works*, 2 vols (Dublin, 1791), 1: 93; on Johnson, ibid., 1: 185.

10   Ibid., 2: 21, 89, 91, 92, 99, 100, and 114 consecutively.

11   *Literary Magazine* 2: 171.

12   Ibid., 301–2.

13   Ibid., 302.

Chapter 14   The *Idler*

1   Saunders Welch, Clifford, *Dictionary Johnson*, 191, citing E. L. McAdam, Jr, 'Dr Johnson and Saunders Welch's *Proposals*', *Review of English Studies*, new series, 4 (October 1953), 337–45. I continue to rely on Clifford for biographical information and for information on Johnson's earnings on Fleeman, 'Revenue of a Writer'.

2   W. J. Bate remarks this in his preface to the *Idler*, *Yale* 2: xxvii.

3   *Idler*, *Yale* 2: 84; *Rambler*, *Yale* 5: 110–11.

4   *Yale* 2: 3–4.

5   Minorca, ibid., 19; the British army, ibid., 28.

6   *Yale* 10: 273 and 277. I draw again on Greene's introductions.

7   *Yale* 2: 319–20.

8   For the publication history of *Idler* 22, see *Yale* 2: 317 n. 1; Johnson to Mulso, *Posthumous Works of Mrs Chapone* (London, 1807), 1: 72–4 (I take the incident and the citation from Clifford, *Dictionary Johnson*, 120); More, *Hints*, 2 vols (1805; 4th edn, London: T. Cadell and W. Davies, 1809), 2: 166.

9   *Yale* 2: 22–3.

10   'Journals are daily multiplied', ibid., 23–4; *Idler* 30, ibid., 94–5.

11   I am indebted throughout this section to James F. Woodruff, 'The Allusions in Johnson's *Idler* no. 40', *Modern Philology*, 76 (1979), 380–9; wash ball, *Yale* 2: 125; Mohawk, ibid., 126.

12 *Idler* 40, ibid., 127; *Adventurer* 115, ibid., 458–9; on Clarendon's *History*, ibid., 201 and 204.

13 Ibid., 70.

14 Ibid., 186, 189, and 191–3.

15 Respectively in *Idlers* 70, 66, 77, 72 and 44, 78, and 83.

16 'One of the peculiarities . . .', *Yale* 2: 264–5; 'the continual multiplication . . .', ibid., 291. Johnson's anxiety about the publishing market is at variance with the findings of J. C. Mitchell, who documents a mid-century drop in production; see 'The Spread and Fluctuation of Eighteenth-Century Printing', *Studies in Voltaire and the Eighteenth Century*, 230 (1985), 305–21, cited by Kernan, *Samuel Johnson and the Impact of Print*, 60–1.

17 'The time of life . . .', *Yale* 2: 261; 'the writer of his own life . . .', ibid., 263; 'Nothing detains . . .', 312.

Chapter 15   *Rasselas*

1 Johnson to his mother, *Letters* 1: 177 (no. 123); his dream of Nathaniel, *Yale* 1: 67; 'art of forgetfulness', *Yale* 2: 139. I rely on Clifford, *Dictionary Johnson*, for biographical details throughout this chapter. For the specific events leading up to the composition of *Rasselas* and for all the information on publication, however, see Gwin Kolb's introduction, *Yale* 16: xix–lxx.

2 Johnson to Strahan, *Letters* 1: 178–9 (no. 124); cf. *Yale* 16: xix and facing page. According to Fleeman, 'Revenue of a Writer', Johnson received £100 for the first and £25 for the second edition. For a detailed account see Gwin Kolb, '*Rasselas*: Purchase Price, Proprietors, and Printings', *Studies in Bibliography*, XV (1962), 256–9, and *Yale* 16: xxiv–xxvi.

3 Editor's conclusion, *Yale* 16: xxxviii; Owen Ruffhead, ibid., xlviii. On the relationship between *Rasselas* and the Bible, particularly Ecclesiastes, see Thomas R. Preston, 'The Biblical Context of Johnson's Rasselas', *PMLA*, 84 (1969), 274–81.

4 On the history of the genre see Martha Pike Conant, *The Oriental Tale in the Eighteenth Century* (New York: Columbia University Press, 1908).

5 *Yale* 16: 14. In drawing attention to these kinds of irony in the text and the problems of reading that they suggest, I am in agreement with and indebted to the following articles: Earl Wasserman, 'Johnson's *Rasselas*: Implicit Contexts', *Journal of English and Germanic Philology*, 74 (1975), 1–25; Howard D. Weinbrot, 'The Reader, the General, and the Particular', *Eighteenth-Century Studies*, 5 (1975), 80–95; Nicholas Hudson, ' "Open" and "Enclosed" Readings of *Rasselas*', *The Eighteenth Century*, 31 (1990), 47–67. The best article on Johnson's fiction remains Lawrence Lipking's essential 'Learning to Read Johnson: *The Vision of Theodore* and *The Vanity of Human Wishes*', to which I am deeply indebted.

6 *Yale* 16: 44–6.

7 Ibid., 24–5.

8 The Stoic, ibid., 71; 'The prince . . .', ibid., 76.

9 Ibid., 85–7.

10 Ibid., 110.

11 Ibid., 118–19.

12 'Surely this man is happy', ibid., 143; Rasselas's decision, 141; 'To indulge . . .', 151–2.
13 Ibid., 174.
14 Ibid., 175–6. On the last resolves, see Hawkins, *Life of Samuel Johnson*, 330. Ellis Cornelia Knight, a young friend to whom Johnson inscribed a copy of *Rasselas* in 1784, published in 1790 a sequel called *Dinarbas* (*Yale* 16: lxii–lxv).
15 Clifford, *Dictionary Johnson*, 236–8; Boswell, *Life* 1: 350 n. 3.
16 On Johnson's involvement with benevolent societies, see Clifford, *Dictionary Johnson*, 226–30. For a detailed analysis of the debate on the Blackfriars bridge, see Morris R. Brownell, *Samuel Johnson's Attitude to the Arts* (Oxford: Clarendon Press, 1989), 107–26.
17 Society of Arts preface, Hazen, *Prefaces and Dedications*, 204–5; *British Magazine*, *Yale* 10: 283–4 (I draw on Greene's notes for my interpretation of the piece); Brumoy's *Theatre*, Johnson's *Works* (1806), 3: 30.
18 Brumoy, ibid., 65; Committee on French Prisoners, *Yale* 10: 288; Hollis, *Life* 4: 97 and 490–1; *The World Displayed*, Hazen, *Prefaces and Dedications*, 224, 227, and 236.
19 *Early Biographical Writings*, 498, 511.
20 Burke, *Annual Register* 2: 479, cited in *Yale* 16: xlvii and Clifford, *Dictionary Johnson*, 216; Smart, *Universal Visiter and Memorialist* 1: 4. On Bute and Wedderbourne, see Clifford, *Dictionary Johnson*, 262–77.
21 *Life* 1: 374–5 and n. 1.

Chapter 16   Shakespeare

1 *Yale* 16: 249.
2 *Yale* 7–8: 69 n. 5.
3 On Johnson's reading of Shakespeare for the *Dictionary*, see E. J. Thomas, 'A Bibliographical and Critical Analysis', 66; Bronson, *Yale* 7–8: xiv.
4 Ibid., 110.
5 Ibid., 106, 108, and 111. For an assessment of Johnson's place in the history of English bibliographical scholarship, see Robert E. Scholes, 'Dr Johnson and the Bibliographical Criticism of Shakespeare', *Shakespeare Quarterly*, 11 (1960), 163–71.
6 Clifford, *Dictionary Johnson*, 285–6.
7 *Life* 1: 379.
8 'Life of Collins', *Early Biographical Writings*, 518; Kennedy's *Chronology*, Hazen, *Prefaces and Dedications*, 77.
9 *Yale* 7–8: 65, 82–3; for other discussions of Johnson's attitude toward fiction in the Preface, see Murray Krieger, 'Fiction, Nature, and Literary Kinds in Johnson's Criticism of Shakespeare', *Eighteenth Century Studies*, 4 (1970), 184–98, and Leopold Damrosch, *The Uses of Johnson's Criticism*. I am indebted to both of these fine works.
10 *Yale* 7–8.
11 Ibid., 70–1.
12 Preface, ibid., 66; 'Ascham', *Early Biographical Writings*, 508.
13 *Hamlet*, *Yale* 7–8: 1002, with additions from Johnson's *Shakespeare* 8: 281 (cf. *Yale* 7–8: 1043); *All's Well*, *Yale* 7–8: 400; *Henry V*, ibid., 542.

14   *1 Henry VI*, ibid., 575–6; *3 Henry VI*, ibid., 607.
15   Ibid., 302–3.
16   Preface, ibid., 61; *Merchant*, ibid., 218; watches, ibid., 317; South Sea voyages,
     ibid., 254; rushes, ibid., 884; traveller's tale, ibid., 407–8; *King John*, ibid., 417.
17   'Satirical Slave', Johnson's *Shakespeare* 8: 189; *Yale* 7–8: 975 facing; *Shrew*, *Yale*
     7–8: 344; *Othello*, ibid., 1015 and n. 3 (in the replacement leaf Johnson cut
     'perhaps . . . and').
18   Parry, ibid., 540; 'bill', ibid., 368; 'mortal', ibid., 248; 'quat', ibid., 1044.
19   *Richard II*, ibid., 429–30; *Coriolanus*, ibid., 811.
20   *Cymbeline*, ibid., 898–9 (this is added in the edition of 1773, where Johnson
     continued the process of moralizing Shakespeare); *1 Henry IV*, ibid., 488;
     Measure for Measure, ibid., 193.
21   'To know a man well', *Yale* 7–8: 1007; 'to be or not to be', ibid., 981; patterns
     of guilt and sorrow, ibid., 902, 298, and 458; *Much Ado*, ibid., 362.
22   Juliet, ibid., 953 – see the treatment of this comment in G. F. Parker, *Johnson's
     Shakespeare*, 7–8 and 134–52; Desdemona, *Yale* 7–8: 1032–33.
23   Ibid., 985.

Chapter 17   *Lectures on the English Law*

1   Shakespeare, above, p. 230; to Warton, *Letters* 1: 256 (no. 176); see Bertram
    H. Davis, 'Johnson's 1764 Visit to Percy', in Korshin (ed.), *Johnson After Two
    Hundred Years*, 25–41; on the Club, see *Life* 1: 477 and 552–3.
2   Murphy, *Life* 1: 493 n. 3; 'home', *Letters* 1: 284 (no. 190).
3   Hawkins, *Life of Samuel Johnson*, 395; Boswell, *Life* 2: 332 n. 1; exceptions, *Life*
    4: 79, 268 (cf. letter no. 952.1) and letter no. 927.1; *Lives*, 'Lyttelton', 22; 'Watts',
    28.
4   Prayers, *Yale* 1: 96–8; also see *Letters* 1: 258–9, 275–8 (180, 187.1, and 187.3),
    which suggest that Johnson was working for an MP; 'Considerations', *Yale* 10:
    300–12; Johnson and Chambers, Chambers, *A Course of Lectures on the English
    Law* 1: 12. I rely on Thomas Curley's introduction for my information on this
    episode in Johnson's life, but E. L. McAdam was the first to demonstrate
    Johnson's part in the work: 'Dr. Johnson's Law Lectures for Chambers: An
    Addition to the Canon', *Review of English Studies*, 15 (1939), 385–91; ibid., 16
    (1940), 159–68, and *Dr Johnson and the English Law* (Syracuse, New York:
    Syracuse University Press, 1951).
5   A letter from Boswell to Johnson soliciting legal help distinguishes between a
    'particular point of law' and a 'general matter' in such a way as to suggest that
    Johnson overtly described his own competence as limited to the latter (*Life* 2:
    145). In a conversation recorded by Boswell, Johnson made a related distinc-
    tion between legal 'precedents' and legal 'principles' and indicated his clear
    preference for the latter (*Life* 2: 158).
6   The effects of legal study in Johnson's later writing, Chambers, *A Course of
    Lectures on the English Law* 1: 68–79; on Coke, ibid., 116. For information on
    quotations in the fourth edition of the *Dictionary* I rely on the Gove–Liebert
    file in the Sterling Memorial Library at Yale University, which is admittedly
    incomplete, but voluminous. This reference to Coke is in part 1, lecture 12,
    where it specifically states, 'if a gentlewoman be named spinster in any original

writ, appeal or indictment, she may abate and quash the same' (2 *Institutes*, 668): see Chambers, *A Course of Lectures on the English Law* 1: 253.

7 Chambers, *A Course of Lectures on the English Law* 1: 129.

8 *Yale* 7–8: 469. On the other hand, the *Lectures* do praise George III by saying, 'the present king . . . generously gave up to the public . . . the hereditary excise' (*Lectures* 1: 175), and the 'trainbands or militia' are distinguished as the 'constitutional forces established for the defence of the realm' (ibid., 159).

9 Shakespeare, *Yale* 7–8: 606; *Lectures* 2: 30.

10 Ibid., 1: 240.

11 'Rebellions', ibid., 1: 175; marriage, ibid., 2: 22–3, 118–19.

12 On Johnson's contribution to the historical part of the Lectures, see Thomas Curley's introduction, Chambers, *Lectures* 1: 39; 'in surveying . . .', ibid., 1: 130.

13 Blackstone, *Commentaries on the Laws of England*, 4 vols (1765–9; facs. rpt Chicago: University of Chicago Press, 1979), 1: 145; *Lectures* 1: 133; 'Ascham', *Early Biographical Writings*, 508 (above, p. 224).

14 Chambers, *Lectures* 1: 133–4.

15 Ibid., 1: 193.

16 'The impossibility . . .', ibid., 1: 205; 'Political society . . .', ibid., 1: 249.

17 In summarizing Johnson's contribution, I am again indebted to Thomas Curley's introduction to the Lectures; 'by its extent . . .', ibid., 1: 83; McNair, *Dr Johnson and the Law*, 79.

18 *Life* 2: 430 and 10 respectively; James Reibman discusses Johnson's affinities with Grotius, Aquinas, and other spokesmen for natural law in 'Dr Johnson and the Law' (D.Phil. dissertation, University of Edinburgh, 1979), 200 and following. Reibman also astutely discusses Johnson and Chambers's collaboration, distinguishing nicely between their respective prose styles.

Chapter 18   Late Political Writings

1 I follow Donald Greene in attributing changes in Johnson's politics to the accession of George III. On George III's book-collecting, see J. H. Plumb, *New Light on the Tyrant George III* (Washington, DC: Anderson House, 1978), 8, and John Brooke, *King George III* (New York: McGraw-Hill, 1972), 304–6.

2 To Barnard, *Letters* 1: 314 (no. 206); to Drummond, ibid., 268–71 (no. 184); Johnson reading law in the King's library, Chambers, *Lectures* 1: 20–1 (Curley mistakenly calls it the Queen's library); Boswell, *Life* 2: 33.

3 George's conversational habits, John Brooke, *King George III*, 296–7; the conversation, *Life* 2: 33–40; Kernan, *Samuel Johnson and the Impact of Print*, 35–47.

4 On the background of the pamphlet, see Greene, *Yale* 10: 313–17. For Boswell's dinners with Johnson and Wilkes, see *Life* 3: 64–78 and 4: 101–5. For Johnson's harshest reported comments on Wilkes, see Boswell's *Tour to the Hebrides, Life* 5: 339 and n. 5.

5 *False Alarm, Yale* 10: 320–1; on Parliament, Chambers, *Lectures* 1: 127 and 145 (in his *Dictionary* Johnson defines 'amesnable', the French form of 'amenable', as 'responsible; subject so as to be liable to enquiries or accounts'); on the House of Commons, ibid., 1: 204; Blackstone, *Commentaries on the Laws of England*, 4 vols (1765–9; facs. rpt; Chicago: University of Chicago Press, 1979), 1: 158–9.

6　*Yale* 10: 317–18, 328.
7　Ibid., 341, 344.
8　Ibid., 335.
9　Greene very plausibly attributes the purer motives to the late political writings in *The Politics of Samuel Johnson. False Alarm, Yale* 10: 319 and n. 3 (Martial, 6.19).
10　Evidence of Johnson's campaigning for Thrale in the election of 1768 appears in a letter to Richard Penneck dated 3 March 1768, *Letters* 1: 294 (no. 196). See Greene on the Grenville Act, *Yale* 10: 387–8; Johnson on 'patriot', ibid., 390.
11　Ibid., 396.
12　Perceval, ibid., 356; Byron, ibid., 356 n. 8; Byron's report, ibid., 356–7; MacBride's account, ibid., 357; Hunt's experience, ibid., 358.
13　'If the rudder . . .', ibid., 380; 'To proportion . . .', ibid., 349.
14　Ibid., 370–1.
15　Ibid., 371 and 384; Johnson's pamphlet was reprinted in full in 1948 as a response to the Falklands crisis of that time, as Greene notes, and parts of it were reprinted again during the Falklands war of 1982.
16　Ibid., 386.
17　Ibid., 452–3.
18　'The loudest yelps', ibid., 454; emancipation, ibid., 452.
19　The constitutional basis of *Taxation No Tyranny*, Chambers, *A Course of Lectures* 1: 74–6; lecture 15, ibid., 1: 268 and 283; 'The *moral* part of this question . . .', ibid., 1: 291; *Taxation No Tyranny, Yale* 10: 433, 418, and 411 consecutively.
20　Ibid., 438, 428, 432 and 421 consecutively; Greene points out the similarity to Johnson's introduction to *The World Displayed*, ibid., 421, n. 5.
21　Ibid., 430.
22　Ibid., 410–11 for Greene's bibliographical summary; to Strahan, *Letters* 2: 184–5 (no. 381, cited by Greene).
23　On Johnson and the Astons, see Clifford, *Young Sam Johnson*, 229, and *Life* 3: 341; 'If by the fortune . . .', *Yale* 10: 455, textual note s.
24　'Like the elephant . . .', *Life* 2: 137 n. 3, citing Hawkins and Croker; *Thoughts on Falkland's Islands* troubled North sufficiently that he tried to stop the sale of the first run (*Letters* 1: 356, no. 246); Maxwell, *Life* 2: 118.
25　Prayer, *Yale* 1: 125; history of melancholy, ibid., 119; manacles, ibid., 140.
26　'Intellectual nature . . . abhors a vacuum', *Letters* 1: 363 (no. 250); Johnson's reading projects, e.g. *Yale* 1: 135, and the resolution to read 200 verses every Sunday (ibid., 145). About 1771 the Thrales established a laboratory for Johnson at Streatham, which was sophisticated enough to permit smelting in its furnaces (*Johnsonian Miscellanies* 1: 307; *Letters* 1: 371, no. 259). He recommeded laboratory work for people with troubled minds, particularly John Taylor (*Letters* 1: 395, no. 277).
27　For Steevens's appeals for assistance, see Sherbo, *Samuel Johnson, Editor of Shakespeare*, 108 n. 15; Johnson on Burke, ibid., 110, citing *The Works of Shakespeare* (1773), 8: 367 n. 6. I rely on Sherbo's account of the revision, ibid., 106–13 and Appendix F.
28　To Langton, *Letters* 1: 381–2 (no. 268); to Taylor, *Letters* 1: 396–7 (no. 278); Johnson's good spirits, *Yale* 1: 147, 154 – for a similar view of how the revision helped Johnson psychologically, see Arthur Sherbo, 'Dr Johnson's Revision of His *Dictionary*', *Philological Quarterly*, 31 (1952), 372–82; Chambers's *Cyclopedia*,

Life 2: 203–204 n. 3; Johnson's watch, *Life* 2: 57 and n. 4, *Yale* 1: 118, and Hawkins, *Life of Samuel Johnson*, 408. Hawkins says Johnson soon decided that the dial-plate was pedantic and traded it for a plain one. This does not necessarily mean that it was any less representative of Johnson's feelings. He may simply have been embarrassed about the public display of such feelings in the ethically problematic context of jewellery. It also may be that he could not stand the mistake in the engraving, μ for ν, which Hawkins reports.

29 For my account of Johnson's revisions I rely mainly on Reddick, *The Making of Johnson's Dictionary*, 89–178. Peyton is mentioned in Johnson's diary (*Yale* 1: 150). Johnson was still trying to find support for Peyton and one or the other Macbean in 1775 (*Letters* 2: 207–8 (nos 393–4). Reddick provides a list of the sources of new quotations (*The Making of Johnson's Dictionary*, 121–2). In '1773: the Year of Revision' (*Eighteenth-Century Studies*, 7 (1973): 18–39), Arthur Sherbo accepts the estimate of 3000 new quotations given by Theodore Stenberg in *Texas Studies in English* (1944), 197–210.

30 M., Sherbo, 'Dr Johnson's Revision'. I think Reddick overestimates the importance of Johnson's changes in determining the politics and the overall meaning of his work. On similarities between the two revisions of 1773, see Sherbo, 'The Year of Revision', 23–8.

31 The classic psychological studies are George Irwin, *Samuel Johnson: A Personality in Conflict*, and Katherine C. Balderston, 'Johnson's Vile Melancholy'. Also see John Wiltshire, *Johnson in the Medical World*, 43–9, and James Gray, 'Arras/Hélas', in Korshin (ed.), *Johnson after Two Hundred Years*, 85–6. Evidence of masochism, *Letters* 2: 37–9 (nos 284a, 307.1, 311.1). Another courtly letter in French, *Letters* 1: 321–2 (no. 213); Bate, *Samuel Johnson*, 439–40; 'Iron Dominion', Chapman's letter no. 403a.

Chapter 19 *A Journey to the Western Islands of Scotland*

1 I rely on the chronology in Appendix C of David Fleeman's edition of the *Journey*, and I am indebted throughout this section to various parts of his remarkable work. For precursors to Johnson's *Journey*, see ibid., 341; also *Life* 5: 222 where Johnson defends Pennant warmly from Boswell's charges of superficiality.

2 To Mrs Thrale, *Letters* 2: 50 (no. 318); 'We came thither too late', *Journey*, 46; Parliamentary acts of 1746 and 1748, *Journey*, 36 and n. 5.

3 Conception of the narrative, ibid., 31–2; to Mrs Thrale, *Letters* 2: 73 (no. 326, cited by Fleeman, *Journey*, 172).

4 Skye ode, *Yale* 6: 279; *Journey*, 130.

5 Bertrand Bronson, 'Johnson, Traveling Companion, in Fancy and Fact' (Bronson precedes me in seeing that the *Journey* exhibits a tension between Johnson's demand for fact and his receptivity to fiction); *Journey*, 74–5.

6 Coll, ibid., 106; Boswell, *Life* 5: 324.

7 Advantages of a central legal system, *Journey*, 76–7; standard currency, ibid., 84 and 94; 'Without intelligence . . .', ibid., 113; 'As there subsists . . .', ibid., 92.

8 The history of the race . . .', ibid., 93; Macpherson, ibid., 95–8 and Fleeman's notes; also see *Letters* 2: 176–8, 180–2 (nos 378 and 380).

9   *Journey*, 99.
10 Castles, ibid., 130; *Fingal's Table*, ibid., 122; Boswell, *Life* 5: 331–2.
11 *Journey*, 90–1.
12 'Knox's reformation', ibid., 3 (also see the cancelled leaf D8 where Johnson refers to plans to melt the lead of Lichfield Cathedral to raise money for renovations as formed by 'a body of men, not less decent or virtuous than the Scotish council. . . . What they shall melt, it were just that they should swallow' – ibid., lvi, and *Letters* 2: 156–7, no. 364); St Andrews, *Journey*, 2–3; '. . . the ruins of *Iona*', ibid., 123–4 (for the textual question of the exclamation point, see 149–50).
13 Women of Skye, ibid., 68–9; Boswell quoting Johnson, *Life* 5: 334.
14 'To sooth his imagination . . . so soon forgotten', *Journey*, 126; storm, ibid., 132; Auchinleck, ibid., 135; college for the deaf, ibid., 137.
15 *Life* 5: 408 n. 4 and 2: 300.
16 Ibid., 5: 344; for Scott's note, see ibid., 382 n. 2.
17 *Letters* 2: 75 (no. 326); diary, *Yale* 1: 160–1.
18 Ode to Mrs Thrale, *Yale* 6: 280.
19 To Chambers, *Letters* 2: 86 (no. 329.1).
20 Solitude, *Yale* 1: 175; gloom, ibid., 213; cave, ibid., 168; Caernarfon, ibid., 204; to Boswell, *Letters* 2: 149 (no. 360). Johnson's Welsh journal was edited and published after his death by his friend Richard Duppa.
21 Against publishing the French journal, *Letters* 2: 274 (no. 438); 'Rhinoceros . . .', *Yale* 1: 242.
22 'Michel Angelo . . .', ibid., 248; books, ibid., 245–8; 'This house struck me', ibid., 232; '. . . I am little pleased', ibid., 238.

Chapter 20   The *Lives of the Poets*

1   On the the deaths of the young Thrales, see *Letters* 2: 311–19 (nos 465–70). On the genesis of the familiar title, see Donald Greene, *Johnsonian News Letter*, 45–6 (September–December 1985 and March 1986), 25–7. But Johnson himself referred to them as 'the lives of the poets' in his diary (*Yale* 1: 292) and in many letters.
2   To Vice-Chancellor Fothergill, *Letters* 2: 196 (no. 385); to the Lord Chamberlain, ibid., 320 (no. 472); Bolt Court, *Life* 2: 427 – this was Johnson's last move in London (for a list of his seventeen places of residence in London, see *Life* 3: 405 and 534–6); Johnson's application for funds to winter in Italy, *Life* 4: 348–50; government neglect, *Life* 4: 116; ibid., 2: 317 n. 1 (Robert Chambers was paid £6000 a year for serving on the Supreme Court in Bombay, beginning in 1773 – letter no. 795). For a table of all of Johnson's travels, see *Life* 3: 450–9.
3   *Life*, 3: 139 n. 4 and 140 n. 2. I rely on *Life* 3: 139–48, the notes, and appendix F (p. 496) for my account of the Dodd affair.
4   *Yale* 14: 302 and 309.
5   To Boswell, *Letters* 3: 20 (no. 515); Johnson's additions, *Life* 3: 370–1; to Nichols, *Letters* 3: 226–7 (no. 670).
6   *Yale* 1: 279.
7   *Lives*, 'Swift', 139; 'Waller', 120–1.

8 Aristotelian code, *Life* 4: 35–6; on Johnson's formal matrix, see my article 'Johnson's Form of Evaluation', *Studies in English Literature*, 19 (1979), 501–14; 'inelegantly splendid', *Lives*, 'Milton', 205.

9 'Those little pieces...', ibid., 207; 'Poetry is the art of uniting pleasure with truth...', ibid., 208, 212; faults, 252 and 264.

10 *Yale* 1: 278. He repeated the experiment in 1779 (ibid., 297).

11 *Lives*, 'Prior', 5 (as Hill notes, Malone thought the anecdote true and traced its transmission to reliable sources – *Lives* 2: 182, n. 4); 'Congreve', 2–3.

12 'Cowley', 5; 'Milton', 37, 42.

13 'King', 2.

14 'Pope', 273 (see also *Letters* 2: 89, no. 559) and 285.

15 'Pope', 199.

16 Johnson's written enquiries, e.g. *Letters* 3: 120–1 (no. 578.1), to the Sheriff of London; legal business in the Midlands, letter no. 807; Dobson, 'Pope', 291; a niece of Mrs Fermor, 'Pope', 54 (cf. *Yale* 1: 236).

17 'Addison', 98; Hill notes the reference to Horace, *Odes* 2.1.7.

18 Michael Johnson, 'Dryden', 109, and 'Sprat', 19; Corbett, 'Addison', 2; Ford, 'Fenton', 13; Elizabeth, 'Gay', 27; Mr Ing, 'A. Philips', 34; Boswell, 'Thomson', 39; Dyer, 'Watts', 25; Tonson, 'Milton', 175; Mrs Thrale, 'Young', 163; Shiels, 'Hammond', 1; Goldsmith, 'Parnell', 1; Hawkesworth, 'Swift', 1; Warton, 'Pope', 344 and n. 2 (cf. *Letters* 3: 259–60, no. 668); Pembroke, 'Shenstone', 5; Walmesley, 'Smith', 72–6; see Hill's index for the rest of the references.

19 Richardson, 'Rowe', 8; Osborne, 'Pope', 238.

20 'Lyttelton', 3, 5; Johnson wrote Lyttelton's speech on the motion to remove Walpole, for example, *Gentleman's Magazine* 13: 172–3.

21 Johnson and Lyttelton, Clifford, *Young Sam Johnson*, 85, *Johnsonian Miscellanies* 2: 208, Reade, *Johnsonian Gleanings* 3: 161, *Life* 4: 57; *Lives*, 'Akenside', 3 (cf. 'Thomson', 22); 'I disregarded all power', *Life* 1: 73–4.

22 *Letters* 3: 156 (no. 606).

23 *Lycidas, Lives*, 'Milton', 181; 'Hammond', 6; 'Prior', 59; 'Smith', 49; 'Gray', 41.

24 'Addison', 130; 'Gay', 30; 'Cowley', 14; 'Pope', 342 and 320.

25 Ruling passion, 'Pope', 203, 205; 'Waller', 69.

26 'Dryden', 72; 'Waller', 136, 141; 'Watts', 33.

27 'Pope', 309; 'Swift', 113; 'The great source of pleasure is variety', 'Butler', 35; 'Dryden', 312.

28 For this analysis I am indebted to Paul Fussell, *Samuel Johnson and the Life of Writing*, 265–78; Mrs Thrale, one of the first readers of the *Lives*, also noticed Johnson's treatment of the deaths (letter no. 743a).

29 *Lives*, 'Halifax', 10; 'A. Philips', 33; 'Otway', 14; 'Pope', 261.

30 Johnson's vernal muse, *Yale* 1: 158; *Lives*, 'Milton', 124; 'Gray', 26.

31 'Pope', 374; 'Gray', 48, 51; 'Butler', 41; I draw on my treatment of Johnson's common reader in 'The Ideal Reader: A Critical Fiction', *PMLA*, 93 (1978), 463–74. Also see Clarence R. Tracy, 'Johnson and the Common Reader', *Dalhousie Review*, 57 (1977), 405–23.

32 *Lives*, 'Cowley', 183; 'Prior', 66.

Chapter 21   Final Years

1   *Yale* 1: 292, 303–4.
2   *Letters* 3: 285 (no. 686).
3   Johnson's meetings with the rich and famous, *Life* 4: 116 and 326; Mrs Siddons, ibid., 241–3; offers of support, e.g. letter no. 905; to Mrs Thrale, letter no. 922.
4   Diary, *Yale* 1: 304; *Letters* 3: 330, 334 (nos 717 and 721).
5   Diary, *Yale* 1: 351; Mrs Thrale's intentions, *Life* 4: 502–4; Johnson to Thrale, letters no. 970 and 972.
6   *Letters* 3: 371 and 287–9 (nos 748 and 686.2).
7   'Wear the gown', *Yale* 6: 306; Johnson's Anacreon, ibid., 296–8; *Thraliana* 1: 232–3; *Anacreontis Teii*, ed. Valentino Rose (Leipsig: Teubner, 1890), 15–17; letter no. 972.
8   *Yale* 6: 302, 298–9.
9   Ibid., 314–15.
10   Letters no. 759 and 757.
11   *Letters* 3: 140 (no. 591), nos 759, 839.1, and 879.2 successively; on Johnson's household, see *Life* 3: 462–4.
12   Letter no. 892.
13   To Nichols, letters no. 1026 and 1042; Johnson's 'minute literary information', *Life* 4: 307.
14   Letters no. 827, 928 (twice), and 835.1 successively.
15   Opium, *Yale* 1: 312; to Thrale, letter no. 954.
16   *Greek Anthology*, 10.124, Loeb edn, trans. and ed. W. R. Paton, 5 vols (London: Heinemann, 1929), 4: 63; Boethius, *Yale* 1: 356; Sallust, ibid., 367.
17   The Thrales' well, *Life* 4: 21–2; to Thrale, letter no. 850. The last thought in this paragraph is not original, but I cannot remember to whom I owe it.
18   Classical editions, letter no. 974; 'In Rivum', *Yale* 6: 342; Uttoxeter, *Life* 4: 373.
19   'The town is my element', letter no. 1029; 'Spring's Return', *Yale* 6: 343.
20   For the fate of the diaries, see *Life* 4: 405–6; John Wiltshire, *Johnson in the Medical World*, best summarizes Johnson's lancings and lettings, which may have included a stab at his testicular tumour; 'I will be conquered', *Life* 4: 374.
21   *Yale* 1: 417–18. He also composed on this date a prayer in Latin verse (*Yale* 6: 351).
22   Death mask, Paul Korshin, 'Johnson's Last Days: Some Facts and Problems', *Johnson After Two Hundred Years*, 60. See *Life* 4: 421–5 and 447–72 for paintings, engravings, and monuments of Johnson. Also see Herman W. Liebert, 'Portrait of the Author: Lifetime Likenesses of Samuel Johnson'.
23   For some of the fictions about Johnson, see *Life* 4: 167–8; Boswell, *Life* 4: 383n.; 250 tightly printed pages, James L. Clifford and Donald J. Greene (eds), *Samuel Johnson: a Survey and Bibliography of Critical Studies*; another 100 pages, Donald J. Greene and John A. Vance (eds), *Samuel Johnson Bibliography, 1970–1985*; letter no. 775.

Bibliography

I Johnson's Works

(Co-author) *Catalogus Bibliothecae Harleianae*. 5 vols. London: Thomas Osborne, 1743–5.

(Co-author) Chambers, Sir Robert. *A Course of Lectures on the English Law*. Ed. Thomas Curley. 2 vols. Madison: University of Wisconsin Press, 1986.

The Complete English Poems. Ed. J. David Fleeman. New Haven: Yale University Press, 1982.

(Trans.) Crousaz, Jean Pierre de. *A Commentary on Mr Pope's Principles of Morality*. 1739; rpt New York: Garland, 1974.

Debates in Parliament. 2 vols. London: John Stockdale, 1787.

A Dictionary of the English Language. 2 vols. London: Strahan et al., 1755; 4th edn, 1773.

(Contributor) Dodsley, Robert. *The Preceptor*. 2 vols. 1748; 5th edn, London: Robert Dodsley, 1769.

(Contributor) *The Harleian Miscellany or, a Collection of Scarce, Curious, and Entertaining Pamphlets and Tracts. . . .* 8 vols. London: Thomas Osborne, 1744–6.

Early Biographical Writings of Dr Johnson. Ed. J. David Fleeman. Westmead, Farnborough, Hants: Gregg, 1973.

A Journey to the Western Islands of Scotland. Ed. J. David Fleeman. Oxford: Clarendon Press, 1985.

Letters of Samuel Johnson, LL.D. Ed. George Birkbeck Hill. 2 vols. Oxford: Clarendon Press, 1892.

The Letters of Samuel Johnson. Ed. R. W. Chapman. 3 vols. Oxford: Clarendon Press, 1952.

The Letters of Samuel Johnson. Ed. Bruce Redford. Vols 1–3. Princeton: Princeton University Press, 1992.

The Life of Richard Savage. Ed. Clarence Tracy. Oxford: Clarendon Press, 1981.

(Contributor) *Literary Magazine: or, Universal Review*. London: J. Richardson, 1756–8. Rpt ed. Donald Eddy. 3 vols. New York: Garland, 1978.

Lives of the Poets. Ed. G. B. Hill. 3 vols. Oxford: Clarendon Press, 1905.

The Plays of William Shakespeare. 8 vols. London: J. and R. Tonson et al., 1765.

The Poems of Samuel Johnson. Ed. David Nichol Smith and Edward L. McAdam. Oxford: Clarendon Press, 1941.

(Contributor) *Universal Visiter and Memorialist.* 1756; facsimile reprint, New York: Garland, 1979.

The Works of Samuel Johnson, LL.D. Ed. John Hawkins. 11 vols. London: J. Buckland et al., 1787.

The Works of Samuel Johnson. Ed. Arthur Murphy. 12 vols. London: J. Johnson, 1806.

The Works of Samuel Johnson. Oxford English Classics. 9 vols. London and Oxford: William Pickering, and Talboys and Wheeler, 1825.

The Yale Edition of the Works of Samuel Johnson. New Haven: Yale University Press, 1958– . 1: *Diaries, Prayers and Annals,* ed. E. L. McAdam, Jr, with Donald and Mary Hyde. 2: *The Idler and The Adventurer,* ed. Walter J. Bate, John M. Bullitt, and L. F. Powell. 3–5: *The Rambler,* ed. Walter J. Bate and Albrecht B. Strauss. 6: *Poems,* ed. E. L. McAdam, Jr, with George Milne. 7–8: *Johnson on Shakespeare,* ed. Arthur Sherbo with an introduction by Bertrand Bronson. 9. *A Journey to the Western Islands of Scotland,* ed. Mary Lascelles. 10: *Political Writings,* ed. Donald J. Greene. 14: *Sermons,* ed. Jean H. Hagstrum and James Gray. 15: *A Voyage to Abyssinia,* ed. Joel J. Gold. 16: *Rasselas and Other Tales,* ed. Gwin J. Kolb.

II Biographical Studies and Collections

Balderston, Katherine C. 'Johnson's Vile Melancholy'. In *The Age of Johnson: Essays Presented to Chauncy Brewster Tinker,* pp. 3–14. Ed. F. W. Hilles. New Haven: Yale University Press, 1949.

Bate, Walter Jackson. *Samuel Johnson and the Life of Writing.* New York: Harcourt Brace Jovanovich, 1971.

Boswell, James. *Boswell's Notebook, 1776–1777.* Ed. R. W. Chapman. London: Humphrey Milford, 1925.

—— *The Correspondence and Other papers of James Boswell relating to the Making of the Life of Johnson.* Ed. Marshall Waingrow. New York and Toronto: McGraw-Hill, n.d.

—— *The Life of Samuel Johnson.* Ed. G. B. Hill; rev. L. F. Powell. Second edition. 6 vols. Oxford: Clarendon Press, 1934–64.

Brack, OM, Jr, and Kelley, Robert E. *The Early Biographies of Samuel Johnson.* Iowa City: University of Iowa Press, 1974.

Clifford, James. *Dictionary Johnson: The Middle Years of Samuel Johnson.* New York: McGraw-Hill, 1979.

—— *Young Sam Johnson.* New York: McGraw-Hill, 1955.

Hawkins, John. *The Life of Samuel Johnson, LL.D.* Dublin: Chamberlain et al., 1787 (rpt of the London edition of the same year). There is a modern edition, edited and abridged by Bertram Davis (New York: Macmillan, 1961), but it excludes some important passages.

Irwin, George. *Samuel Johnson: A Personality in Conflict.* New York: Oxford University Press, 1971.

Johnsonian Miscellanies. Ed. G. B. Hill. 2 vols. New York: Harper and Brothers, 1897.

Kaminski, Thomas. *The Early Career of Samuel Johnson.* New York: Oxford University Press, 1987.

Liebert, Herman W. 'Portrait of the Author: Lifetime Likenesses of Samuel Johnson'. In *English Portraits of the Seventeenth and Eighteenth Centuries,* pp. 47–88. Ed. J.

Douglas Stewart and Herman W. Liebert. Los Angeles: William Andrews Clark Memorial Library, 1974.

Reade, Aleyn Lyell. *Johnsonian Gleanings.* 11 vols. London: Francis, 1909–52.

Thraliana. Ed. Katherine C. Balderston. 2 vols. Oxford: Clarendon Press, 1942.

Wiltshire, John. *Samuel Johnson in the Medical World.* Cambridge: Cambridge University Press, 1991.

III INTERPRETIVE STUDIES

Alkon, Paul. *Samuel Johnson and Moral Discipline.* Evanston: Northwestern University Press, 1967.

Allodoli, Ettore. 'Poliziano e Johnson'. *La Rinascita,* 5 (September 1942), 459–72.

Bloom, Edward and Lillian. 'Johnson's "Mournful Narrative": the Rhetoric of "London"'. In *Eighteenth-Century Studies in Honor of Donald F. Hyde,* pp. 107–44. Ed. W. H. Bond. New York: Grolier Club, 1970.

Bronson, Bertrand H. 'Johnson's "Irene": Variations on a Tragic Theme'. 1944. Rpt in *Johnson Agonistes and Other Essays,* pp. 100–55. Berkeley: University of California Press, 1965.

—— 'Johnson, Traveling Companion, in Fancy and Fact'. In *Johnson and His Age,* pp. 163–87. Ed. James Engell. Cambridge, Mass.: Harvard University Press, 1984.

Damrosch, Leopold. *The Uses of Johnson's Criticism.* Charlottesville: University of Virginia Press, 1976.

DeMaria, Robert, Jr. *Johnson's Dictionary and the Language of Learning.* Chapel Hill: University of North Carolina Press, 1986.

Folkenflik, Robert. *Samuel Johnson, Biographer.* Ithaca, New York: Cornell University Press, 1978.

Fussell, Paul. *Samuel Johnson and the Life of Writing.* New York: Harcourt Brace Jovanovich, 1971.

Giddings, Robert. 'The Fall of Orgilio: Samuel Johnson as Parliamentary Reporter'. In *Samuel Johnson: New Critical Essays,* pp. 86–106. Ed. Isobel Grundy. London: Vision Press, 1984.

Gray, James. *Johnson's Sermons.* Oxford: Clarendon Press, 1972.

Greene, Donald. *The Politics of Samuel Johnson.* New Haven: Yale University Press, 1960.

Grundy, Isobel. *Samuel Johnson and the Scale of Greatness.* Athens, Georgia: University of Georgia Press, 1986.

Hilles, Frederick. *New Light on Dr Johnson.* 1959; rpt Hamden, Conn.: Archon Books, 1967.

Hudson, Nicholas. *Samuel Johnson and Eighteenth-Century Thought.* Oxford: Clarendon Press, 1988.

Kernan, Alvin. *Samuel Johnson and the Impact of Print.* 1987; rpt Princeton: Princeton University Press, 1989.

Korshin, Paul (ed.). *Johnson After Two Hundred Years.* Philadelphia: University of Pennsylvania Press, 1986.

Lipking, Lawrence. 'Learning to Read Johnson: *The Vision of Theodore* and *The Vanity of Human Wishes*'. *English Literary History,* 43 (1976), 517–37. Rpt in *Modern Essays on Eighteenth-Century Literature,* pp. 335–54. Ed. Leopold Damrosch, Jr. New York: Oxford University Press, 1988.

McNair, Arnold. *Dr Johnson and the Law*. Cambridge: Cambridge University Press, 1948.

Parker, G. F. *Johnson's Shakespeare*. Oxford: Clarendon Press, 1989.

Schwartz, Richard. 'Johnson's "Mr Rambler" and the Periodical Tradition'. *Genre*, 7 (1974), 196–204.

Sitter, John. 'To *The Vanity of Human Wishes* through the 1740s'. *Studies in Philology*, 74 (1977), 445–64.

Wimsatt, William K. *Philosophic Words*. New Haven: Yale University Press, 1948.

—— *The Prose Style of Samuel Johnson*. New Haven: Yale University Press, 1941.

IV BIBLIOGRAPHICAL STUDIES

Clifford, James L. and Greene, Donald J. (eds). *Samuel Johnson: a Survey and Bibliography of Critical Studies*. Minneapolis: University of Minnesota Press, 1970.

Courtney, William Prideaux and Smith, David Nichol. *A Bibliography of Samuel Johnson*. With Chapman, R. W., 'Johnsonian Bibliography, A Supplement to Courtney'. 1915 and 1939; rpt New Castle, Delaware: Oak Knoll Books and M. Goldberg, 1984.

Eddy, Donald D. *Samuel Johnson, Book Reviewer in the Literary Magazine: or, Universal Review 1756–1758*. New York and London: Garland, 1979.

Fleeman, J. D. *A Preliminary Handlist of Copies of Books associated with Samuel Johnson*. Oxford Bibliographical Society Occasional Publications, no. 17. Oxford: Oxford Bibliographical Society, 1984.

—— *A Preliminary Handlist of Documents & Manuscripts of Samuel Johnson*. Oxford Bibliographical Society Occasional Publications, no. 2. Oxford: Oxford Bibliographical Society, 1967.

—— 'The Revenue of a Writer: Samuel Johnson's Literary Earnings'. *Studies in the Book Trade in Honour of Graham Pollard*, pp. 211–30. Oxford: Oxford Bibliographical Society, 1975.

Greene, Donald (ed.). *Samuel Johnson's Library: An Annotated Guide*. English Literary Studies Monograph Series, no. 1. Vancouver: University of British Columbia, 1975.

Greene, Donald J. and Vance, John A. (eds). *Samuel Johnson Bibliography, 1970–1985*. English Literary Studies, no. 39. Victoria, British Columbia: University of Victoria Press, 1987.

Hazen, Allen T. *Samuel Johnson's Prefaces and Dedications*. New Haven and London: Yale and Oxford University Presses, 1937.

Hoover, Benjamin Beard. *Samuel Johnson's Parliamentary Reporting*. Berkeley and Los Angeles: University of California Press, 1953.

Reddick, Allen. *The Making of Johnson's Dictionary 1746–1773*. Cambridge: Cambridge University Press, 1990.

Sherbo, Arthur. *Samuel Johnson, Editor of Shakespeare, with an Essay on the Adventurer*. Illinois Studies in Language and Literature, 42. Urbana, University of Illinois Press, 1956.

Sledd, James and Kolb, Gwin. *Dr Johnson's Dictionary: Essays in the Biography of a Book*. Chicago: University of Chicago Press, 1955.

Thomas, E. J. 'A Bibliographical and Critical Analysis of Johnson's Dictionary'. D.Phil. diss. University of Aberystwyth, 1974.

Index

In order to provide brief identifications of the many persons mentioned in the book, I have indexed even those for whom the text provides little information. I have also tried not to repeat in the index the information that is given in the text. While the relatively obscure persons in the book are cited on the strength of mere appearance in the text, the principals – Johnson, Boswell, Hester Thrale, and a few others – are more selectively indexed.